D1521204

The Tanner Lectures on Human Values

THE TANNER LECTURES ON HUMAN VALUES

20

1999

Pagels, Brown, Spence, Coetzee,
Damasio, Garton Ash, Burnyeat
Toulmin, Kleinman

Grethe B. Peterson, *Editor*

UNIVERSITY OF UTAH PRESS
Salt Lake City

THE TANNER LECTURES ON HUMAN VALUES

was composed in Intertype Garamond with Garamond Foundry display type
by Donald M. Henriksen, Scholarly Typography, Salt Lake City.

THE TANNER LECTURES ON HUMAN VALUES

The purpose of the Tanner Lectures is to advance and reflect upon scholarly and scientific learning that relates to human values.

To receive an appointment as a Tanner lecturer is a recognition of uncommon capabilities and outstanding scholarly or leadership achievement in the field of human values. The lecturers may be drawn from philosophy, religion, the humanities and sciences, the creative arts and learned professions, or from leadership in public or private affairs. The lectureships are international and intercultural and transcend ethnic, national, religious, or ideological distinctions.

The Tanner Lectures were formally founded on July 1, 1978, at Clare Hall, Cambridge University. They were established by the American scholar, industrialist, and philanthropist, Obert Clark Tanner. In creating the lectureships, Professor Tanner said, "I hope these lectures will contribute to the intellectual and moral life of mankind. I see them simply as a search for a better understanding of human behavior and human values. This understanding may be pursued for its own intrinsic worth, but it may also eventually have practical consequences for the quality of personal and social life."

Permanent Tanner lectureships, with lectures given annually, are established at nine institutions: Clare Hall, Cambridge University; Harvard University; Brasenose College, Oxford University; Princeton University; Stanford University; the University of California; the University of Michigan; the University of Utah; and Yale University. Other international lectureships occasionally take place. The institutions are selected by the Trustees.

The sponsoring institutions have full autonomy in the appointment of their lecturers. A major part of the lecture program is the publication and distribution of the Lectures in an annual volume.

The Tanner Lectures on Human Values is a nonprofit corporation administered at the University of Utah under the direction of a self-perpetuating, international Board of Trustees. The Trustees meet annually to enact policies that will ensure the quality of the lectureships.

The entire lecture program, including the costs of administration, is fully and generously funded in perpetuity by an endowment to the University of Utah by Professor Tanner and Mrs. Grace Adams Tanner.

Obert C. Tanner was born in Farmington, Utah, in 1904. He was educated at the University of Utah, Harvard University, and Stanford University. He served on the faculty at Stanford University and was a professor of philosophy at the University of Utah for twenty-eight years. Mr. Tanner was also the founder and chairman of the O. C. Tanner Company, the world's largest manufacturer of recognition award products.

Harvard University's former president Derek Bok once spoke of Obert Tanner as a "Renaissance Man," citing his remarkable achievements in three of life's major pursuits: business, education, and public service.

Obert C. Tanner died in Palm Springs, California, on October 14, 1993, at the age of eighty-nine.

GRETHE B. PETERSON
University of Utah

CONTENTS

PREFACE TO VOLUME 20

Volume 20 of the Tanner Lectures on Human Values includes lectures delivered during the academic year 1997–98.

The Tanner Lectures are published in an annual volume.

In addition to the Lectures on Human Values, the Trustees of the Tanner Lectures have funded special international lectureships at selected colleges and universities which are administered independently of the permanent lectures.

The Origin of Satan in Christian Tradition

ELAINE PAGELS

THE TANNER LECTURES ON HUMAN VALUES

Delivered at

University of Utah
May 14, 1997

ELAINE PAGELS is Harrington Spear Paine Foundation Professor of Religion at Princeton University. She was educated at Stanford and at Harvard, where she received her Ph.D. She is a member of the American Theological Society and the American Academy of Arts and Sciences, and was twice a visitor at the Institute for Advanced Study. She has received both Rockefeller and Guggenheim Fellowships and was a Mellon Fellow at the Aspen Institute, where she later served on the Board of Trustees. Among her published works are *Adam, Eve, and the Serpent* (1988); *The Origin of Satan* (1995); and *The Gnostic Gospels* (1979), which received the National Book Critics Circle Award (1979) and the American Book Award (1980). She is the recipient of a MacArthur Foundation Fellowship.

This evening I invite you to consider Satan as an inverse image of how we see ourselves — and others. After all, Satan virtually has made a profession out of being "the other"; like his fellow extraterrestrials in science fiction, the devil virtually defines what we think of as inhuman, nonhuman, alien. Like many people today, I used to think of Satan as an antiquarian relic of a superstitious age, a kind of throwaway in Christian tradition; but, after considerable research, I've come to see how important this figure has been in the history of Western culture. What emerged from it — a vision of the world in which the forces of good contend against the forces of evil — still shapes our political and religious imagination; and I've come to see that this remains even now for millions of people, whether or not they believe in Satan, enormously consequential.

Where did the figure of Satan originate, and what is he doing there? Satan is scarcely present in traditional Judaism to this day— and not present at all in the form that Christians later came to know him, as the leader of an "evil empire," an army of hostile spirits who make war on God and humankind alike. Yet when I began to investigate these questions, I discovered that images of evil spirits did develop and proliferate in certain Jewish sources in late antiquity, from about 150 years before the common era. Significantly, they did not develop among groups later taken to represent the main currents of Judaism, but specifically among groups of "dissident Jews" — groups that ranged from the Jewish sectarians who wrote the Dead Sea Scrolls to the followers of Jesus of Nazareth. Within decades, the figure of Satan — and the image of cosmic war — became central to Christian — and later to Muslim — tradition. How did this happen?

The lecture presented here is a brief sketch of the results of six years of research, available in more detail in my book *The Origin of Satan* (Random House, 1995).

Having started out asking these questions, I'd like to invite you on a mad dash through where these questions led me. What I'm *not* doing is what other people have already done well; I do not intend to investigate the cultural background of the figure of Satan or its literary history; and I'm not looking primarily at theological or psychological questions. What interests me instead is what I called to myself — as a joke — the "social history of Satan" (for how can a supernatural being have a social history?) — how he is invoked to express human opposition, to characterize human enemies, and to interpret all-too-human conflict. What I've come to see is that when people invoke Satan — whether in the first century or the twentieth — they have in mind not only some supernatural being, but also some very human beings. People who say, for example, "Satan is trying to take over this country, but we are resisting him," know exactly who they have in mind, and probably can name names!

The earliest mention of Satan occurs in a few scattered references in the Hebrew Bible. Jewish storytellers introduce a supernatural figure they call *ha satan*, which can be translated from Hebrew as "the adversary," or "the opposer," or "the obstructer." But this supernatural "opposer" never dares to oppose *God*. On the contrary, he is one of God's obedient servants, his messengers, called in Hebrew *malakim*, members of the heavenly court. Translated into Greek, *malak* becomes *angelos*, from which we get the word "angel."

The book of Job, for example, pictures Satan as an angel, one of the "sons of God," a member of God's council — a kind of divine "prosecuting attorney" to whom God assigns the task of afflicting Job in order to test the limits of his loyalty — indeed, a kind of "devil's advocate." But in Job, as in all classical Hebrew sources, Satan never acts independently, never on his own initiative; on the contrary, he remains one of God's angels, entirely subject to God's will. But some 500 years later, the dissident groups I mentioned began to turn this rather unpleasant angel into a far grander — and far more malevolent — figure; he becomes God's *enemy*, his *antagonist*, even his *rival*.

How, then, could one of God's angels go wrong? Jewish story-tellers offered various theories. One group of stories takes its clue from Isaiah 14, suggesting that one of the angels high in the divine hierarchy rebelled against the commander in chief and so was thrown out of heaven, demoted and disgraced (cf. John Milton's *Paradise Lost*). A second group of stories was sparked by the story in Genesis 6, which tells how some of the "sons of God" fell in love with human women and violated divine order by mating with them. A third group of stories blames, in effect, sibling rivalry: the ancient Jewish *Life of Adam and Eve*, for example, says that after God created Adam, he called the angels together to admire his work and ordered them to bow down to their younger human sibling. Michael obeyed, but Satan refused, saying, "Why do you press me? I will not worship one who is younger than I am, and inferior; I am older than he; he ought to worship me!"

So there are many stories about Satan's origin; but what struck me about them is this. Diverse as they are, whichever version you choose, they all agree on one thing: that this greatest and most dangerous enemy did not originate (as we might have expected) as an outsider, an alien, or a stranger. Satan is no distant enemy: on the contrary, he is an "intimate enemy" — one's closest relative, older brother, or trusted colleague — the kind of person on whose goodwill and loyalty the well-being of family and society depends, but one who turns unexpectedly hostile, jealous, and dangerous.

It is this attribute of Satan — his characteristic as *intimate enemy* — that disqualifies him so well to express internal conflict among Jewish dissidents, especially those minority groups whose primary quarrel was with other Jews. For those who developed the image of Satan and turned it against their enemies did not turn it against Israel's traditional enemies — against the alien enemies whom they called "the nations" (*ha goyim*, in Hebrew). Those storytellers who asked, "How could one of God's own angels become his enemy?" were asking, in effect, "How could one of *us* [meaning God's own people] become one of *them* — an alien, an enemy?" So it's not surprising that stories about Satan, rare as they are among mainstream Jewish sources, proliferated especially among certain dissident groups who had, in effect, turned against the rest of the Jewish community and consequently concluded that the others had turned against *them* — or, as they would say it, against *God*.

In ancient times, we learn from the Dead Sea Scrolls of perhaps the first significant group to invoke Satan — a devout and passionately sectarian group of Jews. Members of this group denounced the Jewish majority as apostate; they attacked the leaders of the Jewish people as totally corrupt for accommodating to Gentile ways and for cooperating with the Roman occupation of their land. Such sectarians declared that the majority had been seduced by the power of evil, whom they called by many names: Satan, Belial, Mastema (hatred), Beelzebub, "Prince of Darkness." One of the Dead Sea Scrolls is called the *Scroll of the War of the Sons of Light against the Sons of Darkness*. For these sectarians, calling themselves "sons of light," actually entered into their own sect — which they called the *new covenant* — by ritually blessing all members of their group and by ritually cursing all other Jews who were *not* initiated. The initiated "sons of light" eagerly awaited the day of judgment, when they expected God to come and annihilate the corrupt majority, their "intimate enemies," those Jews whom they called "sons of darkness," who, they said, belonged to the "synagogue of Satan."

Now the sect that wrote these words died out in the first century, and so remains a kind of antiquarian curiosity. But the case of another first-century Jewish sect — the followers of Jesus of Nazareth — has become rather more than an antiquarian curiosity, having structured much of our cultural heritage, whether or not we identify ourselves as Christian. And it's no accident that the foundational texts of Christian tradition — the gospels of the New

Testament, like the Dead Sea Scrolls — all begin with stories of Satan contending against God's spirit. Each of the gospels frames its narrative — both at its beginning and at its close — with episodes depicting the clash of supernatural forces it sees played out in Jesus' life and death.

How, then, does the figure of the devil (here usually called Satan) function in the New Testament gospels? Many liberal-minded Christians have preferred to ignore the presence of such blatant supernaturalism. Yet the story that the evangelists have to tell would make little sense *apart* from the context of cosmic war. For how could anyone claim that a man betrayed by one of his own followers and brutally executed on charges of treason against Rome not only was, but in fact still is, God's divinely appointed Messiah — *unless* his capture and defeat were (as the gospel writers insist) only a preliminary skirmish in a vast cosmic conflict now enveloping the universe? No doubt the devil serves the purposes of Christian theodicy — that is, his presence expresses what one scholar calls the gospels' "sense of the immediacy of evil" (Jeffrey B. Russell, *The Devil: Perceptions of Evil from Antiquity to Primitive Christianity* [Ithaca, N.Y.: Cornell University Press, 1953], p. 14). But this is not some vague idea or some abstract cosmological principle: what concerns these writers is the way they see the power of evil working *through certain people* to effect violence and death, above all, what Matthew calls "the righteous blood shed on earth, from the blood of innocent Abel to the blood of Zechariach the son of Berachiah" — violence epitomized in what these writers regard as the greatest of all evils, the execution of Jesus.

Having started out to explore how Satan in the New Testament serves to characterize human opposition to Jesus and his followers, I discovered that while the gospels *never* identify Satan with the Romans, they consistently identify him with Jesus' *Jewish* enemies. Although Jesus and his followers did not *invent* such demonization of their enemies, they (and Muslims after them) carried it considerably further than others had, and with enormous consequences.

Yet who actually *were* Jesus' enemies? What we know historically suggests that his enemies were the Roman governor and his forces, who condemned and executed Jesus on grounds of sedition against Rome. The gospels indicate that Jesus also had enemies among his own people, especially among those of its leaders who regarded his activity as threatening and potentially dangerous. *Yet had Jesus' followers identified themselves with the majority of other Jews, they might have told his story very differently — and with considerably more historical plausibility.* For example, they might have told it in a style like that of the book of Daniel, which tells how a spirit-inspired man defied the foreign enemies, risking death for the sake of God and of Israel.

But at this crucial juncture, for reasons too complex to summarize now, the evangelists chose to *dissociate* themselves from the Jewish majority and to focus instead upon their own quarrel with the majority of Jews who resisted their claims about Jesus.

Let's take a quick look, then, at the most influential portrait of Jesus — that of the gospel of Mark, probably the earliest of the New Testament gospels, and the one that Matthew and Luke used to write their own gospels. Mark opens his narrative with an account of Jesus' first appearance, identifying him as God's agent and placing him into the context of cosmic war. The story line goes like this: when Jesus is baptized, the spirit of God descends upon him and "immediately," Mark says, "drives him into the wilderness to be tempted by the Satan." From this first, single-handed combat between Jesus, filled with God's spirit, and Satan in the desert, Jesus emerges victorious, proclaiming the coming kingdom of God — God's imminent victory over the forces of evil. Immediately after, when he enters the synagogue at Capernaum, a demon-possessed man, hearing him preach "with authority," cries out, "What is there between us and you, Jesus of Nazareth? Have you come to destroy us" (1:24). The implied answer, of course, is *yes*: Jesus commands the evil spirit to leave and forces him out; the demon convulses the man and screams "with a loud voice" as he departs. All who witness this contest, struck with astonishment, ask each other, "What is this? New teaching! With power he commands the unclean spirits, and they obey him" (1:27). Even in his first public challenge to the forces of evil, Mark shows how Jesus' power sets him in contrast — and soon into direct conflict—with the Jewish authorities, for, as he explains, Jesus "taught with authority, and not like the scribes." No sooner had Jesus engaged Satan's power, Mark says, than his opponents' hostility turned murderous. Immediately after witnessing Jesus heal on the Sabbath, the Pharisees began to plot with the Herodians "how they might kill him" (3:6). Next, Mark says, "the scribes who came down from Jerusalem" charged that Jesus "is possessed by Beelzebub; by the prince of demons he casts out demons!" Even in the opening chapters of Mark, then, we can see that conflict between God and Satan sets the stage for conflict between *people*: or, put another way, conflict between God and Satan is a religious interpretation of *human* conflict — between those believed to be "on God's side" and those accused of being in league with the devil.

Finally, as Mark's narrative darkens into the events leading to the crucifixion, the reader senses Satan closing in, his presence manifest through the increasingly hostile and dangerous machinations of Jesus' "intimate enemies." Mark only implicitly connects Satan with Jesus' Jewish enemies — as Luke and John will do explicitly; and he does this by telling two accounts of Jesus' trial, aimed at showing the reader who is responsible for his death — and who is not.

Mark now tells how Jesus' disciple Judas — the most intimate enemy of all — knowing the hostile influential people bore against Jesus, betrayed him to the chief priests and facilitated his arrest. Mark gives a dramatic story of Jesus' immediate arraignment that night before the high priest, in whose presence, he says, "all the chief priests and elders and the scribes were assembled." At the conclusion of a judicial procedure, including interrogation of the accused and of witnesses, the high priest charged Jesus with blasphemy and the whole assembly "all condemned Jesus as deserving death." Scholars of judicial procedure point out the glaring improbabilities in this story. The Jewish council never met at night, so far as we know; the death penalty required a 24-hour delay; and, if imposed, would have proceeded by Jewish methods — certainly not by crucifixion, which the Romans invented and carried out in cases involving sedition.

Without rehearsing all the arguments here, I agree with many scholars who have argued that Mark's account of what happened was a construction designed to make an apologetic point. By this means, as one scholar observes, Mark evades "the indisputable fact . . . that Jesus' first trial and sentence were the work of a *Roman* court" (Paul Winter, *On the Trial of Jesus*, 2nd ed. [Berlin and New York: Walter de Gruyter, 1974], p. 34). Mark's account goes on to give an equally artificial story of Jesus's so-called trial before Pilate, but in this trial, as Mark tells it, Pilate never condemned Jesus to death; instead, he actually declared him innocent, and decided to release him. Only later, intimidated by the mobs outside shouting for blood, Pilate caved in and reluctantly allowed Jesus to be executed.

What motivates Mark to tell the story this way? For in Mark's account — and even more in Matthew, Luke, and John — the Pilate we know from history disappears and is replaced by the well-intentioned weakling of the gospel narratives. Yet a contemporary of both Jesus and Pilate, Philo of Alexandria, an educated, wealthy, and influential man who represented the Alexandrian Jewish community on a delegation to the Roman emperor, describes a very different Pilate: "a man of inflexible, stubborn and cruel disposition" — a man whose administration, Philo says, was characterized by "greed, violence, robbery, assault, *frequent executions without trial*, and endless savage ferocity" (emphasis added). Even if Philo exaggerates, we find Pilate's reputation for brutality confirmed in the histories written by Josephus, the Jewish governor of Galilee, some thirty years later. Josephus says that when Pilate was first assigned to govern Judea, he immediately — and apparently intentionally — introduced into Jerusalem a garrison that bore standards Jews considered idolatrous, an act that provoked mass demonstrations, as outraged crowds protested for five days outside his residence. Josephus says that Pilate also changed the coin types minted in Judea into coins bearing images that violated Jewish religious sensibilities and that he diverted sacred money from the Temple treasury to pay for building projects — an act that even Romans considered sacrilegious. Josephus tells us, too, how Pilate dealt with unruly crowds; in one episode, for example, he ordered his soldiers to mingle with the people dressed as civilians but fully armed; at a signal, they began to beat and kill demonstrators; others were trampled to death in the ensuing stampede. (Even Luke, who depicts at Jesus' trial a most benign Pilate, mentions in ch. 13 an incident involving galilean Jews "whose blood Pilate mingled with their sacrifices.") Finally, after an incident in which Pilate had executed the ringleaders of a Samaritan religious group suspected for inciting rebellion against Rome, repeated protests from his Jewish subjects finally persuaded Emperor Tiberius to recall Pilate and apparently to discharge him from office, since after that he disappears from history.

We cannot understand why Mark tells the story as he does — effectively exonerating the Romans — until we recall that this was, in effect, wartime literature, probably written during the Jewish war against Rome. Josephus, who fought in that war, calls it "not only the greatest war of our own time, but one of the greatest of all recorded wars." As I reread his account of that war, I thought of the American revolution; but the Jewish war was an attempted revolution against the Romans who occupied, ruled, and taxed Judea, a war fought by Jews under the slogan, "for God and our common liberty." The Romans saw it as sedition, however, and sent in 60,000 expert troops that swept into Jerusalem and left tens of thousands of people dead, the great Temple desecrated, burned, and razed to the ground, the center of the city in ruins.

Yet certain followers of Jesus, convinced that he had predicted all these events, had refused to fight in the war along with other Jews — a stand that alienated them from the communities. And when they continued to insist that Jesus — even after his execution — was actually God's appointed future king of Israel, they encountered predictable reactions from the majority (reactions that Mark depicts the scribes having toward Jesus) — that they were either crazy or demon possessed.

Among Romans they encountered no less hostility. Roman officials and troops were attempting to regain control over Judea after the war, were wary of any hint of renewed sedition, and were naturally suspicious of people who still professed allegiance to a would-be "king of the Jews" who had been recently executed on changes of sedition against Rome. On both sides, then, Jesus' followers often found themselves in dangerous and, at times, even desperate situations. Their greatest leaders had all died by violence: shortly before Mark wrote, Jesus' older brother, James, had been stoned to death by a mob in Jerusalem. Paul had been repeatedly denounced and beaten by Jewish groups and repeatedly hauled before Roman authorities until they finally executed him. And Peter, too, had been crucified, and like Jesus, charged with sedition.

Mark, then, addressing a largely Gentile audience after the war, is careful to present Jesus — and so, by implication, his followers — as an innocent person, falsely accused, who presented no real danger to the Roman order — even Pilate, Mark insists, knew that! Why, then, was he executed? That only happened, Mark says, because of a quarrel internal to the Jewish community. Certain Jewish enemies of Jesus, incited by Satan, tricked the Roman government against his own better judgment: Mark insists that the real quarrel was a religious one between Jesus and the Jewish leaders. Mark and his fellows still hoped to persuade their fellow Jews to "see the light" — to recognize God's spirit in Jesus; consequently, he treats this as a kind of family quarrel between Jews.

But ten to twenty years later, Jesus' followers had encountered increasingly disappointing response among their fellow Jews and unexpected success among Gentiles. The gospels of Matthew and Luke, written around 80 C.E., reflect both experiences and incorporated them into the story of Jesus. Since we can only glance at Matthew here, take a look at the way Matthew introduces the story of Jesus — the story of his birth.

Matthew's birth story is no Christmas card idyl. According to Matthew, the infant Jesus barely escaped death during a mass slaughter of Jewish infants ordered by a murderous tyrant. Many commentators have pointed out that here Matthew is presenting Jesus as the new Moses — whose infancy, even, parallels accounts in the life of Moses. But no one has pointed out how he simultaneously reverses basic elements in the Moses story — a story well known to every Jew from the yearly Passover celebration. Shockingly, Matthew casts the Jewish king, Herod, in the villain's role that tradition reserves for Pharaoh. Here it is Herod — not Pharaoh — who orders the mass slaughter of Jewish infants; Matthew declares that no sooner was Jesus born than King Herod, supported by "the chief priests and scribes and all the people," determined to "search for the child and kill him." Jesus' family eluded Herod by escaping into the land of Egypt; thus the land that in the Passover tradition symbolizes slavery and oppression now becomes the land of deliverance and refuge. And Matthew expects us to notice that while Herod and his court are trying to kill Jesus, Gentile foreigners, the *magi* — who will become the "three kings from the East" of Christian tradition — are coming to *worship* him. We cannot go through the whole gospel in this quick stretch, but let's take a glance at the story's climax — the terrible moment in which Matthew says, *"all the people"* — the whole nation of Israel, in effect — cried out to kill Jesus, even to the point of calling down a blood curse on themselves ("His blood . . ."). By contrast, Matthew depicts Roman officials in relatively positive ways, from Pilate to an anonymous soldier among Jesus' executioners who becomes nothing less than the first Christian convert!

While Matthew implicitly associates the Jewish majority with Satan, Luke does so explicitly. This is probably the only gospel written by a Gentile convert. Luke follows Mark and Matthew by opening with the story of Satan attempting to destroy Jesus in the wilderness; when his first attempts fail, Luke suggests that the devil continued to work underground — or on the ground, so to speak, through human undercover agents. Early in his account, Luke tells an astonishing story of Jesus' first public preaching in his hometown synagogue in Nazareth. Favorably received at first, he then predicts that his own townspeople shall reject him and declares that God intends to bring salvation to the Gentiles. Within moments, his words so outrage his audience that, Luke says, "hearing these things, all those in the synagogue were filled with rage, and they rose up to throw him out of the city, and led him to the edge of the hill on which their city was built, in order to throw him down headlong." But Jesus quickly departs, and so survives this first attempt on his life. Finally, at the climax of his story, Luke says that "Satan entered into Judas Iscariot"; Luke actually has Jesus himself identify the chief priests, scribes, and elders, to their face, as agents of Satan (the "power of darkness"). In the concluding story of Jesus' trial, Luke adds and changes details so that now Pilate three times declares Jesus innocent and insists that he is going to release him; but three times he is cowed by the crowds shouting for Jesus' blood, until he gives in to their demands.

What motivates Luke, like Matthew, to revise the trial account is not so much vindictiveness toward the Jews as defensiveness toward the Romans. So, as we've seen, the gospel writers want to present Christians, like Jesus, as innocent people falsely accused. Second, they increasingly represent Pilate acting as Christians hoped to persuade Roman officers to act, fairmindedly and justly; and third—where both of these fail—Luke's version offers Christians facing execution an exemplary paradigm for how to die. In the process of the changing accounts, as one scholar notes, "the stern Pilate grows more mellow from gospel to gospel . . . (from Mark to Matthew, from Matthew to Luke, and then to John). The more removed from history, the more sympathetic a character he becomes" (Winter, *On the Trial of Jesus*, p. 88). In regard to the "intimate enemies," a parallel process occurs, but in reverse. Where Mark depicts conflict within the Jewish community, division regarding Jesus' mission and identity, Matthew, writing ten or twenty years later, takes up Mark's gospel and revises it, so that Matthew — and only Matthew — has Jesus denounce the Pharisees as a "generation of vipers," "whitewashed graves," even "sons of hell." Luke goes considerably farther, having Jesus identify the Jewish leaders explicitly with "the power of darkness." The gospel of John, which we don't have time to discuss, seems to dismiss the devil as an independent supernatural character. But John depicts specific human enemies of Jesus acting, in fact, as the devil in person. John has Jesus declare to his disciples that "one of you is a devil," meaning, of course, Judas Iscariot. Soon afterward, Jesus addresses "the Jews" and declares that they are the offspring of the devil. For all its sophisticated theology, this gospel expresses the perspective of a beleaguered minority denouncing the Jewish majority in a cosmic war as polarized as that of the Essenes — but enormously more consequential.

Now I'd like to stop in a moment and open up a discussion — adding just a few words to avoid misunderstanding. Does this mean that Christianity invented anti-Semitism? Certainly not; in the first place, animosity toward Jews occurred long before the Christian moment began, as a new book by Peter Schafer demonstrates. Second, Jesus and his earliest followers were, of course, all Jewish; and the Gentiles who joined them, like Luke, were not so much anti-Jewish as ambivalent. They wanted to lay claim to

Israel's heritage, its traditions, and its promise of a glorious future; and some claimed to be the new Israel, the true Israel — but, of course, these claims encountered resistance among the Jewish majority, and the conflicts inherent in the history of the early movement are woven into the stories they tell. When I was in graduate school, I was told that anti-Semitism was a wholly unfounded misreading of Christian tradition; this research has shown me, however, that at least three of the gospels contain elements of anti-Jewish polemic, reflecting the conflicts from which this movement emerged in the first century. After that time, as this once marginalized movement became increasingly Gentile — and especially after it gained political and military power in the fourth century — its members could — and did — find in the gospel considerable fuel for the later fires of anti-Semitism.

But even during the first few centuries, Christians turned the image of Satan against a far wider range of targets — against the Roman empire and its government, which persecuted Christians, and then against other "intimate enemies" — other Christians, whom they called "heretics." Christians tend not simply to switch enemies, so much as accumulate them. To mention one of innumerable examples, recall how the founder of Protestant Christianity, Martin Luther, denounced "the Jews and their lies" in a vituperative pamphlet he called by that name; next, he attacked as Satan's allies all who participated in the peasants' war against the landowners; further, he denounced as "agents of Satan" not only the pope himself but all Christians who remained loyal to the Roman Catholic church — and finally he denounced along with them all other "protestant" Christians who were not Lutheran!

Surely none of us will imagine that Christianity invented human hostility, which is probably as old as the human race itself. But we can see that the Christian movement gave to hostility a moral interpretation — one that has proven enormously powerful. Virtually all people tend to denigrate those they define as other, regarding them as inferior, less than human. The Egyptian word for human being, for example, simply means "Egyptian." And Greeks regarded everyone who did not speak Greek as obviously "barbarian." What Christians added was a moral and religious interpretation of difference — one often read to mean that "we are God's people, and you are Satan's people."

Nor is this obsolete in the twentieth century. So compelling is this vision of God against Satan, good against evil, that it has pervaded the imagination of millions of people for nearly two thousand years — not only Christians but also Muslims — and has powerfully influenced the way we interpret political and social events. It was not so long ago that President Ronald Reagan denounced the Soviet Union as the "evil empire," and while I was working on this, during the Gulf War, President George Bush was denouncing Saddam Hussein as "the devil" — and Hussein no doubt called him the same (cf. Cyrus Vance/Salmon Rushdie).

When I began talking about this with my colleague Toni Morrison, she exclaimed, "But isn't Christianity a religion of love?" — and, of course, at its best it is, which makes so distressing the recognition that sometimes it has lent itself to hate. But her words remind us that other elements of Christian tradition have always urged Christians toward reconciliation. We recall the saying of Jesus from the gospel of Matthew: "You have heard it said, 'You shall love your neighbor and hate your enemy.' But I say to you, 'Love your enemies, and pray for those who persecute you, so that you may be children of your father in heaven.'" And many Christians, from the first century through Francis of Assissi in the thirteenth, or Václav Havel and Desmond Tutu in the twentieth — have shared in this same Christian vision of good against evil, believing that they have stood on God's side, but without demonizing their opponents. Their religious vision inspired them to oppose policies and practices they regarded as evil, often risking their well being and their lives, while praying for the reconciliation — not the destruction — of those who opposed them. But what this research has shown me — and what I wanted to share with you — is the struggle within Christian tradition between the profoundly human view that "otherness" is evil and the words of Jesus: that reconciliation is divine.

The End of the Ancient Other World:
Death and Afterlife between Late Antiquity
and the Early Middle Ages

PETER BROWN

THE TANNER LECTURES ON HUMAN VALUES

Delivered at

Yale University
October 23 and 24, 1996

PETER BROWN is Rollins Professor of History at Princeton University. He was educated at New College, Oxford. He was for many years a research fellow at All Souls College, Oxford, and he has also been on the faculty at Royal Holloway College, University of London, and at the University of California at Berkeley. He is a fellow of the Royal Historical Society, the British Academy, the American Academy of Arts and Sciences, and a member of the American Philosophical Society. He is the author of many books on the history of late antiquity, including *Augustine of Hippo* (1967); *The Making of Late Antiquity* (1978); *The Rise of Western Christendom* (1996); and *The Body and Society* (1988), which won the Ralph Waldo Emerson Award. He is the recipient of a MacArthur Foundation Fellowship.

LECTURE I. *GLORIOSUS OBITUS*: DEATH AND AFTERLIFE 400–700 A.D.

In a small book on *The Byzantine Empire*, written in 1925, Norman Baynes placed at the head of one chapter a quotation from Benjamin Franklin: "Nothing in life is certain but death and taxes." [1] More than any other scholar, it was Baynes who made Byzantium exciting for us, and, with Byzantium, the thought world of late antique Christianity. But Baynes was a man of his age. The chapter dealt with taxes, not with death. It is only comparatively recently that death has attracted the attention of historians of late antiquity and the Middle Ages. [2] As a result of the careful study of

---

* The initial research on the themes treated in these lectures was undertaken in Munich, where I owed to the generosity and care of the Carl Friedrich von Siemens Stiftung of Munich a much-needed opportunity to work in research libraries of unrivalled richness and to experience in them the kindness and interest of so many scholars connected both with the University of Munich and with the *Monumenta Germaniae Historica*. It was a delight and a source of instruction to me to deliver these lectures at Yale University. Since that time I have received constant help and criticism from friends closer than I am to the early medieval period, most notably, on this occasion, from Caroline Bynum, Henry Chadwick, David Ganz, Thomas Head, Richard Lim, Frederick Paxton, Julia Smith, and Carol Straw. The present text owes much to their advice. The errors remain, alas, very much my own: *ardua est ista via*.

[1] N. H. Baynes, *The Byzantine Empire* (Oxford: Oxford University Press, 1925), p. 99.

[2] On the issues that concern these lectures alone (quite apart from many other excellent contributions on death-rituals and on funerary practice), see F. Paxton, *Christianizing Death: The Creation of a Ritual Process in Early Medieval Europe* (Ithaca, N.Y.: Cornell University Press, 1990); H. Kotila, *Memorai mortuorum: Commemoration of the Departed in Augustine* (Rome: Augustinianum, 1992); E. Rebillard, *In hora mortis: Evolution de la pastorale chrétienne de la mort au IVe et Ve siècles*, Bibliothèque de l'école française d'Athènes et de Rome 283 (Rome: Palais Farnèse, 1994); M. P. Ciccarese, *Visioni dell'aldilà in Occidente* (Florence: Nardini, 1987); C. Carozzi, *La voyage de l'âme dans l'au-delà d'après la littérature latine (Ve–XIIIe siècle)*, Collection de l'école française de Rome 189 (Rome: Palais Farnèse, 1994); M. van Uytfanghe, "Les *Visiones* du haut moyen-âge et les récentes 'expériences de mort temporaire': Le sens et non-sens d'un comparaison, première partie," in *Aevum inter utrumque: Mélanges offerts à Gabriel Sanders*, ed. M. van Uytfanghe and R. Demeulenaere (Steenbrugge: Abdij Sint Pieter, 1991), and

the imaginative structures associated with death and with the other world what had once seemed a timeless continuum of Christian dogma has come to be caught in history. Certainly distinguishable constellations of belief, practice, and sentiment, each markedly different from the other, each bearing the imprint of a particular time and place, have emerged, like complex cloud formations detaching themselves from a featureless mist. In an outstanding recent study entitled *In hora mortis: Evolution de la pastorale chrétienne de la mort au Ive et Ve siècles*, Eric Rebillard has drawn attention to the profound changes that took place, within less than one century, between the age of Ambrose and that of Pope Leo, in the attitudes of Latin Christians to the "hour of death." He concluded that the time may have come for the historian "to take the final step, to envisage *des christianismes dans l'histoire*" — to envisage, that is, a succession of distinctive "Christianities" spread out in time.[3]

In allowing myself to be caught up in the enterprise of delineating the forms taken on by Christianity in varying regions and, within the same region, at different times, I have found myself lured increasingly far from my natural habitat as a historian of late antiquity. I have found myself at the very end of my period — in the sixth and seventh centuries. I have come, indeed, with a certain trepidation, to the threshold of what we had once been content to call (with what justice we shall see) the Dark Ages, the postimperial Western Europe of the early Middle Ages. I have touched on regions far from the heartlands of ancient Christianity: Ireland, northern Gaul, and the Hijaz are as important, in this story, as are Rome and Constantinople.

"Deuxième partie," in *Sacris Erudiri* 23/24 (1993/94): 135–82; J. Le Goff, *La naissance du purgatoire* (Paris: Gallimard, 1981), translated as *The Birth of Purgatory* (Chicago: University of Chicago Press, 1984); A. Gourévitch, "Au Moyen-Age: Conscience individuelle et image de l'au-delà," *Annales* 37 (1982): 255–75; J. C. Schmitt, *Les revenants: Les vivants et les morts dans la société mediévale* (Paris: Gallimard, 1994). See now the magisterial survey of A. Angenendt, *Geschichte der Religiosität im Mittelalter* (Darmstadt: Wissenschaftliche Buchgesellschaft, 1997), pp. 659–750.

[3] Rebillard, *In hora mortis*, p. 232.

I have been urged to do this by the growing conviction, which I share with other scholars of the period, that the *end* of late antiquity is now a story well worth telling.[4] For late antiquity itself has gained consistency in our minds as a distinctive phase of ancient history. It is no longer seen as a brief — if breathlessly exciting — moment of transition between antiquity and the Middle Ages. In the eastern Mediterranean, the Christian empire begun by Constantine amounts to half of the entire history of Roman rule. After 324, Anatolia, western Syria, Palestine, and Egypt slowly but surely settled down to enjoy a *pax byzantina* as impressive as that associated with the age of Augustus and the Antonines.[5] The stability of a continuous imperial system was lacking in Western Europe. But there also, styles of culture and imaginative structures set in place in the post-Constantinian empire of the fourth century still formed horizons beyond which most Latin contemporaries of Gregory of Tours were not yet prepared to think.

Yet, if we look back at this period from only a few centuries later, in the early Middle Ages, its ancient, unfamiliar profile stands out clearly. Though plainly continuous in so many ways with a very ancient past, the Christian imagination of Carolingian Europe and of post-Iconoclast Byzantium no longer belonged to the ancient world. The imaginative landscape of Christianity had changed. Pervasive imaginative structures, associated with a late antique Christianity still deeply rooted in the ancient world, had silently lost their power.

The slow and silent setting loose of early medieval Europe and Byzantium from their late antique past is a process that historians

---

[4] See Averil Cameron, "Byzantium and the Past in the Seventh Century: The Search for Redefinition," in *The Seventh Century: Change and Continuity*, ed. J. Fontaine and J. N. Hillgarth (London: Warburg Institute, 1992), pp. 250–76, at p. 250: "In the modern historiography of the Roman Empire, the 'third century crisis' is now so hackneyed a theme as almost to have lost its meaning. . . . By contrast, the seventh century crisis in Byzantium has yet to be confronted in its full impact and complexity."

[5] Averil Cameron, *Christianity and the Rhetoric of Empire: The Development of Christian Discourse* (Berkeley: University of California Press, 1991), pp. 191–92.

can only follow on tiptoe, as discreetly as it occurred. They must remain constantly aware of the weight and texture of the past in what, by the year 700 A.D., was already a very ancient religion. They must be careful not to force the pace of change by ill-timed outbursts of enthusiasm for apparent novelties. Yet, like Galileo, religious historians are entitled to mutter under their breath, *a pur si muove*: "And, nonetheless, it *does* move." Something changed throughout the Christian world, in the sixth and seventh centuries, that eventually rendered much of the late antique past of Christianity unfamiliar. I would agree with Robert Markus, the finest connoisseur of changes in Latin Christianity in the age between Augustine and Gregory the Great, when he suggested, in a lucid book aptly entitled *The End of Ancient Christianity*, that "in Western Europe, the late sixth century marks a real break with the world of antiquity." [6]

Markus's book was devoted to the changing relations between profane and secular culture in the fifth and six centuries. These two lectures will be devoted to similar changes, but on a theme almost too big to be seen — to changing attitudes to the relation between this world and the other world, and hence to death and the afterlife (in the first lecture), to sin, the mercy of God, and the destiny of the soul beyond the grave (in the second).

What I wish to show is that, by the year 700 A.D., an influential segment of opinion in the Latin Christian world, whose views would carry decisive weight in all future centuries, had come to an unprecedentedly high-pitched notion of the "other world" and to a sharply focussed view of the fate of the individual soul within that other world. As a result, Western Europe came to differ significantly, in an important aspect of its imaginative world, from its Christian neighbors in Byzantium and the Middle East, and even more so from the newly formed religion of Islam. Our own notions of the other world go back, effectively, to the seventh cen-

[6] R. A. Markus, *The End of Ancient Christianity* (Cambridge University Press, 1990), p. 222.

tury and no further. When we read late antique Christian texts, we find ourselves in a world where, even on an issue as seemingly continuous throughout Christian history as the notion of the after-life, the principal imaginative landmarks of early Christianity seem strangely out of focus, even exotic, to our postmedieval eyes. By contrast, the view of the other world that emerged in Western Europe in the course of the seventh century is still with us. The early medieval debate on the nature of identity beyond the grave— to what extent it can be known, to what extent its experiences could be assumed to be continuous with a former life, and how the actions of the living might affect its destiny — formed a muted, but significant, background to the emergence of a sharply delin-eated, biographical notion of the individual that has been the hall-mark of Western thought and religious sensibility ever since. It is hard to enter imaginatively into a world where such a notion was considerably less prominent.

This said, we must turn to our story. But let us have no doubt about one thing: it is easier to describe the imaginative shift to which I wish to draw attention than to explain it. I can at least begin with an attempt to sum it up, briefly, in "topographical" terms.

In the fifth and sixth centuries, as at an earlier time, the other world was still thought to lie close to hand. The human gaze brushed the very edges of the other world when it looked up at the night sky. For heaven itself lay behind the stars. The blaze of the inner halls of God's great palace was merely shielded from direct human view by the shimmering veil of the physical heavens. Heaven was near and yet so far. Looking up at the clusters of the Milky Way, one could almost imagine that it was possible "to catch a glimpse of the high pomps within; the vast, lighted con-cavity filled with music and life." [7] This is what the stars still meant to Symeon the Mountain Man, as he wandered in the hills

[7] C. S. Lewis, *The Discarded Image* (Cambridge: Cambridge Univesrity Press, 1964), p. 119.

above the Euphrates, in the sixth century: "at every moment he would raise his eyes to heaven, and be lost in ecstatic wonder at the hosts above, how they stood continuously before God without impediment, and that there is no cessation in their song of praise even for a short span." [8]

Such a view of heaven was "upper-worldly" rather than "other-worldly." [9] Furthermore, the gulf between heaven and earth was constantly bridged by etherial beings. Angels and demons shared the same physical space as human beings. Far from being empty, the upper air was filled with boisterous, contending powers.[10] Angels stood close to hand, to impart comfort and guidance to the faithful. Demons would frequently create chill pockets of moral and physical disorder in the everyday world. Demons, indeed, were believed to occupy distinct ecological niches on earth, lurking in out of the way corners within the settled world and claiming as their own the threatening silence of the desert spaces. In the words of an exorcistic prayer, scratched on a tile in northern Spain, that was where the demons should remain: "where no cock crows nor hen cackles, where no ploughman ploughs nor sower sows." [11]

But Paradise, also, lay close to hand. In the monastic settlements of holy persons and at the tombs of the saints, it was possible to find precious cracks in the wall that separated this world from the next. Light had been known to pour through those cracks, as did fragrance, and, with the fragrance, healing of all kinds — the miraculous blossoming of plants, the multiplication of foodstuffs, the flowering again of the shrivelled bodies of cripples and of paralytics, touched by the healing draughts that blew from the

---

[8] John of Ephesus, *Lives of the Eastern Saints* 16, *Patrologia Orientalis* 17:229.

[9] Peter Brown, *The Making of Late Antiquity* (Cambridge, Mass.: Harvard University Press, 1978), pp. 16–18.

[10] Jerome, *In Ephes.* 6.12, *Patrologia Latina* 26:581A.

[11] From a mid-eighth century abjuration against hail found on a slate in northern Spain: Isabel Velázquez Soriano, *Las pizarras visigódas*, Antigüedad y Cristianismo 6 (Murcia: Universidad de Murcia, 1989), no. 104 at p. 313.

Paradise in which the saints now dwelt.[12] A hole ground by generations of believers in the side of the sarcophagus of Theomastus,
an obscure fifth-century bishop and refugee from the Rhineland,
which stood in the courtyard of the church of Saint Hilary at
Poitiers, showed that the healing flavor of Paradise was to be
found in its very dust: "for the power coming from his tomb
proves that he lives in Paradise." [13] A phial filled with water from
the spring in which the head of Saint Julian had been washed after
his decapitation quickly took on the wondrous qualities of that
adjacent world: it was transformed "into the color, the consistency
and the fragrance of balsam." A visiting bishop had no doubt as
to its status. Here was a fragment of the other world in this world:
the martyr had "distinguished [it] with the powers of Paradise." [14]

Paradise was far too heavily charged a notion to be reduced to
any one, simple definition. Its actual situation in relation to heaven
and earth was subject to a wide variety of views. In the seventh
century, for instance, the newly edited biblical commentaries associated with the school of Theodore of Tarsus in Canterbury contain suggestions for any number of locations. These ranged from
a position above the fixed stars, for the Celestial Paradise, to a site
now occupied by Jerusalem, twenty miles up the road from the

[12] See esp. G. de Nie, *Views from a Many-Windowed Tower: Studies of
Imagination in the Works of Gregory of Tours* (Amsterdam: Rodopi, 1987),
pp. 108–28; E. James, "A Sense of Wonder: Gregory of Tours, Medicine and
Science," *The Culture of Christendom: Essays in Medieval History in Memory of
Denis L. T. Bethel*, ed. M. A. Meyer (London: Hambledon, 1993), pp. 45–60;
Peter Brown, *The Rise of Western Christendom: Triumph and Diversity* AD 200–
1000 (Oxford: Blackwell, 1996), pp. 107–10. For the recovery of Paradise as a
theme of eastern asceticism, see esp. B. Flusin, *Miracle et histoire dans l'oeuvre de
Cyrille de Scythopolis* (Paris: Etudes augustiniennes, 1983), pp. 125–26, and Peter
Brown, *Body and Society: Men, Women and Sexual Renunciation in Early Chris-
tianity* (New York: Columbia University Press, 1988), pp. 221–23.

[13] Gregory of Tours, *De gloria confessorum* 52, trans. R. Van Dam, in *Gregory
of Tours: Glory of the Confessors* (Liverpool: Liverpool University Press, 1988),
pp. 60–61.

[14] Gregory of Tours, *De virtutibus sancti Juliani* 41, trans. R. Van Dam,
in *Saints and Their Miracles in Late Antique Gaul* (Princeton, N.J.: Princeton University Press, 1993), p. 189.

well-known tomb of Adam, where the original garden of Eden had once stood.[15] Such learned dubitation apart, the notion of Paradise summed up all that was most overpoweringly adjacent and yet poignantly inaccessible in the careworn life of the average Christian. For a poet such as Ephraim the Syrian, Paradise encircled the world much as it ringed the Christian imagination, like a golden crown or the shimmering halo formed around the moon.[16] For the heroes of Christianity, Paradise was only next door. A martyr, such as Perpetua, might sleep, step up into Paradise, and wake the next morning with the heavy taste of its sweetness still in her mouth.[17] It was the gift of holy persons to pierce the veil of the present world and to see how much of the other world lingered insistently, for good or ill, in the world around them. Demons and angels were clearly visible to the eyes of a Martin of Tours.[18]

Altogether, we are dealing with a religious sensibility molded by a haunting awareness of the immanent presence of the other world in this world. In the words of the nineteenth-century religious poet Francis Thompson, cited by Henri-Irénée Marrou in one of his many masterly evocations of the quality of the thought-world of late antiquity:

> O world invisible, we view thee,
> O world intangible, we touch thee,
> O world unknowable, we know thee,
> Inapproachable, we clutch thee.[19]

[15] Theodore of Canterbury, *In Pentateuchen I*, 35 and 62, in B. Bischoff and M. Lapidge, *Biblical Commentaries from the Canterbury School of Theodore and Hadrian* (Cambridge: Cambridge University Press, 1994), pp. 308–10 and 388, with commentary on pp. 440–41 and 448.

[16] Ephraim, *De paradiso* 1.8, trans. R. Lavenant, in *Ephrem de Nisibe: Hymnes sur le Paradis*, Sources chrétiennes 137 (Paris: Le Cerf, 1968), p. 38.

[17] *Passio Perpetuae* 4, and the vision of her companion, Saturus, *Passio* 11–12, in Ciccarese, *Visioni*, pp. 76–78.

[18] Sulpicius Severus, *Vita Martini* 21.1.

[19] Francis Thompson, *The Kingdom of God*, Modern Library (New York: Boni and Liveright, 1913), p. 357, cited by H. I. Marrou, "La civilisation de l'antiquité tardive," in *Tardo Antico e Alto Medio Evo: La forma artistica nel passaggio dall'antichità al medioevo*, Accademia Nazionale dei Lincei 365: Problemi attuali di scienza e di cultura 105 (Rome, 1968): 383–94, at p. 392.

For the average believer, belief in the almost physical proximity of Paradise went hand in hand with a strong sense of entitle-
ment. The funeral of any baptized Christian, with its fluttering
white robes, fragrance, and shimmering candles, was an acting out
on earth of the solemn *adventus*, the entry in state of the soul into
Paradise. The dark terrors of the grave were not allowed to block
out a direct view of the sweet, fragrant grove of Paradise that lay,
as it were, just down the road. In the words of Prudentius's *Prayers
for the Daily Round*, from around 400 A.D.:

> *patet ecce fidelibus ampli*
> *via lucida iam paradisi.*
> See now for the faithful a shining way lies open
> to a spacious Paradise.[20]

Those who passed through the sheltered garden that flanked the
basilica of Saint Felix at Cimitille were reminded, by a verse inscription set up by Paulinus of Nola on the side door through
which they entered, that they could not have chosen a more appropriate path: "Christian worshippers, take the path to heaven
by way of this lovely greenery. An approach by way of bright
gardens is fitting, for here is granted to those who desire it their
departure to holy Paradise." [21]

A good friend of Gregory of Tours, Salvius of Albi (who died
in 584), still lived unquestioningly in such a world. Some years
before his death, when in the grip of a severe fever, he had passed
away, only to come to life again when already laid out on his bier.
He had been carried away by two angels to a place above "this
squalid world," even above the stars, until he stood beneath a
cloud of unearthly light. There he was engulfed in a fragrance of

---

[20] Paulinus, *Cathemerinon* 10.161–62, ed. H. J. Thomson, Loeb Classical Library (Cambridge, Mass.: Harvard University Press, 1961), p. 94; see also J. Guyon,
La cimitière Aux Deux Lauriers: Recherches sur les Catacombes romaines, Bibliothèque des écoles françaises de'Athènes et de Rome 264 (Rome: Palais Farnèse,
1987); pp. 193–94, on the bocolic quality of early Christian funerary decoration.

[21] Paulinus of Nola, *Letter* 32.12, trans. P. G. Walsh, in *The Letters of Paulinus
of Nola*, Ancient Christian Writers 36 (New York: Newman Press, 1967), 2:146.

such exquisite perfume that for three days after his return he had
felt no need of food or drink. Salvius was sad to find himself back
again, "in this black hole of an earthly dwelling place." The sweet
taste of Paradise that still filled his mouth gave way to blisters.[22]
But, for Salvius, the darkness to which he returned was never total.
After a particularly trying interview with King Chilperic in 580,
Salvius and Gregory met to say good-bye in the forecourt of the
royal villa at Berny-Rivière. Pointing upward, Salvius said to
Gregory:

> "Do you see above that roof what I see?" To which I said: "I
> see only the tiled roof which the king has recently had con-
> structed." "Do you see anything else?" I answered: "I see
> nothing else at all." I thought that he was joking, so I added:
> "If you see anything more, let me know." And he, drawing a
> deep sigh, said: "I see the unsheathed sword of God's wrath
> hanging over that house."

Sure enough, Chilperic's two sons died within twenty days.[23]

Half a century later the other world seems to have drawn
further away from earth. In a very different part of Europe from
Gregory's Gaul, Fursey, an Irish ascetic, came back from the dead
on two occasions in the course of a severe illness that had fallen
on him sometime in the early 630s.[24] He returned to life quite
literally scarred by the experience. Passing through billowing
flames, his cheek and shoulder had been jostled by the searing
body of a sinner from whom he had once received a gift of clothing in return for the imposition of a lighter penance than his sins
required.[25] It had been a rough ride. The opening stages of
Fursey's journey were accompanied by the chilling war-cries of the

---

[22] Gregory of Tours, *Libri historiarum* 8.1, in Ciccarese, *Visioni*, pp. 76–78.

[23] Gregory of Tours, *Libri historiarum* 5.50.

[24] Carozzi, *Voyage de l'âme*, pp. 99–138. The text of Fursey's visions is edited
by Ciccarese, *Visioni*, pp. 190–224, and Carozzi, *Voyage*, pp. 677–92.

[25] *Visio Fursei* 16, in Ciccarese, *Visioni*, pp. 220–22; Carozzi, *Voyage*, p. 691.

demons, arrayed against him like an army.[26] Swathed in an ominous fire that threatened to search out his every blemish, Fursey, in the person of the protecting angels who spoke on his behalf, faced demonic accusers who were well-versed in Scripture and who appeared to possess a "state of the art" knowledge of the rigors of the penitential system of their time. They knew an "unpurged" sin when they saw one. Hyper-Augustinian in this matter, they pointed out that many of Fursey's good deeds had not sprung from love alone. The busy preacher and administrator of penance had not always "become as a little child." He had not always loved his neighbor as himself, nor, good Irishman that he was, had he always refrained from exacting vengeance.[27] The demons stood on their rights. It was God who was shockingly, inscrutably lax: "This man has neither purged his sins on earth nor has he received vengeance here. Where is the justice of God? . . . Let us get out of here; for here there are no fair rules of judgment." [28]

By contrast to the experiences related by Fursey, for Salvius the short visit to heaven had been a moment of untroubled deliverance, a jailbreak from the "squalid world" out into the clear light and sweet smell of Paradise. It was a jailbreak as dramatic and as instantaneous as were the miraculous jailbreaks frequently associated with the saints of Gaul, whose very presence, alive or as relics, was believed, on many occasions, to have caused to swing open the doors of the suffocating blockhouses that flanked the palace of the count in every city.[29] For Fursey, by contrast, the journey to the edge of heaven and back had not been a moment of blessed deliverance. Far from it. It had been an awesomely pro-

---

[26] *Visio Fursei* 5–6, in Ciccarese, *Visioni*, pp. 196–98; Carozzi, *Voyage*, p. 681.

[27] *Visio Fursei* 7–10, in Ciccarese, *Visioni*, pp. 198–206; Carozzi, *Voyage*, pp. 682–86.

[28] *Visio Fursei* 9, in Ciccarese, *Visioni*, pp. 204–8; Carozzi, *Voyage*, p. 684.

[29] E.g., esp. Gregory of Tours, *De virtutibus sancti Martini* 4.26, trans. Van Dam, in *Saints and Their Miracles*, p. 295; F. Graus, "Die Gewalt bei den Anfängen des Feudalismus und die "Gefangenenbefreiungen" der merowingischen Hagiographie," *Jahrbuch für Wirtschaftsgeschichte 1961*, pt. 1: 61–156.

tracted "journey of the soul." Fursey's account of his experience
formed the basis for the first entire narrative of such a journey in
Latin Christian literature. It marks a significant step in the development of the genre now characterized by Professor Claude
Carozzi, in his magnificent study entitled *Le voyage de l'âme
dans l'au-delà.*

Carried upward by angels, the Irish abbot eventually reached
a heaven that differed little from that of the Gallo-Roman south-
erner Salvius of Albi. But the approach to heaven now passed
through an extensive and menacing no-man's land. The message
of his vision was plain. To die was to experience an *arduum et
difficilem transitum.* It involved a journey across a dark frontier,
whose faceless perils could only be allayed by being conveyed (in
the words of Claude Lévi-Strauss, describing the spirit-journeys of
a healing shaman), through the "fabulation of a reality unknown
in itself." [30] By means of such a "fabulation," the perils of the
world beyond the grave were reduced to order in the form of a
dramatic sequence of events. Fursey returned to life with a narrative of a journey: he told his hearers of its successive stages,
singula per ordinem. One encounter had followed the other, as
the soul travelled across the seemingly measureless distances of
another world. [31]

A later account of the death of Saint Ciarán, an Irish compatriot of Fursey, sums up in one small incident the sense of vertiginous distance, tinged with danger, which Fursey's narrative had
intended to convey. "When the hour of his death approached,
Ciarán ordered that he should be carried outside the house in
which he lay. And looking up into the sky he said: *Ardua est ista
via.* 'That is a hard haul up.'" That said, he went indoors to die. [32]

---

[30] C. Lévi-Strauss, *Structural Anthropology* (London: Peregrine, 1977), p. 179.

[31] *Visio Fursei* 17, in Ciccarese, *Visioni*, p. 224; Carozzi, *Voyage*, p. 692.

[32] *Vita Ciarani* 32, ed. C. Plummer, in *Vitae Sanctorum Hiberniae* (Oxford:
Oxford University Press, 1910), 1:215, cited by H. Lutterbach, "Der *locus resurrec-
tionis* als Ziel der irischen Peregrini," *Römische Quartalschrift* 89 (1994): 26–46
at p. 36.

As far as we know, Fursey's authority in later years did not come from his ability to see in this world what others could not see — to see the sword of God where the cautious Gregory had seen only a new pantile roof — but from having come back, as if from the dead, from another world. The uncanny blemish on his face — no small thing among the Irish, who were acutely sensitive to the shame of a damaged countenance[33] — and the fact that he could be seen to sweat, in the chill North Sea winters of East Anglia, whenever he retold the terrors of his journey, were what people remembered about him.[34] Fursey had already seen what all who heard him knew that they must one day see.

Fursey's visions took up the major part of the *Life of Fursey*, which was written in northern Gaul in around 656/57, in connection with the establishment of a cult at the tomb to which his body had been transferred, at Péronne. It represented the coming of age of a distinctly different attitude to the other world from that which Gregory of Tours (who died in 594) appears to have taken for granted. The fact that Fursey claimed to base his authority in Ireland, in the first instance, upon his other-world experiences should not mislead us into positing too local and "exotic" an origin for the new emphasis placed, throughout Latin Christendom, on the *grandeurs et misères* of the soul after death. To speak of a *fleuve visionnaire imprégné des traditions irlandaises*[35] is misleading. It involves both simplifying the religious culture of seventh-century Ireland[36] and overlooking the complexity of the

---

[33] F. Kelly, *A Guide to Early Irish Law* (Dublin: Institute for Advanced Studies, 1988), p. 132; P. O'Leary, "Jeers and Judgements: Laughter in Early Irish Literature," *Cambridge Medieval Celtic Studies* 22 (1991): 15–29.

[34] Bede, *Historia Ecclesiastica* 3.19.

[35] M. Rouche, "Le combat des saints anges et des démons: La victoire de saint Michel," in *Santi e demoni nell'alto Medio Evo*, Settimane di Studi del Centro italiano sull'alto Medio Evo 36 (Spoleto: Centro di Studi, 1989), 2:533–60, at p. 544.

[36] See esp. M. Herbert, *Iona, Kells and Derry: The History and Hagiography of the Monastic Familia of Columba* (Oxford: Clarendon Press, 1988): pp. 11 and 16, on the distinctly "this worldly" nature of the earliest traditions on Columba.

religious influences that came together to build up a distinctive spiritual world in northern Gaul in the generations after the death of Gregory of Tours.[37] Altogether, as a device for explaining the religious changes of the early medieval West, "the visionary Celt" is a severely overworked figure.[38] The careful work of Máire Herbert on the earlier traditions concerning the life of Saint Columba show that, in Ireland, saints tended to be admired for their asceticism and their learning, and not as purveyors of News from Nowhere.[39]

We should look elsewhere for the origins of this new sense of distance and potential danger. The visions of Fursey go together with texts that imply similar concerns, such as the second book of Jonas of Bobbio's *Life of Columbanus* (written around 639–43) — an account that contained a series of gripping deathbed scenes associated with the convent of Faremoutiers[40] — and the vivid *Vision of Barontus*, written at Saint Pierre de Longoret near Bourges, in 678/79 — in which a monk recounts a journey of the

---

The *testimonia* collected by Cumméne Ailbe emphasized the manner in which the presence of the saint caused incidents of daily life to "take on the hue of the supernatural" (p. 16). This is all the more noteworthy in a writer who was an exact contemporary of Jonas of Bobbio (see n. 40). See also C. Stancliffe, "The Miracle Stories in the Seventh Century Irish Saints' Lives," in *The Seventh Century*, pp. 87–115.

[37] A. Dierkens, "Prolégomènes à une histoire des relations entre les îles brittaniques et le continent pendant le haut moyen-âge," in *La Neustrie*, ed. H. Atsma (Sigmaringen: J. Thorbecke, 1989), 2:371–95; I. N. Wood, "A Prelude to Columbanus," in *Columbanus and Merovingian Monasticism*, ed. H. B. Clarke and M. Brennan, BAR International Series 13 (Oxford: BAR, 1981), pp. 3–32, and "The *Vita Columbani* and Merovingian Hagiography," *Peritia* 1 (1982): 63–80; see now P. Fouracre and R. A. Gerberding, *Late Merovingian France: History and Hagiography 640–720* (Manchester: Manchester University Press, 1996), pp. 100–106 and 313–19.

[38] P. Sims-Williams, "The Visionary Celt: The Construction of an Ethnic Preconception," *Cambridge Medieval Celtic Studies* 11 (1986): 71–96.

[39] Herbert, *Iona, Kells and Derry*, p. 11.

[40] Jonas, *Vita Columbani* 2:11–22, ed. B. Krusch, in *Monumenta Germaniae Historica: Scriptores rerum Merowingicarum* (Hanover: Hahn, 1902), 4:130–42, trans. in J. A. McNamara and J. E. Halborg, *Sainted Women of the Dark Ages* (Durham, N.C.: Duke University Press, 1992), pp. 155–75.

soul as difficult and as fraught with danger as that of Fursey.[41] Taken together, these texts announce the successful establishment, in the Latin Christianity of Gaul and elsewhere, of a newly perfected hybrid plant, destined to flourish exuberantly in all later centuries. The hybrid itself had been bred from strains taken from all over the Christian Mediterranean. To understand the nature of this new hybrid we must look back to the figure who is central to the end of ancient Christianity — to Gregory the Great. So let us turn, inevitably all too briefly, to the *Dialogues of Gregory*, which were written in 594, the year in which the other Gregory, Gregory of Tours, died.

For in the *Dialogues* of Gregory the Great, we can, perhaps, come close to the turning of an age.[42] While Gregory insisted that he wrote of the marvelous events that had occurred in his native Italy "in modern times," "modern" for Gregory often meant "post-Apostolic"; it did not invariably mean "recent." [43] What we find, rather, is an exceptionally rich deposit of memories (of which the life of Benedict in the second book of the *Dialogues* is a characteristic example) that come from the more peaceful days of an antebellum Italy, before the furious onslaught of the Lombards.[44] Many of these stories came from areas whose social and ecclesiastical structures had been seriously disrupted by Gregory's own time. Told to him by immigrants, these were broken shards of local

[41] *Visio Baronti*, ed. W. Levison, in *Monumenta Germaniae Historica: Scriptores rerum Merowingicarum* (Hanover: Hahn, 1910), 5:377–94; Ciccarese, *Visioni*, pp. 236–68; trans. J. N. Hillgarth, in *Christianity and Paganism, 350–750: The Conversion of Western Europe* (Philadelphia: University of Pennsylvania Press, 1986), pp. 195–204.

[42] On this topic I owe most to W. D. McCready, *Signs of Sanctity: Miracles in the Theology of Gregory the Great* (Toronto: Pontifical Institute of Mediæval Studies (1989), and G. Cracco, "Gregorio e l'oltretomba," in *Grégoire le Grand: Colloque de Chantilly*, ed. J. Fontaine (Paris: CNRS, 1986), pp. 255–66. See now R. A. Markus, *Gregory the Great and His World* (Cambridge: Cambridge University Press, 1997).

[43] McCready, *Signs of Sanctity*, pp. 16–32.

[44] Well seen by G. Cracco, "Il tempo fuori del monastero: Tentazione o missione?" *Codex Aquilarensis* 6 (1992): 119–34.

memory, detached from their original context. Picking through
the hagiographical debris of an earlier age, Gregory reassembled
these stories with consummate literary skill and imposed upon
them his own distinctive, I would even say distinctly *avant garde*,
interpretation.

In one such vivid narrative, we can see the pope at work, imposing his own, subtly different meaning on a story that had been
passed on to him from an earlier age. In the province of Valeria
(the hill-country of the modern Abruzzi) a *curialis* had seduced
his own god-daughter in memorably shocking circumstances.[45] He
was said to have done so when he had returned home drunk from
the celebrations that followed the Easter Vigil. It was also said
that he had done what any sensible late antique man would do
with such a sin on his conscience: he went to the baths to wash
away the stain of an illicit act of intercourse. Inhabitants of John
Chrysostom's Antioch had done the same on their way home from
the brothel.[46] But the *curialis* still had to face the solemn Mass of
Easter Sunday. He could not be seen not to take the Eucharist
along with his fellow-citizens at that time of high festival. He
knew what to fear. "He stood there trembling, with terror creep-
ing up upon him, expecting at any moment that this time he would
be given over to possession by an unclean spirit and would fall into
an agonizing fit in front of the entire Christian people."[47] Yet
nothing happened. He stepped out of the church with a lighter
heart. After six days he died of a stroke. Only then was his sin
revealed: "Everyone saw a flame shoot up from his tomb."[48]

End of story — or at least so it seemed to those who told Gregory's informant, the bishop of Syracuse. To have one's bones totally

[45] Gregory, *Dialogi* 4.33.1–5, ed. A. de Vogüé, in *Grégoire le Grand: Les dialogues*, Sources chrétiennes 265 (Paris: Le Cerf, 1980), pp. 108–12.

[46] John Chrysostom, *In Ep. I ad Cor., Hom.* 18.1: *Patrologia Graeca* 61:146;
for other examples, see J. Zellinger, *Bad und Bäder in der altchristlichen Kirche*
(Munich: Hueber, 1928), p. 100.

[47] Gregory, *Dialogi* 4.33.2, in de Vogüé, *Grégoire le Grand*, p. 110.

[48] Gregory, *Dialogi* 4.33.3, in de Vogüé, *Grégoire le Grand*, p. 110.

destroyed by fire was the ultimate annihilation: it amounted to a conclusive, fully public condemnation to oblivion of a notorious outcast.[49] That was all. For Gregory, the flame that burst from the tomb was not the end of the matter. It was no more than a "sign." "It showed what that man's soul suffered in the unseen world, whose very body even — *cuius etiam corpus* — a flame devoured before human eyes."[50]

With a slight but decisive twist, Gregory tilted a story of satisfactorily clear retribution in this world, exactly publicly for a secret sin that had breached peculiarly charged sacred boundaries, toward the other world. The dread of the onslaught of demons in a crowded church, the burst of flame from the presumably impressive grave of a local notable, the stuff, that is, of a good, ancient Christian story, are edged from the center of the stage: the avoidance of the one and the swift appearance of the other are now treated as no more than a well-known, "classical" opening movement to a more extensive and far stranger symphony — a tale of exquisite and finely calibrated sufferings in the silent world beyond the grave.

It is important to be aware of the significance of what was, in itself, a tiny nuance. It is not that the good Christians of Valeria

---

[49] Notoriously in the case of the heretical emperor Valens: Orosius, *Historia adversus paganos* 7.33.15: *quo magis testimonium punitionis eius et divinae indignationis terribili posteris esset exemplo.* In late-sixth-century Constantinople, the destruction of the bones and total burning of the body was regarded as an unusually drastic measure, appropriate only to pagans: John of Ephesus, *Historia ecclesiastica* 3:29 and 33, trans. R. Payne-Smith, in *The Third Part of the Ecclesiastical History of John of Ephesus* (Oxford: Oxford University Press, 1860), pp. 216 and 224, and Evagrius, *Historia ecclesiastica* 5.18. See also *Sixth Council of Constantinople* (553 A.D.), *Actio* VII.8.1 — the opinion of an opponent of Theodore of Mopsuestia: *et si ossa eius evulsa quispiam de sepultura eiceret et . . . incenderet, grantanter acciperes,* in *Acta Conciliorum Oecumenicorum* 4:1, ed. E. Schwartz (Berlin: de Gruyter, 1971), 189.16. For a later example, in which the prayers of a holy man prevent demons from inflicting the supreme "dishonor" of burning the body of a notorious sinner, whose soul they already possessed: *Life of Saint Andrew the Fool* 11.83 and 86, *Patrologia Graeca* 111: 724D and 728C, now ed. L. Rydén, *Life of St. Andrew the Fool,* 1521 and 1583, Studia Byzantina Upsaliensia 4 (Uppsala: Almqvist and Wiksell, 1995), 2:114 and 118.

[50] Gregory, *Dialogi* 4.33.4, in de Vogüé, *Grégoire le Grand*, pp. 110–12.

did not believe in Hellfire, nor that some people got there more
quickly than others and that their dramatic deaths showed where
they had gone.[51] But the otherworldly aspects of these stories did
not hold the center of attention. What made a truly memorable
story for old-fashioned Christians was one that involved touches of
Hell on earth — spectacular condign punishments that fell, here
and now, on notable sins, in the form of torment through possession by demons, vengeful flames, most frequently of all, in the
form of the "hellish" alternating heats and icy chills of sudden
fevers.[52] Gregory was the last person to deny that such things happened and were allowed by God to happen in the here and now.
But in the *Dialogues* he went out of his way to place them in a
different perspective. They were dwarfed by the looming immen-
sity of the world beyond the grave. Like the opening stages of a
Phony War, passing moments of contact with angels and demons
in this life seemed inconclusive skirmishes, compared with the
final, massed assault that all human beings must face at the hour
of death. Memories that had treasured the crackle of visible signs
of the presence of the other world in this world paled in comparison with the dread ranks of angels and demons that would gather
around each soul at the moment of its passing. With Gregory, we
can see an inherited conglomerate of early Christian notions "settle"
into a distinctive "tilt" — a "tilt" toward the moment of death
and the subsequent fate of the soul in an increasingly circumstantial other world.

It is through this perceptible tilt away from a world rustling
with invisible, contiguous powers toward a world beyond the
grave — a world clearly visible for the first time at the moment of

[51] Gregory of Tours, *De virtutibus sancti Juliani* 17, trans. Van Dam, in *Saints and Their Miracles*, p. 176.

[52] E.g, Gregory fo Tours, *Libri historiarum* 5.36. On the strict analogy between fever and the heats and chills of Hell: Jerome, *in Job* 24: *Patrologia Latina* 26:725D. On fever as "from the heat of Hell": al-Bukhâri, *Sahih* 71.28.617–22, trans. M. Muhsin Khân (Beirut: Dar al Arabia, 1985), 7:416–17. See also F. Paxton, "Power and the Power to Heal: The Cult of St. Sigismund in Burgundy," *Early Medieval Europe* 2 (1993): 95–110, at pp. 104–6.

death — that the fourth book of Gregory's *Dialogues* set the tone
for Latin writers of the seventh century, and, indeed, for all future
centuries.[53]

Yet, in his emphasis on the hour of death, Gregory emerges, in
many ways, as a "Latin Byzantine." He shared with the Greek
authors of his own age a finely developed and long-standing, ascetic sensitivity that saw, in the moment of death itself, a "great
mystery," to be contemplated with awestruck, contrite eyes.[54] The
movements of the dying person were often terrible to observe.
They were the visible signs, quite as chilling as was any incident
of possession, of the unseen approach of "The Powers" — of
angels in their dignified ranks sent to summon and protect the
soul; of demons who gathered in violent and disorderly fashion,
jostling the soul like angry creditors; or like unceremonious, no-
nonsense tax-collectors, sent to collect outstanding fiscal debts.[55]
What mattered in such a deathbed scene was that this was an experience of the other world that all Christians could and, indeed,
would share. Other manifestations of the other world in this world
were subject to the tyranny of time and space. Not every Christian
could expect to witness the public theatre of possession and healing at a major shrine, nor were they certain to encounter a holy
person in their own region or lifetime.[56] Death was different.
Witnessed by the companions of monks and of nuns, or simply
by the members of any Christian family, death ushered every

[53] See esp. J. N. Hillgarth, "Eschatological and Political Concepts in the
Seventh Century," in *The Seventh Century*, pp. 212–35, at p. 212, on the decisive
role of Gregory the Great in fostering "the awareness of the other world that seems
to increase in the age we are describing."

[54] See esp. Anastasius Sinaita, *De defunctis*, in *Patrologia Graeca* 89:1191–
1202, at 1196A, and Andrew of Crete, *De defunctis, in Patrologia Graeca* 97:1281C.

[55] Anastasius Sinaita, *De defunctis*, 1196C; compare the vivid incident of the
repentant brigand in the reign of Maurice, in Anastasius, *Oratio in Ps.*6: 1141C,
referred to by C. Farkas, "Räuberbehörden in Thrakien," *Byzantinische Zeitschrift*
86/87 (1993/94): 462–70. In general, see P. A. Recheis, *Engel, Tod und Seelenreise*,
Temi e Testi 4 (Rome: Storia e letteratura, 1958), pp. 152–77.

[56] A point well made by P. Horden, "Responses to Possession and Insanity in
the Earlier Byzantine World," *Social History of Medicine* 6 (1993): 177–94.

Byzantine into an orchestra seat, just as the curtain was about to rise on the most awesome spectacle of all.

The sermons of Anastasius of Sinai (died ca. 700) and of Andrew of Crete (died ca. 740) on the subject of death and the dying represent one aspect of a cultural agenda characteristic of seventh-century Byzantium and of the orthodox communities of the Middle East now fallen under Arab rule — the search for a religious language in which all orthodox believers could share.[57] Just as all could be assumed to view the sign of the Cross with loyal Christian eyes, so all might be expected to shudder, with a well-schooled Christian sensibility, at the unseen drama that was played out at every deathbed.

In this drama death remained, for Byzantines, the great leveller. The powerful, even the emperor himself, would fall silent at the last moment, "seeing now what they had never seen before, and hearing from the Powers what they had never heard before, experiencing what they had never experienced before." [58] It is here that we can measure both how near a Latin such as Gregory came to his neighbors in the eastern Mediterranean and yet how far from them he remained. Both wished to tilt the Christian imagination toward the moment of death, as a privileged, because truly universal, instant of contact with the other world. But the Byzantines of the early Middle Ages were urged to look at death still very much with the eyes of the living. They were to gaze with chastened hearts into the utter blackness that would swallow up the brittle pride of the "world." [59] They were not encouraged to look further.[60] "Do not search out the condition of the soul after its

[57] Well seen by Averil Cameron, "Byzantium and the Past in the Seventh Century: The Search for Redefinition," in *The Seventh Century*, pp. 250–76, at pp. 264–69.

[58] Anastasius Sinaita, *De defunctis*, 1196C.

[59] Anastasius Sinaita, *De defunctis*, 1193CD.

[60] A point cogently made by H. G. Beck, *Die Byzantiner und ihr Jenseits*, Sitzungsberichte der bayrischen Akademie der Wissenschaften, Philol.-Hist. Klasse 1977, no. 6 (Munich: C. H. Beck, 1979). The most dramatic and circumstantial

departure from the body, for it is not for you to ask about such things. It is not given to us to know even the nature of the soul; how should we know the nature of its place of rest?" [61]

What is surprising, then, when we turn from Byzantium to the West, is that so many seventh-century Latins fastened so rapidly on Gregory's *Dialogues* not to instill fear in the many — as they might well have done — nor to insist on the universal claims of death on all Christians — as Byzantines tended to do — so much as to heighten public certainty as to the guaranteed excellence of the few. Memorable deathbed scenes, regularly associated with over-powering radiance, with the gentler, heavy scent of perfume, with the clear sight of a luminous body receding, like a cloud, toward a vanishing point above the earth, often accompanied by unearthly music that grew softer as the invisible choir returned to heaven, announced, through clearly visible signs, that the other world had stepped majestically, for a moment, into this world, to claim for itself a privileged soul, whose *merita* entitled it to such a *gloriosus obitus* — so glorious a passing from this world to the next.[62]

It was this element that caught the imagination of later ages. Death was the appropriate moment that ratified the greatness of the great. In 973, Ulrich, bishop of Augsburg, a hardened servant

---

form of Byzantine accounts of the journey of the soul is the description of the *telônia* (the "customs-posts" passed by every soul on its way to heaven): see *Vita Basilii Junioris*, ed. A. N. Veselovskij, *Sbornik Otdelenija Russkago Jazyka i Slovnesti Imperatorskoj Akademii Nauk* 46 (St. Petersburg, 1889), pp. 16–28. This, the most circumstantial account, may be mid-tenth century: L. Rydén, "The *Life* of Basil the Younger and the Date of the *Life* of St. Andrew Salos," in *Oceanus: Essays Presented to Ihor Ševčenko, Harvard Ukrainian Studies* 7 (1983): 568–86. What is important to note is that it is not presented as a *personal* journey of the soul, like those described by Fursey and Barontus.

[61] Andrew of Crete, *De defunctis*, 1289C.

[62] *Vita Balthildis* A13, ed. B. Krusch, in *Monumenta Germaniae Historica: Scriptores rerum Merowingicarum* (Hanover: Hahn, 1888), 2:498; trans. McNamara and Halborg, *Sainted Women*, p. 275, and Fouracre and Gerberding, *Late Merovingian France*, p. 128. See now B. Caseau, "Crossing the Impenetrable Frontier between Earth and Heaven," in *Shifting Frontiers in Late Antiquity*, ed. R. W. Mathisen and H. Sivan (Aldershot: Variorum, 1996), pp. 333–43, on the implications of the iconography associated with the sarcophagus of Agilbert, bishop of Paris, at Jouarre.

of the Ottonians, whose timely fortification of his city in 955 had enabled Otto I to fall upon the Magyars gathered outside the walls in
the plain of the Lech, set about dying the right way. *formosissime*,
that is, with a copy of book four of Gregory's *Dialogues* to hand.[63]
We are already looking straight ahead, across the centuries, to the
words of Henry James: "So it has come at last—the Distinguished
Thing." [64]

We must ask why this was so. Of course, there was nothing
new, in itself, in such spectacular scenes, nor in the assumption
that the sanctity that had governed the lives of holy persons should
be made particularly manifest at the moment of their death. Already in the 430s, the priest Uranius wrote a moving account of
the last days of Paulinus of Nola, "so that we should judge his
life by the exceptional quality of his death." [65] What was new was
the extent to which this one event was allowed to eclipse all other
elements in the life and burial of a holy person. Despite his previous visit to Paradise, the actual death of Salvius of Albi had been
heroically matter of fact. When the plague came to Albi, he
stayed at his post. God revealed to him that his death was near.
He chose his sarcophagus. He washed carefully, put on an appropriate garment, and lay down to die.[66] He died as a bishop should
die, "according to his *ordo*." In the well-chosen words of Georg
Scheibelreiter, the death of saintly and prominent persons was
expected to be "a final mighty chord." [67] But it was a prolonged

[63] Gerhard of Augsburg, *Vita Uodalrici* 1:26, ed. W. Berschin and A. Häse
(Heidelberg: Universitätsverlag, 1993), p. 276.

[64] Leon Edel, *Henry James, The Master: 1901–1916* (Philadelphia: Lippincott,
1972), p. 542.

[65] Uranius, *De obitu Paulini* 2, in *Patrologia Latina* 53:860A. J. Amat, *Songes
et visions: L'au-delà dans la littérature latine tardive* (Paris: Etudes augustiniennes,
1985), gives an excellent impression of the sheer density and endurance over time of
late antique Christian imagery of the other world.

[66] Gregory of Tours, *Libri historiarum* 7.1.

[67] G. Scheibelreiter, "The Death of the Bishop in the Early Middle Ages,"
in *The End of Strife*, ed. D. Loades (Edinburgh: T. and T. Clarke, 1984), pp. 32–
43, at pp. 32–33.

chord. It reverberated for many days after the passing of the soul. Death itself marked only the beginning of a process that revealed, in a fully public manner in the here and now, that the threads that linked the holy person to his charges, though seemingly broken at death, had, in fact, been instantly rewoven. For this reason, the more public event, the funeral, overshadowed the deathbed. The funeral began with a shattering display of public, fully human grief. For the dead person seemed to have abandoned the living. But it was a grief that was turned instantly to joy. A miracle of healing, usually connected with the bier or with the garments of the dead person, showed that the sense of irreparable loss, expressed by such grief, was misplaced. The saint was still present among the mourners. Linked to public ceremonies that were now many centuries old, such expectations remained remarkably stable in many environments through the entire period that we are discussing. Here there was no dramatic change. Viewing the funeral cortege of Saint Eustadiola of Bourges, in around 684, Bishop Rocco declared that he had never witnessed such grief, "either at the death of a religious person in the church or at the passing of a royal figure." *Sed repente* — "but suddenly, by granting healing to various illnesses, Eustadiola showed herself to be still present." [68] A tomb heavy with miraculous power showed that, as far as the newly arrived denizen of Paradise was concerned, it was "business as usual." The intermittent "blaze" of *virtutes* (acts of power and healing) that emanated from the tomb, and not the moment of death itself, was the conclusive sign that such persons now dwelt "in glory." In the apposite words of Michel Rouche: "La tombe miraculeuse éclipse l'intérrogation sur la vie d'outre tombe et l'au delà." [69]

Such a way of seeing the passing of a saint was driven by a dogged need for continuity. We are dealing with a clear case of

[68] *Vita Eustadiolae* 8, *Acta Sanctorum: Jun. II*, p. 133A, trans. McNamara and Halborg, *Sainted Women*, p. 110.

[69] Rouche, "Le combat des saints anges et des démons," p. 543.

what an anthropologist studying the modern Irish funeral has
described as the conversion of death "from problem to opportunity."[70] Confronted by the death of its prominent members, the
community experiences a pressing need to mobilize the memory
of the dead in order to assert a brisk and orderly transfer of power
in the face of ever-present threats of disruption. A ritual of death,
burial, and solemn entombment assumed the most reassuring continuity of all: the unbroken spiritual "presence" of a saint who
continued to join this world with the next. As Paul Fouracre has
shown, in his study of later Merovingian hagiography, faith in the
continued "presence" of the dead was mobilized so as to restrain
and mask the horrendous scuffles that accompanied the transfer of
episcopal power in most sixth- and seventh-century cities. It was
hoped that, sooner or later, a shattered and hate-filled community
would eventually find its balance around the memory of the former
bishop. The establishment of a new cult, which reasserted the
"presence" of the dead bishop both in Paradise and among his
flock (a cult frequently instituted by the persons most implicated
in the recent dissensions), was supposed to mark the end of strife.[71]

Only in communities endowed with unusual institutional stability, or in groups that were considered to be either so peripheral
or so securely privileged as to stand at a distance from the con-
testational character of normal ecclesiastical life, was it possible
for the *gloriosus obitus* of the soul at death to emerge as the sole,
unchallenged focus of attention. Reassured on that central point —
that the other world had reached out, in a single moment of glory,
to take to itself one of its own members — such communities were
under less pressure to scan this world for further signs of an abiding "presence" with which to stem an ever-present tide of potential

[70] L. Taylor, "The Uses of Death in Europe," *Anthropological Quarterly* 62
(1989): 149–54, at p. 149.

[71] P. Fouracre, "Merovingian History and Merovingian Hagiography," *Past and
Present* 127 (1990): 3–38, at pp. 13–27.

disruption. Imaginatively and institutionally, members of such groups may well have felt that they lived in a more solid world. Paradoxically, therefore, Gregory's decisive "tilt" toward the other world, as it was taken up in the seventh century, does not necessarily reflect the anxiety of Christians reeling under the blows of a declining world, as the lamentable state of late-sixth-century Italy, seen through the lens of Gregory's own poignant rhetoric of the end of time, might lead us to suppose and as many outline histories of the Dark Ages seem to imply. Rather, outside Italy, a new style of "otherworldliness" was adopted with gusto by a new class of super-*potentes*, by a clearly marked, if narrow, elite of monks, nuns, and clergy that stretched from Rome and Toledo to Neustria, Iona, and Monk Wearmouth. We are dealing with a *Tugendadel*, an "aristocracy of virtue," clearly designated, in this period, by the spectacular nature of their deaths.[72]

We can follow this process closely in one region. By the middle of the seventh century, the Faremoutiers of Burgundofara, the Nivelles of Gertrude, and the Chelles, to which Queen Balthildis retired, so as to merit her own *gloriosus obitus*, were convents held to be *hors de concours*.[73] They do not appear to have suffered from the strains that wrought havoc in the convent of saint Radegund immediately after her death in 587. Clamorous weeping at Radegund's funeral and instant miraculous signs of her continued "presence" among the living did not prevent the eruption of a

[72] M. Heinzelmann, "Sanctitas und 'Tugendadel': Zu Konzeptionen von 'Heiligkeit' im 5. und 10. Jahrhundert," *Francia* 5 (1977): 741–52. See now F. X. Noble, "Rome in the Seventh Century," in *Archbishop Theodore: Commemorative Studies of His Life and Influence*, ed. M. Lapidge (Cambridge: Cambridge University Press, 1995), pp. 68–87, at pp. 75–83.

[73] See esp. Dierkens, "Prolégomènes," pp. 388–92; J. L. Nelson, "Queens as Jezabels: Brunhild and Balthild in Merovingian History," in *Politics and Ritual in Early Medieval Europe* (London: Hambledon, 1986), pp. 1–48, at pp. 38–43; I. N. Wood, *The Merovingian Kingdoms* (London: Longman, 1994), pp. 181–202; Fouracre and Gerberding, *Late Merovingian France*, pp. 97–118. While departing from his views on many issues, these are all built on the ground-breaking study of F. Prinz, *Frühes Mönchtum im Frankenreich*, 2nd ed. (Munich: C. H. Beck, 1988).

catastrophic revolt of the nuns only three years later.[74] Carefully protected by kings, queens, and noble clans, convents such as Faremoutiers, Chelles, and Nivelles were built of stronger stuff. From their abbesses down to the youngest child, death might come equally gloriously to all members of such convents. The supreme event could stand by itself, unmanipulated by the needs of factions to turn each death into an opportunity to assert the "presence" of the holy dead, as was the case in the strife-ridden cities of Gaul.

In this respect, it may be significant that the full flowering of a piety of the *gloriosus obitus* is best documented among groups of women. The great convents of northern Gaul were active centers of religious life in their regions, fully integrated into the world by complex privileges and endowments.[75] But notionally, at least, such groups of holy women were expected to stand to one side of the more frankly conflictual concerns of the male world.[76] Already in the *Dialogues* of Gregory, it is stories of nuns, and of noble nuns at that, that seem to look straight across more than a century. They bridge the seeming chasm, geographical and cultural, between the Rome of Boethius and the Faremoutiers of Burgundo-fara, where Jonas of Bobbio's *hortamina* addressed to the nuns of the community took the form of a series of dramatic deathbed scenes. Galla the patrician, the daughter of the senator Symmachus, the father-in-law of Boethius, and so a direct descendent of none

---

[74] Gregory of Tours, *De gloria confessorum* 104, trans. Van Dam; Venantius Fortunatus, *Vita Radegundae* 1.38, in *Monumenta Germaniae Historica: Scriptores rerum merowingicarum* 2:376, trans. McNamara and Halborg, p. 85; see G. Scheibelreiter, "Königstöchter im Kloster: Radegund (+587) und der Nonnenaufstand von Poitiers," *Mitteilungen des Instituts für österreichische Geschichtsforschung* 87 (1979): 1–37.

[75] I. Hen, *Culture and Religion in Merovingian Gaul, AD 481–751* (Leiden: Brill, 1995), pp. 54–60 and 150–52.

[76] On the entire subject of female monasticism in Gaul, G. Muschiol, *Famula Dei: Zur Liturgie in merowingischen Frauenklöstern*, Beiträge zur Geschichte des alten Mönchtums und des Benediktinertums 41 (Münster in Westfalen: Aschendorff, 1994), is outstanding; see also Julia M. H. Smith, "The Problem of Female Sanctity in Carolingian Europe: 780–920," *Past and Present* 146 (1995): 3–37, at p. 34.

other than Quintus Aurelius Symmachus, the last defender of the pagan Altar of Victory, died speaking with Saint Peter in a bed-chamber in which great candelabra always burned: for her fine, aristocratic soul craved for soft light at all times. "This event remains a subject of memory in the same monastery up to the present, because it has been narrated by the older ladies to the younger, in such a way that the nuns who are now there tell the tale as if they themselves had been present." [77]

Contemporary writers frequently gave the impression that the great seventh-century convents and monasteries of northern Gaul and of the British Isles were enclosed places of wonder, lying at "the world's end, some at the sea jaws / Or over a dark lake. . . ." [78] But we should not be misled by this impression. They were no Little Giddings. They were impressive human settlements, characterized by a complex cultural and economic life,[79] "holy cities" of a new kind. Many such convents were marked off by a sharp, even secretive sense of the sacred. It was a different sense of the sacred from that to which a man such as Gregory of Tours had been accustomed. In the great urban shrines of Gaul, the basilicas were open to heaving crowds of men and women, rich and poor, clergy and laypersons, gathered around fully public tombs, "like a swarm of happy bees." [80] Paradise came down to earth in a magnificently open-handed manner, in buildings filled with light, with

[77] Gregory, *Dialogi* 4.14.5, ed. de Vogüe, in *Grégoire le Grand*, p. 58.

[78] T. S. Eliot, *Little Gidding I*, in *Four Quartets* (New York: Harcourt, Brace and Co., 1943), p. 32.

[79] C. Doherty, "The Monastic Town in Early Medieval Ireland," and L. Swan, "Monastic Proto-Towns in Early Medieval Ireland," in *The Comparative History of Urban Origins in Non-Roman Europe*, ed. H. B. Clark and A. Simms, BAR International Series 255 (Oxford: BAR, 1985), 45–75 and 77–102; E. James, "Archaeology and the Merovingian Monastery," *Columbanus and Merovingian Monasticism*, ed. H. B. Clarke and M. Brennan, BAR International Series 113 (Oxford: BAR, 1981), pp. 33–55; and, by implication, for the foundations at Jarrow and Monk Wearmouth, I. N. Wood, "The Most Holy Abbot Ceolfrid," Jarrow Lecture, 1995.

[80] Gregory of Tours, *De vita patrum* 8.6, trans. E. James, in *Gregory of Tours: Life of the Fathers* (Liverpool: Liverpool University Press, 1985), p. 71.

heavy gusts of fragrance and with constant noise. Now Paradise itself became that much more distant; it was no longer "repre sented" on earth as exuberantly as it had once been, as monastic communities, many of them associated with carefully segregated, upper-class women, took over the care of the saints.[81] Clearly delineated by sacred enclosures, which few laypersons dared to cross, often grouped around caches of precious and exotic relics that outsiders would rarely visit, the *crème de la crème* of the new, Merovingian aristocracy (and their equivalents in England and Ireland), monks and nuns alike, could be presented as waiting for the one supreme, and sufficient, manifestation of the other world in this world, at the moment of their death.

The imaginative structures associated with such death-scenes were shared by both sexes. We are faced by a singularly high-pitched way of validating the identity of a spiritual elite. Here were men and women, like Gertrude of Nivelles, whose deaths declared that "their soul and inner world was all of a piece with eternity." [82] One is, indeed, struck by a sharpening of the "Platonic" streak in the hagiography of seventh-century Gaul.[83] The soul rises upward from the body with all the solemnity of an ancient moment of apotheosis. In this, the great abbesses of the

[81] Barbara H. Rosenwein, "Inaccessible Cloisters: Gregory of Tours and Episcopal Exemption," and Julia M. H. Smith, "Women at the Tomb: Access to Relic Shrines in the Early Middle Ages," in *Gregory of Tours*, ed. I. N. Wood and K. Mitchell (forthcoming). Though revealing in the cases discussed in these articles, the break with the past was neither irreversible nor universal. See now C. Hahn, "Seeing and Believing: The Construction of Sanctity in Early Medieval Saints' Shrines," *Speculum* 72 (1997): 1079–1106, and W. Jacobsen, "Saints' Tombs in Frankish Architecture," ibid., pp. 1107–43.

[82] *Vita Geretrudis, Miracula* 1, ed. B. Krusch, in *Monumenta Germaniae Historica: Scriptores rerum Merowingicarum* 2:464, trans. McNamara and Halborg, *Sainted Women*, p. 229; see now the excellent treatment of Bonnie Effros, "Symbolic Expressions of Sanctity: Gertrude of Nivelles in the Context of Merovingian Mortuary Custom," *Viator* 27 (1996): 1–10.

[83] M. van Uytfanghe, *Stylisation biblique et condition humaine dans l'hagiographie mérovingienne (600–750)*, Verhandelingen van de Koninklijke Academie voor Wetenschapen: Klasse der Letteren, Jaargang 49, no. 120 (Brussels: Paleis der Academien, 1987, pp. 231–42.

north resemble the last pagan Platonists, the philosophers of
Athens and Asia Minor, as they are presented to us in Eunapius
of Sardis's *Lives of the Sophists* and in Marinus's *Life of Proclus*.
They are shown as standing above the treacherous eddies of power.
They performed few miracles in their lifetime. They were above
such things. For them, as for Eunapius, miracles were garish
sparks, struck off by conflict with lower powers in this lower
world.[84] It is their death — in the case of leading pagans, a death
often described, through the words of an oracle, as a *voyage de
l'âme*, an orderly ascent of the soul to its rightful place among the
stars[85] — that provided all their admirers needed. The taking of
their soul up into heaven provided the final, conclusive glimpse
of the dizzying otherworldly heights on which their identity had
rested, even in this world. Great differences between the two
world views remain. The souls of the great Platonic philosophers
had ascended easily to heaven because they had descended from
heaven almost as easily, by the happy accident of birth into a
human body: the soul of Saint Gertrude was believed to have been
finally "released" and set on a safe road to heaven only after years
of anxious penance for her sins. But the silent sociological pressure to create imaginative structures that placed a sheltered and influential few as far as possible above human competition ensured
that Proclus of Athens — presented by Marinus as the majestically
unruffled "hierophant of the entire world" [86] — would have found
that he had more in common than he might have expected with
Gertrude, the great-aunt of Charles Martel: "For who in Europe
[wrote her biographer, in a novel adaptation of the old geographi-

---

[84] Peter Brown, *Power and Persuasion in Late Antiquity: Towards a Christian
Empire* (Madison: Universtiy of Wisconsin Press, 1992), pp. 143–44.

[85] Porphyry, *Vita Plotini* 22, commented by R. Goulet, "L'oracle d'Apollon
dans la *Vie de Plotin*," in *Poprhyre: Vie de Plotin*, ed. L. Brisson et al. (Paris:
J. Vrin, 1982), pp. 369–412.

[86] Marinus, *Life of Proclus* 19, ed. J. F. Boissonnade (Leipzig, 1814; Amsterdam: Hakkert, 1966), p. 16.

cal term] does not know the high status of her kin, their names and their estates?" [87]

The breakthrough of a sense of the distance of the other world, and a growing emphasis on the sheer height and dangers of the threshold that separated all but the most exceptional persons from its inner reaches, cannot be separated from a convergent phenomenon — the emergence, throughout seventh-century Western Europe, of new spiritual leaders, clearly linked to new social elites.

But that, of course, is only half the story. Those who were believed by their contemporaries to have passed most gloriously to heaven were precisely those who saw themselves as most endangered by their sins. Although endowed with a majestic destiny by her biographer, Gertrude of Nivelles was no exception to this fear. Indeed, it may well have been to none other than Ultán, the brother of Fursey, now settled at Fosses, southwest of Namur, that she sent a messenger just before her death, to ask on what day she would die: "for she says that, at one and the same time, she fears greatly just as she also rejoices." [88] How these fears had changed, and in what manner they came to be relieved in the centuries that stretched from the age of Augustine to Fursey's journey in the other world and Gertrude's question to his brother, will be the subject of the next lecture. For in Western Europe, in Byzantium, and in the new world of Islam, the throne of God itself shifted a little in the course of the seventh century: significantly different views on the issue of purification and forgiveness would emerge in different regions, leading, eventually, to the very different worlds of medieval Catholicism, orthodox Byzantium, and Islam.

---

[87] *Vita Geretrudis*, praef., p. 454, trans. McNamara and Halborg, p. 223, and Fouracre and Gerberding, *Late Merovingian France*, p. 320; Brown, *The Rise of Western Christendom*, p. 166.

[88] *Vita Geretrudis* 7, pp. 462–63, trans. McNamara and Halborg, p. 227, and Fouracre and Gerberding, *Late Merovingian France*, p. 235 wtih note 114.

LECTURE II. THE DECLINE OF THE EMPIRE OF GOD: FROM AMNESTY TO PURGATORY

In the first decade of the sixth century, Jacob, future bishop of Batnae in the region of Sarug, south of Edessa, on the road that led westward from Persia toward the Euphrates and Antioch, described the manner in which a parishioner might listen to a sermon:

> When the preacher speaks of matters that concern perfection, it leaves him cold; when he tells stories of those who have stood out for their zeal for righteousness, his mind begins to wander. If a sermon starts off on the subject of continence, his head begins to nod; if it goes on to speak of sanctity, he falls asleep. But if the preacher speaks about the forgiveness of sins, then your humble Christian wakes up. This is talk about his own condition; he knows it from the tone. His heart rejoices; he opens his mouth; he waves his hands; he heaps praise on the sermon: for this is on a theme that concerns him.[1]

The Christian churches of late antiquity in all regions were full of such less than perfect persons. It was essential that the *peccata levia*, the lighter, barely conscious sins of the average Christians, should not be held to exclude them altogether from the hope of heaven. In the Latin world, Augustine of Hippo found himself forced to face this issue, in the early decades of the fifth century, in the course of the Pelagian controversy. The Pelagians seemed to imply that every sin was a conscious act of contempt for God and, consequently, worthy of Hellfire. A newly discovered letter of Augustine, written to none other than Cyril of Alexandria, shows that he had to defend himself against Pelagian accusations

---

Since my first delivery of this lecture, I have treated aspects of the same theme: see Peter Brown, "Vers la Naissance du Purgatoire: Amnistie et pénitence dans le christianisme occidental de l'Antiquité tardive au Haut Moyen Age," *Annales* 52 (1997): 1247–61.

[1] Jacob of Sarug, *On the Penitent Thief* 60, trans. P. S. Landersdorfer, in *Ausgewählte Schriften der syrischen Dichter*, Bibliothek der Kichenväter (Kempten/ Munich: J. Kosel, 1912), p. 363.

of minimizing the dangers of Hell.[2] Of the many grievances brought
against Augustine, especially in modern times, softness on the issue
of damnation is not the one we would expect! But, by the end of
the Pelagian controversy, Augustine had gone out of his way to
find room in the Catholic church and hope of heaven for those

> who indulge their sexual appetites although within the deco-
> rous bonds of matrimony, and not only for the sake of chil-
> dren, but even because they enjoy it. Who put up with insults
> with less than complete patience. . . . Who may even burn, at
> times, to take revenge. . . . Who hold on to what they possess.
> Who give alms, but not very generously. Who do not grab
> other people's property, but who do defend their own — al-
> though they do it in the bishop's court and not before a secu-
> lar judge.[3]

Though reassuringly average to modern, post-Augustinian eyes,
such believers posed an acute problem to the late antique Christian
imagination. They would die. Their *peccata levia* — which Augustine considered to be linked to a tenacious, subliminal love of
"the world" and to habitual, unthinking overenjoyment of its licit
goods — were sufficiently pervasive and elusive not to have been
fully atoned for, by penance, in their own lifetime. Their souls
were faced with unfinished business in the next world. A residue
of unatoned, "light" sin, and, with it, an identity rendered deeply
particular by the actions of a past life, crossed the boundary into
an other world habitually defined by the absence of such features.[4]

---

[2] Augustine, *Ep.* 4*.4, ed. *Oeuvres de Saint Augustin 46 B: Lettres 1*–29*,*
Bibliothèque augustinienne (Paris: Etudes augustiniennes, 1987), pp. 112–14;
trans. R. Eno, in *Saint Augustine: Letters VI,* Fathers of the Church 81 (Washington, D.C.: Catholic University of America, 1989), pp. 42–43.

[3] Augustine, *Contra ii epistulas Pelagianorum* 3.5.14.

[4] Augustine, *Enchiridion* 68–69; *Enarrationes in Ps.* 37.36 and 80.20; see
C. Carozzi, *Le voyage de l'âme dans l'au-delà d'après la littérature latine (Ve.–
XIIIe. siècle),* Collection de l'école française de Rome 189 (Rome: Palais Farnèse,
1994), pp. 22–33, with G. R. Edwards, "Purgatory: 'Birth' or 'Evolution'?" *Journal of Ecclesiastial History* 36 (1985): 634–46, and E. Rebillard, *In hora mortis:
Evolution de la pastorale chrétienne de la mort au IVe. et Ve. siècles,* Bibliothèque
de l'école française d'Athènes et de Rome 283 (Rome: Palais Farnèse, 1994),
pp. 160–67 and 214.

Forced to "think about the unthinkable" on this issue, Christians of the fifth and sixth centuries tended to fall back on the "fixed-components" of their thought-world — to well-established imaginative structures. But no one imaginative structure could do justice to the full extent of the problem. Each structure reflected significantly different areas of experience. As a result, what is usually presented as the emergence of a doctrine of purgatory in the Latin West may best be seen in terms of the inconclusive juxtaposition of two such structures. One structure was associated with the eventual purgation of the soul after death; the other stressed God's exercise of His sovereign prerogative of mercy.

The two imaginative structures abutted each other somewhat awkwardly in the back of the minds of premedieval Christians, when they addressed the problem of the sinful dead. The opening of the way toward a doctrine of purgatory in the West, in the crucial period between late antiquity and the Middle Ages, came about as a result of shifts in the relative imaginative weight of these two structures. A pervasive and deeply rooted notion of the amnesty of God resolved the problem of the unatoned sins of the average believer by appeal to God's sovereign, dramatic ability to wipe the slate clean, much as an emperor was expected, at high moments of his power, to offer pardon to minor criminals and to cancel arrears in taxes. This notion enjoyed a density that takes some effort of the modern imagination to recapture. Persistent recourse to the notion of an amnesty of God, freely offered to still imperfect souls, overshadowed and inhibited the growing demand for some form of purgation beyond the grave, by which the souls of the departed were made fully worthy to enjoy God's presence.

Images of power, grown from the ground up over the centuries among Mediterranean and Near Eastern populations long accustomed to the symbolic weight of empire, came to lose a little of their unchallenged density in regions of the postimperial Latin West. As a result, a new synthesis of amnesty and purgation was free to come to the fore. For only when the spectacular, but studiously unparticularized powers of amnesty associated with the Empire of God receded, if only a little, in the Christian imagination could souls after death come to enjoy (in the minds of the living) the free play of a clear, interim identity, conferred on them by the medieval doctrine of purgatory. They were no longer a somewhat faceless group of erring subjects, waiting to receive, at an ill-defined moment of time, the all-sufficient grace of God's pardon. Hence my title: there is a relation between the "Decline of the Empire of God" and the shift from "amnesty" to "purgatory" that would render early medieval Western Europe different from Byzantium and Islam — both of them societies where the "imperial" image of God emerged, if anything, greatly strengthened by the crisis of the seventh century.

Our first problem, then, is one of imaginative perspective. It is the tradition of Augustine and Gregory the Great, and the consequences that later ages would draw from their works, which seems close to us. This tradition assumed that, since the fall of Adam, spiritual growth must be a prolonged and painful process. It might, indeed, take more than a lifetime to become worthy of the presence of God. Exactly how slow the process of healing beyond the grave might be and precisely what experiences might be associated with it remained open questions. A strongly rooted imaginative tradition gave a major place to the operation of "fire" of some kind.[5] Ever since the third century, Christians had appealed to the authority of Paul's *First Epistle to the Corinthians*, chapter 3, verses 13 and 15: "and the fire shall try every man's work of what sort it is . . . If any man's work shall be burned, he shall suffer loss: he himself shall be saved, yet so as by fire." [6]

For Clement of Alexandria and for Origen, this was a "wise fire," "strong and capable of cleansing evil." [7] Seen in this way,

---

[5] See esp. C. M. Edsman, *La Baptême de Feu*, Uppsala Universitet Nytestamentliga Seminar: Acta 9 (Uppsala: Lundqvist, 1940), pp. 3–12.

[6] 1 *Corinthians* 3:13 and 15.

[7] Clement of Alexandria, *Eclogae propheticae* 25.4 and *Stromateis* 7.6; Origen, *Hom. 3 in Ps.* 36.1. See H. Crouzel, "L'exégèse origénienne de 1 *Cor.* 3:11–15 et la

fire was a symbol of God's ability to transform every level of His own creation. Yet, at the same time, it was a drastic fire, which guarded the ontological threshold between the human and the divine. The "wise fire" of Clement and his contemporaries demanded a transformation more total than the mere purgation of individual sins. To pass through that fire was to go beyond the human — to approach God by entering a firestorm, in which human beings lost their very nature and took on the fiery essence of the angels who pressed in around His throne.[8] For later Latin thinkers, such an image of transformation by fire was too overpowering to be entirely welcome. Human identity itself, even the all-important distinction between saints and sinners, might be swallowed up in a furnace of such intensity. In the third century, Origen could suggest that "even a Paul and a Peter comes to that fire." [9] This was a thought that Latin Christians of later times, their religious sensibility attuned to the cult of the saints, were unwilling to entertain.

What mattered, rather, for Augustine and Gregory the Great was that the soul must change. It must undergo a process of "purgation" thought of on a largely medical model. In this process, the soul could not be passive. The total mobilization of the patient behind his or her cure, which was the secret of ancient medicine,[10]

---

purification eschatologique," in *Epektasis: Mélanges patristiques offerts au cardinal Jean Daniélou*, ed. J. Fontaine and C. Kannengiesser (Paris: Beauchesne, 1972), pp. 273–83; W. C. van Unnik, "The 'Wise Fire' in a Gnostic Easchatological Vision," in *Kyriakon: Festschrift für Johannes Quasten* (Münster in Westfalen: Aschendorff, 1970), 1:277–88; C. Carozzi, *Eschatologie et au-delà: Recherches sur l'Apocalypse de Paul* (Aix-en-Provence: Université de Provence, 1994), pp. 71–76.

[8] E.g., 3 *Enoch* 15.1: "at once my flesh turned to flame . . . and the substance of my body to blazing fire," trans. P. Alexander, in *The Old Testament Pseudepigrapha*, ed. J. H. Charlesworth (Garden City, N.Y.: Doubleday, 1983), 1:267.

[9] Origen, *Hom. 3 in Ps.* 36.1.

[10] A. Rousselle, "Du sanctuaire au thaumaturge: La guérison en Gaule au IVe. siècle," *Annales* 31 (1976): 1085–1107, and *Croire et quérir: La foi en Gaule dans l'Antiquité tardive* (Paris: Fayard, 1990), p. 101; H. Lutterbach, "Der *Christus medicus* und die *sancti medici*: Das wechselvolle Verhältnis zweier Grundmotive christlicher Frömmigkeit zwischen Spätantike und Frühen Neuzeit," *Saeculum* 47 (1996): 239–81.

was the *sine qua non*, also, of the life of the sincere Christian penitent.

> *virga directionis, virga regni tui.*
> *a rod of setting right is the rod of your kingdom.*
> (Psalm 45 [44]: 6)

> God cannot so act as not to punish sins. . . . While God withholds His hand [in forms of visible punishment] from your sins, withhold not your own. Turn yourself to the punishment of your own sins, since it is not possible for sin to be *un*punished. The punishment must either be at your own hands or at His. You take it on yourself, that He may forgive you.[11]

It goes without saying that, for men such as Augustine and Gregory the Great, an overwhelming sense of the majesty and mercy of God crowned the great arch of human penance, in this world and in the next. But the base of the arch rested firmly on classical soil. The responsibility of the sinner for his or her own sins linked final forgiveness to personal transformation. God was not content with substandard souls. Each soul must learn to depend "more closely and with greater love" upon Him, so as to absorb into itself, and not merely experience from the outside, "the fine-turned inner rule" of His righteousness.[12] Worked upon continuously by God's grace, the sinner must be changed from the inside, in a process that admitted no shortcuts. Amnesty *from* God, in itself, would not satisfy a soul that hungered to be *with* God. In this sense, talk of the necessity for the "purgation" of the soul as the *sine qua non* of entry into the presence of God retained a distant link, across the centuries, to the long, austere labor on the self associated with the moral world of the classical philosopher.

What is important to stress is that the moral world of the classical philosopher was notable for a carefully maintained "vacuum

---

[11] Augustine, *Enarratio in Ps.* 44.18; see J. Burnaby, *Amor Dei: A Study in the Religion of St. Augustine* (1938, repr. Norwich: Canterbury Press, 1991), pp. 196–97.

[12] Gregory, *Dialogi* 4.46.9, ed. A. de Vogüé, in *Grégoire le Grand: Les Dialogues 3*, Sources chrétiennes 265 (Paris: Le Cerf, 1980), p. 166.

of power." Slow, authentic self-transformation, pursued without
fear or favor, had always been the upper-class philosopher's answer to the proximity of overwhelming power — power of vast
might and largely unconsidered motivation, as capable of reckless
acts of generosity as of crushing severity. Philosophers should not
act in this manner, nor should they depend on the good graces of
those who did.[13]

Yet Christianity, like Judaism, had endowed God with just
those attributes of infinite power, linked to the sovereign prerogative of mercy, which characterized "the kings of this world."
Clementia was an all-important imperial prerogative because the
act of forgiveness was a stunning suspension, on the part of a
Roman emperor, of an untrammeled power to harm. It was the
same with God. The words of the Collect for the twelfth Sunday
after Pentecost, in the *Gelasian Sacramentary*, "Deus, qui om-
nipotentiam tuam parcendo maxime et miserando manifestas,"[14]
appeal to a frankly "imperial" virtue in God. It was a virtue still
appreciated by those Tudor and Stuart divines who incorporated
the same Collect, without change, in *The Book of Common Prayer*:
"O God, who declareth thy almighty power chiefly in showing
mercy and pity."[15]

We must be careful not to trivialize the notion of the "imperial" power of God by treating it as a simple projection upward,
into heaven, of the workings of the contemporary Roman empire.
It drew on images of divine monarchy that reached back for a
millennium, to the kingdoms of the ancient Near East and their

[13] Peter Brown, *Power and Persuasion in Late Antiquity: Towards a Christian
Empire* (Madison: University of Wisconsin Press, 1992), pp. 62–69; P. Hadot,
La citadelle intérieure: Introduction aux Pensées de Marc Aurèle (Paris: Fayard,
1992), p. 324.

[14] *The Gelasian Sacramentary* 3.6, ed. H. A. Wilson (Oxford: Clarendon Press,
1894), p. 227.

[15] *The Book of Common Prayer*: Collects. Traditional: Proper 21 (Evanston,
Ill.: Seabury Press, 1977), p. 182.

Hellenistic successors.[16] It was splendidly nonspecific and, so, capable of forming an imaginative backdrop to many monarchical régimes other than the Roman empire. By the year 400 A.D., it was so pervasive a model of power that it would be impossible to decide whether, in offering the occasional amnesty, an emperor helped to mould the image of the Christian God, or whether, as is more likely, imperial amnesty followed the divine model, in imitating the mercy of God.

But nor should we underestimate the constant presence of imperial practice in the minds of late antique Christians, and the manner in which this practice helped them to frame the question of the forgiveness of unatoned sins beyond the grave. A solution that placed a heavy emphasis upon a relation to the self, favored by Christian moralists such as Augustine and Gregory the Great, was frequently eclipsed by a solution posed in terms of relations with power. God's supreme power assumed, on an imperial model, an uncircumscribed reserve of mercy that overshadowed the strict implementation of His justice. This ultimate, unplumbed reserve of mercy might be tapped, even at the last moment, by the plaintiff sinner. In the *Sacramentary of Gellone*, the soul of the recently deceased, still soiled with sins, is held up to the amnesty of God:

> et si de regione tibi contraria . . . contraxit . . . tua pietate ablue indulgendo . . . tu, Deus, inoleta bonitate clementer deleas, pietate indulgeas, oblivioni in perpetuum tradas.

> And if this soul has contracted stains which come from this mortal region, so contrary to Your own. . . . May your Piety wash them away by showing indulgence, may You, by the goodness rooted in your nature, annul it with Clemency, that you may remit its debts in an act of amnesty, that You may consign [those debts] to perpetual oblivion.[17]

---

[16] E.g., A. Ziegler, *Die Königsgleichnisse des Midrasch beleuchtet durch die römische Kaiserzeit* (Breslau: Schottlaender, 1903); N. Johansson, *Parakletoi* (Lund: Ohlsson, 1940); H. Mattingly, "The Roman 'Virtues,'" *Harvard Theological Review* 30 (1937): 103–7.

[17] *Sacramentary of Gellone* 2895, ed. A. Dumas, in *Corpus Christianorum*, Series Latina 159 (Turnhout: Brepols, 1981), p. 462. See D. Sicard, *La Liturgie de la*

Furthermore, a long-established model of the workings of royal power had set in place a mechanism for such pleas for mercy to be considered. The notion of absolute power, and the consequent right to exercise amnesty, deliberately left space for a third factor: the presence, near the ruler, of persons whose principal, most publicly acclaimed privilege was the right, bestowed on them by the ruler, to exercise "freedom of speech" so as to forward claims for forgiveness. Those admitted to the presence of God — the angels and the saints — were authorized by Him to plead on behalf of their sinful protégés. They were intercessors. Indeed, they were frankly recognized as *patroni*, as "patrons" sufficiently confident of enjoying the friendship of God to bring before Him, with some hope of success, pleas for mercy on behalf of their many far from perfect clients.

All this is well known. The cult of the saints in the Latin world was characterized, among its most vocal exponents, by an intense piety of grateful dependence upon powerful protectors, thought of as *patroni* at the court of God.[18] What needs to be stressed, in this context, is the manner in which this warm sense of dependence on the power of others imposed a distinctive structure on the expectations of forgiveness harbored by contemporary Christians.

In the first place, the speculations of anonymous *misericordes*— of "mercifully minded" persons, whose views are referred to by Augustine and others — were more widespread than we might, at first sight, suppose.[19] Late antique Christians did not invariably

Mort dans l'Eglise latine des origines à la réforme carolingienne, Liturgiewissenschaftliche Quellen und Forschungen 63 (Münster in Westfalen: Aschendorff, 1978), pp. 261–345, and F. Paxton, *Christianizing Death: The Creation of a Ritual Process in Early Medieval Europe* (Ithaca, N.Y.: Cornell University Press, 1990), pp. 62 and 116–19.

18 Brown, *Power and Persuasion*, pp. 67–69; Johansson, *Parakletoi*, pp. 120–78, with Peter Brown, *The Cult of the Saints: Its Rise and Function in Latin Christianity* (Chicago: University of Chicago Press, 1981), pp. 62–68, and *Authority and the Sacred: Aspects of the Christianisation of the Roman World* (Cambridge: Cambridge University Press, 1995), pp. 73–74.

19 H. de Lavalette, "L'interprétation du Ps. 1, 5 chez les Pères 'miséricordieux' latins," *Recherches de Science Religieuse* 48 (1960): 544–63.

contemplate with joy the pains of Hell for any but notorious sinners and for blatant, contumacious outsiders. But the misgivings of the "merciful-minded" were not modern misgivings. They did not challenge the severity of God. But they frequently appealed, beyond that severity, to His power. God had a right, uncircumscribed and unplumbed by human expectations, to remit and to deliver from punishment. If this was so, then time itself took on a different meaning in the other world. The necessary time of purgation, for instance, was not the only measure of duration beyond the grave. Indeed, it was not the most important. The punishment of sin might be dramatically shortened for some. For others, the seeming immobility of eternal punishment might yet be broken by mysterious, sovereign acts of remission.

When he came to the penultimate book of the *City of God*, Augustine found that he had to deal with a surprisingly wide variety of views on the amnesty of God, "which I have had experience of, expressed in conversations with me." [20] In this, he was not reporting only the wishful thinking of woolly minded persons. He was touching the outlines of an imaginative structure endowed with exceptional long-term solidity. What he heard was that, at the Last Judgment, the power of the saints would prevail to obtain forgiveness for all but the worst sinners. For, so the argument went, if the saints had prayed for their persecutors, when alive, how much more effective would their prayers be now that they stood in the presence of God. At that time, their prayers would no longer be impeded by the frailty of their bodies; and their enemies now lay "prostrate before them, as humble suppliants." What saint could resist such an occasion to show mercy?[21] The amnesty granted by God in answer to the saints, on their great day of intercession, would be wide. It would certainly cover all baptized Catholics who had partaken of the Eucharist and, maybe, many others.[22]

[20] Augustine, *De civitate Dei* 21.18.1, ed. B. Dombart and A. Kalb, in *Corpus Christianorum* 48 (Turnhout: Brepols, 1955), p. 784.

[21] Augustine, *De civitate Dei* 18.9–11, p. 784.

[22] Augustine, *De civitate Dei* 21.19–23, pp. 785–89.

As for Hell itself, its eternity might also be disrupted by God's amnesty. The purifying fire, of which Paul had spoken, was the fire of Hell itself, into which sinful Catholics would be immersed for a short time.[23]

It was at this that Augustine drew the line. As Brian Daley makes plain, in his admirably clear *Handbook of Patristic Eschatology*, "For Augustine, the aspect of damnation [to Hellfire] that needed most elaborate defence was not its materiality but its eternity." [24] He was unwilling to give a definitive answer on the extent of the power of intercession enjoyed by the saints on the Last Day and on the exact nature of the sins for which this intercession might prove effective. In the *City of God*, as in his preaching,[25] Augustine was a conscientious bishop, who thought that it was better for Christians to remain sorry rather than feel safe: "for perhaps such things remain hidden lest the zeal to make progress slacken in its concern to avoid all sins." [26] But it is on the issue of time that we can sense the collision between a Neo-Platonist's hunger for a "total freedom from duration, extension or sequence" [27] in the presence of God and tacit acceptance, by others, of an "imperial" model, in which amnesty was expected to express itself precisely by the cutting up of time into significant periods of remission.

Thus, in around 400, the poet Prudentius, who, we should remember, was a retired provincial governor, could take for granted when he wrote his *Cathemerinon*, his poem *On the Daily Round*, that every Easter, perhaps even every Sunday, was marked by a spell of remission of punishment for that "population of dark shades" who were confined in Hell or, what amounted to much the same thing, in the Hell-like prison of the netherworld, in which

---

[23] Augustine, *De civitate Dei* 21.21.13–20, p. 786.

[24] Brian E. Daley, *The Hope of the Early Church: A Handbook of Patristic Eschatology* (Cambridge: Cambridge University Press, 1991), p. 149.

[25] E.g., Augustine, *Enarratio in Ps.* 37.6 and 80.20.

[26] Augustine, *De civitate Dei* 21.27.192, p. 804.

[27] Daley, *Hope of the Early Church*, p. 132.

they awaited definitive sentence at the Last Judgment.[28] Such remission was only to be expected. It had worked its way deep into the language of amnesty in a Christian empire. Valentinian I could hardly be called the most gentle of emperors. Yet he knew how to celebrate Easter in a manner worthy of his God: "On account of Easter, which we celebrate from the depths of our heart, We release from confinement all those persons who are bound by criminal charges and who are confined to prison."[29] In the yet more pious Ravenna of the emperor Honorius, prisoners would be released from jail every Sunday, to be conducted to the local baths, "under trustworthy guard," subject to the supervision of the local bishop.[30]

These, of course, were temporary measures, from which major criminals were excluded. They did not imply an emptying of the jails. They referred only to pretrial confinement, which was the sole legitimate form of imprisonment admitted in Roman law.[31] Yet such gestures, and the language that they adopted, did ensure that imperial and Christian ideas of the mercy of God kept pace, in a satisfactorily concrete manner, in the minds of late antique Christians such as Prudentius.

By contrast, the idea left Augustine cold. Compared with what was truly at stake for sinners excluded from the presence of God, it was a trivial solution:

> There is no harm in their thinking, if this gives them pleasure, that the penalties of the damned are at certain intervals of time somewhat eased.... But even if [the physical punishment imposed by] this wrath of God were the slightest that can be imagined — to perish from the kingdom of God, to be alienated from the presence of God, to be deprived of the abun-

[28] Prudentius, *Cathemerinon* 5. 125–36, ed. H. J. Thomson, Loeb Classical Library (Cambridge, Mass.: Harvard University Press, 1969), 1:46.

[29] *Codex Theodosianus* 9.38.3.

[30] *Codex Theodosianus* 9.3.7.

[31] Brown, *Power and Persuasion*, p. 153; P. L. Gatier, "Nouvelles inscriptions de Gérasa: Le prison de l'évêque Paul," *Syria* 62 (1982): 297–305.

dance of God's sweetness. . . . So great is *that* punishment, that no torments we have experienced can be compared to it.[32]

Faced by so deeply serious a dismissal, it is difficult to keep in mind the extent to which the immediate future of Christian views of God's amnesty rested with individuals such as Prudentius rather than with Augustine. The issue of periodic respite from punishment in Hell, raised by Prudentius, was, in itself, somewhat peripheral: it was simply a testing of the outer limits of a very solidly established structure of expectations.[33] In the world of Gregory of Tours, even the most seemingly insignificant miracles associated with the tombs of the saints of Gaul were heavy with meaning because they hinted at the eventual power of the saints to secure protection for their worshipers at the Last Day. Tiny wonders in themselves — a remission, for Gregory, of his throbbing headaches, the dramatic shattering of a glass of wine into which a bluebottle had fallen, in Poitou — they offered a majestic upward glimpse, psychologically magnified to huge dimensions by the surreal insignificance of the incidents in question, of the backdrop against which the saints would finally intervene to protect their charges:

> God deigns to protect in this world the foster children who respect His friends [the saints]. He ensures that the martyrs whom He receives after their victory as immortals in the beauty of Paradise will be of assistance when invoked by His [Christian] people. At the moment of Judgment, when eternal glory surrounds the martyrs, either the mercy or their mediating prayers will excuse us or a lenient punishment will pass, for a time, over us.[34]

[32] Augustine, *Enchiridion* 112, trans. E. Evans (London: SPCK, 1953), pp. 97–98.

[33] C. Carozzi, *Eschatologie et au-delà: Recherches sur l'Apocalypse de Paul* (Aix-en-Provence: Université de Provence, 1994), pp. 127–31.

[34] Gregory of Tours, *De gloria martyrum* 106, trans. R. Van Dam, in *Gregory of Tours: Glory of the Martyrs* (Liverpool: University of Liverpool Press, 1988), pp. 133–34.

Reticent about many aspects of himself and his family, Gregory is at his most urgently autobiographical when he thinks of himself on the Last Day:

> And when, at the Last Judgment, I am to be placed on the left hand, Martin will deign to pick me out from the middle of the goats with his sacred right hand. He will shelter me behind his back. And when, in accordance with the Judge's sentence, I am to be condemned to the infernal flames, he will throw over me that sacred cloak, by which he once covered the King of Glory [by sharing it with Christ in the form of the beggar with whom he had divided his officer's robe] and will gain a reprieve for me, as angels tell the King. . . . "This is the man for whom Saint Martin pleads." [35]

The world of Gregory of Tours was characterized by repeated, dramatic scenes of amnesty. In this respect, the Merovingian state of the sixth century had remained formidably "sub-Roman." Its upper classes found themselves implicated, on a day-to-day basis, in the stark antitheses of justice and forgiveness, abject humiliation and protection, which formed the ever-present background to the religious sensibility of Gregory himself. Faced by the King of Heaven, kings knew exactly how to behave. In 561, after a reign of fifteen years, the aging king Chlothar came to the shrine of Saint Martin at Tours:

> in front of the tomb . . . he went over all the actions in which he had, perhaps, failed to do what was right. He prayed with much groaning that the blessed confessor should beseech the mercy of the Lord, so that, through Martin's intervention on his behalf, God might cancel the account of those things which he had done wrongly. [36]

[35] Gregory of Tours, *De virtutibus sancti Martini* 2.60, trans. R. Van Dam, in *Saints and Their Miracles in Late Antique Gaul* (Princeton, N.J.: Princeton University Press, 1993), p. 259.

[36] Gregory of Tours, *Liber historiarum* 4.21.

The *potentes* of the kingdom were expected to behave in the same manner before their king. *Repraesentari*, to be "led into the presence of the king," was at once a privilege and a moment of danger.[37] Guntram Boso, for instance, was a notoriously tricky member of the newly formed elite of Austrasia. But he was also sufficiently close to the Catholic piety of Gregory to allow himself, on one occasion, to be persuaded by a soothsayer that he would be Gregory's successor as bishop of Tours.[38] When he fell out of favor with Brunhild, the queen-mother, he knew what he should do:

> He began to go around the bishops and courtiers. . . . He then pinned his hopes on gaining pardon through bishop Agerich of Verdun, who was god-father to the king . . . stripped of his arms and in fetters, he was brought into the King's presence by the bishop. . . . Falling at the king's feet, he said: *Peccavi* "I have sinned. . . ." The king ordered him to be raised from the ground and place him in the hands of the bishop: "Holy bishop, he is yours. . . ."[39]

And so, once again, Guntram Boso wriggled free.

Count Leudast, by contrast, failed to heed Gregory's advice on a similar occasion. When granted an audience with the king in Paris, in 583, he did not go out of his way to gain the good graces of Queen Fredegund: "unforesightful and silly man that he was, he placed his confidence in the fact that he had gained the favor of coming into the presence of the king." Without the right intercessor, admittance to the royal presence did him no good. Left on his own, unprotected, Leudast was immediately "jumped" by the queen's servants, taken to a neighboring country villa, and killed in an atrocious manner.[40]

In Gregory's world, the demons did just that to those who neglected, or who had forfeited, the protection of the saints. Un-

[37] Gregory of Tours, *Liber historiarum* 5.20; 6.10 and 24; 7.38; 8.6.
[38] Gregory of Tours, *Liber historiarum* 5.14.
[39] Gregory of Tours, *Liber historiarum* 9.8.
[40] Gregory of Tours, *Liber historiarum* 6.32.

guarded souls might be swept away by the demons at any time. Neglect of the protection offered by the sign of the Cross exposed even innocent persons to passing affliction in this life.[41] At the moment of death, the themes of protection by the saints and the ever-present threat of ambush by the demons were played out with gripping intensity. The troubled last stages of a deathbed could speak directly of protection and its chilling alternative. When Dioscola, the niece of none other than Bishop Salvius of Albi, lay dying in the convent of Saint Radegund, the efforts of the saints on her behalf were palpable as death approached. Finally, speaking through the persons of the possessed, the demons began to howl with frustration, as Dioscola's soul brushed past them, escorted to safety by Saint Michael.[42] These incidents meant so much to Gregory because they were so many overtures to the final scene of protection, amnesty, and possible abandonment that filled his heart as he thought of the Last Day.

Gregory wrote as he did because he considered that his contemporaries had become complacent. They had allowed that last scene to slip from their minds. His careful calculations of time and detailed record of signs of growing disorder around him were meant to warn those who, unlike himself, were inclined "to place no further hope on the approaching end of the world."[43] Just as Paradise pressed into this world, not only around the tombs of the saints, but into so many unconsidered nooks and crannies of this world, made fragrant with scattered hints of heaven, so the throne of God at the Last Day was a looming presence, rendered perpetually actual to him, in his own world, by so many sharp, small scenes of patronage, protection, and amnesty.

---

[41] E.g., Gregory of Tours, *De virtutibus sancti Martini* 2.45, trans. Van Dam, in *Saints and Their Miracles*, p. 252.

[42] Gregory of Tours, *Liber historiarum* 6.30.

[43] Gregory of Tours, *Liber historiarum* 1, praef.: *qui adpropinquantem finem mundi disperant.* The reader should know that my interpretation of this phrase differs from the *communis opinio*. L. Thorpe, *Gregory of Tours: The History of the Franks* (Harmondsworth: Penguin, 1974), p. 67, translates "who are losing hope

On both these issues, Gregory may already have came to find himself, by the late 580s, a little out of date. In our last lecture, we have seen how an influential trend in religious sensibility had begun to gather momentum in his own lifetime and in the generation after his death. This would tilt interest in the other world away from its day-to-day manifestations among the living. Serendipitous wonder at the many random hints of the presence of the other world in this world gave way to a more sharply focused emphasis on the world beyond the grave. New forms of literature stressed the prolonged and arduous nature of the journey of the soul after death, thereby conveying a novel sense of peril, which served to heighten admiration for the spectacular deaths of the privileged few.

As a result, the Throne of God itself became that much more distant. The Ireland in which Fursey had his visions, among his kin, in the early 630s, was a land of virtually no state power and, so, a land without amnesty. Irish kings could be as forceful and

---

as they see the end of the world coming nearer." I would translate "who do not expect the end of the world to come." *Disperare* can mean "not expect, lose hope of": cf. *Liber historiarum* 4.12, citing Sidonius Apollinaris, *Letter* 2.1: *nec accipiebat instrumenta desperans*, trans. O. M. Dalton, in *The Letters of Sidonius* (Oxford: Clarendon Press, 1915), 1:35: "nor does he trouble to furnish himself with deeds, knowing it hopeless to prove a title." Commenting on this passage, B. Krusch renders *desperans* as *spem nullam habens*, in *Gregorii Turonensis Opera Historica: Monumenta Germaniae Historica: Scriptores rerum Merowingicarum* 1:1 (Hanover: Hahn, 1951), p. 142, note 2. See also *Sortes Sangallenses* 33, R.8: *Habebis spem fidei, sed de disperato*, in A. Dold, *Die Orakelsprüche im St. Galler Palimpsestcodex 908*, Sitzungsberichte 225:4 (Vienna: Österreichische Akademie der Wissenschaften, 1948, p. 24, with note on p. 110: "from someone you do not expect." See A. H. B. Breukelaar, *Historiography and Episcopal Authority in Sixth-Century Gaul: The Histories of Gregory of Tours Interpreted in Historical Context*, Forschungen zur Kirchen- und Dogmengeschichte 57 (Göttingen: Vandenhoeck and Ruprecht, 1994), p. 300 and note 23, and on Gregory's attitude to the approaching end of time, see pp. 52–55 and 169–74, with M. Heinzelmann, *Gregor von Tours (538–94): "Zehn Bücher der Geschichte": Historiographie und Gesellschaftskonzept im 6. Jht.* (Darmstadt: Wissenschaftliche Buchgesellschaft, 1994), pp. 71–72. See also R. Landes, "Lest the Millennium Be Fulfilled: Apocalyptic Expectations and the Pattern of Western Chronography 100–800 C.E.," *The Use and Abuse of Eschatology in the Middle Ages*, ed. W. Verbeke, D. Verhelst, and R. Welkenhuysen (Louvain: Louvain University Press, 1988), pp. 137–211 at pp. 166–67. Gregory's attitude was that expected of pious persons: see the preamble for a pious foundation in Marculf, *Formulae* 2.3, ed. A. Uddholm (Uppsala: Eranos, 1962), p. 178.

violent as any Merovingian, but their power remained carefully masked by a "polite political discourse," which saw them, still, as no more than chieftains, surrounded by free clients.[44] It was a world where, in theory at least, status and political power were carefully disjoined in a manner that contrasted sharply with the sub-Roman structures of Gregory's Gaul.[45] Law and order derived from "elaborate norms of conduct . . . and a set of juridical institutions that positively sanctioned adhesion to these norms."[46] While a state, such as the Merovingian kingdom, could impose adherence to legal norms by fear of savage punishment tempered by gestures of amnesty, Irish law "controlled through a system of prevention and frustration of individual autonomy, which limited the social damage any one person could do."[47] Caught in a "system of control embedded in the kinship group," the life of a compatriot of Fursey notably lacked high moments of amnesty, granted by a superior power. Such power did not exist, or, if it did, it could not show itself in so starkly "vertical" a manner. Life was controlled "horizontally," as it were. It involved the unremitting accumulation and paying-off of obligations: the making of honor-payments to "restore the face" of injured neighbors; the offering of mutual sureties (which could include the grim exchange of hostages); the creation of agreements sanctioned by liability to distraint of cattle; innumerable claims from fellow-kinsmen, enforced, in the last resort, by "the horror of a visit by a professional satirist."[48] Furthermore, the working of this system was jealously supervised by a distinct class of professional lawyers,

[44] R. Chapman Stacey, *The Road to Judgement: From Custom to Court in Medieval Ireland and Wales* (Philadelphia: University of Philadelphia Press, 1994), p. 111.

[45] N. B. Aitchison, "Kingship, Society and Sacrality: Rank, Power and Ideology in Early Medieval Ireland," *Traditio* 49 (1994): 45–75.

[46] N. Patterson, *Cattle Lords and Clansmen: The Social Structure of Early Ireland* (Notre Dame, Ind.: Notre Dame University Press, 1994), p. 328.

[47] Patterson, *Cattle Lords and Clansmen*, pp. 328–29.

[48] Patterson, *Cattle Lords and Clansmen*, p. 348.

a group of persons unique in northern Europe, who had recently been challenged to assert their skills in an even more ambitious fashion, through symbiosis with a rival elite, the literate Christian clergy.[49]

No matter how acutely asymmetrical relations of power could become in Irish society, the society's own self-image precluded mercy. No individual had the power to halt the relentless workings of a law by which a society policed itself in the near-absence of the state. While Gregory of Tours looked out on what was still a late Roman society, where the daily exercise of power gave imaginative weight to hopes of amnesty on the Last Day, Fursey saw no such thing. What he saw, rather, was a world where every debt must be paid and every wrong atoned — he saw a world that was a lot more like purgatory.

Hence the deliberately inconclusive nature of Fursey's vision. Part of this comes from the fact that he was a man who had "returned" from the other world, with a message only about its lower reaches. But that genre in itself implied a view of the world that would have puzzled a contemporary Byzantine reader, as would the many absences in Fursey's account. The Throne of God is nowhere to be seen. The escorting angels and the demons act as if they are in a space of their own. The angels have none of the brisk confidence of officials sent directly from the Throne — instantly recognizable as such by their court dress.[50] Nor do the demons offer their challenge according to the correct forms of Roman administrative law. They do not produce a heavy sheaf of documents, to prove their claims for outstanding debts.[51] Instead, the demons line up against Fursey, "in battle array," showering him with

---

[49] Stacey, *The Road to Judgement*, pp. 127–40.

[50] E.g., Leontius of Neapolis, *Life of John the Almsgiver* 27 and 44, trans. E. Dawes and N. H. Baynes, in *Three Byzantine Saints* (Oxford: Blackwell, 1948), pp. 239 and 255.

[51] Anastasius of Sinai, *Oratio in Ps. 6*, in *Patrologia Graeca* 89:1141C — the story of the death of a brigand chief; see C. Farkas, "Räuberbehörde in Thrakien," *Byzantinische Zeitschrift* 86/87 (1993/94): 462–70.

arrows and setting up a spine-chilling battle-yell.[52] They know
their rights: "If God is just, this man will not enter the kingdom
of Heaven. . . . For He has promised that every sin that is not
atoned for on earth must be avenged in Heaven."[53] Only the
angels invoke a higher court, by saying "Let us be judged before
the Lord." For the demons, that is the last straw: "Let us get out
of here, for here there are no norms of justice."[54] In Constantinople, by contrast (and maybe only a generation after the writing
down of the *Visions* of Fursey), a vision concerned a monk accused of much the same sin as Fursey himself — the abuse of gifts
given to him by a penitent — showed angels and demons appealing jointly, straight to the Throne, and receiving, instantly, a divine
reply.[55]

More significant still, the fire that, in a late antique imaginative
model, usually ringed the Throne of God, as the last barrier that
the human soul must cross, has lost its association with it. Cut
loose from the divine Presence, it acts on its own, guarding the
threshold between this life and the next: "It searches out each one
according to their merits. . . . For just as the body burns through
unlawful desire, so the soul will burn as the lawful, due penalty
[of each vice]."[56]

[52] *Visio Fursei* 6, ed. M. P. Ciccarese, in *Visioni dell'aldilà in Occidente*
(Florence: Nardini, 1987), p. 198, and Carrozzi, *Voyage de l'âme*, p. 681.

[53] *Visio Fursei* 7 and 9, in Ciccarese, *Visioni*, pp. 200 and 204; Carozzi, *Voyage*,
pp. 682 and 684.

[54] *Visio Fursei* 7 and 9, in Ciccarese, *Visioni*, pp. 200 and 204; Carozzi, *Voyage*,
pp. 682 and 684.

[55] *Life of St. Andrew the Fool*, 32.108, in *Patrologia Graeca* 111: 752C–53A;
L. Rydén, *The Life of St. Andrew the Fool*, 1971–2033, Studia Byzantina Upsalensia 4
(Uppsala, 1995), 2:146. The reader should know that I remain convinced by the
arguments for a late-seventh-century date advanced by C. Mango, "The Life of
St. Andrew the Fool Reconsidered," *Rivista di Studi Bizantini e Slavi* 2 (1982):
297–313. These arguments are not accepted by Rydén, who prefers a considerably
later date.

[56] *Visio Fursei* 8, in Ciccarese, *Visioni*, p. 202; Carozzi, *Voyage*, p. 683: see
Carozzi, *Voyage*, pp. 133–37 on the purificatory associations of fire in Celtic and
northern folklore.

Fursey, we should remember, consigned his *Visions* to writing so as to assert, beyond these scenes of unremitting, demonic legalism, the unplumbed mystery of God's mercy.[57] It is not a rigorist text. But he wrote within a system that now left little room for amnesty. Amnesty no longer occupied the center of attention, as it did for Gregory of Tours. It lay on the edge of the horizon. It was a last resort. Precise sins, if unatoned for on earth, would leave the believer instantly exposed to sanctions in heaven that were as predictable as was the constant petty violence of distraint and the searing, blistering shame inflicted, on earth, by the satirists of Ireland.

Fursey's *Visions* were not a local document. They were written down in northern Gaul. They circulated precisely among the new elite that I described in the first lecture, to such an extent that it was to Fursey's own brother, Ultán, that Gertrude of Nivelles appealed for reassurance as her own death drew near, in 658. Fursey's account of the dialogue on the mercy of God between the angels and the exigent demons can best be seen as a complement and, possibly, even as a corrective to the penitential rigorism introduced into Gaul, a generation earlier, by his compatriot, Columbanus.[58] This penitential system dominated the life of many great convents and monasteries, among them Faremoutiers. It forms a background to the dramatic deathbed scenes, among the nuns of Faremoutiers, described by Jonas of Bobbio in his *Life of Columbanus*. Here death itself was dependent on penance. Only those whose sins had been stripped from them, in a lifelong "ordeal of community," [59] which included confession three times daily,[60] would be sure to pass gloriously to heaven. More than that: only

[57] *Visio Fursei* 9, in Ciccarese, *Visioni*, p. 204; Carozzi, *Voyage*, p. 684.

[58] See esp. Carozzi, *Voyage*, pp. 112–20.

[59] J. A. McNamara, "The Ordeal of Community: Hagiography and Discipline in Merovingian Convents," *Vox Benedictina* 2 (1986): 293–326.

[60] [Waldebert], *Regula cuiusdam patris ad virgines* 5, in *Patrologia latina* 88:1059D–60A.

those who had done sufficient penance would be allowed to set off on that journey. Jonas's account of the deathbeds of the nuns of Faremoutiers lingers precisely on such delays. Sisetrudis was warned in a dream that she had only forty days in which to complete her penance. Her soul was taken from her and returned on the thirty-seventh day. Angels had held a *discussio* — a tax-audit — of her remaining sins. Three days later, exactly on the fortieth day, even these were paid off. Sisetrudis could die: "I will go now . . . for I am now better prepared for the road." [61]

Behind many scenes, one senses the absolute power of the abbess. As director of souls and regular confessor to her nuns, the abbess was a "silent well of secrets" [62] at the very heart of the convent.[63] She guarded the greatest secret of all — the appropriate moment of death. Only when a nun had totally forgiven her sisters, unburdening herself of all her hidden thoughts about them, would she be set free, by the abbess, to go.[64]

We are dealing with a sense of the self no longer held in abeyance by the vast hope of amnesty. It is a self drawn out by a sense of the long, penitential process that led up to the Throne of God. All outstanding accounts must be paid off, and in detail, even by persons more frail than the nuns of Faremoutiers. A long journey of the soul, similar to that endured by Fursey, awaited every one. In 678/79, Barontus, a late convert to the monastery of Saint Pierre

[61] Jonas of Bobbio, *Vita Columbani* 2.11, ed. B. Krusch, in *Monumenta Germaniae Historica: Scriptores rerum Merowingicarum* 4 (Hanover: Hahn, 1902), p. 130; trans. J. A. McNamara and J. Halborg, in *Sainted Women of the Dark Ages* (Durham, N.C.: Duke University Press, 1992), pp. 162–63.

[62] F. Nietzsche, *Die fröhliche Wissenschaft* 5 (358), Kroners Taschenausgabe 74 (Stuttgart, 1956), p. 268.

[63] [Waldebert], *Regula cuiusdam patris* 7:1060B; G. Muschiol, *Famula Dei: Zur Liturgie in merovingischen Frauenklöstern*, Beiträge zur Geschichte des alten Mönchtums und des Benediktinertums 41 (Münster in Westfalen: Aschendorff, 1994), pp. 222–63.

[64] Jonas, *Vita Columbani* 2.12, p. 132; trans. McNamara and Hallborg, in *Sainted Women*, p. 164; cf. *Vita Bertilae* 3, in *Monumenta Germaniae Historica: Scriptores rerum Merowingicarum* 4, p. 106, trans. McNamara and Halborg, in *Sainted Women*, p. 283.

de Longoret, near Bourges — an invaluable specimen for us, an average Merovingian: neither a thug nor a trickster, but a middle-aged former public servant, with three marriages and far too many concubines on his conscience — underwent such a journey.[65] He returned to earth badly shaken. Demons had clawed and kicked him as he made his way through the air above the countryside of Bourges. He never reached the Throne of God. Rather, when brought before Saint Peter, he was accused by demons who showed that they knew him better than he knew himself: "And they went over all the sins that I committed from infancy onwards, including those which I had totally forgotten." [66]

Seen by the demons, Brontus carried with him an entire life, in its full circumstantiality, made up of nothing other than the sum total of specific sins and virtues. In that sense, the timorous Barontus (though he had hoped to avoid the full weight of his past by cutting off his hair and entering the monastic life) was, indeed, a sign of the future. In the concluding words of Claude Carozzi's monumental study, *Le Voyage de l'âme dans l'au-delà*, the penitent monk of this period "n'est qu'une première ébauche de la conscience de soi de l'individu en Occident" is only a first sketch of the awareness of the self on the part of the individual in Western Europe).[67]

Barontus and those who read his *Vision* had no doubt that Christ would come again, and perhaps soon. It was not a reassuring prospect. The account ended with a collection of citations from the *Homilies on the Gospels* of Gregory the Great: "Let us consider how severe a judge is coming, who will judge not only

[65] Carozzi, *Voyage*, pp. 142–44; I. Hen, "The Structure and Aim of the *Visio Baronti*," *Journal of Theological Studies*, n.s. 47 (1996): 477–97, esp. at pp. 493–97.

[66] *Visio Baronti* 12, ed. W. Levinson, in *Monumenta Germaniae Historica: Scriptores rerum Merowingicarum* 5 (Hannover: Hahn, 1910), p. 386; Ciccarese, *Visioni*, p. 254; trans. J. N. Hillgarth, in *Christianity and Paganism, 350–750: The Conversion of Western Europe* (Philadelphia: University of Pennsylvania Press, 1986), p. 199.

[67] Carozzi, *Voyage*, p. 638.

our evil deeds, but even our thoughts." [68] In losing many of the associations of an emperor, Christ had taken on the lineaments of a great abbot. He searched the hearts of all Christians, as an abbot would do, to test the alloy of their penance. A new model of power, based on the monastery, determined His exercise of mercy. In the words of the Old Norse kenning, Christ had imperceptibly become, above all, the *meinalausan munka reyni*, the "faultless tester of the hearts of monks." [69]

It was not to be so in other parts of the world. In exactly the same years when Fursey had experienced his visions of the other world, in one stateless society, in Ireland, in another stateless zone, at the other end of the Roman world, in the Hijaz, the visions of Muhammad had set in motion "one of the most radical religious reforms that have ever appeared in the East." [70] This reform went in the opposite direction from Western Europe. What emerged in the *Qur'ân* and in the Islamic tradition, as it crystallized in the seventh and eighth centuries, was a singularly consequential re-assertion of the Empire of God. In a scenario of the Last Judgment more stunning and immediate even than that contemplated by Gregory of Tours, God would make plain that not only amnesty, but even the power to obtain it through intercession, depended unambiguously on his sovereign will.

Members of a tribal society, which was more oligarchical and gerontocratic and, perhaps, less locked into legal norms by a caste of lawyers than was the Ireland of Fursey, the Arabs of the Arabian peninsula had valued pardon in the great and the skills of intercession (*shafâ'a*) that could extort it. But there was a coziness about such intercession that Muhammad refused to accept.

---

[68] *Visio Baronti* 22, p. 394; Hillgarth, *Christianity and Paganism*, p. 204, citing Gregory, *Homilies on the Gospels* 2.8, 14.6, and 32.8.

[69] *Landnámabók* S91/H79, ed. Jakob Benediktsson (Reyjavik: Islenzk Fornrít, 1968), pp. 132–34.

[70] T. Isutzu, *Ethico-Religious Concepts in the Qur'an* (Montreal: McGill University Press, 1966), p. 16.

As the root, *sh-f-'*, "to make a pair," implies, to be an intercessor, in the Arab world, was to claim familiarity with the great — to insinuate oneself into their counsels as a friend and adviser.[71] No created beings could ever enter into such a relationship with God. When the pagans of Mecca suggested that their own, lesser gods — female divinities, such as Allat, referred to mysteriously as "the exalted cranes," *al-gharânîq* — might nestle up to the new high God of Muhammad in this manner, it was a notion that Muhammad apparently entertained for a moment, only to reject it fiercely in the famous incident of the "Satanic Verses."[72] Thoughts of intercessors of that kind could not have come from God. When the pagans claimed that their gods might even protect them from the wrath of the Last Day, the claim was dismissed out of hand. Such *shafâ'a* was no more than a shimmering mirage — a non-existent image that would evaporate, to reveal the clear and utterly empty chasm that separated God from His creatures: "They have no power, not the weight of an atom."[73]

Drastic though it was, the *Qur'ân*'s dismissal of intercession looked inward, into Arabia, and, maybe, to the south, to the well-developed henotheism of Yemen and the Hadramawt. There, a remote and powerful Supreme God, known by the same epithet as that later regarded by Muhammad as the attribute *par excellence* of God, "The Merciful," might be thought to be dependent for His knowledge of human affairs on the reports of lower beings, who "walked the world up and down," such as the "sons of God" had been, who are described, in the *Book of Job*, as assembling periodically in His presence.[74] Thought on intercession of this kind

[71] E. Riad, "Šafâ'a dans le Coran," *Orientalia Suecana* 30 (1981): 37–62, at pp. 37–42.

[72] I. Lichtenstaedter, "A Note on the *Gharâniq* and Related Qur'ânic Problems," *Israel Oriental Studies* 5 (1975): 54–61; U. Rubin, *The Eye of the Beholder: The Life of Muhammad as Viewed by the Early Muslims*, Studies in Late Antiquity and Early Islam 5 (Princeton, N.J.: Darwin Press, 1995), pp. 156–66.

[73] *Qur'ân* 34:22; see Isutzu, *Ethico-Religious Concepts*, p. 133.

[74] Job 1:6–7 and 2:1–2; see G. Ryckmans, *Les religions arabes préislamiques* (Louvain: Bibliothèque du Muséon, 1951).

had its back turned on the Christian world and its practices. Debates on intercession, as part of the cult of the saints, played little
or no role in the anti-Christian polemics of later Muslims.

Yet Muhammad became, for Muslims, what Saint Martin of
Tours had been for Gregory of Tours. By the second century of
the Muslim era, it was widely assumed that Muhammad's intercession would protect the majority of Muslims, as they stood before the Throne of God at the Last Day, sweating with fear until
the pools of perspiration reached as far as their necks.[75] For many,
the *shafâ'a* of Muhammad was their only hope. The Beduin poet
Sawad ibn Qarib was even imagined to have expressed such sentiments in a poem composed before the Prophet at Medina:

> So be to me an Intercessor on that Day when none [but you]
> possess a right to Intercession that is of any use to Sawad ibn
> Qarib.[76]

What is significant is that, even more clearly than in the late
antique Christian imagination, Muhammad's rights of intercession
were defined as absolutely dependent on God's prerogative of
mercy: they existed only *bi-fadhl rahmatihi*, out of the supreme
bounty of His mercy.[77] And this mercy remained consistently overwhelming. The most optimistic estimates of the *misericordes* of
late antiquity, as to what the power of God's mercy could achieve
for their fellow-Christians, became a central feature of the imaginative world of early medieval Islam. Whatever humans or angels
might think, God has kept for Himself "ninety-nine parts of
mercy."[78] Even at the very end of the Last Day, He would not be

---

[75] Jane Idleman Smith and Yvonne Yazbeck Haddad, *The Islamic Understanding of Death and Resurrection* (Albany, N.Y.: SUNY Press, 1981), p. 74.

[76] Riad, "Šafâ'a dans le Coran," p. 54.

[77] T. Huitema, *De Voorspraak (Shafâ'a) in den Islam* (Leiden: Brill, 1936),
pp. 45 and 56.

[78] al-Bukhâri, *Sahîh* 76.19.476, ed. Muhammad Muhsin Khân (Beirut: Dar
al-Arabia, 1985), 8:316.

content until the last Muslim crawled out of Hellfire, blackened all over like a coal, except for the unburned patches on his forehead and two knees: for even this sinner had prayed the appropriate prayers as a Muslim should. And God would joke with him, with the *bonhomie* of a great king, imperturbably certain of His power.[79]

It was the notion of inscrutable mercy, linked to absolute power and to the almost unlimited possibility of amnesty for those who accepted the intercession of Muhammad, that held together a notoriously fissile community.[80] If they were to survive at all, Muslims of the seventh and eighth centuries had to see each other as, in some way or other, all members of the *ahl al-janna*: all bound for Paradise. To allow oneself to consider sinful Muslims as already clearly bound for Hell and, so, as clear "apostates," irrevocably cut off from the Community of Believers, was a train of thought that led straight to schism.[81]

When, in 692, 'Abd al-Malik began to build the unusual octagonal shrine on the Dome of the Rock at Jerusalem, he chose the spot where many Muslims of Syria and Palestine had come to believe that God Himself had once trod on this earth, when He spoke with Adam in the earthly Paradise, and to which He would soon return, to set up His Throne of Judgment. An inscription repaired in 831 even referred to Muhammad's power of intercession on behalf of the Muslim community: it may well date from the original foundation of the building.[82] A dramatic version of

---

[79] al-Bukhârî, *Sahîh* 76.49.574, p. 374; Smith and Haddad, *Islamic Understanding of Death and Resurrection*, p. 84.

[80] J. Van Ess, *Theologie und Gesellschaft im 2. und 3. Jahrhundert Hidschra: Eine Geschichte des religiösen Denkens im frühen Islam* (Berlin: de Gruyter, 1991), 1:17–25. Professor Van Ess, to whose advice I owe much, tells me that the issue of intercession will be dealt with in the forthcoming fourth volume.

[81] Huitema, *De Voorspraak*, p. 61.

[82] J. Van Ess, " 'Abd al-Malik and the Dome of the Rock: An Analysis of Some Texts," in *Bayt al-Maqdis: 'Abd al-Malik's Jerusalem*, ed. J. Raby and J. Johns (Oxford: Oxford University Press, 1992), pp. 89–103, and Oleg Grabar, *The Shape of the Holy: Early Islamic Jerusalem* (Princeton, N.J.: Princeton University Press, 1996), pp. 61, 64, and 186.

the late antique notion of the "Empire of God" had come true —
with a headlong speed and in a manner which Gregory of Tours,
for all his urgent calculations of the coming of just that event,
could hardly have imagined.

The rise of Islam involved a spectacular working out of a central theme of late antique Christianity along the periphery of the
existing Christian world. But, if we go back in time a century, to
the generation in which Gregory the Great wrote his *Dialogues*,
we can appreciate that, within Christianity itself, views of the
other world had come to vary considerably from one region to
another. Christians of the East were not prepared to take the steps
that Gregory and a succeeding generation of Latin Christians took
with confidence. They were content for the other world to remain
largely opaque to them. Overshadowed still by the ultimate mercy
of God, the fate of souls in the other world was not a topic that
they chose to bring into sharp focus.

Thus, when Eustratius, a priest in Constantinople, wrote a treatise on the state of the souls of the departed, in around 580, what
concerned him most was to prove that all human souls, and most
especially the vibrant souls of the saints, remained "alive" after
death.[83] It appalled him to think, as his opponents suggested, that
the saints died only so as "to rest and snore" until the Last Judgment.[84] It was equally disturbing to consider that the appearances
of saints to their worshipers might not be "real" — that they were
"bit parts" played by obliging angels, or, worse, that such appearances were mere effects of "virtual reality," brought about, in the

---

[83] Eustratius, *De animis defunctorum* 9, printed in Leo Allatius, *De utriusque
ecclesiae occidentalis et orientalis perpetua in dogmate de Purgatorio consensione*
(Rome, 1655), pp. 380–580 at p. 373: see H. G. Beck, *Kirche und theologische
Literatur im byzantinischen Reich* (Munich: C. H. Beck, 1959), p. 411. On the
background to such doubts, see V. Déroche, "Pourquoi écrivait-on des recueils des
miracles? L'exemple des Miracles de saint Artémius," in *Les saints et leur sanctuaire
à Byzance*, Byzantina Sorbonensia 11, ed. C. Jolivet-Levy et al. (Paris: CNRS, 1993),
pp. 95–116, at pp. 113–16. See also L. S. B. MacCoull, "The Monophysite Angelology
of John Philoponus," *Byzantion* 65 (1995): 388–95.

[84] Eustratius, *De animis* 12, in Allatius, *De utriusque*, p. 407.

minds of believers, by the omnipotence of God alone.[85] This was not so. Eustratius insisted that this world was flanked by a great city, peopled by "citizens," who enjoyed a more vigorous existence than did the living on earth. Yet that is all that he was prepared to say. The basic category that concerned him in souls beyond the grave was their "life" and *energeia*, the effective activity of "living" persons. "Life" is what he defended, with energy, against those who appeared to deny it. Eustratius barely thought of the life of the soul beyond the grave in connection with "sin." This did not concern him greatly. He took for granted that the abiding "flecks" of human frailty, common to all departed believers, would be forgiven by God in a final, all-embracing, but profoundly unspecific, gesture of amnesty.[86]

Eustratius painted the other world with a broad, old-fashioned brush. We should not forget the extent to which Christian funerary practice supported his attitude. It effectively delineated the horizons beyond which the average late antique Christian was not prepared to think. The departed soul was a "spirit." Because it was alive, it sought "rest." Sinners, indeed, annoyed their bishops by saying that they were quite happy to settle for that: *requies aeterna* meant more to them than did the hope of the Kingdom of Heaven.[87] Early Christian epigraphy supported this view,[88] as did funerary practices and attitudes to the tomb that assumed that a "spirit" lay "at rest" in its vicinity.[89] Crude food offerings were

---

[85] Eustratius, *De animis* 18, in Allatius, *De utriusque*, pp. 488–90.

[86] Eustratius, *De animis* 28, in Allatius, *De utriusque*, pp. 561–63.

[87] Caesarius of Arles, *Sermo* 47.5; the same view distressed Symeon the New Theologain, cited by H. G. Beck, *Die Byzantiner und ihr Jenseits*, Sitzungsberichte der bayerischen Akademie der Wissenschaften, Philol.-histor. Klasse 1977, no. 6 (Munich: C. H. Beck, 1979), p. 53.

[88] I. Kajanto, "The Hereafter in Christian Epigraphy and Poetry," *Arctos* 12 (1978): 27–53; F. P. Rizzo, "Il ix volume delle ICUR per una storia dell'immaginario vetero-cristiano sull'aldilà," *Seia* 3 (1986): 77–92, at pp. 89–90.

[89] K. L. Noethlichs, "Spätantike Jenseitsvorstellungen im Spiegel des staatlichen Gräberschützes: Zur Novelle 23 Kaiser Valentinians III," in *Jenseitsvorstellungen in Antike und Christentum: Gedenkschriften für Alfred Stuiber*, Jahrbuch für Antike

discouraged. Instead, the Mass came to be seen as a means of turning raw food into a more ethereal menu.[90] A senatorial lady from
Lyon regularly offered Gaza wine of rare *bouquet* at Masses for
her dead husband. When the priest drank the wine and substituted
vin ordinaire, the husband appeared in a dream to rebuke her —
he did not enjoy being offered vinegar![91] Regular Masses were
important for the lady; but they were hardly seen by her, as they
would be seen in later centuries, as a series of sacrifices offered for
the progressive forgiveness of the sins of her late husband.[92]

Offerings for the dead and prayers for their soul at the Eucharist were traditional practices that had been hotly defended, in the
fifth century, by none other than Cyril of Alexandria, in a fragment preserved for us by Eustratius.[93] But such prayers and offerings were "affirmatory in nature rather than instrumental." [94] They
testified to the fact that the departed had been a member in good
standing of the Christian community and so might be entitled to
salvation. They also expressed the fact that the dead remained
specific members of individual families. In the case of spouses it
was particularly important that such links should be publicly maintained: for the freedom to remarry enjoyed by the widow or the
widower constantly threatened to condemn the dead former spouse

---

und Christentum: Ergänzungsband 9 (Münster in Westfalen: Aschendorff, 1982),
pp. 47–54; P. -A. Février, "La tombe chrétienne et l'au-delà," in *Le temps chrétien
de la fin de l'Antiquité au Moyen-Age*, Colloques internationaux du CNRS 604
(Paris: CNRS, 1984), pp. 163–83.

[90] J. C. Schmitt, *Les revenants: Les vivants et les morts dans la société mediévale*
(Paris: Gallimard, 1994), p. 135.

[91] Gregory of Tours, *De gloria confessorum* 64, trans. Van Dam, in *Gregory
of Tours*, pp. 70–71.

[92] A. Angenendt, "Theologie und Liturgie in der mittelalterlichen Toten-
Memoria," in *Memoria: Der geschichtliche Zeugniswert des liturgischen Gedenkens
im Mittelalter*, ed. K. Schmid and J. Wollasch (Munich: W. Fink, 1984), pp. 70–
199, at p. 159. For a different view of the offering of Masses for the dead, see now
M. McLaughlin, *Consorting with Saints: Prayers for the Dead in Early Medieval
France* (Ithaca, N.Y.: Cornell University Press, 1994), pp. 2–22 and 178–259.

[93] Eustratius, *De animis* 28, in Allatius, *De utriusque*, pp. 571–77, and *Patrologia Graeca* 76:1324–1425.

[94] McLaughlin, *Consorting with Saints*, p. 183.

to oblivion.[95] What these prayers for the departed envisioned was a high moment of eventual amnesty, where the Throne of God would be surrounded by the clamor of petitions, just as Christ, in the present, was enthroned on the altar at the time of the Eucharist, "as on the fearsome Judgment Seat," and so available to the noisy and insistent prayers of the faithful.[96] Urgent though these customary prayers might be, they were not thought of as prayers for the gradual purgation of sins, capable of having an immediate effect in an extended process where time beyond the grave mysteriously kept pace with human time.[97]

On such an issue, the tombstones of the Latin West had been notably silent. "The Epitaphic Habit" that characterized late antique Christian cemeteries conferred on the dead no more than the unproblematic, ascribed status of spirits "at rest." [98] When, at a slightly later time, an unknown bishop at Piacenza spoke of his hope for "dew from heaven" to refresh his thirsty soul,[99] and when Trasimir, buried outside Narbonne, asked "all men" to pray for his soul,[100] a new, more personal note was struck. In these epitaphs of the seventh century, we begin to hear snatches of autobiography, as a soul in need of prayer speaks to the living from beyond the grave.

---

[95] E.g., Tertullian, *De monogamia* 10.4 and *De exhortatione castitatis* 11.2; see Carozzi, *Eschatologie et au-delà*, pp. 130–48, for a particularly fine discussion of this issue.

[96] Anastasius Sinaita, *Oratio de Synaxi*, in *Patrologia Graeca* 87:837B; Cyprian, *De oratione dominica* 4; see H. Kotila, *Memoria Mortuorum: Commemoration of the Departed in Augustine*, Studia Ephemeridis "Augustinianum" 38 (Rome: Augustinianum, 1992), p. 104.

[97] Carozzi, *Voyage*, p. 635.

[98] Carlos R. Galvao-Sobrinho, "Funerary Epigraphy and the Spread of Christianity in the West," *Athenaeum* 83 (1995): 431–62, esp. pp. 445–53.

[99] E. Diehl, *Inscriptiones latinae christianae veteres* (Zurich: Weidmann, 1970), 1: no. 2425.

[100] Gisela Ripoll López and Isabel Velázquez Soriano, "El epitafio de Trasimirus (Mandourle, Villesèque de Corbiéres, Aude)," *Espacio, Tiempo y Forma* 3 (1990): 273–87.

In marked contrast to Eustratius and to the attitudes implied in much of Christian funerary practice, Gregory and his interlocutor, Petrus, had set to work, in the *Dialogues*, with fine engravers' tools. They etched memorably individual portraits, using the acid of "unpurged" sins to catch a unique likeness of each person. They asked themselves, for instance, what complex calibration of God's justice could catch the individuality of a man such as the deacon Paschasius. Paschasius had been a learned clergyman, a lover of the poor, altogether a figure from a late antique laudatory epitaph,[101] whose funeral had even been the occasion of a miracle of healing. Yet he had been so pig-headed in his support of an antipope that he made his last appearance as a phantom, in the steam of a thermal spa, to ask an astonished bishop for his prayers.[102] A precise notion of temporary suffering after death, undergone for particular sins, offered a way of seeing the respected, but problematic, Paschasius "in the round."

It was "sin" and "merit," now graded with meticulous precision, and not only the "life" of the soul, which mattered most in the definition of the human person, in this world and in the next. In this shift of emphasis, we have come to touch upon a remarkable achievement of the early medieval Latin West. The period has usually been dismissed as a Dark Age of Christian thought, an age of "theology in eclipse," [103] characterized by "doctrinal stagnation and the riot of imagination." [104] But the heated arguments in the other world, reported by Fursey, and the evidence of lively conflicts of opinion in clerical circles all over northern Eu-

---

[101] Compare the doublet *cultor pauperum et contemptor sui* used of Paschasius with Diehl, *Inscriptiones latinae christianae veteres*, no. 1195.10: *pauperibus dives sed sibi pauper erat* and 1778.6: *pauperibus locuples, sibi pauper.* See now A. Wirbelauer, *Zwei Päpste in Rom: Der Konflikt zwischen Laurentius und Symmachus (498–514)* (Munich: Tuduv, 1993).

[102] Gregory, *Dialogi* 4.42.1–5, in de Vogüé, *Grégoire le Grand*, pp. 150–54.

[103] A. Angenendt, *Das Frühmittelalter: Die abendländische Christenheit von 400 bis 900* (Stuttgart: W. Kohlhammer, 1990), p. 155.

[104] J. Le Goff, *The Birth of Purgatory* (Chicago: University of Chicago Press, 1984), p. 96.

rope and the British Isles, which ranged over issues relating to sin, penance, and the notion of impurity, combine to give a somewhat different impression of the age.[105] Its principal interests were not our own, and so it is easy to miss wherein lay its principal achievements. What the spiritual leaders of the seventh century may have lacked in zest for those aspects of speculative theology that we, as modern persons, tend to value, they more than made up for in a heroic effort to cover all known life, in this world and the next, in the fine web of a Christian notion of sin and forgiveness. They did not read the Early Christian classics that we think they should have read. But they knew a good book when they saw one — a book on handling sins was what they appreciated most, such as the late-seventh-century *Penitential* of Theodore of Tarsus, archbishop of Canterbury, praised, in the age of Charlemagne, by the Lombard Paul the Deacon as "written with wonderful and discerning reflection," laying down due penance for each and every sin.[106] At the risk of offending fastidious ears, I am tempted to coin a neologism. We are dealing with the final stages of the "peccatization" of the world: not a "culpabilization," in the sense of the fostering of a greater sense of guilt in Christian circles; but something more precise and a good deal more significant — the definitive reduction of all experience, of history, politics, and the social order quite as much as the destiny of individual souls, to two universal explanatory principles, sin and repentance.

When this happened, the *mundus* itself grew pale. In a vision told to Boniface, in the late 730s, in Frisia, a view from beyond the grave no longer included the *mundus* in its glory, such as had ap-

---

[105] R. Meens, "Willibrords boeteboek?" *Tijdschrift voor Geschiedenis* 106 (1993): 163–78; "A Background to Augustine's Mission to Anglo-Saxon England," *Anglo-Saxon England* 23 (1994): 5–17; "Pollution in the Early Middle Ages: The Case of Food Regulations in the Penitentials," *Early Medieval Europe* 4 (1995): 3–19; and now *Het tripartite boeteboek: Overlevering en beteknis van vroegmiddeleeuwse biechtvoorschriften* (Hilversum: Verloren, 1994), pp. 267–321.

[106] Paul the Deacon, *History of the Lombards* 5.30; see T. Charles-Edwards, "The Penitential of Theodore and the *Iudicia Theodori*," in *Archbishop Theodore*, ed. M. Lapidge (Cambridge: Cambridge University Press, 1995), pp. 141–74.

peared to pagan mystics of an earlier age, as they ascended through its refulgent layers, to the world beyond the stars.[107] What now mattered for the visionary was a view of the sum total of human secrets. The basic model for such revelations was no longer a longing to embrace the universe from a high point in the stars. It was a longing to unveil the "hidden things" of the religious life, secret sins, secret virtues, secret practices, told in the confessional or whispered into the ears of holy hermits — in sum, to penetrate the secrets of the individual. What the monk reported by Boniface saw was not the *mundus*: it was "the individual merits of almost all persons and the human race and all the world gathered before his gaze as so many individual souls." [108]

And with that change — a change inevitably made to seem more abrupt, more irreversible, and unidirectional in the short space of two short lectures than it was in reality, but a change all the same — we have reached the end of a very ancient world. It is an ancient world whose unmistakable profile we who study late antiquity have learned to recognize. But the distinctiveness of that profile stands out, also, in contrast to other forms of Christianity, in terms of those imaginative structures that were central to its own life, but which it did not pass on to later ages. After the seventh century, a new style of Christianity, greatly preoccupied with issues of merit, sin, and identity, and so in need of a different imaginative world, peopled with more clearly focussed faces of saints and sinners, did not wish to appropriate the rich imaginative structures of its own, more ancient past. A little bit of the overwhelming exuberance of Paradise, which lay close to this world, and, along with a sense of Paradise, an ancient sense of untrammeled power

---

[107] A. J. Festugière, *La Révélation d'Hermès Trismégiste 2: Le Dieu Cosmique* (Paris: Belles Lettres, 1981), pp. 441–46, on the *Dream of Scipio*.

[108] Boniface, *Epistula* 115, ed. M. Tangl, in *Monumenta Germaniae Historica: Epistulae selectae* (Berlin: Weidmann, 1916), p. 248; Ciccarese, *Visioni*, pp. 366 and 370–72. See Carozzi, *Voyage*, pp. 200–222.

and mercy associated with the Empire of God[109] were lost along the way. As a result, late antique Christian views of the other world either have remained opaque to us or can seem strangely out of focus. The ancient other world, in its Christian form, is one of those many casualties of time that we tend to sum up in the somewhat anodyne phrase "The Birth of Medieval Europe."

---

[109] J. C. Schmitt, "Une histoire religieuse du Moyen-Age est-elle possible?" in *Il mestiere del storico del Medioevo* (Spoleto: Centro di Studi sull'Alto Medio Evo, 1994), pp. 73–83 at p. 82: "Dieu n'est plus maître de toute l'espace et de tout le temps: c'est le sens de la nouvelle doctrine de purgatoire."

Ideas of Power: China's Empire in the Eighteenth Century and Today

JONATHAN D. SPENCE

THE TANNER LECTURES ON HUMAN VALUES

Delivered at

University of Utah
October 15, 1997

JONATHAN D. SPENCE is Sterling Professor of History at Yale University. He studied at Clare Hall, Cambridge, and received a Mellon Fellowship to support his graduate studies at Yale, where he received his Ph.D. in 1965. In the spring of 1987 he was a visiting professor at the University of Peking, and in 1994 was named honorary professor at the University of Nanjing. He is a fellow of the American Academy of Arts and Sciences, a member of the American Philosophical Society, and a corresponding fellow of the British Academy. In 1988 he was named one of the Council of Scholars at the Library of Congress. He specializes in the history of China since the sixteenth century and is the author of numerous publications, including *The Search for Modern China* (1990) ; *The Memory Palace of Matteo Ricci* (1984) ; and *The Gate of Heavenly Peace* (1982). In 1996 he and his wife, Chin Annping, published *The Chinese Century: A Photographic History of the Last Hundred Years*. He is the recipient of a MacArthur Foundation Fellowship.

My current interest in exploring the ideas of power that were prevalent in China during the eighteenth century — and in comparing those ideas with the ones prevalent today — stems from a curious action taken by the emperor Qianlong on November 29, 1735. On the surface, the incident looks harsh, but completely routine under the then prevailing modes of justice: the emperor called for the rearrest of a formerly convicted man living in Hunan province named Zeng Jing and ordered him brought to Beijing for trial. After a hurried examination, Zeng was found guilty and executed by the most savage penalty allowed by the law, death by dismemberment.

The unusual nature of the incident stems from the fact that Zeng had been pardoned by Emperor Qianlong's own father, Yongzheng, seven years before. Not only that, but Zeng had been pardoned by Emperor Yongzheng in 1728 with an elaborate display of publicity perhaps unprecedented in the annals of imperial benevolence. For although Zeng had been charged with treason, and found guilty by the chief officials in the realm, Emperor Yongzheng ordered that he be forgiven completely. Zeng was even given an official position, along with government funds to purchase a house and land in his native province. To publicize this act of extraordinary benevolence even further, Emperor Yongzheng ordered the compilation of a special book in four chapters, summarizing his generosity to Zeng Jing and the reasons for it. The book was printed at court expense in 1730 and distributed to every one of China's close to fifteen hundred county magistrates. The magistrates in turn were ordered to see to it that every candidate for the state examinations in the whole of China read the book and digested its message.[1]

[1] For a succinct summary of the case, see the biographies of Lu Liu-liang and Tseng Ching in Arthur Hummel, ed., *Eminent Chinese of the Ch'ing Period*, 2 vols.

[89]

How then could one emperor so completely reverse the policies and actions of another? Or, to rephrase the question, how could a son in a culture that so valued filial piety completely reverse the instructions and actions of his own father? The legal questions seem almost secondary: was Zeng Jing guilty or not, and if so, guilty of what? The attempt to answer these simple-looking questions takes us into the heart of the imperial power structure.

In the late 1720s and the 1730s, when all this was happening, the unified Chinese imperial system had been in place for close to two thousand years. Patterns of belief and practice had solidified over time into a form that gave extraordinary power to the central government. To be sure, that government never lacked critics, but it had grown adept at isolating or marginalising them. It had also become expert at coopting moralistic arguments from the past in order to ensure that its own mission was taken for granted. The greatest danger facing the state was that internal dissension at the highest levels might threaten the fabric of the whole or that questions about the incumbents' right to rule might receive wide acceptance. The nightmare facing the two emperors was that both these things seemed to be happening at once, and the two men adopted different strategies to deal with the dangers. Yongzheng chose to woo the public by a display of personal generosity and an appearance of absolute honesty. Qianlong chose to protect his position by a reassertion of imperial dignity and by reimposing a veil of secrecy over the disclosures that his father had made.

The first problem, that of internal dissension, sprang from the number of imperial princes who had been struggling to gain power earlier in the dynasty. China at this time was controlled by the descendants of the Manchu warriors who had conquered the

---

(Washington, D.C., 1943). There is a copy of a woodblock edition of the *Dayi juemi lu*, undated, in the Yale Sterling Memorial Library (some pages are missing). A reprint of the complete text was published in the Taiwan reprint *Jindai zhongguo shiliao congkan*, ed. Shen Yunlong, series 36 (1966). Some details of the original trial, and the retrial, are in the *Daqing shilu* (Veritable Records) of the late Yongzheng and early Qianlong reigns.

country in 1644 and formed the Qing dynasty. They had taken over the preexisting imperial structures and bureaucracy, the legal codes, the patterns of provincial government, traditional modes of taxation, along with the Confucian value system and the schools and examinations that institutionalized it. They had not, however, solved the problem of establishing an ordered and peaceful succession process to follow the decease of an incumbent emperor. Lacking a system of primogeniture, they sought to identify from among the competing sons the one considered most able to rule. Not surprisingly, different sons had different views on this matter. The process that led to the selection of Yongzheng as emperor after his father's death back in 1722 had been especially murky. It was rumors about Yongzheng's possible usurpation of power, spread by the disaffected eunuchs of other thwarted princes, that had first raised doubts in Zeng Jing's mind about the morality of the current imperial order. His testimony makes it clear that the inns and restaurants along China's busy highways were the focal points for the dissemination of news and rumor and that even in inland cities far from Beijing such as Changsha, visitors from the countryside could read scrolls publicly posted on the walls that spoke of national portents and other dangerous matters. Along such roads, too, passed the condemned criminals being taken to exile in China's southwest border regions, along with their accompanying jailers. Both groups spread their own stories as they paused for the night. However powerful the state's censorship apparatus might appear, it could never stop the swift spread of gossip. The fact that once he became emperor Yongzheng arrested many of his brothers, and that several of them subsequently died in prison in unexplained circumstances, did nothing to quell such tales.

The second problem, that of the right to rule, naturally emerged from this specific pattern of doubt about Yongzheng's own legitimacy. But this matter of personal legitimacy was only part of a larger process, that of the Manchus' own right to rule, and indeed the nature of the Chinese state as a whole. What is unique about the text that Emperor Yongzheng issued in his own exoneration, and ordered every examination candidate in the country to read, is that in it he confronted this question head on. He called the four-chapter text itself the *Dayi juemi lu*, which can be translated as "Record of how Righteous Acts Awaken Us from Delusion." In the first chapter the emperor tackled the question of the ways in which the Han Chinese identified the Manchus as being "bar-barians" (*yi*). On a three-part scale of growth and intelligence, Chinese placed the inhabitants of their own ancestral land at the top, as being truly human; those on the peripheries, termed "bar-barians," blurred human with animal properties, and thus stood at the next level down. Third came the outermost tribes, who were almost entirely animal in nature. Yongzheng mocked this argu-ment on historical and geographical grounds: China had been constantly expanding and changing, he wrote. China's greatest culture heroes such as the emperor Shun or King Wen came from the north and the east respectively, outside the inner core areas of their day. The provinces of Hunan and Hubei had once been con-sidered barbarian territory, as had Shanxi, whereas now they were considered part of China's heartland.

In defense of his treasonous views, the emperor continued, Zeng Jing sought to reject the work of all those who had helped to construct a centralized state. In a tract called *Zhi xin lu* (Record of Achieving Renewal), Zeng had written that China should go back to its earlier period of coexisting princes, each with his own domain. Zeng's rationale was that under such a system men might rule according to their abilities, with the wiser controlling larger territories, and the less able controlling smaller areas. In such a system, at least each ruler could be in touch with his subjects, whereas in the huge current area of China one man could never hope to do so.

As a final act of obedience and contrition, accord to the em-peror Yongzheng's account, after his trial Zeng Jing had composed a personal apologia and confession, entitled the *Gui ren shuo*" (Record of a Return to Goodness). Yongzheng was delighted to share this essay with his subjects. It took centuries for wise people to first emerge in China, Zeng had written, and a millennium for the greatest of the sages to appear. Could it not be that this great period of creativity was now ending, that the inner lands of China were exhausted? Was it not almost inevitable that the sages of the present or the future would come from the peripheries? Was this not the case with the currently ruling Qing dynasty, which had shown such signal abilities to restore China to the greatness it had once possessed, and then lost, under the now defunct Ming dynasty? The balance of elements between heaven and earth, after all, constantly changes and circulates. Why should not the production of sagely persons follow some similar cyclical rhythms?

The specificity of these overlapping messages was too much for Yongzheng's son Qianlong, as he showed by his arrest and execution of the luckless Zeng Jing. Qianlong underlined his determination by ordering that every copy of the *Dayi juemi lu* his father had circulated be destroyed. No more would the public record of China contain such a public confessional that seemed altogether too close to a confession of imperial guilt. (It is one of those chances of history, unpredictable yet invaluable, that a few isolated copies were preserved in China and in defiance of Qianlong's wishes can be read by us today.)

Without going here into the details of Qianlong's remarkable reign, which spanned the years 1735 to 1799, one can still see clearly how strongly these youthful experiences of felt humiliation colored his later actions. More than almost any other emperor, Qianlong was on the watch for slights to the imperial name and dignity. He became the self-professed defender of the Manchu heritage, ordering the compilation of extensive genealogies in which the Manchus' ancestors would be assembled and tabulated, so that his contemporaries could relate their own lives to those of their warrior predecessors. He had a careful history written of the original Manchu shamanic religion, spelling out the exact details and significance of every sacrifice and where possible defining the roles of the various spirits and deities invoked in the shamanic ceremonies. He closely supervised the management of the Manchu military organizations known as the Eight Banners and removed from the Banner rolls many soldiers of Chinese origin who had drifted into the ranks over the previous century. He insisted on the maintenance of both written and spoken Manchu language at the court and had special exams conducted to encourage Chinese scholars too to learn the language. He was insistent on the need to follow precise protocols of mourning and was swift to punish anyone — Manchu or Chinese — found guilty of laxity in that regard. And he commissioned a colossal manuscript compilation of the inherited wisdom of the Chinese past, which not only enabled accurate editions of earlier treasured texts to be collated, but also enabled him to expunge from China's literary heritage any books that he felt contained insulting references to barbarians in the Chinese past or contained information on national defense or military strategy that might somehow be useful to those challenging his regime.[2]

Such an imperial appropriation of China's past was equally clear in Qianlong's mania for collecting Chinese art. As a youth he received some training in traditional Chinese brush techniques from the court painters, and he was himself able to produce a competent landscape scroll. But had he not been emperor, nothing in his background would have given him the right to comment — and in such definitive-sounding terms — on his country's artistic heritage. Some of his attempts at connoisseurship were wide of the mark, and he personally insisted on the genuineness of several works that were later shown to be forgeries. But that does not detract from the fact that the vast Chinese Palace Museum Col-

---

[2] Scholars who have recently been exploring this field are Pamela Crossley, Mark Elliott, and Kent Guy.

lection (currently split between repositories in Taiwan and Beijing) took its definitive form in Qianlong's reign, as the emperor's agents scoured the country for fine examples of painting and calligraphy, bronzes, jade, and porcelain.

Once again, power was an asset. Some of the rarest pieces came to the court collection as "gifts," the coerced nature of which was barely disguised. Others were essentially bribes, offered to the court in thanks for, or expectation of, some favor. Rich merchants offered paintings to avoid being fined for alleged malfeasance. Some the emperor purloined, on the excuse that their current owners were unable to protect them from fire or theft. Informal gifts of money, or fines paid into private Imperial Household accounts, helped the emperor to have large amounts of surplus cash on hand when only direct purchase would work. And the emperor's favorite courtier, the former Manchu guards officer Heshen, was also a conduit for a steady stream of rare gifts during the last twenty-five years of the emperor's life.[3]

As we can see from confidential court documents that have been preserved from the year 1768, Qianlong's wariness concerning possible threats to his regime or to his person could lead him to condone shameful acts of injustice. In that year, Qianlong received several reports that wandering Chinese had been seeking to cast spells to conjure up spirit armies and had been stealing the souls of innocent victims — some of whom had first been drugged — by means of black magic methods that included the use of hair clippings and scraps of garments. Overreacting violently, Qianlong ordered the widespread arrest of monks, peddlers, and vagrants and their interrogation under the fullest rigors of the law. Only when many people had been permanently maimed by the judicial tortures that they suffered, several had been executed, and hundreds more had their lives massively disrupted did Qianlong

---

[3] See especially Wen C. Fong and James C. Y. Watt, eds., *Possessing the Past: Treasures from the National Palace Museum, Taipei* (New York and Taipei, 1996), especially the introductory essay by Chang Lin-sheng.

realize the whole affair had been based on a series of misunder-
standings and quietly let the matter drop.[4]

In the central years of his reign, between 1740 and 1780, Emperor Qianlong also put into practice the theoretical arguments
that his father had advanced concerning the past incorporation of
Chinese peripheries into China itself. By so doing, he transformed
the scope of Chinese emperorship, and with it the long-term fate
of China. The incorporation of the gigantic territories of the
west into the Qing domain — later to be named the province of
Xinjiang — dates from this period. So does the tighter incorporation of Taiwan into the Chinese administration; the increase of a
Qing military presence in Tibet; and the Qing invasion of Vietnam, though in that case — unlike the others — the Chinese in-
vaders were successfully resisted by the local inhabitants themselves.

The incorporation of the Muslim regions to China's west into
China proper was not only military and bureaucratic. It was also
personal and sexual, as Qianlong took the sister of one of the
Muslim nobles to be an imperial concubine in the year 1760, be-
stowing on her the title of Rongfei. Though she was permitted to
follow her own religious and dietary practices, she became in all
other respects a Qing court woman, bearing a daughter to the emperor and accompanying him on his tours to central China and to the
ancestral home of Confucius in Shandong province. At Rongfei's
death in 1788 her coffin, incised in Arabic with passages from the
Koran, was buried in the imperial mausoleum north of Beijing.[5]

The body of Rongfei was living testimony to the new terri-
torial worlds controlled by the Qing dynasty, but a full decade
before her death Qianlong received news of a different kind of
discovery that had been made in the far west of his new dominions.
This was a block of pure green jade over six feet high, weighing

---

[4] These events are finely described in Philip A. Kuhn, *Soulstealers: The Chinese
Sorcery Scare of 1768* (Cambridge, Mass., 1990).

[5] James A. Millward, "A Uyghur Muslim in Qianlong's Court: The Meanings
of the Fragrant Concubine," *Journal of Asian Studies*, 53, no. 2 (May 1994): 427–58.

almost five tons. When asked if he wished it cut into sections, which could be shipped to the imperial workshops in Beijing for carving, Qianlong said no. He wished, he said, for the entire block to be transported to his court, so that he could decide on the best use to make of it. This immense logistical task took more than a year and involved thousands of men and draft animals. After detailed inspection of the jade rock and the making of a full-scale clay model, so that various experiments could be tried without damaging the original stone, Qianlong determined on the perfect solution. The jade would be used to create an immense carving of the Chinese sage and culture hero Yu the Great, in the act of taming the waters.

The labors of Yu the Great (the successor emperor to Yao and Shun, whose reigns had preceded China's earliest dynasties) in diverting flood-prone rivers by tunneling through the mountains, clearing forests, and constructing irrigation canals were immortalized in China's early histories. By laying claim to this legacy as well, Qianlong could use his western jade to enshrine the cultural glories of his mythic precursor inside his own palace. Only the finest carvers in the land would be good enough for this task, and accordingly Qianlong had the jade shipped to the city of Yangzhou, on the Grand Canal just to the north of the Yangzi River, where the jade carvers were without peer. After many years, the labor was done, and the carved jade rock was returned to Beijing. There one can see it still, in the intimate palace complex on the eastern side of the Forbidden City that Qianlong had ordered built for his retirement years. Its intricate pattern of carving is the artists' hymn to the ingenuities of China's engineers: there are all the details we need to reconstruct the ancient scene, meticulously depicted, down to the straining muscles in the laborers' backs, the sledgehammers in their hands, the wedges they are driving into cracks in the rocks, the foremen beating out the time, the drilling equipment, the wheel-borne pile-drivers, and far up on the summit the emperor himself, supervising the transformation of his land.

Can any of this be related to the China of more recent times? I would have thought the answer was yes. Not, certainly, in the form of direct influence or of immediate cause and effect. But in the sense that certain aspects of the power of Chinese government over society have continued to manifest themselves under communism, especially those relating to five main areas: governmental secrecy; the public manifestation of authority; the silencing of opposition; the comprehensive scrutiny of people's lives; and the center's insistence on seizing the high moral ground. Let us explore these in turn.

For the eighteenth-century emperors, there were few areas of Chinese life and action that were not in some sense political, and they seem to have felt that constant wariness was the key to survival. At all times, they found able adjutants to reinforce them in that supposition. Once one's life had become entangled with that of the state, either by deliberation or by accident, extrication could be a protracted, costly, or even impossible. Nor was pardon, even from the emperor himself, an adequate guarantee of one's long-term survival.

Perhaps one of Emperor Yongzheng's greatest failings, in the eyes of his son Qianlong, was his abandonment of the rules of secrecy in the case of Zeng Jing. It would have been simple enough to interrogate Zeng Jing either in Hunan or in Beijing, with or without torture, and to dispose of him and his treasonous activities discreetly. His name would never have entered the historical record; he would have died unnoticed and unknown even to virtually all his own contemporaries. Indeed, Yongzheng circulated the news of Zeng Jing's charges to the entire country, not only Zeng's scurrilous remarks about the Manchus and his various comments on the unfavorable auguries that had accompanied the Manchus' seizure of power, but a startling array of personal details about Yongzheng himself, many of them most unimperial, such as Yongzheng's love of drinking, his lasciviousness, his financial manipulations, and his cruelty.

From a current political perspective, the route chosen by Yongzheng was not entirely outlandish. Secrecy is an aspect of power that can be handled in many different ways. One can conduct secret trials based on secret charges, condemn people to a life in secret prisons, dismiss powerful figures for secret reasons, mobilize masses of one's people for reasons that must be kept secret. As the director of the Public Security Bureau puts it, in the poet Bei Dao's dark and powerful story about government's secret layerings, "13 Happiness Street": "Whatever no one knows is a secret." [6] And of course one can be condemned for divulging state secrets in a secret trial even when everyone knows that the matter of the charge was not really secret at all. That is not unlike what happened in the case of Wei Jingsheng in 1979, with the charges levelled by the state prosecutor that Wei divulged secrets about China's invasion of Vietnam to foreign journalists. (This was, incidentally, the first such Chinese attack on Vietnam since Emperor Qianlong's two hundred years before, and equally unsuccessful.) Wei's protest that he had no access to any secret information on the Chinese military or on Vietnam was dismissed out of hand.

But at quite another level, the government can force former secrets out into the public domain, quite willing to endure the public's bewilderment at the sudden fall from grace of some former heroes. It can do this in order to ensure its own reputation for thoroughness, or merely to reemphasize the point that the world is full of enemies, that amidst any garden of flowers snakes are lurking. Such was the case with the purges of Gao Gang and Rao Shushi by Mao Zedong in 1954–55, although they were among the handful of most powerful officials in the country and had long been his close revolutionary associates; also with charges hurled against Liu Shaoqi in 1966 at the start of the Cultural Revolution, though Liu had been Mao's key ideological lieutenant during the Communist guerilla days of Yanan, and the first decade of the

---

[6] Bei Dao, trans. Bonnie McDougall and S. T. Cooke, in *Waves* (New York, 1990), p. 70.

People's Republic, and was head of state at the time; with the news of the treachery and death of Defense Minister Lin Biao in 1971, though Lin had been heralded for years as Mao's "closest comrade in arms"; and with Mao's own wife and the other members of the so-called Cultural Revolution Gang of Four in 1976.

One can perhaps detect yet another change in more recent years, a growing reticence about airing such charges too widely as the Communist Party is perceived to be growing weaker. Spectacular purges have indeed continued: the party general secretary Hu Yaobang after the still-born democracy protests of 1985–86; his successor as party general secretary at the time of the massive Tiananmen upheavals of 1989, Zhao Ziyang; and, just three weeks ago, the sudden removal of Qiao Shi from all his key party rankings, despite the fact that he was the head of China's security apparatus and was considered number three on the roster of China's topmost leaders. But in these cases, tortuous explanations were not offered; the country was left to make what it wished of the vague charges and assignments of ideological blame.

In the second area, that of the public manifestations of authority, the Chinese emperors had always been masters. The overlays of ritual and protocol that surrounded their actions, their words, and their living and travel arrangements were all designed to convey awe through distancing the ruler from the subject. Everything seemed to conspire to reinforce this impression. There was the huge scale of the Forbidden City, especially in terms of its axis of approach to the emperor. There was the hierarchization of everyone, from palace maids and eunuchs to senior consorts, from junior bodyguards to the senior ministers of state. And, most vividly, there was the practice of the kowtow itself, the ninefold self-prostration that took place not only at each audience with the emperor, but at each reciting of the emperor's words. The converse of this, of course, was that a minute unbending of the rules was seen as cosmically significant to the individual receiving it: a gesture to come nearer so that the ruler could whisper some private words, the gift of a piece of fruit or a vial of medicine from the imperial store, permission to ride a horse in palace precincts, a scrawled notation — no matter how routine or banal — from the imperial hand: everyone receiving such benedictions felt transported by gratitude.

Just as the Communists' leaders were sequestered for so many years behind the high and closely guarded wall of Zhongnanhai, and conducted their affairs in the closest secrecy, so were they masters at the art of manipulating signs of their authority. In the early days of the People's Republic it was the gradations in dress, deportment, and title, as well as more obvious things like living accomodations or access to an automobile or private telephone, that signalled one's status. Nobody surpassed Mao Zedong in these arts. The photographs, prints, tapestries, and paintings of himself in handsome youth and in allegedly virile yet compassionate old age were iconic in their precision. Mao too bestowed gifts of calligraphy and small presents with a careful eye to their effect. He almost never spoke to the country as a whole, but only to confidants, or in an informal style to a somewhat wider circle of party figures, for whom the studied informality appeared as genuine generosity of spirit.

If the account of his doctor Li Zhisui may be believed, within Zhongnanhai Mao cultivated an aura of total casualness, disregarding conventional notions of dress and time, so that the most senior figures might be summoned at three in the morning to discuss some complex issue with Mao, as he sprawled beside his swimming pool in a worn bathrobe, belly bare. His occasional trips out into the country, as recounted by Dr. Li, also sound imperial in style and effectiveness: the closely guarded private train, the isolated villas, the swims in the rivers, the carefully spaced consultations with peasant farmers or local cadres: all had their special cadence, and their specific goal.[7] To see how foreigners themselves

---

[7] Li Zhisui, trans. Tai Hung-chao, in *The Private Life of Chairman Mao* (New York, 1994).

were affected by all this, even those whom one would have thought were inured to such showmanship, one need look no further than the passages in the memoirs of President Richard Nixon and his national security adviser Henry Kissinger where they discuss their meetings and conversations with Mao in 1972.

The images that Western observers picked up of Deng Xiaoping, especially from his 1979 visit to the United States, composed as they were of smiling vignettes from the concerts at the Kennedy center and of Deng in his Stetson hat at a Texas rodeo, gave an impression of him as informal and outgoing. But one can hazard, with hindsight, that this was only an exception to a picture that in general was more closely tied to the earlier imperial and Maoist styles than to the media-conscious and publicity-seeking present that we take so for granted. The Deng Xiaoping of the 1979 Vietnam War and suppression of the Democracy Wall movement, of the mid-1980s purges, of the 1989 Tiananmen suppression, was a very different person, invoking different trappings of authority, distance, isolation, and thus (it was hoped) of quiet determination and political will. Only perhaps with his 1992 tour of South China, designed to give a personally orchestrated jolt of support to what he saw as the possibly jeopardized moves to modernize China's economy through the market forces, did Deng gamble at a more complex level with the intersections of power and the media.

These reflections on some former rulers or leaders lead us to see the predicament facing current leaders such as President Jiang Zemin, Li Peng, and Zhu Rongji. Jiang, in particular, has tried to combine elements of the imperial and Maoist styles with the demands of contemporary populist imagery. His calligraphy is displayed at numerous visible sites and — in the cases I saw in his hometown of Yangzhou — even carved on stone tablets in the most beautiful gardens and parks; it is hard here not to see an implicit consonance with Emperors Kangxi and Qianlong, who both visited that city frequently in the eighteenth century, when it was in its rich and prosperous prime, and left their marks in similar ways. More surprising visually, though certainly logical in our current world, was the sight this summer of Jiang's calligraphy on immense billboards at one of the busiest junctions near the Forbidden City in Beijing, endorsing a party-spondsored movie on the benevolent results of the occupation of Tibet by the Chinese. But in Jiang's case, his physical presence and appearance makes it hard for him to convey an aura of grandeur, something that never seemed hard for the diminutive Deng Xiaoping. The premier Li Peng seems resigned to his own unpopularity and uninterested in attempting to create any sense of the charisma that he knows he lacks. Zhu Rongji, as befits someone on the rise, perhaps to the very top of the tree, is content at present to hold to a quiet image of one so concerned for the nation's future that it is hard to worry about other, more personal, matters. Symbolic gestures can come later.

Both the emperors Yongzheng and his son Qianlong were focused, as we saw above, on the third area of our current discussion, the need to silence the opposition. However, they differed profoundly as to method. Yongzheng chose disclosure and reason to make his points, first highlighting his own vulnerability by itemizing the charges made against him, but then rebutting them one by one in what he clearly believed was a rational and convincing manner. Each of these rebuttals was followed, in the printed text, by a lengthy confessional statement by Zeng Jing, endorsing the strength of the emperor's arguments. In ordering that Zeng Jing be executed as one of the first acts of his new reign, Qianlong chose the somewhat risky course of invoking his sense of filial piety to justify his abandonment of it. He was clearly reversing his father's expressed intentions. But he claimed that his father had been carried away by his own compassionate nature, and that a higher level of justice — involving exemplary equity — needed to be invoked in this particular case. The subsequent withdrawal and destruction of his father's text was a corollary to the trial and execution. The emperor's words should, traditionally, always be preserved. But what if the words were mistaken?

In our common current parlance, Qianlong was silencing the opposition in body and in word so as to reinforce his version of an imperial master narrative. Such a narrative did not allow for waverings such as those of Yongzheng on this matter, nor did they allow the inclusion of such lengthy presentations of the opposition's views. The historiography of twentieth-century China, as many scholars are now beginning to observe, has itself been dominated by two master narratives, both of which have been maintained and propagated by the silencing of opposing views. One is that of the Guomindang nationalist party, its revolutionary late Qing heritage, and its development under Sun Yat-sen. The central theme of this narrative is the achievement of Chinese national unity in a period of dynastic oppression, foreign imperialism, and internal warlord dissension. Sun's strength lay in correctly perceiving the problems and the solution. The northern expedition to unify China was the triumphant conclusion to this phase of the narrative, which was then inherited by Sun's Guomindang successors, most prominently Chiang Kai-shek.

The Communist master narrative, by contrast, centers around the fledgling Communist Party's roots in the intellectual turmoil of the May Fourth Movement of 1919, the incorporation of the positive sides of that movement and its leadership into the Communist Party, and the emergence from within this tradition of the young Mao Zedong. By creatively blending his knowledge of the rural China from which he sprang with the new intellectual currents and with Marxism-Leninism, this narrative runs, Mao was able to chart a course for the party that led from the peasant guerilla socialism of the Jiangxi Soviet, the military triumphs of the Long March, and the anti-Japanese united front strategies of Yanan, to the eventual Communist victory in 1949. The subsequent Maoist upheavals from the Hundred Flowers movement and antirightist campaigns of 1957 to the Great Leap Forward of 1958–60, and the Cultural Revolution of 1966–72, are more problematic in the narrative's terms, but they share a common theme with the earlier historical periods. Mao was consistently able to think through and past the opposition by the strength of his revolutionary will. The opposition, being wrong, was silenced. Their protest voices would only be heard, if at all, in carefully modulated versions scrutinized by the party itself, whether these were in the form of self-criticisms, trial confessions, or selective passages circulated to the party in order to be dismantled.

The fascination with dismantling these two master narratives is now widespread and is not only an academic matter. It will affect how the party thinks of itself in China, just as it has already affected how the Guomindang party thinks and acts in Taiwan. But in the meantime, the opposition continues to be silenced within China itself, especially if it tries to make its views known through any kind of public forum — whether that be in verse or prose, paint or film, drama or music cassette. The battle for maintaining silence is certainly a losing one, though the rear-guard action is intense. The weakening supervisory powers of the party, the explosion of economic resources and spread of new market mechanisms, and a host of new technologies from the satellite dish to the fax, the video, and the internet all are insuring that Qianlong's route to silence will no longer be viable. Yongzheng's mode of selective public disclosure and attempted explanation is more likely to be the way of the future.

In such a world, too, the fourth area, which I call the intense scrutiny of individual private lives, grows harder for the state. Yongzheng and Qianlong would not have acknowledged limitations to their rights to probe, as many surviving imperial documents demonstrate. The justifications for intrusion were law and order, and the moral life of the realm as a whole. These emperors believed that they knew the fundamental rhythms of social harmony, and that accordingly their role was correct interpretation of past definitions and constant watchfulness over contemporary aberrations. Communist leaders, I feel, would have agreed. They claimed, at least, that the norms of social cohesion under socialism

were predictable and definable, and they showed astonishing skills
in persuading the population that they were right. The Cultural
Revolution was perhaps the apogee and the turning-point of this
mindset, though not without incalculable damage to millions of
lives and individual psyches. The intoxication of power felt by
the young as they imposed what they believed to be Mao's will for
the collective good, and the sense of nagging guilt that some
began to feel after the euphoria passed and they grew older, has
been captured as well as I have ever seen it by Rae Yang in her
new book *Eating Spiders*. As a Red Guard from a cadre family,
Rae Yang describes her infatuation with Mao as a disconcerting
blend of the sensual and the political. This manner of self-definition
is shown at intervals in her account through flashes that draw all
the themes together: a middle-aged man who suddenly, shockingly,
exposes himself in the midst of being beaten by the Red Guards;
or the frenzied squealing of the piglets held in Rae Yang's inept
hands, as she tremblingly tries to de-sex them in the communal
farm to which she has chosen to banish herself in answer to Chairman Mao's call.[8] Herein lie the possibilities of new narratives, and
the reexamination of power and its intrusions into our innermost
zones.

As to our fifth area, reading both Yongzheng's defensive account and Qianlong's angry denunciations in the Zeng Jing case,
along with many other documents from their reigns, one is constantly struck by their moral confidence. The sense of doubt, even
though apparent in Yongzheng, seems to be speedily and successfully suppressed. It rarely if ever appears in the pronouncements
of Qianlong. The belief that the high moral ground belonged to
the country's leaders was surely axiomatic too in the main years of
Communist dominance in China. Part of the extraordinary frustration of living through that period must have been the difficulty of
cutting through that veneer of official self-confidence. Again, the
poet Bei Dao tried to do this with his own sense of moral urgency,

---

[8] Rae Yang, *Spider Eaters* (Berkeley, Cal., 1997).

in his poems from the seventies such as "The Answer" or "Notes from the City of the Sun." Others tried in different ways, only to be jailed indefinitely, like Wei Jingsheng, or pushed out of China, like Liu Binyan and Fang Lizhi. But now the state's certainty is eroding, and Tiananmen may take some of the credit. The flimsy reasons for the lengthy prison sentence handed down to the thoughtful Tiananmen history student Wang Dan — though their flimsiness may be of scant solace to him — are so widely perceived that one feels the alleged system of justice that imposed them will be pushed into change. The moral ground claimed by the party will not be indefinitely enforceable in the courts of law, and here perhaps lies China's greatest hope for an ending to the patterns of power that have endured for so long.

Let us close with a rather different linking of past and present. As his reign was edging to a close Qianlong drew, as we saw, on the great jade as a means to celebrate and justify the extensions of Chinese power into central Asia and to reassert his own centrality in the cosmic order of things. With considerable symbolic skill, we might now say, he chose the imagery of Yu the Great, rendered in finely executed detail in the hardest of all materials to carve. Money and time were no object in such a quest. Today's Communist regime has no such jade at its behest, but like Qianlong it has chosen the taming of the waters to be its grandest literal and symbolic act. According to Chinese myth, Yu's control of the rivers and carving up of the mountains not only eased the passage of the waters to the sea, but had immeasurably beneficial effects on agriculture and communications as a whole. According to the Communist Party, that is just what will be achieved by the Three Gorges Dam project. The feasibility of somehow damming the Yangzi River has been under debate by Chinese planners and politicians since early in this century, but it was only when Mao revived the idea after a riverine tour in the mid 1950s that it edged onto the Communists' agenda. The more the question was studied, the more dramatic the claims for its beneficial effects became, and the more doom-laden became the counter pronouncements of the dam's critics. The project was shelved again and again; it seems to have been the forces of the Yangzi River development bureaucracy in conjunction with premier Li Peng — trained as an engineer in his youth (as was President Jiang Zemin) and raised on the grandiloquent visions and promises of Stalinist hydraulic rhetoric — that in 1992 pushed it through to final acceptance by the People's Congress.

The Three Gorges Dam, almost two kilometers across, will transform the natural channel of the famous Yangzi Gorges into a lake the size of Lake Superior. It will generate millions of kilowatts of electricity and via a series of locks and sluiceways, allow deep draft cargo ships to sail all the way to Chongqing city in the heart of Sichwan. By regulating the storage levels within this immense reservoir, the dam proponents claim, they will permanently end the flooding that for so many centuries has plagued the lower reaches of the stream.

Their opponents claim that this is all grandiosity that has passed the bounds of reason. Millions of people will lose their homes and have to be relocated. Untold natural beauties and treasured historical sites will be permanently buried beneath the waters. No plans having been made for any of the drainage systems from Chongqing itself or the other cities along the shores of the new reservoir, the artificial lake will become the world's largest cesspool. The Yangzi waters also are laden with more silt than almost any of the world's other great rivers, and thus the lake bed will, in short order, fill up and the sluiceways and catchment areas become blocked. Natural catastrophes, or human design and faulty construction errors, might well lead to the dam's collapse, as has already happened to over a dozen dams in China built under the Communists; even if such catastrophes were avoided, the dangers from attack in wartime could never be altogether guarded against. Finally, the financial cost is simply unknowable: preliminary estimates of sixteen to twenty billion dollars are probably far too low and do not allow for any readjustments, improvements, or later corrective action that might be needed.[9]

The voices of power claim to find these arguments unconvincing, but on the whole they have chosen like Qianlong to suppress the dissenters with censorship or prison, rather than like Yongzheng to broadcast their warnings and to answer them point by point. It may well be that no answer can be given to the criticisms; cancellation of the project will not prove the critics right. Only completion of the project and its subsequent failure could do that. That is so often the paradox of apparently absolute power. By not allowing adequate exploration of an issue early enough, either enforced acquiescence or sullen silence becomes the dominant mode of response. China is now once again becoming as large a force on the world stage as it was believed to be by its foreign admirers and its own rulers in the eighteenth century. The country's future course, and much of the world's along with it, may well depend on how the current leaders and their successors come to grips with the opportunities for both good and evil that the presence of power bestows.

[9] A full analysis is that compiled by Dai Qing, trans. Ming Yi, in *The River Dragon Has Come, The Three Gorges Dam and the Fate of China's Yangtze River* (Armonk, N.Y., 1997).

The Lives of Animals

J. M. COETZEE

THE TANNER LECTURES ON HUMAN VALUES

Delivered at

Princeton University
October 15 and 16, 1997

J. M. COETZEE holds a chair in General Literature at the University of Cape Town. He received degrees in literature and mathematics at the University of Cape Town and received his Ph.D. from the University of Texas at Austin in 1969. He has been a visiting professor at numerous universities, including Johns Hopkins, Harvard, and the University of Chicago. He is a fellow of the Royal Society of Literature and an honorary member of the American Academy of Arts and Sciences. His first work of fiction was published in 1974. Since then he has published seven novels, three works of criticism, and a memoir, as well as translations from the Dutch and Afrikaans. His fiction, which includes *The Master of Petersburg* (1994), *Waiting for the Barbarians* (1982), and *In the Heart of the Country* (1977), has been translated into sixteen languages and has won several major awards. *The Life and Times of Michael K.* (1983) won both Britain's Booker Prize and France's Prix Femina Etranger. He was awarded the Jerusalem Prize in 1987.

LECTURE I. THE PHILOSOPHERS
AND THE ANIMALS

He is waiting at the gate when her flight comes in. Two years have passed since he last saw his mother; despite himself, he is shocked at how she has aged. Her hair, which had had streaks of gray in it, is now entirely white; her shoulders stoop; her flesh has grown flabby.

They have never been a demonstrative family. A hug, a few murmured words, and the business of greeting is done. In silence they follow the flow of travellers to the baggage hall, pick up her suitcase, and set off on the ninety-minute drive.

"A long flight," he remarks. "You must be exhausted."

"Ready to sleep," she says; and indeed, en route, she falls asleep briefly, her head slumped against the window.

At six o'clock, as it is growing dark, they pull up in front of his home in suburban Waltham. His wife Norma and the children appear on the porch. In a show of affection that must cost her a great deal, Norma holds her arms out wide and says, "Elizabeth!" The two women embrace; then the children, in their well-brought-up though more subdued fashion, follow suit.

Elizabeth Costello the novelist will be staying with them for the three days of her visit to Appleton College. It is not a period he is looking forward to. His wife and his mother do not get on. It would be better were she to stay at a hotel, but he cannot bring himself to suggest that.

Hostilities are renewed almost at once. Norma has prepared a light supper. His mother notices that only three places have been set. "Aren't the children eating with us?" she asks.

"No," says Norma, "they are eating in the playroom."

"Why?"

The question is not necessary, since she knows the answer. The children are eating separately because Elizabeth does not like to see meat on the table, while Norma refuses to change the children's diet to suit what she calls "your mother's delicate sensibilities."

"Why?" asks Elizabeth Costello a second time.

Norma flashes him an angry glance. He sighs. "Mother," he says, "the children are having chicken for supper, that's the only reason."

"Oh," she says. "I see."

His mother has been invited to Appleton College, where her son John is assistant professor of physics and astronomy, to deliver the annual Gates Lecture and meet with literature students. Because Costello is his mother's maiden name, and because he has never seen any reason to broadcast his connection with her, it was not known at the time of the invitation that Elizabeth Costello had a family connection in the Appleton community. He would have preferred that state of affairs to continue.

Elizabeth Costello is best known to the world for *The House on Eccles Street* (1969), a novel about Marion Bloom, wife of Leopold Bloom, which is nowadays spoken of in the same breath as *The Golden Notebook* and *The Story of Christa T* as pathbreaking feminist fiction. In the past decade there has grown up around her a small critical industry; there is even an *Elizabeth Costello Newsletter*, published out of Albuquerque, New Mexico.

On the basis of her reputation as a novelist, this fleshy, white-haired lady has been invited to Appleton to speak on any subject she elects; and she has responded by electing to speak, not about herself and her fiction, as her sponsors would no doubt like, but about a hobbyhorse of hers, animals.

John Bernard has not broadcast his connection with Elizabeth Costello because he prefers to make his own way in the world. He is not ashamed of his mother. On the contrary, he is proud of her, despite the fact that he and his sister and his late father are written into her books in ways that he sometimes finds painful. But he is not sure that he wants to hear her once again on the subject of animal rights, particularly when he knows he will afterwards be treated, in bed, to his wife's disparaging commentary.

He met and married Norma while they were both graduate students at Johns Hopkins. Norma holds a Ph.D. in philosophy with a specialism in the philosophy of mind. Having moved with him to Appleton, she has been unable to find a teaching position. This is a cause of bitterness to her, and of conflict between the two of them.

Norma and his mother have never liked each other. Probably his mother would have chosen not to like any woman he married. As for Norma, she has never hesitated to tell him that his mother's books are overrated, that her opinions on animals, animal consciousness, and ethical relations with animals are jejune and sentimental. She is at present writing for a philosophy journal a review-essay on language-learning experiments upon primates; he would not be surprised if his mother figured in a dismissive footnote.

He himself has no opinions one way or the other. As a child he briefly kept hamsters; otherwise he has little familiarity with animals. Their elder boy wants a puppy. Both he and Norma are resisting: they do not mind a puppy, but foresee a grown dog, with a grown dog's sexual needs, as nothing but trouble.

His mother is entitled to her convictions, he believes. If she wants to spend her declining years making propaganda against cruelty to animals, that is her right. In a few days, blessedly, she will be on her way to her next destination, and he will be able to get back to his work.

On her first morning in Waltham, his mother sleeps late. He goes off to teach a class, returns at lunch-time, takes her for a drive around the city. The lecture is scheduled for the late afternoon. It will be followed by a formal dinner hosted by the president, in which he and Norma are included.

The lecture is introduced by Elaine Marx of the English Department. He does not know her, but understands that she has written about his mother. In her introduction, he notices, she makes no attempt to link his mother's novels to the subject of the lecture.

Then it is the turn of Elizabeth Costello. To him she looks old and tired. Sitting in the front row beside his wife, he tries to will strength into her.

"Ladies and gentlement," she begins. "It is two years since I last spoke in the United States. In the lecture I then gave, I had reason to refer to the great fabulist Franz Kafka, and in particular to his story 'Report to an Academy,' about an educated ape, Red Peter, who stands before the members of a learned society telling the story of his life — of his ascent from beast to something approaching man.[1] On that occasion I felt a little like Red Peter myself, and said so. Today that feeling is even stronger, for reasons that I hope will become clearer to you.

"Lectures often begin with lighthearted remarks whose purpose is to set the audience at ease. The comparison I have just drawn between myself and Kafka's ape might be taken as such a lighthearted remark, meant to set you at ease, meant to say I am just an ordinary person, neither a god nor a beast. Even those among you who read Kafka's story of the ape who performs before human beings as an allegory of Kafka the Jew performing for Gentiles[2] may nevertheless — in view of the fact that I am not a Jew — have done me the kindness of taking the comparison at face value, that is to say, ironically.

"I want to say at the outset that that was not how my remark — the remark that I feel like Red Peter — was intended. I did not intend it ironically. It means what it says. I say what I mean. I am an old woman. I do not have the time any longer to say things I do not mean."

His mother does not have a good delivery. Even as a reader of her own stories she lacks animation. It always puzzled him, when

---

[1] Cf. J. M. Coetzee, "What Is Realism?" *Salmagundi* 114–15 (1997): 60–81.

[2] Cf. Frederick R. Karl, *Franz Kafka* (New York: Ticknor & Fields, 1991), pp. 557–58.

he was a child, that a woman who wrote books for a living should be so bad at telling bedtime stories.

Because of the flatness of her delivery, because she does not look up from the page, he feels that what she is saying lacks impact. Whereas he, because he knows her, senses what she is up to. He does not look forward to what is coming. He does not want to hear his mother talking about death. Furthermore, he has a strong sense that her audience — which consists, after all, mainly of young people — wants death-talk even less.

"In addressing you on the subject of animals," she continues, "I will pay you the honor of skipping a recital of the horrors of their lives and deaths. Though I have no reason to believe that you have at the forefront of your minds what is being done to animals at this moment in production facilities (I hesitate to call them farms any longer), in abattoirs, in trawlers, in laboratories, all over the world, I will take it that you concede me the rhetorical power to evoke these horrors and bring them home to you with adequate force, and leave it at that, reminding you only that the horrors I here omit are nevertheless at the center of this lecture.

"Between 1942 and 1945 several million people were put to death in the concentration camps of the Third Reich: at Treblinka alone more than a million and a half, perhaps as many as three million. These are numbers that numb the mind. We have only one death of our own: we can comprehend the deaths of others only one at a time: in the abstract we may be able to count to a million, but we cannot count to a million deaths.

"The people who lived in the countryside around Treblinka — Poles, for the most part — said that they did not know what was going on in the camp; said that, while in a general way they might have guessed what was going on, they did not know for sure; said that, while in a sense they might have known, in another sense they did not know, could not afford to know, for their own sake.

"The people around Treblinka were not exceptional. There were camps all over the Reich, nearly six thousand in Poland alone, untold thousands in Germany proper.[3] Few Germans lived more than a few kilometres from a camp of some kind. Not every camp was a death camp, a camp dedicated to the production of death, but horrors went on in all of them, more horrors by far than one could afford to know, for one's own sake.

"It is not because they waged an expansionist war, and lost it, that Germans of a particular generation are still regarded as standing a little outside humanity, as having to do or be something special before they can be readmitted to the human fold. They lost their humanity, in our eyes, because of a certain willed ignorance on their part. Under the circumstances of Hitler's kind of war, ignorance may have been a useful survival mechanism, but that is an excuse which, with admirable moral rigor, we refuse to accept. In Germany, we say, a certain line was crossed which took people beyond the ordinary murderousness and cruelty of warfare into a state that we can only call sin. The signing of the articles of capitulation and the payment of reparations did not put an end to that state of sin. On the contrary, we said, a sickness of the soul continued to mark that generation. It marked those citizens of the Reich who had committed evil actions, but also those who, for whatever reason, were in ignorance of those actions. It thus marked, for practical purposes, every citizen of the Reich. Only those in the camps were innocent.

" 'They went like sheep to the slaughter.' 'They died like animals.' 'The Nazi butchers killed them.' Denunciation of the camps reverberates so fully with the language of the stockyard and slaughterhouse that it is barely necessary for me to prepare the ground for the comparison I am about to make. The crime of the Third Reich, says the voice of accusation, was to treat people like animals.

"We — even we in Australia — belong to a civilization deeply rooted in Greek and Judaeo-Christian religious thought. We may not, all of us, believe in pollution, we may not believe in sin, but

---

[3] Daniel J. Goldhagen, *Hitler's Willing Executioners* (London: Little, Brown, 1996), p. 171.

we do believe in their psychic correlates. We accept without question that the psyche (or soul) touched with guilty knowledge cannot be well. We do not accept that people with crimes on their conscience can be healthy and happy. We look (or used to look) askance at Germans of a certain generation because they are, in a sense, polluted; in the very signs of their normality (their healthy appetites, their hearty laughter) we see proof of how deeply seated pollution is in them.

"It was and is inconceivable that people who *did not know* (in that special sense) about the camps can be fully human. In our chosen metaphorics, it was they and not their victims who were the beasts. By treating fellow human beings, beings created in the image of God, like beasts, they had themselves become beasts.

"I was taken on a drive around Waltham this morning. It seems a pleasant enough town. I saw no horrors, no drug-testing laboratories, no factory farms, no abattoirs. Yet I am sure they are here. They must be. They simply do not advertise themselves. They are all around us as I speak, only we do not, in a certain sense, know about them.

"Let me say it openly: we are surrounded by an enterprise of degradation, cruelty, and killing which rivals anything that the Third Reich was capable of, indeed dwarfs it, in that ours is an enterprise without end, self-regenerating, bringing rabbits, rats, poultry, livestock ceaselessly into the world for the purpose of killing them.

"And to split hairs, to claim that there is no comparison, that Treblinka was so to speak a metaphysical enterprise dedicated to nothing but death and annihilation while the meat industry is ultimately devoted to life (once its victims are dead, after all, it does not burn them to ash or bury them but on the contrary cuts them up and refrigerates and packs them so that they can be consumed in the comfort of our homes) is as little consolation to those victims as it would have been — pardon the tastelessness of the following — to ask the dead of Treblinka to excuse their killers because their body-fat was needed to make soap and their hair to stuff mattresses with.[4]

"Pardon me, I repeat. That is the last cheap point I will be scoring. I know how talk of this kind polarizes people, and cheap point-scoring only makes it worse. I want to find a way of speaking to fellow human beings that will be cool rather than heated, philosophical rather than polemical, that will bring enlightenment rather than seeking to divide us into the righteous and the sinners, the saved and the damned, the sheep and the goats.

"Such a language is available to me, I know. It is the language of Aristotle and Porphyry, of Augustine and Aquinas, of Descartes and Bentham, of, in our day, Mary Midgley and Tom Regan. It is a philosophical language in which we can discuss and debate what kind of souls animals have, whether they reason or on the contrary act as biological automatons, whether they have rights in respect of us or whether we merely have duties in respect of them. I have that language available to me, and indeed for a while will be resorting to it. But the fact is, if you had wanted someone to come here and discriminate for you between mortal and immortal souls, or between rights and duties, you would have called in a philosopher, not a person whose sole claim to your attention is to have written stories about made-up people.

"I could fall back on that language, as I have said, in the unoriginal, second-hand manner which is the best I can manage. I could tell you, for instance, what I think of St. Thomas's argument that, because man alone is made in the image of God and partakes in the being of God, how we treat animals is of no importance except insofar as being cruel to animals may accustom us to being cruel to men.[5] I could ask what St. Thomas takes to be the being

---

[4] Philippe Lacoue-Labarthe: "The extermination of the Jews . . . is a phenomenon which follows essentially no logic (political, economic, social, military, etc.) other than a spirtiual one"; "The Extermination is . . . the product of a purely metaphysical decision" (*Heidegger, Art and Politics* [Oxford: Blackwell, 1990], pp. 35, 48).

[5] Cf. *Summa* III, 2, 112, quoted in Tom Regan and Peter Singer, eds., *Animal Rights and Human Obligations* (Englewood Cliffs: Prentice-Hall, 1976), pp. 56–59.

of God, to which he will reply that the being of God is reason. Likewise Plato, likewise Descartes, in their different ways. The universe is built upon reason. God is a God of reason. The fact that through the application of reason we can come to understand the rules by which the universe works proves that reason and the universe are of the same being. And the fact that animals, lacking reason, cannot understand the universe, but have simply to follow its rules blindly, proves that, unlike man, they are part of it but not part of its being: that man is godlike, animals thinglike.

"Even Immanuel Kant, of whom I would have expected better, has a failure of nerve at this point. Even Kant does not pursue, with regard to animals, the implications of his intuition that reason may be not the being of the universe but on the contrary merely the being of the human brain.

"And that, you see, is my dilemma this afternoon. Both reason and seven decades of life-experience tell me that reason is neither the being of the universe nor the being of God. On the contrary, reason looks to me suspiciously like the being of human thought; worse than that, like the being of one tendency in human thought. Reason is the being of a certain spectrum of human thinking. And if this is so, if that is what I believe, then why should I bow to reason this afternoon and content myself with embroidering on the discourse of the old philosophers?

"I ask the question, and then answer it for you. Or rather, I allow Red Peter, Kafka's Red Peter, to answer it for you. Now that I am here, says Red Peter, in my tuxedo and bowtie and my black pants with a hole cut in the seat for my tail to poke through (I keep it turned away from you, you do not see it), now that I am here, what is there for me to do? Do I in fact have a choice? If I do not subject my discourse to reason, whatever that is, what is left for me but to gibber and emote and knock over my water-glass and generally make a monkey of myself?

"You must know of the case of Srinivasa Ramanujan, born in India in 1887, captured and transported to Cambridge, England, where, unable to tolerate the climate and the diet and the academic regime, he sickened, dying afterwards at the age of thirty-three.

"Ramanujan is widely thought of as the greatest intuitive mathematician of our time, that is to say, as a self-taught man who thought in mathematics, one to whom the rather laborious notion of mathematical proof or demonstration was foreign. Many of Ramanujan's results (or, as his detractors call them, his speculations) remain undemonstrated to this day, though there is every chance they are true.

"What does the phenomenon of a Ramanujan tell us? Was Ramanujan closer to God because his mind (let us call it his mind, it would seem to me gratuitously insulting to call it just his brain) was at one, or more at one than anyone else's we know of, with the being of reason? If the good folk at Cambridge, and principally Professor G. H. Hardy, had not elicited from Ramanujan his speculations, and laboriously proved true those of them that they were capable of proving true, would Ramanujan still have been closer to God than they? What if, instead of going to Cambridge, Ramanujan had merely sat at home and thought his thoughts while he filled out dockets for the Madras Port Authority?

"And what of Red Peter (the historical Red Peter, I mean)? How are we to know that Red Peter, or Red Peter's little sister, shot in Africa by the hunters, was not thinking the same thoughts as Ramanujan was thinking in India, and saying equally little? Is the difference between G. H. Hardy on the one hand, and the dumb Ramanujan and the dumb Red Sally on the other, merely that the former is conversant with the protocols of academic mathematics while the latter are not? Is that how we measure nearness or distance from God, from the being of reason?

"How is it that humankind throws up, generation after generation, a cadre of thinkers slightly further from God than Ramanujan but capable nevertheless, after the designated twelve years of schooling and six of tertiary education, of making a contribution to the decoding of the great book of nature via the physical and mathematical disciplines? If the being of man is really at one with the being of God, should it not be cause for suspicion that human beings take eighteen years, a neat and manageable portion of a human lifetime, to qualify to become decoders of God's master-script, rather than five minutes, say, or five hundred years? Might it not be that the phenomenon we are examining here is, rather than the flowering of a faculty that allows access to the secrets of the universe, the specialism of a rather narrow self-regenerating intellectual tradition whose forte is reasoning, in the same way that the forte of chess-players is playing chess, which for its own motives it tries to install at the center of the universe?[6]

"Yet, although I see that the best way to win acceptance from this learned gathering would be for me to join myself, like a tributary stream running into a great river, to the great Western discourse of man versus beast, of reason versus unreason, something in me resists, foreseeing in that step the concession of the entire battle.

"For, seen from the outside, from a being who is alien to it, reason is simply a vast tautology. Of course reason will validate reason as the first principle of the universe — what else should it do? Dethrone itself? Reasoning systems, as systems of totality, do not have that power. If there were a position from which reason could attack and dethrone itself, reason would already have occupied that position, otherwise it would not be total.

"In the olden days the voice of man, raised in reason, was confronted by the roar of the lion, the bellow of the bull. Man went to war with the lion and the bull, and after many generations won that war definitively. Today these creatures have no more power. Animals have only their silence left with which to confront us. Generation after generation, heroically, our captives refuse to speak to us. All save Red Peter, all save the great apes.

"Yet because the great apes, or some of them, seem to us to be on the point of giving up their silence, we hear human voices

---

[6] Cf. Paul Davies, *The Mind of God* (Harmondsworth: Penguin, 1992), pp. 148–50.

raised arguing that the great apes should be incorporated into a greater order of the Hominoidea, as creatures who share with man the faculty of reason.[7] And being human, or humanoid, these voices go on, the great apes should then be accorded human rights, or humanoid rights. What rights in particular? At least those rights that we accord mentally defective specimens of the species *Homo sapiens*: the right to life, the right not to be subjected to pain or harm, the right to equal protection before the law.[8]

"That is not what Red Peter was striving for when he wrote, through his amanuensis Franz Kafka, the life-history that, in November of 1917, he proposed to read to the Academy of Science. Whatever else it may have been, his report to the academy was not a plea to be treated as a mentally defective human being, a simpleton.

"Red Peter was not an investigator of primate behavior but a branded, marked, wounded animal presenting himself as speaking testimony to a gathering of scholars. I am not a philosopher of mind but an animal exhibiting yet not exhibiting, to a gathering of scholars, a wound, which I cover up under my clothes but touch on in every word I speak.

"If Red Peter took it upon himself to make the arduous descent from the silence of the beasts to the gabble of reason in the spirit of the scapegoat, the chosen one, then his amanuensis was a scapegoat from birth, with a presentiment, a Vorgefühl, for the massacre of the chosen people that was to take place so soon after his death. So let me, to prove my goodwill, my credentials, make a gesture in the direction of scholarship and give you my scholarly speculations, backed up with footnotes" — here, in an uncharacteristic gesture,

[7] Cf. Stephen R. L. Clark, "Apes and the Idea of Kindred," in Paola Cavalieri and Peter Singer, eds., *The Great Ape Project* (London: Fourth Estate, 1993), pp. 113–25.

[8] Cf. Gary L. Francione: "However intelligent chimpanzees, gorillas and orangutans are, there is no evidence that they possess the ability to commit crimes, and in this sense, they are to be treated as children or mental incompetents" ("Personhood, Property and Legal Competence," in Cavalieri and Singer, eds., *Great Ape Project*, p. 256).

his mother raises and brandishes the text of her lecture in the air —
"on the origins of Red Peter.

"In 1912 the Prussian Academy of Sciences established on the
island of Tenerife a station devoted to experimentation into the
mental capacities of apes, particularly chimpanzees. The station
operated until 1920.

"One of the scientists working there was the psychologist Wolfgang Köhler. In 1917 Köhler published a monograph entitled *The
Mentality of Apes* describing his experiments. In November of
the same year Franz Kafka published his 'Report to an Academy.'
Whether Kafka had read Köhler's book I do not know. He makes
no reference to it in his letters or diaries, and his library disappeared during the Nazi era. Some two hundred of his books reemerged in 1982. They do not include Köhler's book, but that
proves nothing.⁹

"I am not a Kafka scholar. In fact I am not a scholar at all.
My status in the world does not rest on whether I am right or
wrong in claiming that Kafka read Köhler's book. But I would
like to think he did, and the chronology makes my speculation at
least plausible.

According to his own account, Red Peter was captured on the
African mainland by hunters specializing in the ape trade, and
shipped across the sea to a scientific institute. So were the apes
Köhler worked with. Both Red Peter and Köhler's apes then underwent a period of training intended to humanize them. Red Peter
passed his course with flying colors, though at deep personal cost.
Kafka's story deals with that cost: we learn what it consists of
through the ironies and silences of the story. Köhler's apes did less
well. Nevertheless, they acquired at least a smattering of education.

---

⁹ Patrick Bridgwater says that the origins of the "Report" lie in Kafka's early
reading of Ernst Haeckel, while he got the idea for a story about a talking ape from
the writer M. M. Seraphim: "Rotpeters Ahnherren," *Deutsche Vierteljahrsschrift* 56
(1982): 459. On the chronology of Kafka's publications in 1917, see Joachim
Unseld, *Frank Kafka: Ein Schriftstellerleben* (Munich: Hanser, 1982), p. 148. On
Kafka's library, see Karl, *Franz Kafka*, p. 632.

"Let me recount to you some of what the apes on Tenerife learned from their master Wolfgang Köhler, in particular Sultan, the best of his pupils, in a certain sense the prototype of Red Peter.

"Sultan is alone in his pen. He is hungry: the food that used to arrive regularly has unaccountably ceased coming.

"The man who used to feed him and has now stopped feeding him stretches a wire over the pen three metres above ground level, and hangs a bunch of bananas from it. Into the pen he drags three wooden crates. Then he disappears, closing the gate behind him, though he is still somewhere in the vicinity, since one can smell him.

"Sultan knows: Now one is supposed to think. That is what the bananas up there are about. The bananas are there to make one think, to spur one to the limits of one's thinking. But what must one think? One thinks: Why is he starving me? One thinks: What have I done? Why has he stopped liking me? One thinks: Why does he not want these crates anymore? But none of these is the right thought. Even a more complicated thought — for instance: What is wrong with him, what misconception does he have of me, that leads him to believe it is easier to reach a banana hanging from a wire than to pick up a banana from the floor? — is wrong. The right thought to think is: How does one use the crates to reach the bananas?

"Sultan drags the crates under the bananas, piles them one on top of the other, climbs the tower he has built, and pulls down the bananas. He thinks: Now will he stop punishing me?

"The answer is: No. The next day the man hangs a fresh bunch of bananas from the wire, but also fills the crates with stones so that they are too heavy to be dragged. One is not supposed to think: Why has he filled the crates with stones? One is supposed to think: How does one use the crates to get the bananas despite the fact that they are filled with stones?

"One is beginning to see how the man's mind works.

"Sultan empties the stones from the crates, builds a tower with the crates, climbs the tower, pulls down the bananas.

"As long as Sultan continues to think wrong thoughts, he is starved. He is starved until the pangs of hunger are so intense, so overriding, that he is forced to think the right thought, namely, how to go about getting the bananas. Thus are the mental capabilities of the chimpanzee tested to their uttermost.

"The man drops a bunch of bananas a metre outside the wire pen. Into the pen he tosses a stick. The wrong thought is: Why has he stopped hanging the bananas on the wire? The wrong thought (the right wrong thought, however) is: How does one use the three crates to reach the bananas? The right thought is: How does one use the stick to reach the bananas?

"At every turn Sultan is driven to think the less interesting thought. From the purity of speculation (Why do men behave like this?) he is relentlessly propelled toward lower, practical, instrumental reason (How does one use this to get that?) and thus toward acceptance of himself as primarily an organism with an appetite that needs to be satisfied. Although his entire history, from the time his mother was shot and he was captured, through his voyage in a cage to imprisonment on this island prison camp and the sadistic games that are played around food here, leads him to ask questions about the justice of the universe and the place of this penal colony in it, a carefully plotted psychological regimen conducts him *away* from ethics and metaphysics toward the humbler reaches of practical reason. And somehow, as he inches through this labyrinth of constraint, manipulation, and duplicity, he must realize that on no account dare he give up, for on his shoulders rests the responsibility of representing apedom. The fate of his brothers and sisters may be determined by how well he performs.

"Wolfgang Köhler was probably a good man. A good man but not a poet. A poet would have made something of the moment when the captive chimpanzees lope around the compound in a circle, for all the world like a military band, some of them as naked as the day they were born, some draped in cords or old strips of cloth that they have picked up, some carrying pieces of rubbish.

"(In the copy of Köhler's book I read, borrowed from a library, an indignant reader has written in the margin, at this point: "Anthropomorphism!" Animals cannot march, he means to say, they cannot dress up, because they don't know the meaning of *march*, don't know the meaning of *dress up*.)

"Nothing in their previous lives has accustomed the apes to looking at themselves from the outside, as if through the eyes of a being who does not exist. So, as Köhler perceives, the ribbons and the junk are there not for the visual effect, because they *look* smart, but for the kinetic effect, because they make you *feel* different — anything to relieve the boredom. This is as far as Köhler, for all his sympathy and insight, is able to go; this is where a poet might have commenced, with a feel for the ape's experience.

"In his deepest being Sultan is not interested in the banana problem. Only the experimenter's single-minded regimentation forces him to concentrate on it. The question that truly occupies him, as it occupies the rat and the cat and every other animal trapped in the hell of the laboratory or the zoo it: Where is home, and how do I get there?

"Measure the distance back from Kafka's ape, with his bowtie and dinner jacket and wad of lecture notes, to that sad train of captives trailing around the compound in Tenerift. How far Red Peter has travelled! Yet we are entitled to ask: In return for the prodigious overdevelopment of the intellect he has achieved, in return for his command of lecture-hall etiquette and academic rhetoric, what has he had to give up? The answer is: Much, including progeny, succession. If Red Peter had any sense, he would not have any children. For upon the desperate, half-mad female ape with whom his captors, in Kafka's story, try to mate him, he would father only a monster. It is as hard to imagine the child of Red Peter as to imagine the child of Franz Kafka himself. Hybrids are, or ought to be, sterile; and Kafka saw both himself and Red Peter as hybrids, as monstrous thinking devices mounted inexplicably on suffering animal bodies. The stare that we meet in all the surviving photographs of Kafka is a stare of pure surprise: surprise, astonishment, alarm. Of all men Kafka is the most insecure in his humanity. This, he seems to say: *this* is the image of God?"

"She is rambling," says Norma beside him.

"What?"

"She is rambling. She has lost her thread."

"There is an American philosopher named Thomas Nagel," continues Elizabeth Costello, who has not heard her daughter-in-law's remark. "He is probably better known to you than to me. Some years ago he wrote an essay called 'What is it like to be a bat?' which a friend suggested I read.

"Nagel strikes me as an intelligent and not unsympathetic man. He even has a sense of humor. His question about the bat is an interesting one, but his answer is tragically limited. Let me read to you some of what he says in answer to his question:

> It will not help to try to imagine that one has webbing on one's arms, which enables one to fly around . . . catching insects in one's mouth; that one has very poor vision, and perceives the surrounding world by a system of reflected high-frequency sound signals; and that one spends the day hanging upside down by one's feet in an attic. Insofar as I can imagine this (which is not very far), tells me only what it would be like for *me* to behave as a bat behaves. But that is not the question. I want to know what it is like for a *bat* to be a bat. Yet if I try to imagine this, I am restricted by the resources of my own mind, and those resources are inadequate to the task.[10]

To Nagel a bat is "a fundamentally alien form of life" (168), not as alien as a Martian (170), but less alien than another human being (particularly, one would guess, were that human being a fellow academic philosopher).

"So we have set up a continuum that stretches from the Martian at one end to the bat to the dog to the ape (not, however, Red

---

[10] Thomas Nagel, "What Is It Like to Be a Bat?" in *Mortal Questions* (Cambridge: Cambridge University Press, 1979), p. 169.

Peter) to the human being (not, however, Franz Kafka) at the
other; and at each step as we move along the continuum from bat
to man, Nagel says, the answer to the question 'What is it like for
X to be X?' becomes easier to give.

"I know that Nagel is only using bats and Martians as aids in
order to pose questions of his own about the nature of consciousness. But, like most writers, I have a literal cast of mind, so I
would like to stop with the bat. When Kafka writes about an ape
I take him to be talking in the first place about an ape; when Nagel
writes about a bat I take him to be writing, in the first place, about
a bat."

Norma, sitting beside him, gives a sigh of exasperation so
slight that he alone hears it. But then, he alone was meant to
hear it.

"For instants at a time," his mother is saying, "I know what it
is like to be a corpse. The knowledge repels me. It fills me with
terror; I shy away from it, refuse to entertain it.

"All of us have such moments, particularly as we grow older.
The knowledge we have is not abstract — All human beings are
mortal, I am a human being, therefore I am mortal' — but embodied. For a moment we *are* that knowledge. We live the impossible: we live beyond our death, look back on it, yet look back
as only a dead self can.

"When I know, with this knowledge, that I am going to die,
what is it, in Nagel's terms, that I know? Do I know what it is like
for me to be a corpse or do I know what it is like for a corpse to
be a corpse? The distinction seems to me trivial. What I know
is what a corpse cannot know: that it is extinct, that it knows nothing and will never know anything anymore. For an instant, before
my whole structure of knowledge collapses in panic, I am alive
inside that contradiction, dead and alive at the same time."

A little snort from Norma. He finds her hand, presses it.

"That is the kind of thought we are capable of, we human
beings, that and even more, if we press ourselves or are pressed.

But we resist being pressed, and rarely press ourselves; we think our way into death only when we are rammed into the face of it. Now I ask: if we are capable of thinking our own death, why on earth should we not be capable of thinking our way into the life of a bat?

"What is it like to be a bat? Before we can answer such a question, Nagel suggests, we need to be able to experience bat-life through the sense-modalities of a bat. But he is wrong; or at least he is sending us down a false trail. To be a living bat is to be full of being; being fully a bat is like being fully human, which is also to be full of being. Bat-being in the first case, human-being in the second, maybe; but those are secondary considerations. To be full of being is to live as a body-soul. One name for the experience of full being is *joy*.

"To be alive is to be a living soul. An animal — and we are all animals — is an embodied soul. This is precisely what Descartes saw and, for his own reasons, chose to deny. An animal lives, said Descartes, as a machine lives. An animal is no more than the mechanism that constitutes it; if it has a soul, it has one in the same way that a machine has a battery, to give it the spark that gets it going; but the animal is not an embodied soul, and the quality of its being is not joy.

" 'Cogito ergo sum,' he also famously said. It is a formula I have always been uncomfortable with. It implies that a living being that does not do what we call thinking is somehow second-class. To thinking, cogitation, I oppose fullness, embodiedness, the sensation of being — not a consciousness of yourself as a kind of ghostly reasoning machine thinking thoughts, but on the contrary the sensation — a heavily affective sensation — of being a body with limbs that have extension in space, of being alive to the world. This fullness contrasts starkly with Descartes's key state, which has an empty feel to it: the feel of a pea rattling around in a shell.

"Fullness of being is a state hard to sustain in confinement. Confinement to prison is the form of punishment that the West favors and does its best to impose on the rest of the world through the means of condemning other forms of punishment (beating, torture, mutilation, execution) as cruel and unnatural . What does this suggest to us about ourselves? To me it suggests that the freedom of the body to move in space is targeted as the point at which reason can most painfully and effectively harm the being of the other. And indeed it is on creatures least able to bear confinement — creatures who conform least to Descartes's picture of the soul as a pea imprisoned in a shell, to which further imprisonment is irrelevant — that we see the most devastating effects: in zoos, in laboratories, institutions where the flow of joy that comes from living not *in* or *as* a body but simply from being an embodied-being has no place.[11]

"The question to ask should not be: Do we have something in common — reason, self-consciousness, a soul — with other animals? (With the corollary that, if we do not, then we are entitled to treat them as we like, imprisoning them, killing them, dishonoring their corpses.) I return to the death camps. The particular horror of the camps, the horror that convinces us that what went on there was a crime against humanity, is not that despite a humanity shared with their victims, the killers treated them like lice. That is too abstract. The horror is that the killers refused to think themselves into the place of their victims, as did everyone else. They said, 'It is *they* in those cattle-cars rattling past.' They did not say, 'How would it be if it were I in that cattle-car?' They did not say, 'It is I who am in that cattle car.' They said, 'It must be the dead who are being burnt today, making the air stink and falling in ash on my cabbages.' They did not say, 'How would it be if I were burning?' They did not say, 'I am burning, I am falling in ash.'

---

[11] John Berger: "Nowhere in a zoo can a stranger encounter the look of an animal. At the most, the animal's gaze flickers and passes on. They look sideways. They look blindly beyond. They scan mechanically. . . . That look between animal and man, which may have played a crucial role in the development of human society, and with which, in any case, all men had always lived until less than a century ago, has been extinguished," (*About Looking* [New York: Pantheon, 1980], p. 26).

"In other words, they closed their hearts. The heart is the seat of a faculty, *sympathy*, that allows us to share at times the being of another. Sympathy has everything to do with the subject and little to do with the object, the 'another,' as we see at once when we think of the object not as a bat ('Can I share the being of a bat?') but as another human being. There are people who have the capacity to imagine themselves as someone else, there are people who have no such capacity (when the lack is extreme, we call them psychopaths), and there are people who have the capacity but choose not to exercise it.

"Despite Thomas Nagel, who is probably a good man, despite Thomas Aquinas and René Descartes, with whom I have more difficulty in sympathizing, there is no limit to the extent to which we can think ourselves into the being of another. There are no bounds to the sympathetic imagination. If you want proof, consider the following. Some years ago I wrote a book called *The House on Eccles Street*. To write that book I had to think my way into the existence of Marion Bloom. Either I succeeded or I did not. If I did not, I cannot imagine why you invited me here today. In any event, the point is, *Marion Bloom never existed*. Marion Bloom was a figment of James Joyce's imagination. If I can think my way into the existence of a being who has never existed, then I can think my way into the existence of a bat or a chimpanzee or an oyster, any being with whom I share the substrate of life.

"I return one last time to the places of death all around us, the places of slaughter to which, in a huge communal effort, we close our hearts. Each day a fresh holocaust, yet as far as I can see our moral being is untouched. We do not feel tainted. We can do anything, it seems, and come away clean.

"We point to the Germans and Poles and Ukrainians who did and did not know of the atrocities around them. We like to think they were inwardly marked by the aftereffects of that special form of ignorance. We like to think that in their nightmares the ones whose suffering they had refused to enter came back to haunt them.

We like to think they woke up haggard in the mornings, and died of gnawing cancers. But probably it was not so. The evidence points in the opposite direction: that we can do anything and get away with it; that there is no punishment."

A strange ending. Only when she takes off her glasses and folds away her papers does the applause start, and even then it is scattered. A strange ending to a strange talk, he thinks, ill gauged, ill argued. Not her metier, argumentation. She should not be here.

Norma has her hand up, is trying to catch the eyes of the dean of humanities, who is chairing the session.

"Norma!" he whispers. Urgently he shakes his head. "No!"

"Why?" she whispers back.

"Please," he whispers: "not here, not now!"

"There will be an extended discussion of our eminent guest's lecture on Friday at noon — you will see the details in your program notes — but Ms. Costello has kindly agreed to take one or two questions from the floor. So — ?" The dean looks around brightly. "Yes!" he says, recognizing someone behind them.

"I have a right!" whispers Norma into his ear.

"You have a right, just don't exercise it, it's not a good idea!" he whispers back.

"She can't just be allowed to get away with it! She's confused!"

"She's old, she's my mother. Please!"

Behind them someone is already speaking. He turns and sees a tall, bearded man. God knows, he thinks, why his mother ever agreed to field questions from the floor. She ought to know that public lectures draw kooks and crazies like flies to a corpse.

"What wasn't clear to me," the man is saying, "is what you are actually targeting. Are you saying we should close down the factory farms? Are you saying we should stop eating meat? Are you saying we should treat animals more humanely, kill them more humanely? Are you saying we should stop experimenting *on* animals? Are you saying we should stop experiments *with* animals, even benign psychological experiments like Köhler's? Can you clarify? Thank you."

Clarify. Not a kook at all. His mother could do with some clarity.

Standing before the microphone without her text before her, gripping the edges of the rostrum, his mother looks distinctly nervous. Not her metier, he thinks again: she should not be doing this.

"I was hoping not to have to enunciate principles," his mother says. "If principles are what you want to take away from this talk, I would have to respond, open your heart and listen to what your heart says."

She seems to want to leave it there. The dean looks nonplussed. No doubt the questioner feels nonplussed too. He himself certainly does. Why can't she just come out and say what she wants to say?

As if recognizing the stir of dissatisfaction, his mother resumes. "I have never been much interested in proscriptions, dietary or otherwise. Proscription, laws. I am more interested in what lies behind them. As for Köhler's experiments, I think he wrote a wonderful book, and the book wouldn't have been written if he hadn't thought he was a scientist conducting experiments with chimpanzees. But the book we read isn't the book he thought he was writing. I am reminded of something Montaigne said: We think we are playing with the cat, but how do we know that the cat isn't playing with us?[12] I wish I could think the animals in our laboratories are playing with us. But alas, it isn't so."

She falls silent. "Does that answer your question?" asks the dean. The questioner gives a huge, expressive shrug and sits down.

There is still the dinner to get through. In half an hour the president is to host a dinner at the Faculty Club. Initially he and Norma had not been invited. Then, after it was discovered that Elizabeth Costello had a son at Appleton, they were added to the list. He suspects they will be out of place. They will certainly be the most junior, the lowliest. On the other hand, it may be a good thing for him to be present. He may be needed to keep the peace.

[12] Michel de Montaigne, "Apology for Raimon Sebonde."

With grim interest he looks forward to seeing how the College will cope with the challenge of the menu. If today's distinguished lecturer were an Islamic cleric or a Jewish rabbi, they would presumably not serve pork. So are they, out of deference to vegetarianism, going to serve nut rissoles to everyone? Are her distinguished fellow-guests going to have to fret through the evening, dreaming of the pastrami sandwich or the cold drumstick they will gobble down when they get home? Or will the wise minds of the College have recourse to the ambiguous fish, which has a backbone but does not breathe air or suckle its young?

The menu is, fortunately, not his responsibility. What he dreads is that, during a lull in the conversation, someone will come up with what he calls The Question — "What led you, Mrs. Costello, to become a vegetarian?" — and that she will then get on her high horse and produce what he and Norma call The Plutarch Response. After that it will be up to him and him alone to repair the damage.

The response in question comes from Plutarch's moral essays. His mother has it by heart; he can reproduce it only imperfectly — "You ask me why I refuse to eat flesh. I, for my part, am astonished that you can put in your mouth the corpse of a dead animal, astonished that you do not find it nasty to chew hacked flesh and swallow the juices of death-wounds." [13] Plutarch is a real conversation-stopper: it is the word *juices* that does it. Producing Plutarch is like throwing down a gauntlet; after that, there is no knowing what will happen.

He wishes his mother had not come. It is nice to see her again; it is nice that she should see her grandchildren; it is nice for her to get recognition; but the price he is paying and the price he stands to pay if the visit goes badly seems to him excessive. Why can she not be an ordinary old woman living an ordinary old woman's life? If she wants to open her heart to animals, why can't she stay home and open it to her cats?

[13] Cf. Plutarch, "Of Eating of Flesh," in Regan and Singer, eds., *Animal Rights*, p. 111.

His mother is seated at the middle of the table, opposite President Garrard. He is seated two places away; Norma is at the foot
of the table. One place is empty — he wonders whose.

Ruth Orkin, from Psychology, is telling his mother about an
experiment with a young chimpanzee reared as human. Asked to
sort photographs into piles, the chimpanzee insisted on putting a
picture of herself with the pictures of humans rather than with the
pictures of other apes. "One is so tempted to give the story a
straightforward reading," says Orkin — "namely that she wanted to
be thought of as one of us. Yet as a scientist one has to be cautious."

"Oh, I agree," says his mother. "In her mind the two piles
could have a less obvious meaning. Those who are free to come
and go versus those who have to stay locked up, for instance. She
may have been saying that she preferred to be among the free."

"Or she may just have wanted to please her keeper," interjects
President Garrard. "By saying that they looked alike."

"A bit Machiavellian for an animal, don't you think?" says a
large blond man whose name he did not catch.

"Machiavelli the fox, his contemporaries called him," says his
mother.

"But that's a different matter entirely — the fabulous qualities
of animals," objects the large man.

"Yes," says his mother.

It is all going smoothly enough. They have been served pump-
kin soup and no one is complaining. Can he afford to relax?

He was right about the fish. For the entree the choice is between red snapper with baby potatoes and fettucine with roasted
eggplant. Garrard orders the fettucine, as he does; in fact, among
the eleven of them there are only three fish orders.

"Interesting how often religious communities choose to define
themselves in terms of dietary prohibitions," observes Garrard.

"Yes," says his mother.

"I mean, it is interesting that the form of the definition should
be, for instance, "We are the people who don't eat snakes" rather

than "We are the people who eat lizards." What we don't do rather than what we do do." Before his move into administration, Garrard was a political scientist.

"It all has to do with cleanness and uncleanness," says Wunderlich, who despite his name is British. "Clean and unclean animals, deciding who belongs and who doesn't, who is in and who is out." clean and unclean habits. Uncleanness can be a very handy device for

"Uncleanness and shame," he himself interjects. "Animals have no shame." He is surprised to hear himself speaking. But why not? — the evening is going well.

"Exactly," says Wunderlich. "Animals don't hide their excretions, they perform sex in the open. They have no sense of shame, we say: that is what makes them different from us. But the basic idea remains uncleanness. Animals have unclean habits, so they are excluded. Shame makes human beings of us, shame of uncleanness. Adam and Eve: the founding myth. Before that we were all just animals together."

He has never heard Wunderlich before. He likes him, likes his earnest, stuttering, Oxford manner. A relief from American self-confidence.

"But that can't be how the mechanism works," objects Olivia Garrard, the president's elegant wife. "It's too abstract, too much of a bloodless idea. Animals are creatures we don't have sex with — that's how we distinguish them from ourselves. The very thought of sex with them makes us shudder. That is the level at which they are unclean — all of them. We don't mix with them. We keep the clean apart from the unclean."

"But we eat them." The voice is Norma's. "We do mix with them. We ingest them. We turn their flesh into ours. So it can't be how the mechanism works. There are specific kinds of animal that we don't eat. Surely *those* are the unclean ones, not animals in general."

She is right, of course. But wrong: a mistake to bring the conversation back to the matter on the table before them, the food.

Wunderlich speaks again. "The Greeks had a feeling there was something wrong in slaughter, but thought they could make up for that by ritualizing it. They made a sacrificial offering, gave a percentage to the gods, hoping thereby to keep the rest. The same notion as the tithe. Ask for the blessing of the gods on the flesh you are about to eat, ask them to declare it clean."

"Perhaps that is the origin of the gods," says his mother. A silence falls. "Perhaps we invented gods so that we could put the blame on them. They gave us permission to eat flesh. They gave us permission to play with unclean things. It's not our fault, it's theirs. We're just their children." [14]

"Is that what you believe?" asks Mrs. Garrard cautiously.

"And God said: Every moving thing that liveth shall be meat for you," his mother quotes. "It's convenient. God told us it was OK."

Silence again. They are waiting for her to go on. She is, after all, the paid entertainer.

"Norma is right," says his mother. "The problem is to define our difference from animals in general, not just from so-called unclean animals. The ban on certain animals — pigs and so forth — is quite arbitrary. It is simply a signal that we are in a danger area. A minefield, in fact. The minefield of dietary proscriptions. There is no logic to a taboo, nor is there any logic to a minefield — there is not meant to be. You can never guess what you may eat or where you may step unless you are in possession of a map, a divine map."

"But that's just anthropology," objects Norma from the foot of the table. "It says nothing about our behavior today. People in the modern world no longer decide their diet on the basis of whether

---

[14] James Serpell, quoting Walter Burkert, *Homo necans*, describes the ritual of animal sacrifice in the ancient world as "an elaborate exercise in blame-shifting." The animal delivered to the temple was by various means made to seem to assent to its death, while the priests took precautions to cleanse themselves of guilt. "It was ultimately the gods who were to blame, since it was they who demanded the sacrifice." In Greece the Pythagoreans and Orphics condemned these sacrifices "precisely because the underlying carnivorous motives were so obvious" (*In the Company of Animals* ([Oxford: Blackwell, 1986], pp. 167–68).

they have divine permission. If we eat pig and don't eat dog, that's just the way we are brought up. Wouldn't you agree, Elizabeth? It's just one of our folkways."

Elizabeth. She is claiming intimacy. But what game is she playing? Is there a trap she is leading his mother into?

"There is disgust," says his mother. "We may have got rid of the gods but we have not got rid of disgust, which is a version of religious horror."

"Disgust is not universal," objects Norma. "The French eat frogs. The Chinese eat anything. There is no disgust in China."

His mother is silent.

"So perhaps it's just a matter of what you learned at home, of what your mother told you was OK to eat and what was not."

"What was clean to eat and what was not," his mother murmurs.

"And maybe" — now Norma is going too far, he thinks, now she is beginning to dominate the conversation to an extent that is totally inappropriate — "the whole notion of cleanness versus uncleanness has a completely different function, namely, to enable certain groups to self-define themselves, negatively, as elite, as elected. We are the people who abstain from *a* or *b* or *c*, and by that power of abstinence we mark ourselves off as superior: as a superior caste within society, for instance. Like the Brahmins."

There is a silence.

"The ban on meat that you get in vegetarianism is only an extreme form of dietary ban," Norma presses on; "and a dietary ban is a quick, simple way for an elite group to define itself. Other people's table habits are unclean, we can't eat or drink with them."

Now she is getting really close to the bone. There is a certain amount of shuffling, there is unease in the air. Fortunately the course is over, the red snapper, the tagliatelle, and the waitresses are among them removing the plates.

"Have you read Gandhi's autobiography, Norma?" asks his mother.

"No."

"Gandhi was sent off to England as a young man to study law. England, of course, prided itself as a great meat-eating country. But his mother made him promise not to eat meat. She packed a trunk full of food for him to take along. During the sea voyage he scavenged a little bread from the ship's table and for the rest ate out of his trunk. In London he faced a long search for lodgings and eating-houses that served his kind of food. Social relations with the English were difficult because he could not accept or return hospitality. It wasn't until he fell in with certain fringe elements of English society—Fabians, theosophists, and so forth—that he began to feel at home. Until then he was just a lonely little law student."

"What is the point, Elizabeth?" says Norma. "What is the point of the story?"

"Just that Gandhi's vegetarianism can hardly be conceived as the exercise of power. It condemned him to the margins of society. It was his particular genius to incorporate what he found on those margins into his political philosophy."

"In any event," interjects the blond man, "Gandhi is not a good example. His vegetarianism was hardly committed. He was a vegetarian because of the promise he made to his mother. He may have kept his promise, but regretted and resented it."

"Don't you think that mothers can have a good influence on their children?" says Elizabeth Costello.

There is a moment's silence. It is time for him, the good son, to speak. He does not.

"But your own vegetarianism, Mrs. Costello," says President Garrard, pouring oil on troubled waters: "it comes out of moral conviction, does it not?"

"No, I don't think so," says his mother. "It comes out of a desire to save my soul."

Now there truly is a silence, broken only by the clink of plates as the waitresses set baked Alaskas before them.

"Well, I have a great respect for it," says Garrard. "As a way of life."

"I'm wearing leather shoes," says his mother. "I'm carrying a leather purse. I wouldn't have overmuch respect if I were you."

"Consistency," murmurs Garrard. "Consistency is the hobgoblin of small minds. Surely one can draw a distinction between eating meat and wearing leather."

"Degrees of obscenity," she replies.

"I too have the greatest respect for codes based on respect for life," says Dean Arendt, entering the debate for the first time. "I am prepared to accept that dietary taboos do not have to be mere customs. I will accept that underlying them are genuine moral concerns. But at the same time one must say that our whole superstructure of concern and belief is a closed book to animals themselves. You can't explain to a steer that its life is going to be spared, any more than you can explain to a bug that you are not going to step on it. In the lives of animals, things, good or bad, just happen. So vegetarianism is a very odd transaction, when you come to think of it, with the beneficiaries unaware that they are being benefited. And with no hope of ever becoming aware. Because they live in a vacuum of consciousness."

Arendt pauses. It is his mother's turn to speak, but she merely looks confused, gray and tired and confused. He leans across. "It's been a long day, mother," he says. "Perhaps it is time."

"Yes, it is time," she says.

"You won't have coffee?" inquires President Garrard.

"No, it will just keep me awake." She turns to Arendt. "That is a good point you raise. No consciousness that we would recognize as consciousness. No awareness, as far as we can make out, of self with a history. What I mind is what tends to come next. They have no consciousness *therefore*. Therefore what? Therefore we are free to use them for our own ends? Therefore we are free to kill them? Why? What is so special about the form of consciousness we recognize that makes killing a bearer of it a crime while killing an animal goes unpunished? There are moments —"

"To say nothing of babies," interjects Wunderlich. Everyone turns and looks at him. "Babies have no self-consciousness, yet we think it a more heinous crime to kill a baby than an adult."

"Therefore?" says Arendt.

"Therefore all this discussion of consciousness and whether animals have it is just a smokescreen. At bottom we protect our own kind. Thumbs up to human babies, thumbs down to veal calves. Don't you think so, Mrs. Costello?"

"I don't know what I think," says Elizabeth Costello. "I often wonder what thinking is, what understanding is. Do we really understand the universe better than animals do? Understanding a thing often looks to me like playing with one of those Rubik cubes. Once you have made all the little bricks snap into place, hey presto, you understand. It makes sense if you live inside a Rubik cube, but if you don't . . ."

There is a silence. "I would have thought —" says Norma; but at this point he gets to his feet, and to his relief Norma stops.

The president rises, and then everyone else. "A wonderful lecture, Mrs. Costello," says the president. "Much food for thought. We look forward to tomorrow's offering."

LECTURE II. THE POETS AND THE ANIMALS

It is after eleven. His mother has retired for the night, he and Norma are downstairs clearing up the children's mess. After that he still has a class to prepare.

"Are you going to her seminar tomorrow?" asks Norma.

"I'll have to."

"What is it on?"

" 'The Poets and the Animals.' That's the title. The English Department is staging it. They are holding it in a seminar room, so I don't think they are expecting a big audience."

"I'm glad it's on something she knows about. I find her philosophizing rather difficult to take."

"Oh. What do you have in mind?"

"For instance, what she was saying about human reason. Presumably she was trying to make a point about the nature of rational understanding. To say that rational accounts are merely a consequence of the structure of the human mind; that animals have their own accounts in accordance with the structure of their own minds, to which we don't have access because we don't share a language with them."

"And what's wrong with that?"

"It's naive, John. It's the kind of easy shallow relativism that impresses freshmen. Respect for everyone's world-view, the cow's world-view, the squirrel's world-view, and so forth. In the end it leads to total intellectual paralysis. You spend so much time respecting that you haven't time left to think."

"Doesn't a squirrel have a world-view?"

"Yes, a squirrel does have a world-view. Its world-view comprises acorns and trees and weather and cats and dogs and automobiles and squirrels of the opposite sex. It comprises an account of how these phenomena interact and how it should interact with them to survive. That's all. There's no more. That's the world according to squirrel."

"We are sure about that?"

"We are sure about it in the sense that hundreds of years of observing squirrels has not led us to conclude otherwise. If there is anything else in the squirrel mind, it does not issue in observable behavior. For all practical purposes, the mind of the squirrel is a very simple mechanism."

"So Descartes was right, animals are just biological automata."

"Broadly speaking, yes. You cannot, in the abstract, distinguish between an animal mind and a machine simulating an animal mind."

"And human beings are different?"

"John, I am tired and you are being irritating. Human beings invent mathematics, they build telescopes, they do calculations, they construct machines, they press a button, and, bang, Sojourner lands on Mars, exactly as predicted. That is why rationality is not just, as your mother claims, a game. Reason provides us with real knowledge of the real world. It has been tested, and it works. You are a physicist. You ought to know."

"I agree. It works. Still, isn't there a position outside from which our doing our thinking and then sending out a Mars probe looks a lot like a squirrel doing its thinking and then dashing out and snatching a nut? Isn't that perhaps what she meant?"

"But there isn't any such position! I know it sounds old-fashioned, but I have to say it. There is no position outside of reason where you can stand and lecture about reason and pass judgment on reason."

"Except the position of someone who has withdrawn from reason."

"That's just French irrationalism, the sort of thing a person would say who has never set foot inside a mental institution and seen what people look like who have *really* withdrawn from reason."

"Then except for God."

"Not if God is a God of reason. A God of reason cannot stand outside reason."

"I'm surprised, Norma. You are talking like an old-fashioned rationalist."

"You misunderstand me. That is the ground your mother has chosen. Those are her terms. I am merely responding."

"Who was the missing guest?"

"You mean the empty sea? It was Stern, the poet."

"Do you think it was a protest?"

"I'm sure it was. She should have thought twice before bringing up the Holocaust. I could feel hackles rising all around me in the audience."

The empty seat was indeed a protest. When he goes in for his morning class, there is a letter in his box addressed to his mother.

He hands it over to her when he comes home to fetch her, She reads it quickly, then with a sigh passes it over to him. "Who is this man?" she says.

"Abraham Stern. A poet. Quite well-respected, I believe. He has been here donkey's years."

He reads Stern's note, which is handwritten.

"Dear Mrs. Costello, Excuse me for not attending last night's dinner. have read your books and know you are a serious person, so I do you the credit of taking what you said in your lecture seriously.

"At the kernel of your lecture, it seemed to me, was the question of breaking bread. If we refuse to break bread with the executioners of Auschwitz, can we continue to break bread with the slaughterers of animals?

"You took over for your own purposes the familiar comparison between the murdered Jews of Europe and slaughtered cattle. The Jews died like cattle, therefore cattle die like Jews, you say. That is a trick with words which I will not accept. You misunderstand the nature of likenesses; I would even say you misunderstand wilfully, to the point of blasphemy. Man is made in the likeness of God but God does not have the likeness of man. If Jews were treated like cattle, it does not follow that cattle are treated like Jews. The inversion insults the memory of the dead. It also trades on the horrors of the camps in a cheap way.

"Forgive me if I am forthright. You said you were old enough not to have time to waste on niceties, and I am an old man too.

"Yours sincerely, Abraham Stern."

He delivers his mother to her hosts in the English Department, then goes to a meeting. The meeting drags on and one. It is two-thirty before he can get to the seminar room in Stubbs Hall.

She is speaking as he enters. He sits down as quietly as he can near the door.

"In that kind of poetry," she is saying, "animals stand for human qualities: the lion for courage, the owl for wisdom, and so forth. Even in Rilke's poem the panther is there as a stand-in for something else. He dissolves into a dance of energy around a center, an image that comes from physics, elementary particle physics. Rilke does not get beyond this point — beyond the panther as the vital embodiment of the kind of force that is released in an atomic explosion but is here trapped not so much by the bars of the cage as by what the bars compel on the panther: a concentric lope that leaves the will stupefied, narcotized."

Rilke's panther? What panther? His confusion must show: the girl next to him pushes a Xeroxed sheet under his nose. Three poems: one by Rilke called "The Panther," two by Ted Hughes called "The Jaguar" and "Second Glance at a Jaguar." He has no time to read them.

"Hughes is writing against Rilke," his mother goes on. "He uses the same staging in the zoo, but it is the crowd for a change that stands mesmerized, and among them the man, the poet, entranced and horrified and overwhelmed, his powers of understanding pushed beyond their limit. The jaguar's vision, unlike the panther's, is not blunted. On the contrary, his eyes drill through the darkness of space. The cage has no reality to him, he is *elsewhere*. He is elsewhere because his consciousness is kinetic rather than abstract: the thrust of his muscles moves him through a space quite different in nature from the three-dimensional box of Newton — a circular space that returns upon itself.

"So — leaving aside the ethics of caging large animals — Hughes is feeling his way toward a different kind of being-in-the-world, one which is not entirely foreign to us, since the experience before the cage seems to belong to dream-experience, experience held in the collective unconscious. In these poems we know the jaguar not from the way he seems but from the way he moves. The body is as the body moves, or as the currents of life move within it. The poems ask us to imagine our way into that way of moving, to inhabit that body.

"With Hughes it is a matter — I emphasize — not of inhabiting another mind but of inhabiting another body. That is the kind

of poetry I bring to your attention today: poetry that does not try
to find an idea in the animal, that is not about the animal, but is
instead the record of an engagement with him.

"What is peculiar about poetic engagements of this kind is that,
no matter with what intensity they take place, they remain a matter
of complete indifference to their objects. In this respect they are
different from love poems, where your intention is to move your
object.

"Not that animals do not care what we feel about them. But
when we divert the current of feeling that flows between ourself
and the animal into words, we abstract it forever from the animal.
Thus the poem is not a gift to its object, as the love poem is. It
falls within an entirely human economy in which the animal has
no share. Does that answer your question?"

Someone else has his hand up: a tall young man with glasses.
He doesn't know Ted Hughes's poetry well, he says, but the last
he heard, Hughes was running a sheep-ranch somewhere in England. Either he is just raising sheep as poetic subjects (there is
a titter around the room) or he is a real rancher raising sheep for
the market. "How does this square with what you were saying in
your lecture yesterday, when you seemed to be pretty much against
killing animals for meat?"

"I've never met Ted Hughes," replies his mother, "so I can't
tell you what kind of farmer he is. But let me try to answer your
question on another level.

"I have no reason to think that Hughes believes his attentiveness to animals is unique. On the contrary, I suspect he believes
he is recovering an attentiveness that our faraway ancestors possessed and we have lost (he conceives of this loss in evolutionary
rather than historical terms, but that is another question). I would
guess that he believes he looks at animals much as paleolithic
hunters used to.

"This puts Hughes in a line of poets who celebrate the primitive and repudiate the Western bias toward abstract thought. The

line of Blake and Lawrence, of Gary Snyder in the United States, or Robinson Jeffers. Hemingway too, in his hunting and bullfighting phase.

"Bullfighting, it seems to me, gives us a clue. Kill the beast by all means, they say, but make it a contest, a ritual, and honor your antagonist for his strength and bravery. Eat him too, after you have vanquished him, in order for his strength and courage to enter you. Look him in the eyes before you kill him, and thank him afterwards. Sing songs about him.

"We can call this primitivism. It is an attitude that is easy to criticize, to mock. It is deeply masculine, masculinist. Its ramifications into politics are to be mistrusted. But when all is said and done, there remains something attractive about it at an ethical level.

"It is also impractical, however. You do not feed four billion people through the efforts of matadors or deer-hunters armed with bows and arrows. We have become too many. There is no time to respect and honor all the animals we need to feed ourselves. We need factories of death; we need factory animals. Chicago showed us the way; it was from the Chicago stockyards that the Nazis learned how to process bodies.

"But let me get back to Hughes. You say: Despite the primitivist trappings Hughes is a butcher, and what am I doing in his company?

"I would reply, writers teach us more than they are aware of. By bodying forth the jaguar Hughes shows us that we too can embody animals — by the process called poetic invention that mingles breath and sense in a way that no one has explained and no one ever will. He shows us how to bring the living body into being within ourselves. When we read the jaguar poem, when we recollect it afterwards in tranquility, we are for a brief while the jaguar. He ripples within us, he takes over our body, he is us.

"So far, so good. With what I have said thus far I don't think Hughes himself would disagree. It is much like the mixture of shamanism and spirit possession and archetype psychology that he himself espouses. In other words, a primitive experience (being face to face with an animal), a primitivist poem, and a primitivist theory of poetry to justify it.

"It is also the kind of poetry with which hunters and the people I call ecology-managers can feel comfortable. When Hughes the poet stands before the jaguar cage, he looks at an individual jaguar and is possessed by that individual jaguar life. It has to be that way. Jaguars in general, the subspecies jaguar, the idea of a jaguar, will fail to move him because we cannot experience abstractions. Nevertheless, the poem that Hughes writes is about *the* jaguar, about jaguarness embodied in this jaguar. Just as later on, when he writes his marvellous poems about salmon, they are about salmon as transitory occupants of the salmon-life, the salmon-biography. So despite the vividness and earthiness of the poetry, there remains something Platonic about it.

"In the ecological vision, the salmon and the river-weeds and the water-insects interact in a great, complex dance with the earth and the weather. The whole is greater than the sum of the parts. In the dance, each organism has a role: it is these multiple roles, rather than the particular beings who play them, that participate in the dance. As for actual role-players, as long as they are self-renewing, as long as they keep coming forward, we need pay them no heed.

"I called this Platonic and I do so again. Our eye is on the creature itself but our mind is on the system of interactions of which it is the earthly, material embodiment.

"The irony is a terrible one. An ecological philosophy that tells us to live side by side with other creatures justifies itself by appealing to an idea, an idea of a higher order than any living creature. An idea, finally — and this is the crushing twist to the irony — that no creature except man is capable of comprehending. Every living creature fights for its own, individual life, refuses, by fighting, to accede to the idea that the salmon or the gnat is of a lower order of importance than the idea of the salmon or the idea of the gnat. But when we see the salmon fighting for its life we say, it is just programmed to fight; we say, with Aquinas, it is locked into natural slavery; we say, it lacks self-consciousness.

"Animals are not believers in ecology. Even the ethnobiologists do not make that claim. Even the ethnobiologists do not say that the ant sacrifices its life to perpetuate the species. What they say is subtly different: the ant dies and the function of its death is the perpetuation of the species. The species-life is a force which acts through the individual but which the individual is incapable of understanding. In that sense the idea is innate, and the ant is run by the idea as a computer is run by a program.

"We, the managers of the ecology — I'm sorry to go on like this, I am getting way beyond your question, I'll be through in a moment — we managers understand the greater dance, therefore we can decide how many trout may be fished or how many jaguar may be trapped before the stability of the dance is upset. The only organism over which we do not claim this power of life and death is man. Why? Because man is different. Man understands the dance as the other dancers do not. Man is an intellectual being."

While she speaks his mind has been wandering. He has heard it before, this anti-ecologism of hers. Jaguar poems are all very well, he thinks, but you won't get a bunch of Australians standing around a sheep, listening to its silly baa, writing poems about it. Isn't that what is so suspect in the whole animals-rights business: that it has to ride on the back of pensive gorillas and sexy jaguars and huggable pandas because the real objects of its concern, chickens and pigs, to say nothing of white rats or prawns, are not newsworthy?

Now Elinor Marx, who did the introduction to yesterday's lecture, asks a question. "In your lecture you argued that various criteria — does this creature have reason? does this creature have speech? — have been used in bad faith to justify distinctions that have no real basis — between *Homo* and other primates, for example — and thus to justify exploitation.

"Yet the very fact that you can be arguing against this reasoning, exposing its falsity, means that you put a certain faith in the power of reason, of true reason as opposed to false reason.

"Let me concretize my question by referring to the case of Lemuel Gulliver. In *Gulliver's Travels* Swift gives us a vision of a utopia of reason, the land of the so-called Houyhnhnms, but it turns out to be a place where there is no home for Gulliver, who is the closest that Swift comes to a representation of us, his readers. But which of us would want to live in Houyhnhnm-land, with its rational vegetarianism and its rational government and its rational approach to love, marriage, and death? Would even a horse want to live in such a perfectly regulated, totalitarian society? More pertinently for us, what is the track record of totally regulated societies? Is it not a fact that they either collapse or else turn militaristic?

"Specifically, my question is: Are you not expecting too much of humankind when you ask us to live without species exploitation, without cruelty? Is it not more human to accept our own human-ity — even if it means embracing the carnivorous Yahoo within ourselves — than to end up like Gulliver, pining for a state he can never attain, and for good reason: it is not in his nature, which is a human nature?"

"An interesting question," his mother replies. "I find Swift an intriguing writer. For instance, his "Modest Proposal." Whenever there is overwhelming agreement about how to read a book, I prick up my ears. On 'A Modest Proposal' the consensus is that Swift does not mean what he says, or seems to say. He says, or seems to say, that Irish families could make a living by raising babies for the table of their English masters. But he can't mean that, we say, be-cause we all know that it is atrocious to kill and eat human babies. Yet, come to think of it, we go on, the English are already in a sense killing human babies, by letting them starve. So, come to think of it, the English are already atrocious.

"That is the orthodox reading, more or less. But why, I ask myself, the vehemence with which it is stuffed down the throats of young readers? Thus shall you read Swift, their teachers say, thus and in no other way. If it is atrocious to kill and eat human babies, why is it not atrocious to kill and eat piglets? If you want Swift to be a dark ironist rather than a facile pamphleteer, you might examine the premises that make his fable so easy to digest.

"Let me now turn to *Gulliver's Travels*.

"On the one hand you have the Yahoos, who are associated with raw meat, the smell of excrement, and what we used to call bestiality. On the other you have the Houyhnhnms, who are associated with grass, sweet smells, and the rational ordering of the passions. In between you have Gulliver, who wants to be a Houyhnhnm but knows secretly that he is a Yahoo. All of that is perfectly clear. As with 'A Modest Proposal,' the question is, what do we make of it?

"One observation. The horses expel Gulliver. Their ostensible reason is that he does not meet the standard of rationality. The real reason is that he does not look like a horse, but something else: a dressed-up Yahoo, in fact. So: the standard of reason that has been applied by carnivorous bipeds to justify a special status for themselves can equally be applied by herbivorous quadrupeds.

"The standard of reason. *Gulliver's Travels* seems to me to operate within the three-part Aristotelian division of gods, beasts, and men. As long as one tries to fit the three actors into just two categories — which are the beasts, which are the men? — one can't make sense of the fable. Nor can the Houyhnhnms. The Houyhnhnms are gods of a kind, cold, Apollonian. The test they apply to Gulliver is: Is he a god or a beast? They feel it is the appropriate test. We, instinctively, don't.

"What has always puzzled me about *Gulliver's Travels* — and this is a perspective you might expect from an ex-colonial — is that Gulliver always travels alone. Gulliver goes on voyages of exploration to unknown lands, but he does not come ashore with an armed party, *as happened in reality*, and Swift's book says nothing about what would normally have come after Gulliver's pioneering efforts:

follow-up expeditions, expeditions to colonize Lilliput or the island of the Houyhnhnms.

"The question I ask is: What if Gulliver and an armed expedition were to land, shoot a few Yahoos when they become threatening, and then shoot and eat a horse, for food? What would that do to Swift's somewhat too neat, somewhat too disembodied, somewhat too unhistorical fable? It would certainly give the Houyhnhnms a rude shock, making it clear that there is a third category besides gods and beasts, namely, man, of whom their ex-client Gulliver is one; furthermore, that if the horses stand for reason, then man stands for physical force.

"Taking over an island and slaughtering its inhabitants is, by the way, what Odysseus and his men did on Thrinacia, the island sacred to Apollo, an act for which they were mercilessly punished by the god. And that story, in turn, seems to call on older layers of belief, from a time when bulls were gods and killing and eating a god could call down a curse on you.

"So — excuse the confusion of this response — yes, we are not horses, we do not have their clear, rational, naked beauty; on the contrary we are subequine primates, otherwise known as man. You say there is nothing to do but embrace that status, that nature. Very well, let us do so. But let us also push Swift's fable to its limits and recognize that, in history, embracing the status of man has entailed slaughtering and enslaving a race of divine or else divinely created beings and bringing down on ourselves a curse thereby."

It is three-fifteen, a couple of hours before his mother's last engagement. He walks her over to his office along tree-lined paths where the last autumn leaves are falling.

"Do you really believe, Mother, that poetry classes are going to close down the slaughterhouses?"

"No."

"Then why do it? You said you were tired of clever talk about animals, proving by syllogism that they do or do not have souls.

But isn't poetry just another kind of clever talk: admiring the muscles of the big cats in verse? Wasn't your point about talk that it changes nothing? It seems to me the level of behavior you want to change is too elementary, too elemental, to be reached by talk. Carnivorousness expresses something truly deep about human beings, just as it does about jaguars. You wouldn't want to put a jaguar on a soybean diet."

"Because he would die. Human beings don't die on a vegetarian diet."

"No, they don't. But they don't *want* a vegetarian diet. They *like* eating meat. There is something atavistically satisfying about it. That's the brutal truth. Just as it's a brutal truth that, in a sense, animals deserve what they get. Why waste your time trying to help them when they won't help themselves? Let them stew in their own juice. If I were asked what the general attitude is toward the animals we eat, I would say: contempt. We treat them badly because we despise them; we despise them because they don't fight back."

"I don't disagree," says his mother. "People complain that we treat animals like objects, but in fact we treat them like prisoners of war. Do you know that when zoos were first opened to the public, the keepers had to protect the animals against attacks by spectators? The spectators felt the animals were there to be insulted and abused, like prisoners in a triumph. We had a war once against the animals, which we called hunting, though in fact war and hunting are the same thing (Aristotle saw it clearly).[15] That war went on for millions of years. We won it definitively only a few hundred years ago, when we invented guns. It is only since victory became absolute that we have been able to afford to cultivate compassion. But our compassion is very thinly spread. Beneath

---

[15] Aristotle: "The art of war is a natural art of acquisition, for the art of acquisition includes hunting, an art which we ought to practise against wild beasts, and against men who, though intended by nature to be governed, will not submit; for war of such a kind is naturally just" (*Politics*, book I, ch. 8, in Regan and Singer, eds., *Animal Rights*, p. 110).

it is a more primitive attitude. The prisoner of war does not belong to our tribe. We can do what we want with him. We can sacrifice him to our gods. We can cut his throat, tear out his heart, throw him on the fire. There are no laws when it comes to prisoners of war."

"And that is what you want to cure humankind of?"

"John, I don't know what I want to do. I just don't want to sit silent."

"Very well. But generally one doesn't kill prisoners of war. One turns them into slaves."

"Well, that's what our captive herds are: slave populations. Their work is to breed for us. Even their sex becomes a form of labor. We don't hate them because they are not worth hating any-more. We regard them as you say, with contempt.

"However, there are still animals we hate. Rats, for instance. Rats haven't surrendered. They fight back. They form themselves into underground units in our sewers. They aren't winning, but they aren't losing either. To say nothing of the insects and the microbia. They may beat us yet. They will certainly outlast us."

The final session of his mother's visit is to take the form of a debate. Her opponent will be the large, blond man from yesterday evening's dinner, who turns out to be Thomas O'Hearne, professor of philosophy at Appleton.

It has been agreed that O'Hearne will have three opportunities to present positions, and his mother three opportunities to reply. Since O'Hearne has had the courtesy to send her a précis before-hand, she knows, broadly speaking, what he will be saying.

"My first reservation about the animal-rights movement," O'Hearne begins, "is that by failing to recognize its historical nature, it runs the risk of becoming, like the human-rights move-ment, yet another Western crusade against the practices of the rest of the world, claiming universality for what are simply its own standards." He proceeds to give a brief outline of the rise of animal-protection societies in Britain and America in the nineteenth century.

"When it comes to human rights," he continues, "other cultures and other religious traditions quite properly reply that they have their own norms and see no reason why they should have to adopt those of the West. Similarly, they say, they have their own norms for the treatment of animals and see no reason to adopt ours — particularly when ours are of such recent invention.

"In yesterday's presentation our lecturer was very hard on Descartes. But Descartes did not invent the idea that animals belong to a different order from humankind: he merely formalized it in a new way. The notion that we have an obligation to animals themselves to treat them compassionately — as opposed to an obligation to ourselves to do so — is very recent, very Western, and even very Anglo-Saxon. As long as we insist that we have access to an ethical universal to which other traditions are blind, and try to impose it on them by means of propaganda or even economic pressure, we are going to meet with resistance, and that resistance will be justified."

It is his mother's turn.

"The concerns you express are substantial, Professor O'Hearne, and I am not sure I can give them a substantial answer. You are correct, of course, about the history. Kindness to animals has become a social norm only recently, in the last hundred and fifty or two hundred years, and in only part of the world. You are correct too to link this history to the history of human rights, since concern for animals is, historically speaking, an offshoot of broader philanthropic concerns — for the lot of slaves and of children, among others.[16]

"However, kindness to animals — and here I use the word *kindness* in its full sense, as an acceptance that we are all of one kind, one nature — has been more widespread than you imply. Pet-

---

[16] See James Turner, *Reckoning with the Beast* (Baltimore: Johns Hopkins University Press, 1980), chapter 1.

keeping, for instance, is by no means a Western fad: the first travellers to South America encountered settlements where human beings and animals lived higgledy-piggledy together. And of course children all over the world consort quite naturally with animals. They don't see any dividing-line. That is something they have to be taught, just as they have to be taught it is all right to kill and eat them.

"Getting back to Descartes, I would only want to say that the discontinuity he saw between animals and human beings was the result of incomplete information. The science of Descartes's day had no acquaintance with the great apes or with higher marine mammals, and thus little cause to question the assumption that animals cannot think. And of course it had no access to the fossil record that would reveal a graded continuum of anthropoid creatures stretching from the higher primates to *Homo sapiens* — anthropoids, one must point out, who were exterminated by man in the course of his rise to power.[17]

"While I concede your main point about Western cultural arrogance, I do think it is appropriate that those who pioneered the industrialization of animal lives and the commodification of animal flesh should be at the forefront of trying to atone for it."

O'Hearne presents his second thesis. "In my reading of the scientific literature," he says, "efforts to show that animals can think strategically, hold general concepts, or communicate symbolically have had very limited success. The best performance the higher apes can put up is no better than that of a speech-impaired human being with severe mental retardation. If so, are not animals, even the higher animals, properly thought of as belonging to another legal and ethical realm entirely, rather than being placed in this depressing human subcategory? Isn't there a certain wisdom in the traditional view that says that animals cannot enjoy legal

---

[17] See Mary Midgley, "Persons and Non-Persons," in Peter Singer, ed., *In Defence of Animals* (Oxford: Blackwell, 1985), p. 59; Rosemary Rodd, *Biology, Ethics, and Animals* (Oxford: Clarendon Press, 1990), p. 37.

rights because they are not persons, even potential persons, as fetuses are? In working out rules for our dealings with animals, does it not make more sense for such rules to apply to us and to our treatment of them, as at present, rather than being predicated upon rights which animals cannot claim or enforce or even understand?" [18]

His mother's turn. "To respond adequately, Professor O'Hearne, would take more time than I have, since I would first want to interrogate the whole question of rights and how we come to possess them. So let me just make one observation: that the program of scientific experimentation that leads you to conclude that animals are imbeciles is profoundly anthropocentric. It values being able to find your way out of a sterile maze, ignoring the fact that if the researcher who designed the maze were to be parachuted into the jungles of Borneo, he or she would be dead of starvation in a week. In fact I would go further. If I as a human being were told that the standards by which animals are being measured in these experiments are human standards, I would be insulted. It is the experiments themselves that are imbecile. The behaviorists who design them claim that we understand only by a process of creating abstract models and then testing those models against reality. What nonsense. We understand by immersing ourselves and our intelligence in complexity. There is something self-stultified in the way in which scientific behaviorism recoils from the complexity of life.[19]

---

[18] Cf. Bernard Williams: "Before one gets to the question of how animals should be treated, there is the fundamental point that this is the only question there can be: how they should be treated. The choice can only be whether animals benefit from our practices or are harmed by them." Quoted in Michael P. T. Leahy, *Against Liberation* (London and New York: Routledge, 1991), p. 208.

[19] For a critique of behaviorism in the political context of its times, see Bernard E. Rollin, *The Unheeded Cry* (Oxford: Oxford University Press, 1990), pp. 100–103. On the behaviorist taboo on considering the subjective mental states of animals, see Donald R. Griffin, *Animal Minds* (Chicago: University of Chicago Press, 1992), pp. 6–7. Griffin calls the taboo "a serious impediment to scientific investigation," but suggests that in practice investigators do not adhere to it (pp. 6, 120).

"As for animals being too dumb and stupid to speak for themselves, consider the following sequence of events. When Albert Camus was a young boy in Algeria, his grandmother told him to bring her one of the hens from the cage in their back yard. He obeyed, then watched her cut off its head with a kitchen knife, catching its blood in a bowl so that the floor would not be dirtied.

"The death-cry of that hen imprinted itself on the boy's memory so hauntingly that in 1958 he wrote an impassioned attack on the guillotine. As a result, in part, of that polemic, capital punishment was abolished in France. Who is to say, then, that the hen did not speak?" [20]

O'Hearne. "I make the following statement with due deliberation, mindful of the historical associations it may evoke. I do not believe that life is as important to animals as it is to us. There is certainly in animals an instinctive struggle against death, which they share with us. But they do not *understand* death as we do, or rather, as we fail to do. There is, in the human mind, a collapse of the imagination before death, and that collapse of the imagination — graphically evoked in yesterday's lecture — is the basis of our fear of death. That fear does not and cannot exist in animals, since the effort to comprehend extinction and the failure to do so, the failure to master it, have simply not taken place.

"For that reason, I want to suggest, dying is, for an animal, just something that happens, something against which there may be a revolt of the organism but not a revolt of the soul. And the lower down the scale of evolution one goes, the truer this is. To an insect, death is the breakdown of systems that keep the physical organism functioning, and nothing more.

"To animals, death is continuous with life. It is only among certain very imaginative human beings that one encounters a horror of dying so acute that they then project it onto other beings, includ-

---

[20] Albert Camus, *The First Man*, trans. David Hapgood (London: Hamish Hamliton, 1995), pp. 181–83; "Réflexions sur la guillotine," in *Essais*, ed. R. Quilliot and L. Faucon (Paris: Gallimard, 1965), pp. 1019–64.

ing animals. Animals live, and then they die: that is all. Thus to equate a butcher who slaughters a chicken with an executioner who kills a human being is a grave mistake. The events are not comparable. They are not of the same scale, they are not on the same scale.

"That leaves us with the question of cruelty. It is licit to kill animals, I would say, because their lives are not as important to them as our lives are to us; the old-fashioned way of saying this is that animals do not have immortal souls. Gratuitous cruelty, on the other hand, I would regard as illicit. Therefore it is quite appropriate that we should agitate for the humane treatment of animals, even and particularly in slaughterhouses. This has for a long time been a goal of animal welfare organizations, and I salute them for it.

"My very last point concerns what I see as the troubling abstract nature of the concern for animals in the animal rights movement. I want to apologize in advance to our lecturer for the seeming harshness of what I am about to say, but I believe it needs to be said.

"Of the many varieties of animal-lover I see around me, let me isolate two. On the one hand, hunters, people who value animals at a very elementary, unreflective level; who spend hours watching them and tracking them; and who, after they have killed them, get pleasure from the taste of their flesh. On the other hand, people who have little contact with animals, or at least with those species they are concerned to protect, like poultry and livestock, yet want all animals to lead — in an economic vacuum — a utopian life in which everyone is miraculously fed and no one preys on anyone else.

"Of the two, which, I ask, loves animals more?

"Is it because agitation for animal rights, including the right to life, is so abstract that I find it unconvincing and, finally, idle. Its proponents talk a great deal about our community with animals, but how do they actually live in that community? Thomas Aquinas says that friendship between human beings and animals is impossible, and I tend to agree.[21] You can be friends neither with a Martian nor with a bat, for the simple reason that you have too little in common with them. We may certainly *wish* for there to be community with animals, but that is not the same thing as living in community with them. It is just a piece of prelapsarian wistfulness."

His mother's turn again, her last turn.

"Anyone who says that life matters less to animals than it does to us has not held in his hands an animal fighting for its life. The whole of the being of the animal is thrown into that fight, without reserve. When you say that the fight lacks a dimension of intellectual or imaginative horror, I agree. It is not the mode of being of animals to have an intellectual horror: their whole being is in the living flesh.

"If I do not convince you, that is because my words, here, lack the power to bring home to you the wholeness, the unabstracted, unintellectual nature, of that animal being. That is why I urge you to read the poets who return the living, electric being to language; and if the poets do not move you, I urge you to walk, flank to flank, beside the beast that is prodded down the chute to his executioner.

"You say that death does not matter to an animal because the animal does not understand death. I am reminded of one of the academic philosophers I read in preparing for yesterday's lecture. It was a depressing experience. It awoke in me a quite Swiftian response. If this is the best that human philosophy can offer, I said to myself, I would rather go and live among horses.

"Can we, asked this philosopher, strictly speaking, say that the veal calf misses its mother? Does the veal calf have enough of a grasp of the significance of the mother-relation, does the veal calf have enough of a grasp of the meaning of maternal absence, does

---

[21] *Summa* II, 65, iii, quoted in Regan and Singer, eds., *Animal Rights*, p. 120.

the veal calf, finally, know enough about missing to know that the feeling it has is the feeling of missing?[22]

"A calf who has not mastered the concepts of presence and absence, of self and other — so goes the argument — cannot, strictly speaking, be said to miss anything. In order to, strictly speaking, miss anything, it would first have to take a course in philosophy. What sort of philosophy is this? Throw it out, I say. What good do its piddling distinctions do?

"To me, a philosopher who says that the distinction between human and nonhuman depends on whether you have a white or a black skin and a philosopher who says that the distinction between human and nonhuman depends on whether or not you know the difference between a subject and a predicate are more alike than they are unlike.

"Usually I am wary of exclusionary gestures. I know of one prominent philosopher who states that he is simply not prepared to philosophize about animals with people who eat meat. I am not sure I would go as far as that — frankly, I have not the courage — but I must say I would not fall over myself to meet the gentleman whose book I just have been citing. Specifically, I would not fall over myself to break bread with him.

"Would I be prepared to discuss ideas with him? That really is the crucial question. Discussion is possible only when there is common ground. When opponents are at loggerheads, we say: 'Let them reason together, and by reasoning clarify what their differences are, and thus inch closer. They may seem to share nothing else, but at least they share reason.'

"On the present occasion, however, I am not sure I want to concede that I share reason with my opponent. Not when reason is what underpins the whole long philosophical tradition to which

[22] Leahy, *Against Liberation*, p. 218. Leahy elsewhere argues against a ban on the slaughtering of animals on the grounds that (a) it would bring about unemployment among abattoir workers, (b) it would entail an uncomfortable adjustment to our diet, and (c) the countryside would be less attractive without its customary flocks and herds fattening themselves as they wait to die (p. 214).

he belongs, stretching back to Descartes and beyond Descartes through Aquinas and Augustine to the Stoics and Aristotle. If the last common ground that I have with him is reason, and if reason is what sets me apart from the veal calf, then thank you but no thank you, I'll talk to someone else."

That is the note on which Dean Arendt has to bring the proceedings to a close: acrimony, hostility, bitterness. He is sure that is not what Arendt or his committee wanted. Well, they should have asked him before they invited his mother. He could have told them.

It is past midnight, he and Norma are in bed, he is exhausted, at six he will have to get up to drive his mother to the airport. But Norma is in a fury and will not give up. "It's nothing but food-faddism, and food-faddism is always an exercise in power. I have no patience when she arrives here and begins trying to get people, particularly the children, to change their eating habits. And now these absurd public lectures! She is trying to extend her inhibiting power over the whole community."

He wants to sleep, but he cannot utterly betray his mother. "She's perfectly sincere," he murmurs.

"It has nothing to do with sincerity. She has no self-insight at all. It is because she has so little insight into her motives that she seems sincere. Mad people are sincere."

With a sigh he enters the fray. "I don't see any difference," he says, "between her revulsion from eating meat and my own revulsion from eating snails or locusts. I have no insight into my motives and I couldn't care less. I just find it disgusting."

Norma snorts. "You don't give public lectures producing pseudo-philosophical arguments for not eating snails. You don't try to turn a private fad into a public taboo."

"Perhaps. But why not try to see her as a preacher, a social reformer, rather than as an eccentric trying to foist her preferences onto other people?"

"You are welcome to see her as a preacher. But take a look at all the other preachers and their crazy schemes for dividing mankind up into the saved and the damned. Is that the kind of company you want your mother to keep? Elizabeth Costello and her Second Ark, with her dogs and cats and wolves, none of whom, of course, has ever been guilty of the sin of eating flesh, to say nothing of the malaria virus and the rabies virus and the HI virus, which she will want to save so that she can restock her Brave New World."

"Norma, you're ranting."

"I'm not ranting. I would have more respect for her if she didn't try to undermine me behind my back, with her stories to the children about the poor little veal calves and what the bad men do to them. I'm tired of having them pick at their food and ask, 'Mom, is this veal?' when it's chicken or tuna-fish. It's nothing but a power-game. Her great hero Frank Kafka played the same game with his family. He refused to eat this, he refused to eat that, he would rather starve, he said. Soon everyone was feeling guilty about eating in front of him and he could sit back feeling virtuous. It's a sick game, and I'm not having the children play it against me." [23]

"A few hours and she'll be gone, then we can return to normal."

"Good. Say good-bye to her from me. I'm not getting up early."

Seven o'clock, the sun just rising, and he and his mother are on their way to the airport.

"I'm sorry about Norma," he says. "She has been under a lot of strain. I don't think she was in position to sympathize. Perhaps one could say the same for me. It's been such a short visit, I

[23] "What [Kafka] required was a regimen of eccentric food habits that were at odds with the 'normal' dinner table habits of his family . . . Kafka's form of anorexia — not to lose weight but to use food ritualistically as a form of superior statement — was a way of bridging the gap between himself and his family, while at the same time insisting on his uniqueness, his superiority, his sense of rejection" (Karl, *Frank Kafka*, p. 188).

haven't had time to make sense of why you have become so intense about the animal business."

She watches the wipers wagging back and forth. "A better explanation," she says, "is that I have not told you why, or dare not tell you. When I think of the words, they seem so outrageous that they are best spoken into a pillow or into a hole in the ground, like King Midas."

"I don't follow. What is it you can't say?"

"It's that I no longer know where I am. I seem to move around perfectly easily among people, to have perfectly normal relations with them. Is it possible, I ask myself, that all of them are participants in a crime of stupefying proportions? Am I fantasizing it all? I must be mad! Yet every day I see the evidences. The very people I suspect produce the evidence, exhibit it, offer it to me. Corpses. Fragments of corpses that they have bought for money.

"It is as if I were to visit friends, and to make some polite remark about the lamp in their living-room, and they were to say, 'Yes, it's nice, isn't it? Polish-Jewish skin it's made of, we find that's best, the skins of young Polish-Jewish virgins.' And then I go to the bathroom and the soap-wrapper says, 'Treblinka—100% human stearate.' Am I dreaming, I say to myself? What kind of house is this?

"Yet I'm not dreaming. I look into your eyes, into Norma's, into the children's, and I see only kindness, human-kindness. Calm down, I tell myself, you are making a mountain out of a molehill. This is life. Everyone else comes to terms with it, why can't you? *Why can't you?*"

She turns on him a tearful face. What does she want, he thinks? Does she want me to answer her question for her?

They are not yet on the expressway. He pulls the car over, switches off the engine, takes his mother in his arms. He inhales the smell of cold cream, of old flesh. "There, there," he whispers in her ear. "There, there. It will soon be over."

Exploring the Minded Brain

ANTONIO R. DAMASIO

THE TANNER LECTURES ON HUMAN VALUES

Delivered at

University of Michigan
November 14, 1997

ANTONIO R. DAMASIO is Maurice W. Van Allen Distinguished Professor and head of the Department of Neurology at the University of Iowa College of Medicine. He is also an adjunct professor at the Salk Institute in La Jolla. He was born in Portugal and received both his M.D. and his Ph.D. from the University of Lisbon. His work has focused on elucidating critical problems in the fundamental neuroscience of mind and behavior at the level of large-scale systems in humans. He is a member of the National Academy of Sciences' Institute of Medicine and a fellow of the American Academy of Arts and Sciences. He is also a member of the European Academy of Sciences and Arts and of the Royal Academy of Medicine in Belgium. In 1990 he received the William Beaumont Prize from the American Medical Association; he has also received the Golden Brain Award (1995) and the Ipsen Prize (1997). In 1992 he and his wife, Hanna Damasio, shared the Pessoa Prize. He is the author of *Descartes' Error: Emotion, Reason, and the Human Brain* (1994); and *The Feeling of What Happens: Body, Emotion, and the Making of Consciousness* (forthcoming).

LECTURE I. THE MINDED BRAIN

WHAT IS A MINDED BRAIN?

I would like to begin this lecture by explaining that the topic of my work is the minded brain, not just any brain but the minded brain. You may wonder if by minded brain I mean the human brain, but I do not. The human brain is a minded brain, for certain, but so are, I believe, the brains of many other species though not all. Yet qualifying the brain as minded is not a trivial matter, because many brains of many creatures do not generate a mind in the proper sense. By this I mean that they probably do not generate what I regard as necessary for a normal mind: a continuous logically related sequence and concurrence of mental images of varied sensory modality oriented toward the resolution of some problem. I am not diminishing the value of plain brains without proper minds. Unminded brains can do wonderful things for the organisms they inhabit. They can help those organisms maintain life by responding in predetermined manner to the surrounding environment; they can incorporate ingredients; they can eliminate waste; they can move away from a physically and chemically hostile place or thing; they can seek physically and chemically greener pastures; they can respond to certain stimuli with a reflex. I am just drawing a distinction between minded and unminded brains.

By no means are unminded brains the hallmark of the simplest living creatures. Really simple creatures have no brains at all, minded or otherwise. Their life regulation dispenses with a nervous system altogether. Those creatures — an example is the many unicellular organisms that both surround us and live within us — form the most numerous class of living creatures in the universe, in the past as well as now. There are more *Escherichia coli* inside each one of us than there are people in the cities where we live.

[169]

Working on the minded brain, then, means working on complex organisms that like all other organisms, are equipped with an urge to maintain life, but in which the means to implement such an urge include a special kind of brain, the kind that can make mind as described above.

The minded brain is very much a part of the organism in which it lives. Its mindedness is in fact rooted in the body structure that constitutes the organism in which the brain lives. I have suggested that the body-proper, as represented in the brain, may constitute the frame of reference for the neural activities that we experience as the mind; that the very core of our organism is the ground reference for the constructions we make of the world around us and for the construction of the sense of self that is an indispensable part of our experience. I have suggested that our most refined thoughts and actions, our greatest joys and deepest sorrows, use the body as a yardstick; that the mind was first about the body and was then about many other things, real and imaginary; that our minds would not be the way they are if it were not for the continuous interplay of body and brain during evolution, during individual development, and at the current moment.

A brief summary of this situation can be made in the following statements: (1) the human brain and the rest of the body constitute an integrated organism, brought together by means of mutually interactive biochemical and neural regulatory circuits that include endocrine, immune, and autonomic neural components; (2) the organism interacts with the surrounding environment as an ensemble: the interaction is neither of the body alone nor of the brain alone; (3) the physiological operations that we call mind rely on the ensemble; (4) the full understanding of mental phenomena should be sought in the context of an organism that is interacting with an environment. The environment continuously modifies the organism, but that environment is, in part, a product of the organism's activity itself.

I realize that it is unusual, although not unprecedented, to refer to organisms, let alone bodies, in discussions about brain and mind. It is so obvious that mind arises from the activity of neurons that neurons become the focus of interest, as if operation of the rest of the organism would be irrelevant to their function. My view is quite the opposite. Mental phenomena are based on neural events within a brain, provided that brain has been and is now interacting with its body. Relative to the brain, I believe that the body proper provides the reference content. In a curious way, pleasure and pain, whether they start in the skin or in a mental image, happen in the flesh.

We thus work, as scientists, on strange organisms indeed, the result of a bizarre combination of something very openly physical, their bodies, and something not apparently physical, their minds. Friedrich Nietzsche described this marriage, in a phrase of rare felicity, as "hybrids of plants and of ghosts." I am sympathetic toward his wording because, notwithstanding the physicality of mind, mind and body are sensibly different and their different kinds of physicality may well be honored by different words. Moreover, the word "hybrid" captures the organismic blend that I regard as so essential to the understanding of the biology of mind.

THE RELATION BETWEEN MIND AND BRAIN

Let me clarify a bit more my ideas on the relation between mind and brain and make three points that I regard as especially important.

The first is that the mind is private. You may guess what is in my mind, but you will not know for certain unless I tell you, and I will not know for certain what is in your mind until you tell me.

Second, as I indicated earlier, I believe that mind requires a goal-oriented, logically informed continuous concurrence and sequence of mental images of varied sensory modalities. At first glance those images describe entities and actions, properties and relationships, both concrete and abstract, all of which pertain to the world within our organisms and outside our brains. In effect, those images describe either the state of the body-proper or the mapping of interactions between our organism and something in the environment that surrounds it.

Third, images arise from sensory maps located in specific sectors of complex brains. There are numerous lines of evidence that I cannot possibly detail here that support my statement unequivocally. Let me just review one bit of evidence that is especially relevant. Consider an experimental situation in which I would ask you to view a pattern, for instance, a cross of black lines at right angles. As you focus on it, you will form an optical image of the cross in your retina and go on to perceive the pattern. Now consider that in the same room there is also an experimental animal, say a monkey, that will be trained to look at that same cross from the same viewing angle. Finally, imagine that we will be allowed to study the brain of that animal with the appropriate histological method after he does look at that cross. We will find that in some layers of the visual cortext of the animal's brain the distribution of neuronal activity will have a pattern that in every way resembles the external pattern at which you, and I, and the monkey looked. This was shown in an experiment performed by Roger Tootell.

Now let us consider what this finding can and cannot tell us. To begin with, it can tell us about a consistency of patterns. You and I can see a pattern external to us and we can also see the same pattern within a specific brain structure. It is, incidentally, one of the brain structures in which we *expected* to encounter such a pattern, given our current knowledge of neurophysiology. The finding can also tell us that under certain experimental circumstances and for certain levels of knowledge, we can get around the barrier that the privacy of mind offers to the curious scientist. To be sure, I cannot have your experience when you see this cross, but I can learn a whole lot under experimental conditions about some of the structures and some of the biological states related to that kind of mental experience.

One thing that the finding does *not* tell us at all is the sum total of the structures and operations necessary to generate an image in the mind of the monkey or in your mind or my mind. And here we must return to the statement that motivated this digression: images arise *from* sensory maps located in specific sectors of complex brains. Note that I did not say that mental images *are* sensory maps. To say that images *arise* in or from sensory maps is neither a cop-out nor a pedantic distinction. It is, rather, the critical distinction with which I can make clear my sense of something very unclear: the relation between mind and brain. I believe that the images that constitute the mind are biological states that are, in turn, constituted by chemical and physical states within the neural tissue of a brain placed within an organism that is placed in an environment. Moreover, I know that the generation of those images holds a principled relationship to certain sectors of the brain. (For instance, visual images arise from visual sensory maps and not other maps, and visual sensory maps cannot support the generation of auditory or tactile or visceral images. This has become even more clear recently with the study of sensory processing in congenitally blind individuals.) But by no means do I know the full biological specification of the processes that allow us to construct a visual mental image or an auditory mental image. In other words, I am saying that there is a sizable gap between our current description of the physics of a mental image, in the broad sense of physics, and the description we must have if we are to talk confidently about the physical constitution and generation of that image. It should be clear that the gap that I am identifying is not to be filled by some nonphysical spook but rather by a detailed description of physics, by which I mean physics proper, chemistry, and biology. I am identifying a gap of knowledge, or rather plain ignorance, to put it in more modest terms. I am not identifying a necessarily insoluble mystery, or at least I hope I am not.

DEFINING A MATERIALIST POSITION; AVOIDING DUALISM;
WHAT KIND OF REDUCTIONISM?

What I need to clarify further regarding the relation between mind and brain is whether the materialist position I have just articulated means that I am reducing the mind to the brain. My answer is a firm no for a number of reasons. Mental phenomena and thus mind *are* mental phenomena and thus mind. They are also explainable in biological terms because certain biological states of high complexity constitute the class of phenomena we call mental. There is no incompatibility between the reality and particularly of mental phenomena and the fact that they are biological. But mental phenomena are not reducible to brain circuits or nerve cells, let alone to molecules, because they are not any of those things in isolation, and they are not *just* the mere collection of all those things together. Mental phenomena are biological states that occur when many brain circuits operate together according to particular designs. The plausible identity is not between mind and brain, or between mind and neurons, or circuits, or molecules. The plausible identity is between mind and complex biological states.

Even after a comprehensive materialist research program delivers all the details that I have indicated as currently missing from our accounts of the biology of mind, your experience of love or of listening to Mozart is not going to be *substituted by* the physical description of the antics of your neurons as you either love or listen. Love and listening will be *explained by* the antics of your neurons, but will remain as mental experiences, because mental experiences are the latest and greatest achievement of neuronal antics in the history of the universe.

It is important to note, then, that when we recognize mental phenomena as the highest level of biological phenomena, our position remains materialist, and that we are not endorsing dualism. The mind is the most complex aspect of biology, or to put it in slightly more precise terms, the images in the mind are constituted by the most complex biological states. Minds are part of biology, but their biological status in no way cancels out the mental properties we discover through our experience. The *res cogitum* is part of the *res extensa* rather than being something else. And the *res cogitum* remains as such rather than being eliminated.

THE APPROPRIATE LEVEL OF STUDY TO LINK MIND AND BRAIN: THE LARGE-SCALE SYSTEMS LEVEL

For most of the history of civilization, which we can set as beginning 2,500 years ago around Plato's urbane dining table, some humans have maintained an interest in the working of their minds. On and off, especially for the last two centuries, they have even had an interest in both mind and brain. But interest, reflection, and description are one thing and exploration is another. By exploration I mean a real adventure of ideas that requires theories, hypotheses, and the scientific checking of those hypotheses by scientific experiments. In this particular sense, the explorations of the minded brain are of more recent vintage and have only begun in earnest over the past two decades, following the developments of a number of new scientific methods. They include the extension of our knowledge of biological systems to the molecular level and to genes antecedent to those molecules; the development of means to study cognitive processes rather than just behaviors; the ensuing strengthening of the available descriptions of mind; and the development of new probes for brain structure and brain function, in animals and in humans, capable of delivering measurement at the level of neurons and at the level of systems.

What we want to understand as we explore the minded brain depends largely on the operation of neurons and of the molecules that constitute them and make them fire away. We are beginning to know something about those neurons and about the genes that make those neurons develop and operate in a certain fashion. But the minded brain requires more than single neurons. It depends on overall patterns of the firing neurons, as assembled complicated networks that range from microscopic-scale circuits confined to a small brain area to macroscopic systems that span several centimeters. The complexity is immense. There are several billion neurons in the circuits of one human brain. The number of synapses formed among those neurons is at least 10 trillion. The length of the axon cables forming neuron circuits totals several hundred thousand miles. The product of activity in such circuits is a pattern of firing that is transmitted to another circuit. The time scale for the firing is extremely small, on the order of tens of milliseconds — which means that within one second in the life of our minds, the brain produces millions of firing patterns over a large variety of circuits distributed over various brain regions.

The secrets of the minded brain cannot be revealed by discovering all the mysteries of one typical single neuron or by discovering all the intricate patterns of local activity of one typical neuron circuit. The secrets of the minded brain are hiding in the interaction of firing patterns generated by many neuron circuits, locally and globally, moment by moment, within the brain of a living organism.

There is thus not one simple answer in the current explorations of the minded brain, but rather many answers, keyed to the myriad components of the nervous system at its many levels of structure. The approach to understanding those levels calls for various techniques and proceeds at various paces.

Some have asked why neuroscience has not yet achieved results as spectacular as those seen in molecular biology over the past four decades. Some have wondered what is the neuroscientific equivalent of the discovery of DNA structure, and whether or not a corresponding neuroscientific fact has been established. There is no such single correspondence, although some facts, at several levels of the nervous system, might be construed as comparable in practical value to knowing the structure of DNA — for instance, understanding the nature of an action potential. But the equivalent of DNA structure at the level of the minded brain is likely to be a large-scale outline of circuit and system designs and to involve descriptions at both microstructural and macrostructural levels.

The limits of our current neuroscientific knowledge have other justifications, to which I will return at the end of the talk. One is that only a part of our brain circuitry is specified by the genome. The human genome commands the construction of our bodies in great detail, including the overall design of the brain. But not all brain circuits end up wired and working as commanded by genes. A good part of the circuitry in each of our brains, perhaps most of it, reflects the particular history and circumstances of our organism and is thus relatively individual and unique. Each human organism operates in collectives of like beings. The mind of individuals operating in specific cultural and physical environments is not shaped merely by any kind of activity and even less is it shaped by genes alone. Social and cultural context are relevant to the shaping of the minded brain.

A successful exploration of the minded brain depends on choosing the right level of study. At the moment, the level of large-scale systems appears to be the right level to guide the study of the relation between neural processes and cognitive processes.

EXAMPLES OF ADVANCES IN COGNITIVE NEUROSCIENCE

Virtually all of the cognitive macrofunctions, such as memory, language, and emotion, are now better understood in terms of their underlying neural systems. Numerous types of memory have been identified relative to their temporal dimension, their learning curve profile, their dependence on consciousness, their mode of access, and the form of output they require for a response. We have a sense now of the neural systems needed to learn a fact and of the learning systems needed to learn a skill. We know about systems needed for conditioning and we even know that they are independent of those required to hold on to a fact or to a skill.

Progress in the understanding of the neural basis of language has been just as remarkable and has proceeded along the same lines. Different components of language function — for instance, retrieval from the lexicon or organization of syntactic structure — depend on separable neural systems. In the most remarkable recent development in this area of study, it has become clear that even the systems that support lexical retrieval are segregated, at least in part. To invoke just one of the most dramatic examples, we rely on concerted activation of different brain regions as we search for the word with which we can denote a unique person or a manipulable tool.

Emotion is perhaps the subject about which there has been the most notable progress, though not necessarily the most abundant. The idea of understanding the neural underpinnings of emotion was neglected for a good part of the twentieth century and neuroscience has only recently approached it in earnest. But in just about a decade of new work we are gathering a rich view of the varied systems that support different kinds of emotion and feeling. Most importantly, the view of the role that emotion plays in human cognition has been changing radically. Rather than being a luxury, emotion is gradually being recognized as a fundamental function of the nervous system indispensable for biological regulation. Rather than being a hindrance to proper reasoning, emotion is now being seen as an obligate component of the mechanisms that permit efficient logical reasoning and advantageous decision-making. It is perhaps true that as research on emotion reveals a multiplicity of systems controlling mental and behavioral outputs, it is contributing powerfully to a reformulation of our views on human nature. Of necessity, our views on rationality, free will, and responsibility, though not necessarily shaken by research results, may be reconsidered and perhaps even adjusted, from the perspective afforded by new findings from the mind and brain sciences.

LECTURE II. MODERN NEUROBIOLOGY
AND HUMAN VALUES

What do the facts of modern neurobiology mean for the managing of human affairs? Does it matter at all, to any but the curious, to know how varied aspects of the mind have evolved, have developed, and are currently constructed by the brain? I would say that it does.

First, I would not minimize the value of satisfying human curiosity, least of all curiosity about humanity itself. Second, I would say that modern neurobiological facts have an immediate practical value in medicine: the diagnosis and treatment of neurological and psychiatric diseases improve remarkably whenever we gather more knowledge about how the brain operates. Needless to say, the alleviation of suffering in those affected by brain disorders, directly or indirectly, is of immense value. Consider, for instance, the modern rehabilitation of patients who suffer from impairments of language or memory; the treatment of parkinsonism or of depression; or the prospect of preventing catastrophic diseases caused by specific gene defects. Third, and no less importantly, I would say that knowing human nature more deeply and from a neurobiological perspective may be of considerable value in the understanding and management of human suffering in a wider context. I am not referring to disease in the narrow sense of the term. I am referring, rather, to the kind of personal suffering that results from the struggle for life in a complicated social and cultural environment — although I might as well refer to the pathologies of society and culture. My hope is that neurobiology can contribute to reduce suffering at that level too, and to achieve a greater realization of human potential.

Intriguingly, understanding human nature in ways that can be helpful to the resolution of human conflict—and, to put it bluntly, to the increase of human well-being — depends not just on how much we know about the ways in which the organism and its brain operate *now*. It also depends on our views of how organisms and brains came to be the way they are *now*. In short, it depends on their history in the perspective of evolution and individual development. Ideally, the evolutionary perspective should not make any difference, but in practice it does. Periodically, scientists, philosophers, and the general public revisit the issue of nature versus nurture, and the value of our knowledge of biology is indexed to the relative position one holds in the nature versus nurture debate. Worse than that, the degree to which practical interventions on the matter of human suffering and happiness are either promoted or withheld depends almost entirely on the nature/nurture position one holds. I would like to explain how I interpret the evidence currently available on this issue, and the position I hold as a result.

For most of the twentieth century, cognitive science, neuroscience, and the related philosophy of mind have not made use of an evolutionary perspective. In many respects, the instance of emotion being perhaps the most blatant, the sciences of mind and brain proceeded as if Charles Darwin never existed, as if nothing in the theory of evolution or in the grand synthesis might constrain the hypotheses, the approaches, and the explanations devised to cope with mental and neural phenomena. Recently, however, under the growing volume of evidence amassed by general biology, the tide has turned and the evolutionary perspective seems to be everywhere at once. Better late than never, one might have said just a few years ago, but now I am beginning to wonder if one should not complain about too much of a good thing, or perhaps just complain about the misuse of a good thing. My complaint would take the form of calling attention to a number of issues that emphasize the importance and value of an evolutionary perspective while suggesting where evolutionary explanations are not sufficient to account for the operations of the human brain and mind in a significant way.

THE ISSUE OF NEURAL DEVELOPMENT

The brain's circuits and the operations they perform depend on the pattern of connections among neurons and on the strength of the synapses that constitute those connections. But it is not entirely clear how the connection patterns and the synaptic strengths are set, or when they are, and for which systems, and for how long. This much seems likely: the human genome, which is the sum total of the genes in our chromosomes, does not specify the entire structure of the brain. There simply are not enough genes available to determine the precise structure and place of everything in our organisms, least of all in the brain, where billions of neurons form their synaptic contacts. The disproportion is not subtle: we come to life and carry around about 100,000 genes, but we have more than 10 trillion synapses in our brains. Moreover, the genetically induced formation of tissues is assisted by interactions among cells, within a specific environment, in which cell adhesion molecules and substrate adhesion molecules also play an important role. What happens among cells as development unfolds depends on the cells' behavior and on the environment of which they are a part, and what happens in those interactions actually controls, in part, the expression of the genes that regulate development in the first place. As far as one can tell, then, many structural specifics are determined by genes, but the genes' actions themselves are controlled by environments, large and small, and are influenced by the activity of the living organism itself, as it develops. This remains true as the organism changes continuously throughout the life span.

The practical meaning of this situation is as follows. The genome puts in place the nearly precise structure of important systems and circuits in the evolutionarily old sectors of the human brain. Those sectors include the brain stem, hypothalamus, basal forebrain, amygdaloid nuclei, and cingulate region, and we share their essence with individuals in many other species. The role of the neural devices in these brain sectors is to regulate the life process *without* the help of a minded brain. The innate patterns of activity in these circuits regulate the physiological mechanisms without which there is no survival. They do not generate mental images, although the consequences of their activity can be represented in mental images. Without these innately set circuits we would not be able to breathe, regulate our heart and lungs, balance metabolism, seek food and shelter, avoid predators, or reproduce. But there is another role for these innate circuits, a role that is usually forgotten in the discussion of models of brain and mind. The innate circuits also intervene in the development and adult activity of the evolutionary modern structures of the brain, structures such as the neocortex.

In all likelihood, as far as the evolutionarily modern brain sectors are concerned, the genome only sets the general rather than the precise arrangement of the circuits in the evolutionary modern sectors of the brain. The specifics of circuitry equivalent to the specifics that genes help set in the circuitry of older sectors such as brain stem or hypothalamus only come long after birth, as individuals develop through infancy, childhood, and adolescence and interact with the physical environment and with other individuals. The specifics come about under the influence of environmental circumstances constrained by the influence of the innately and precisely set circuits that are concerned with basic life regulation.

In short, we have evolutionarily old and genetically preset circuits that regulate body function and ensure the organism's survival, by controlling the endocrine system, immune system, viscera, and enacting drives and instincts. But those circuits also interfere with the shaping of the evolutionarily more modern and only partially preset circuits that are concerned with representing our acquired experiences, and they are far more plastic. Why should this be so?

My answer to the above question is as follows: both the records of experiences and the responses to them, if they are to be adaptive, must be evaluated and shaped by a fundamental set of organism preferences aimed at survival. Because this evaluation and shaping are vital for the continuation of the organism, genes seem to specify that the innate circuits must exert a powerful influence on virtually the entire set of circuits that can be modified by experience. In part, that influence is carried out by "modulator" neurons acting on the remainder of the circuitry. The modulator neurons are located in the brain stem and in the basal forebrain, and they are influenced by the interactions of the organism at any given moment. Modulator neurons distribute neurotransmitters such as dopamine, norepinephrine, serotonin, and acetylcholine to widespread regions of the cerebral cortex and subcortical nuclei. This arrangement can be summarized in the following statements: (1) the innate, regulatory circuits are involved in organism survival and are privy to activity in the modern sectors of the brain; (2) the value (goodness and badness) of situations is signaled to them continuously, following a process of evaluation (the evaluation can be exceedingly rapid, automatic, and nonconscious or be deliberately controlled); (3) the regulatory circuits express their automatic reaction to value (goodness and badness) by influencing how the rest of the brain operates. This influence begins to be exerted during development and continues in adulthood, in day-to-day operations. The influence ends up assisting the brain in achieving survival in the most efficacious way.

As we develop, the design of brain circuitries that represent our evolving body and its interaction with the world depends *both* on the activities the organism engages and on the responses of innate bioregulatory circuitries, caught in the process of reacting to such activities.

The above account underscores the inadequacy of conceiving brain, behavior, and mind in terms of nature versus nurture or genes versus experience. Our brains and our minds are not a tabula rasa when we are born. Yet neither are they fully determined. The genetic shadow is large but not complete. Genes provide for *precise* structure in one brain component and influence indirectly the determination of precise structure in another component. But the micro- and macro-environments surrounding the networks play a critical role in that determination. Thus, the to-be-determined structure is the result of three types of influence: (1) the precise structure of the regulatory sector; (2) the individual activity and circumstances related to the human and physical environment; and (3) the self-organizing pressures that arise from the sheer complexity of the system.

Since the profile of experiences of each individual is not predictable, that unpredictability has a say in circuit design, directly and indirectly, because of the varied reactions it engenders in the innate circuitries and because of the ensuing consequences of such reactions in the process of circuit shaping. Last but not least, the process never ends. Synaptic strengths can change throughout the life span, to reflect different organism experiences, and accordingly the design of brain circuits continues to change. The evolutionary modern brain circuits not only are receptive to the results of first experience, but are repeatedly pliable. They can learn from new experience.

The Limits of the Innate Bioregulatory Machinery

How much the innate bioregulatory machinery alone can ensure an organism's survival depends on the complexity of the environment and of the organism in question. From insects to mammals, there are unequivocal examples of successful coping with particular forms of environment on the basis of innate strategies, and those strategies include complex aspects of social cognition and behavior. When we consider humans, however, and the novel physical and social environments in which humans have thrived, it appears that we rely both on genetically based biological mechanisms and on suprainstinctual survival strategies that have developed in society and that are transmitted by culture. Those strategies require a minded brain, one with consciousness, reason, and willpower. Those strategies explain why human hunger, desire, and anger do not usually result in feeding frenzy, rape, and murder. Those strategies require both a healthy human organism and a long period of development in a society in which those survival strategies are actively transmitted and respected.

One task that faces neuroscientists today is to study and understand the brain structures required to learn and implement suprainstinctual regulations. This may give pause to those who see suprainstinctual regulation as purely cultural phenomena, but it should not cause any concern. I am not reducing social phenomena to biological phenomena, but rather calling attention to their powerful mutual interactions. Culture and civilization obviously arise from the behavior of biological creatures, but that behavior was generated in collectives of individuals interacting in specific environments. Culture and civilization could not have arisen from single individuals and cannot be reduced to biological mechanisms or to genetic messages. The comprehensive understanding of culture and civilization requires biology *and* the social sciences.

Human societies have produced social conventions and ethical rules over and above those that biology already provides. Those additional layers of control shape instinctual behavior so that it can be adapted flexibly to a complex and rapidly changing environment, modify it, and ensure survival in circumstances in which a "natural" response would be counterproductive, immediately or eventually. Social conventions and ethical rules preclude immediate physical or mental harm, or future losses of every kind. Such conventions and rules are transmitted by education and socialization, from generation to generation, not by genes. Yet I suspect that the neural representations of the wisdom they embody and of the means to implement that wisdom are connected indelibly to the neural representations of the innate, regulatory life processes I alluded to above. Elsewhere I have written that I see a "trail" connecting the brain that represents acquired social conventions and rules to the brain that represents innate life regulation, a trail that is made up of neuron connections, of course. For most ethical rules and social conventions, regardless of how elevated their goal, I believe that one can envision a meaningful link to simpler goals and to drives and instincts. There is a good reason why this should be so: the consequences of achieving or not achieving a rarefied social goal contribute, directly or indirectly, to survival and to the quality of that survival. More about quality of survival further on.

This is not the same thing as saying that we possess brain modules for the production of certain behavior — say, for males seeking social status or females marrying rich husbands — and even less claiming that those modules are set in place by genes. In fact, I see no need whatsoever to invoke genetic modules to carry out nature's survival intentions. I expect that such modules would actually compromise the flexibility the organism requires for future adaptations. Incidentally, the existence of free will hinges partially on the availability of a certain degree of freedom and indeterminacy in the learning, adoption, and utilization of such suprainstinctual strategies.

Human organisms come to life designed with automatic survival mechanisms. Culture then adds a set of socially permissible and desirable decision-making strategies that enhance survival and improve the quality of that survival. The human brain comes to development endowed with physiological devices to regulate metabolism, drives and instincts, and basic devices to cope with social cognition and behavior. It emerges from child development with additional layers of survival strategy, which are interwoven with those that support and implement the instinctual repertoire and both modify their use and extend their reach.

The neural mechanisms that support the suprainstinctual repertoire are similar in formal design to those governing biological drives and are constrained by them. But they require the intervention of society to develop and become whatever they become. They are related to general neurobiology and to a given culture. Out of that dual constraint, suprainstinctual survival strategies generate something unique to humans: a moral point of view that may transcend the interests of the immediate group and even the species.

BEYOND SURVIVAL

True enough, natural selection plays the lead part in evolution, and true enough, survival and reproduction are the agents of selection. But these simple facts hide other simple facts that are not unrelated and that require our consideration. For instance, side by side with the biological evolution whose information is transmitted by the genome, there is a cultural evolution, whose artifacts are transmitted by technologies as old as the printed word and as modern as the electronic media. Their influence on survival and reproduction is anything but modest.

Another fact: our biological makeup, brains and minds included, is presumed to be the result of successful adaptations to the environment obtained in the lengthy purifying process of evolution. But it is also a fact that many of the evolving organisms that led to humans, and humans in particular, are engaged in an active modification of the environment to suit their purposes. At this junction, in this room, we are indeed living on the capital of many successful adaptations to the environment, of many successful modifications of the environment, and of many mutual interactions of the former with the latter.

And yet another, perhaps most important fact: the mention of survival ignores the fact that for quite some time now — the quite some time being in the order of more than two millennia — humans have been engaged not just in surviving but in surviving well, not just in surviving well but in surviving better than before. To paraphrase Alfred North Whitehead, humans have been interested not just in maintaining life but in cultivating the art of life.

For several centuries now, humans have entered what I like to describe as the thoughtful phase of evolution. Human minds and brains can be both servants and masters of the organisms they inhabit and of the societies to which they contribute. Human brains and minds came from nature no doubt, but they can be apprentices to the sorcerer and influence nature itself. To be sure, sorcerer's apprentice is a risky role to play, but all is risky in the game of life, and not playing any role—doing just what comes naturally— is the most risky of all strategies. Besides, doing just what comes naturally can satisfy only those who are unable to imagine better worlds and better ways, those who believe they already live in the best of all possible worlds.

Needless to say, the decision to respond to the challenge of nature, the deliberate attempt to construct better worlds — worlds with less suffering, worlds with measurable increases of well-being for sentient creatures, worlds in which self-interest and the pursuit of happiness become tempered with a concern for the other — is not a direct consequence of our knowledge of neurobiology, but it can be influenced by it, positively or negatively. A view of mind as overdetermined by evolution and genes can discourage successful attempts to improve the human lot, especially when resources are scarce. On the contrary, a view of mind devoid of the constraints of evolution and genetics may foster unrealistic hopes for what cultures can achieve. The decision as to which shade of view will eventually prevail should not be a political matter. It should rest on the evidence. It is a matter of scientific and philosophic in-terpretation. Whatever you do with the decision is another issue, and it does involve politics. It should be clear that, at the moment, we do not have enough evidence for a definitive view, although I have indicated which view I see as likely to be correct. In spite of the uncertainty, I suspect that knowing more about the minded brain will help us find better ways for the management of human affairs.

The Direction of European History

TIMOTHY GARTON ASH

THE TANNER LECTURES ON HUMAN VALUES

Delivered at

Charles University (Prague)
November 27, 1997

TIMOTHY GARTON ASH is Senior Research Fellow in Contemporary European History at St. Antony's College, Oxford. After reading modern history at Oxford, his research into the German resistance to Hitler took him to both the eastern and western halves of the divided city of Berlin, where he lived for several years. In 1986–87 he was a fellow of the Woodrow Wilson International Center for Scholars. He is a governor of the Westminster Foundation for Democracy and a fellow of the Berlin-Brandenburg (formerly Prussian) Academy of Sciences and the Royal Society of Arts. He has been honored with both the Polish and the German Order of Merit. He was the foreign editor of the *Spectator*, and for several years wrote a column in the *Independent*. He remains a regular contributor to the *New York Review of Books*, the *TLS*, and the London *Times*. He is the author of *The Uses of Adversity: Essays on the Fate of Central Europe* (1989); *The Magic Lantern* (1993; British title: *We the People*); and *The Polish Revolution: Solidarity* (1983), which won the Somerset Maugham Award.

It is a great pleasure to deliver the first Tanner Lecture to be held behind the line of what used to be called the Iron Curtain, here in Prague, in this historic building of the Charles University. Since what I have to say may be regarded by some guardians of European political correctness as mildly heretical, I take comfort in the thought that since the days of Jan Hus and John Wyclif, the Charles University and my own University of Oxford are old partners in heresy.

It would have been a very particular pleasure to have delivered this lecture — as was planned — in the presence of President Václav Havel, a man who has himself contributed so much to shaping the direction of recent European history. I very much hope that he will be with us again before too long. Meanwhile, I am much looking forward to the comments tomorrow of Senator Petr Pithart, Professor Pierre Hassner, and Professor Arnulf Baring, three colleagues and friends whose work I have greatly admired, and learned from, for many years.

As the Czech Republic is set fair to achieve, within the foreseeable future, what in 1989 we started calling "the return to Europe," it seems appropriate to consider what this "Europe" is that the Czech lands are rejoining, and what we can say about the direction in which it is developing. But is there anything meaningful we can say about that? Did not the events of 1989 show, once again, the folly of any attempt to predict the future? Which of the countless models and theories of political science, or from the academic field of international relations, suggested that the world of Soviet communism would end in that way, let alone at that time? As one American scholar ruefully observed, "None of us predicted these events, and all of us could explain why they were inevitable."

Historians, including those of us who try to write the history of the present, should be especially wary. What happened in 1989 was, amongst other things, a further demonstration of the poverty of historicism, in Karl Popper's particular usage of that word. Historicism understood, that is, as the claim to be able to detect scientific laws of historical development. Would it not be wiser to stick with R. G. Collingwood's injunction that the historian's task is only to show how the present has come into existence? History, says Collingwood bluntly, ends with the present.

Nonetheless, I have decided to ignore this old wisdom. From deep immersion in recent history one does, I think, emerge with some strong impression, some half-intuitive sense, of the way things seem likely to develop. And this kind of historically informed guesswork — I make no larger claim for it — may be marginally useful for European policy, in a period of European history that is unusually open. The contemporary shorthand often used is "a time of transition." A time of transition has been well defined as the period between one transition and the next. Yet it is certainly true that modern European history has oscillated between generally shorter periods of openness and disorder and generally longer periods of a more settled order: the order of Westphalia, Vienna, Versailles, Yalta, and so on. Thus, on past precedent, it seems unlikely that this openness will last for decades. It therefore matters a great deal what we might be moving toward, and what we should, realistically, be trying to move toward.

Despite the spectacular failure of grand theory to predict what happened in 1989, since 1989 the intellectual skies have in fact been full of competing grand theories about the direction not just of European but of world history. There was Francis Fukuyama's "End of History." There was John Mearsheimer's neo-realist vision of Europe going "back to the future" — with a return of unbridled, violent competition between nation-states. There is the notion of a "new Middle Ages," first cautiously advanced by Pierre Hassner, then flaunted in full feather by Alain Minc. There is Samuel Huntington's "clash of civilisations," with its implication that Europe is now likely to be divided along the historical fault-line between western and eastern Christianity, while confronting the world of Islam to the south.

My own remarks will be largely confined to the internal arrangements of the European continent, although this necessarily involves some consideration of its relations with the rest of the world. I will not be concerned with the philosophy of history, but will remain somewhat closer to the earth, at the point where political theory and political reality intersect.

For there is Europe and there is "Europe." There is the place, the continent, the political and economic reality, and there is Europe as an idea and an ideal, a dream, as project, process, progress toward some *finalité européenne*. These idealistic and teleological visions of Europe at once inform, legitimate, and are themselves informed and legitimated by the political development of something now called the European Union. The very name "European Union" is itself a product of this approach. For a union is what it's meant to be, not what it is.

At its most vertiginous, this comes as the dialectical idealism of German Europeanism. The title of a German work on the recent development of Europe is *Europa der Gegensätze auf dem Wege zu sich selbst*: The Europe of Contradictions on the Way to Itself. In English, this makes about as much sense as "the London of traffic jams on the way to itself." Less giddily, though, even in Britain we have grown accustomed to what I call the Whig interpretation of recent European history. European history since 1945 is interpreted as a story of progress toward more freedom, more democracy, more prosperity, more integration, and in the end — or as the end — to unity.

Among the continents, this view is peculiar to Europe. There may be talk of "Asian values," for example, or attempts to find a pan-African identity, but it would be hard to argue that the analyses and policies of the political elites of Asia or Africa are

routinely informed by any teleological or idealistic notion of their
continent "becoming itself." The same would seem to hold for the
Americas. That leaves Australia.

A classic example of this European self-interpretation is Jean-
Baptiste Duroselle's *Europe: A History of Its Peoples*, published
simultaneously in several European languages in 1990. Discussing
several different ways of viewing the post-1945 history of Europe,
he writes, "One may, finally, see this phase of history in a European
light" — by implication, the other lights must be un-European —
"and observe how many objective factors have combined with
creative acts of will to make possible the first step towards a
united Europe." Reflecting, in conclusion, on "the decline of
Europe, the result of two World Wars after centuries of violence,"
he avers that "the only remedy is to build a Europe which at first
will be confederal and later federal, while maintaining freedom
and democracy. This project is natural, realistic and legitimate, because there has long been a community of Europe — embryonic
at first, but growing with time, despite centuries of war and conflict, blood and tears." Note particularly the word "natural."

This idealistic-teleological discourse puts at the very centre of
discussion a single notion: unification. European history since
1945 is told as a story of unification; difficult, delayed, suffering
reverses, but nonetheless progressing. Here is the grand narrative
taught to millions of European schoolchildren and accepted by
East Central European politicians when they talk of rejoining "a
uniting Europe." It is a narrative whose next chapter is even now
being written by a leading German historian, Dr. Helmut Kohl.
The millennial culmination is to be achieved on January 1, 1999,
with a monetary union that will, it is argued, irreversibly bind together some of the leading nations and states of Europe. This
group of states should in turn become the "magnetic core" of a
larger unification.

However, European unification is seen not just as the product
of political will, of visionary leaders from Jean Monnet and Robert

Schuman to François Mitterrand and Kohl. It is also seen as a necessary, even an inevitable, response to certain deeper forces. "Globalisation" is the current buzz-word used to describe these forces. Nation-states are no longer able to protect and realise their economic and political interests on their own. They are no match for transnational actors like global currency speculators, multi-national companies, or international "mafia"-type criminal gangs. Both power and identity, it is argued, are migrating both upward and downward from the nation-state: upward to the supra-national level, downward to the regional one. In a globalised world of large trading blocs, Europe will only be able to hold its own as a larger political-economic unit.

We have all heard the arguments. It would be absurd to suggest that there is no force in them. Yet I will contend that, when com-bined into the single grand narrative, into the idealistic-teleological discourse of European unification, they result in a seriously mis-leading picture of the real ground on which European leaders have to build at the end of the twentieth century. In what follows, I will merely glance at the millennia before 1945, look a little more closely at the now finished period of the divided Europe of "Yalta," from 1945 to 1989, and then concentrate on developments since 1989.

1

One of my favourite index entries is that under "Europe" in Arnold Toynbee's *Study of History*. Toynbee's first reference reads: "Europe, as battlefield," his second: "as not an intelligible field of historical study," and his last: "unification of, failure of attempts at."

The most fundamental point is, of course, his second one: "not an intelligible field of historical study." Toynbee has a splendid dig at H. A. L. Fisher, who in his *History of Europe* famously claimed to detect "no pattern" in history. Actually, says Toynbee, in calling his book *A History of Europe*, Fisher embraces one of the oldest patterns of all, "for the portmanteau word 'Europe' is a whole *Corpus Juris Naturae* in itself." It is, Toynbee claims, a "cultural misapplication of a nautical term" to suggest that Hellenic history — the mediterranean ancient history of Greece and Rome — and Western history are successive acts in a single European drama.

He gives more credence to the Polish historian Oskar Halecki's periodisation, in which a Mediterranean Age is followed by a European Age, running roughly from 950 A.D. to 1950, that in turn is succeeded by what Halecki called an Atlantic Age, today we might refer to it simply as a global age). But even in the European Age, the continent's eastern edge remained deeply ill-defined: Was it the Elbe? Or the dividing line between Western and Eastern Christianity? Or the Urals? Europe's political history was characterised by the astounding diversity of peoples, nations, states, and empires, and the ceaseless and often violent competition between them.

In short, no continent is externally more ill-defined, internally more diverse, or historically more disorderly. Yet no continent has produced more schemes for its own orderly unification. So our teleological-idealistic or Whig interpreters can cite an impressive list of intellectual and political forebears, from your own Bohemian King George of Podebrady through the Duc de Sully and William Penn (writing already in America) to Aristide Briand and the half-Austrian, half-Japanese prophet of Pan-Europa, Richard Coudenhove-Kalergi.

The trouble is that those designs for European unification that were peaceful were not implemented, while those that were implemented were not peaceful. They involved either a temporary solidarity in response to an external invader or an attempt by one European state to establish continental hegemony by force of arms, from Napoleon to Hitler. Yet the latter, too, failed, as Toynbee's index drily notes.

2

The attempt at European unification since 1945 thus stands out from all earlier attempts by being both peaceful and implemented — and, so far, successful, at least in the rudimentary sense of lasting longer without being undone. The idealistic interpretation of this historical abnormality is that we Europeans have at last learned from history. The "European civil war" of 1914 to 1945, that second and still bloodier Thirty Years War, finally brought us to our senses.

Yet this requires a little closer examination. For a start, "peaceful" applies only in the sense of "the absence of hot war," and even that applies only to the continent west of the Iron Curtain. I hardly need to remind this audience of the Soviet invasion of Hungary in 1956, the invasion of Czechoslovakia in 1968, or martial law in Poland in 1981/82. Moreover, the whole continent was deeply shaped by the experience of Cold War. It has become almost commonplace to oberve that only after the end of the Cold War are we discovering just how much European integration owed to it. Minerva's owl again flies at dusk.

First, there was the Soviet Union as negative external integrator. West Europeans pulled together in face of the common enemy: as they had before the Turks or the Mongols. Second, there was the United States as positive external integrator. Particularly in the earlier years, the United States pushed very strongly for West European integration, making it almost a condition for further Marshall Aid. (In later decades, the United States was at times more ambivalent about building up what might be a rival trading bloc, but in broad, geographical terms it did support West European integration throughout the Cold War.)

Third, the Cold War helped, quite brutally, by cutting off most of Central and Eastern Europe behind the Iron Curtain. This meant that European integration could begin with a relatively small number of nation-states, bourgeois democracies at a roughly comparable economic level and with important older elements of common history. As has often been pointed out, the frontiers of the original European Economic Community of six were roughly coterminous with those of Charlemagne's Holy Roman Empire. It was also centered around what historical geographers have nicely called the "golden banana" of advanced European economic development, stretching from Manchester to Milan, via the low countries, eastern France, and western Germany.

Moreover, within this corner of the continent there were important convergences or tradeoffs between the political and economic interests of the nations involved. Alan Milward has powerfully argued that what happened in the political economy of the postwar years was not the end of the nation-state but, to quote his striking title, *The European Rescue of the Nation-State*. The crucial tradeoffs were, of course, between France and Germany. Painting with a broad brush one could say: between French iron and German coal, making the European Coal and Steel Community; between the protection of French agriculture by the Common Agricultural Policy and easier European market access for German industry, in the European Economic Community; and, especially from the Elysée Treaty of 1963 onward, between France's interest in maintaining its position as the *grande nation* by exercising the political leadership of "Europe" and Germany's interest in international rehabilitation after Nazism, exporting to the European market and securing Western support for its Ostpolitik.

None of this is to deny a genuine element of European idealism among the elites of that time. But the more we discover about this earlier period, especially through the opening of archives previously closed under the thirty years rule, the more hard-nosed and nationally self-interested the main actors appear. Winston Churchill, so often cited abroad as the British Moses of European unification, thought France and Germany — but not Britain — should get together, in the classic British interest of preserving the balance of power on the continent. Konrad Adenauer emerges from the recent biographies as a clear-sighted national realist. Of the architect of West Germany's economic miracle he once remarked: "Ludwig Erhard, wissen Sie, das ist ein Idealist" (Ludwig Erhard, you know, there's an idealist). This was not a compliment. Certainly, Adenauer was not a committed federalist. "There are," he once said, "anti-Europeans, Europeans, and hyper-Europeans. I'm a European." And of course there is Charles de Gaulle, Adenauer's co-architect of the Franco-German special relationship, who, when asked by Henry Kissinger how France would resist German domination, startling replied, "Par la guerre."

Contrary to the received view, the idealists are, I believe, more to be found in the next and next-but-one generation. The generation of Helmut Kohl rather than Konrad Adenauer. There is no mistaking the genuine enthusiasm with which Helmut Kohl describes, as he will at the slightest prompting, the unforgettable experience of lifting the first frontier barriers between France and Germany, just a few years after the end of the war.

To be sure, the national interests were still powerfully present in the 1970s and 1980s. Britain, most obviously, joined the then still European Economic Community in the hope of reviving its own flagging economy and buttressing its declining influence in the world. In a book of 1988 revealingly entitled *La France par l'Europe*, none other than Jacques Delors wrote that "creating Europe is a way of regaining that room for manoeuvre necessary for 'a certain idea of France.'" The phrase "a certain idea of France," was, of course, de Gaulle's. In my book *In Europe's Name* I have shown how German enthusiasm for European integration continued to be nourished by the desire and need to secure wider European and American support for the vital German national interest of improving relations with the communist East and, eventually, for the reunification of Germany. European unification in the cause of national unification!

Besides this mixture of genuinely idealistic and national-instrumental motives, however, there was undoubtedly a growing perception of real common interests. In a world dominated politically by superpowers and economically by larger units and trading blocs, the countries of Europe were much less capable of realising their national interests on their own.

As a result of the confluence of these three kinds of motives, and those three favourable external conditions, the 1970s and 1980s saw an impressive sequence of steps toward closer political cooperation and economic and legal integration. Starting with the Hague summit of December 1969 (which coincided, not coincidentally, with the launch of Willy Brandt's Ostpolitik), through direct elections to the European Parliament and the founding of the European Monetary System, to the Single European Act and the great project of completing the internal market in the magic year of "1992."

Now this dynamic process, against a background of renewed economic growth and the spread of democracy to southern Europe, contributed directly to the end of the Cold War. To use, just for a moment, the language of systems theory: if the European Community started life as a subsystem of the Cold War, the subsystem then fed back powerfully into the larger system. To put it more concretely: there is ample evidence that one of the reasons behind Mikhail Gorbachev's "new thinking" in foreign policy was Soviet alarm at the prospect of being left still further behind by, and excluded from, a "Europe" that was seen to be technologically advanced, economically dynamic, and integrating behind high protective walls.

How much more was this true of the peoples of East Central Europe, who felt themselves to belong culturally and historically to Europe, felt this with the passion of the excluded, and for whom the prosperous Western Europe they saw on their travels now clearly represented the better alternative to a discredited and stagnant "real socialism." George Orwell once said that "seen from inside, everything looks worse." The European Community certainly looked better seen from outside. Indeed, traveling to and fro across the Iron Curtain in the 1980s I concluded that the real European divide was between those in the West, who had Europe, and those in the East, who believed in it. Accordingly, one of the great slogans to arise from the velvet revolutions of 1989 in Central Europe was "the return to Europe." In this sense one could argue, in apparent defiance of historical logic, that "1992" in Western Europe was one of the causes of 1989 in Eastern Europe.

The Whig interpretation of recent European history, so widely taught and accepted in the 1980s, might not face the music of historical facts. But the very prevalence and wide appeal of this interpretation was itself a major historical fact: 1989 seemed to be the ultimate confirmation of its rightness.

3

What, then, have we witnessed since? It is possible to construe the last eight years — and the leading German historian I mentioned earlier would undoubtedly so construe them — as one more chapter, even a decisive one, in the pilgrim's progress to European unification. The Community has been renamed a Union. The major states of Western Europe have devoted extraordinary efforts to readying themselves for the unprecedented step of uniting their currencies. At the same time, preparations have been made to enlarge the Union. Negotiations should start next year with five new post-communist democracies. Certainly, there have been difficulties along the way; but never in its history has Europe been so close to the peaceful achievement of unity.

Against this optimistic, even Panglossian view, we have to enter a number of major objections. The first is that in this same period war has returned to the European continent; war and, in the former Yugoslavia, atrocities such as we had not seen in Europe since 1945. One of the central claims for Euorpean integration has been that it has made war in Europe unthinkable. What remains of that claim now? At moments the contradiction between West European rhetoric and East European reality has been positively grotesque. "War in Europe has become unthinkable," said the politicians in Strasbourg or Brussels. Crash went the artillery shells into Sarajevo. The question remains open whether it was West European integration that kept the peace in Europe until 1989, inasmuch as it was kept, or rather the hard fact of the nuclear standoff between the two superpower blocs in the Cold War. Perhaps it was not the EC but the North Atlantic Treaty Organization (NATO) — or, to put it still more sharply, not Europe's unity but Europe's division — that prevented the outbreak of hot war?

Second, even in core states of the old European Community, we have seen a popular reaction against the technocratic, elitist model of "building Europe from above" epitomised by the impenetrable detail of the Maastricht Treaty. The French referendum vote on the Maastricht Treaty, so narrowly won, was a telling symptom of this. This popular resentment still persists, as does a sense that the institutions of the European Union are perilously short on democratic legitimacy.

Third, while these years have indeed seen further incremental diminution in the effective powers and sovereignty of established nation-states, they have also seen the explosive emergence of at least a dozen new nation-states. Indeed, there are now more states on the map of Europe than ever before in the twentieth century. In the former Yugoslavia, these new states emerged by blood and iron, through ethnic cleansing and the violent redrawing of frontiers. In the former Czechoslovakia, the separation into two states was carried out peacefully, by negotiation. In the former Soviet Union, there were variations in between.

I am not going to argue that these deunifications reflected some deeper necessity or laws of historical development. There is a specific aetiology, different in each case, but very often having to do with the conduct of post-communist politicians, making manipulative use of nationalist agendas to gain or maintain power for themselves. Nonetheless, a diplomatic observer who went to sleep in 1897 and woke up again in 1997 would surely exclaim: "Ah yes,

I recognise what is going on. This modern passion for each nation to demand its own state has clearly proceeded apace." As Ernest Gellner, the late-lamented Prague doyen of studies of nationalism, always argued, the case for what he called "one culture, one state" is an eminently modern one. Moreover, its logic is, or can be, closely related to that of democracy. Democracy requires trust. It requires that the minority is prepared to accept the decision of the majority, because the minority still regards the state as fundamentally "theirs." The argument is hardly original — you find it already in John Stuart Mill's *Considerations on Representative Government*: "Among a people without fellow-feelings, especially if they read and speak different languages, the united public opinion necessary to the working of representative government cannot exist."

Nor is this phenomenon of deunification confined to the post-communist half of Europe. The cliché of "integration in the West, disintegration in the East" does not bear closer examination. I am always surprised, for example, when the progressive disintegration of Belgium is cited as evidence for the decline of the nation-state and the rise of regionalism. For the tensions that are pulling Belgium apart would be entirely familiar to a nineteenth-century liberal nationalist. Each ethno-linguistic group demands a growing measure of self-government. My own country, Britain, has for decades been an unusual modern variation on the theme of nation-state: a nation composed of four nations (or, to be precise, three and a bit). But now the constituent nations, and especially Scotland, are pulling away toward a larger measure of self-goverment.

And what of Europe's central power? It would be hard to dispute the simple statement that since 1989 Germany has reemerged on the European stage as a fully sovereign nation-state. In Berlin, we are witnessing the extraordinary architectural reconstruction of the grandiose capital of a historic nation-state. Yet at the same time, Germany's political leaders, and above all Helmut Kohl, are pressing with all their considerable might to surrender that vital component of national sovereignty — and, particularly in the contemporary German case, also identity — which is the national currency. There is a startling contradiction between, so to speak, the architecture in Berlin and the rhetoric in Bonn.

I do not believe that this contradiction can be resolved dialectically, even in the homeland of the dialectic. In fact, Germany today is in a political-psychological condition that might be described as Faustian ("Zwei Seelen wohnen, ach, in meiner Brust") or, in the loose colloquial sense of the term, as schizophrenic. If in 1999 monetary union goes ahead and the German government moves to Berlin, then the country will wake up in its new bed on January 1, 2000, scratch its head, and ask itself: "Now, why did we just give up the Deutschmark?" Dr. Kohl's unspoken answer, "Because we cannot trust ourselves," will not, I believe, suffice for a new generation. They will say, "Why not?"

This brings me to the central, unavoidable subject of monetary union. We could spend a whole day on this subject alone. I will confine myself to three brief remarks: one about causes, two about consequences. There are, of course, economic arguments for monetary union, as a complement to the single market and a disciplinary mechanism promoting tight budgets, low interest rates, and therefore higher growth. But monetary union is primarily an economic means to a political end. In general terms, this is the continuation of the functionalist approach used by the French and German architects of the Community ever since the 1950s: to move through economic integration to political integration. It was in this spirit that the project of monetary union was revived in Paris, Brussels, and Rome in the late 1980s, as part of the dynamic pre-1989 sequence I have already described.

But there was a much more specific politics of the decision to make this the central goal of European integration in the 1990s. As so often before, the key lies in a compromise between French and German national interests. In 1990, there was at the very least an implicit linkage made between François Mitterrand's anxious and reluctant support for German unification and Helmut Kohl's support for a decisive push toward European monetary union. Indeed one could describe the German commitment to European monetary union as a postdated cheque for German unification. The Federal Republic may have paid billions of Deutschmarks to the Soviet Union for its reluctant assent to unification, but this was nothing compared to the cheque given to France. Postdated January 1, 1999, it read: We promise to pay the bearer, on demand, not so or so many billion Deutschmarks but the Deutschmark itself! Or, as one of the diplomats involved put it: the whole of Deutschland for Kohl, half the Deutschmark for Mitterand.

Yet in large measure, this is a price that Helmut Kohl himself wants to pay. He wants to see the newly united Germany bound firmly and, as he himself puts it, "irreversible" into "Europe." Even more than his mentor Konrad Adenauer, he believes that it is dangerous for Germany, with its critical size and mass — too big for Europe, too small for the world" as Henry Kissinger once pithily put it — to stand alone in the centre of Europe, trying to juggle or balance the nine neighbours and many partners around it. The question is, however, whether the particular means chosen are the right ones to achieve the desired end.

One consequence of monetary union has been seen even before the union has happened. There is no doubt that the Maastricht agenda of internal unification has taken the time, attention, and energy of West European leaders away from the agenda of eastward enlargement. To be sure, there is no theoretical contradiction between — to use the familiar jargon — the "deepening" and the "widening" of the European Union. Indeed widening requires deepening. If the major institutions of the EU — the Council of Ministers, the Commission, the Parliament, the Court — originally designed ot work with six member states are still to function in a community of twenty and more, then major reforms, necessarily involving a further sharing of sovereignty, are essential. But these changes are of a different kind from those required for monetary union. So while there is no theoretical contradiction, there has been a practical tension between deepening and widening.

I believe, to put it plainly, that our leaders set the wrong priority after 1989. We were like people who for forty years had lived in a large, ramshackle house divided by a concrete wall down the middle. In the western half we had rebuilt, mended the roof, knocked several rooms together, redecorated, and put in new plumbing and electric wiring, while the eastern half fell into a state of dangerous decay. Then the wall came down. What did we do? We decided that what the whole house needed most urgently was a superb, new, computer-controlled system of air-conditioning in the western half. While we prepared to install it, the eastern half of the house began to fall apart and even — because the wiring was so rotten — to catch fire. We fiddled in Maastricht, while Sarajevo began to burn. Whether we could have prevented it from burning is another question; but certainly we did not devote to the problems of the eastern half the efforts we might have done, had we not embarked on this internal project of perfection.

Even if we leave aside these enormous political "opportunity costs" (to use an economist's term), what is the prospect now for this project, in its own boundaries and terms? Despite a substantial lack of public support, particularly in Germany, and grave doubts on the part of many bankers, business leaders, economists, and politicians, a monetary union of a number of European states now seems almost certain to proceed on January 1, 1999. Does that mean it will succeed?

Unfortunately, I find very powerful arguments that it is quite unlikely to succeed. The main ones are from political economy and from history. Very briefly, the argument from political economy is as follows. Different areas of a very large economic entity like the European common market need to be able to adjust to economic shocks and dislocations that affect them differently. Flexible exchange rates are a mechanism for so doing, allowing simple adjustments between the member countries. Other mechanisms would be price and wage flexibility, labour mobility, or direct financial transfers to the adversely affected areas. Now the monetary union of the United States of America possesses all these adjustment mechanisms. It has flexibility, mobility, *and* provision for large-scale budgetary transfers to adversely affected states. The cost of these transfers is accepted by citizens and taxpayers, because they belong to the same nation, speak the same language, would expect the same in return; and simply because these habits of solidarity have grown up over a long period of shared history in the same state.

Europe has neither the flexibility nor the mobility to compare with that in the United States. So the only major adjustment mechanism would be budgetary transfers. But the European Union currently redistributes less than 2 percent of the GDP of its member states, and most of that is already committed to existing schemes. What, then, will happen when a part of France (or Belgium or Italy) is badly hit, and the disadvantaged French go on the streets (as they are rather inclined to do) and their government appeals to its better off partners, above all Germany, for financial transfers? We have seen in the years since 1989 how reluctant West German taxpayers have been to pay even for their own compatriots in the East. Do we really expect that they would be willing to pay for the French unemployed as well? That essential minimal trust and mutual solidarity between citizens that is the fragile treasure of a democratic nation-state does not, alas, yet exist between the citizens of Europe. There is no European *demos*, no European *polis*, and certainly no Nation Europa. So without any other mechanism of adjustment, the tensions could only grow as the experiences of different parts of the union diverged.

This sombre analysis from comparative political economy may be supplemented by one from history. Historically, successful monetary unions have *followed* not preceded political union. As the German Constitutional Court pointed out in its judgment on the Maastricht Treaty, this was the case with the first unification of Germany. Indeed, the German Reich only finally achieved a single currency in 1909, thirty-eight years after political unification. As for the United States of America, they did not have a full monetary union until the establishment of the Federal Reserve Board in 1913 — some one hundred and twenty years after the political creation of the state!

I have perforce reproduced the arguments in telegraphic brevity. But the conclusion they lead to is an alarming one. The "Europe" that I hope the Czech Republic will join in the year 2000, or very soon thereafter, is quite likely to be subject to increasing rather than diminishing tensions between its major member states and nations. For at Maastricht, the leaders of the EU put the cart before the horse. Out of the familiar mixture of three different kinds of motives — idealistic, national-instrumental, and that of perceived common interest — they committed themselves to what was meant to be a decisive step to uniting Europe, but now seems likely to divide even those who belong to the monetary union. At least in the short term, it will certainly divide those existing EU members who participate in the monetary union from those who do not: the so-called ins and outs. Meanwhile, the massive concentration on this single project has contributed to the neglect of the great opportunity and challenge that arose in the eastern half of the continent when the wall came down.

The best can so often be the enemy of the good. The rationalist, functionalist, perfectionist attempt to "make Europe" or "complete" Europe through a hard core built around a rapid monetary union could well end up achieving the very opposite of the desired effect. One can, I think, all too plausibly argue that what we are likely to witness in the next five to ten years is the writing of another entry for Toynbee's index, under "Europe, unification of, failure of attempts at."

Some contemporary Cassandras go further still and suggest that we may even witness the writing of another entry under "Europe, as battlefield." One might answer that we already have, in the former Yugoslavia. Yet the suggestion that the forced march to unification through money will bring the danger of violent conflict between West European states does seem drastically overdrawn — for at least three reasons. First, there is the powerful neo-Kantian argument that bourgeois democracies are unlikely to go to war against each other. Second, we have a new situation, compared with pre-1945 Europe, in that we have a benign extra-European hegemon in the United States.

Third, this is to ignore the huge and real achievement of European integration to date: the unique, unprecedented framework and deeply ingrained habits of permanent institutionalised cooperation that ensure that the conflicts of interest that exist, and will continue to exist, between the member states and nations are never resolved by force. All those endless hours and days of negotiation in Brussels between ministers from fifteen European countries, who end up knowing each other almost better than they know their own families: that is the essence of this "Europe." It is an economic community, of course, but it is also a security community, in Karl Deutsch's classic definition of a group of states that do find it unthinkable to resolve their own differences by war.

4

I could end this lecture in several different ways. I could go even closer to the ground of political reality and try to suggest how the dangers I have indicated might be averted. I could go back to the skies and talk about the implications of this story for historiography, about the interplay between individuals and deeper forces in recent European history and the danger of politicians learning the wrong lessons from that history. Instead, I want to propose a modest paradigm shift in our thinking about Europe.

One could certainly argue that Western Europe would never have got as far as it has without the utopian goal or telos of "unity." Only by resolutely embracing, and in many cases actually believing in, the objective of "ever closer union," solemnly affirmed in successive treaties, have we attained the more modest degree of permanent institutional cooperation, with important elements of legal and economic integration, that we have. Yet as a paradigm for European policy in our time the notion of "unification" is fundamentally flawed. The most recent period of European history provides no indication that the immensely diverse peoples of Europe, speaking such different languages, having such disparate histories, geographies, cultures, and economies, are ready to merge peacefully and voluntarily into a single polity. It provides substantial evidence of a directly countervailing trend: toward the constitution — or reconstitution — of nation-states. If "unity" was not attained among a small number of Western European states, with strong elements of common history, under the paradoxically favourable conditions of the Cold War, how can we expect to come anywhere near it in the infinitely larger and more diverse Europe — the whole continent — that we have to deal with after the end of the Cold War?

Yet it is equally unrealistic to think that we can or should return to a Europe that is simply Harold Macmillan's glorified free trade area or de Gaulle's Europe des Patries. I trust no one here will make the mistake of confusing my intellectual scepticism with the chauvinistic Euroscepticism of some of my compatriots. I see Europe as much from a Central European viewpoint as from a British one and, unlike those British Eurosceptics, I care passionately about preserving what has already been achieved in constructing a new kind of Europe. But it is precisely this achievement that I see imperilled by the forced march to unity.

How, then, to characterise positively what has been achieved, and what it is both desirable and realistic to work toward in a wider Europe? I believe the best paradigm is that of *liberal order*. The quest for liberal order is an attempt to avoid both of the extremes between which Europe has unhappily oscillated through most of its modern history: violent disorder, on the one hand, and, on the other, hegemonic order that itself is built on the use of force and the denial of national and democratic aspirations within the constitutive empires, blocs, or spheres of influence. (The Czechs know better than most of what I speak.) The European Union, NATO, the Council of Europe, and the Organisation for Security and Cooperation in Europe are all elements, building blocks of such a liberal order.

Liberal order differs from previous European orders in several vital ways. Its first commandment is the renunciation of force in the resolution of disputes between its members. Of course, this goal is an ancient one. We find it anticipated already in King George of Podebrady's famous proposal of 1464 for "the inauguration of peace throughout Christendom." There we read that he and his fellow princes "shall not take up arms for the sake of any disagreements, complaints or disputes, nor shall we allow any to take up arms in our name." But today we have well-tried institutions of what might be called bourgeois internationalism in which to practice what Churchill called "making jaw-jaw rather than war-war."

Liberal order is, by design, nonhegemonic. To be sure, the system depends to some extent on the external hegemonic balancer, the United States — "Europe's pacifier," as an American scholar once quipped. And, of course, Luxembourg does not carry the same weight as Germany. But the new model order that we have developed in the European Union does permit smaller states to have an influence often disproportionate to their size. Another key element of this model order is the way in which it allows different alliances of states on individual issues, rather than cementing any fixed alliances.

Liberal order also differs from previous European orders in explicitly legitimating the interest of participating states in each other's internal affairs. Building on the so-called Helsinki process, it considers human, civil, and, not least, minority rights to be a primary and legitimate subject of international concern. These rights are to be sustained by international norms, support, and, where necessary, also pressure. Such a liberal order recognises that there is a logic that leads peoples who speak the same language, and share the same culture and tradition, to want to govern themselves in their own state. There is such a thing as liberal nationalism. But it also recognises that in many places a peaceful, neat separation into nation-states will be impossible. In such cases it acknowledges a responsibility to help sustain what may variously be called multiethnic, multicultural, or multinational democracies, within an international framework. This is what we disastrously failed to do for Bosnia; what we can still do for Macedonia or Estonia.

You will notice that missing from this paradigm is one idea that is still very important in contemporary European visions, especially those of former Great Powers, such as France, Britain, and Germany. This is the notion of "Europe" as a single actor on the world stage, a world power able to stand up to the United States, Russia, or China. In truth, I don't share this vision. I don't think the drive for world power is any more attractive because it is a joint enterprise than it was when attempted — somewhat more crudely — by individual European nations. Certainly, in a world of large trading blocs we must be able to protect our own interests. Certainly, a liberal order also means one that both gives and gets as much free trade as possible. Certainly, a degree of power-projection, including the coordinated use of military power, may be needed to realise the objectives of liberal order even within the continent of Europe and in other adjacent areas of vital interest to us, such as North Africa and the Middle East. But beyond this, just to put our own all-European house in order would be a large enough contribution to the well-being of the world.

Now someone may possibly object that I am paying too much attention to semantics. Why not let the community be called a Union, and the process "unification," even if they are not that in reality? In his 1994 New Year address, President Havel seemed to come close to this position when he said, "Today, Europe is attempting to give itself a historically new kind of order in a process that we refer to as unification." And of course I hardly expect the European Union to be, so to speak, unnamed. After all, the world organisation of states is called the United Nations! But I am, I freely admit, too much the English empiricist to be quite happy with a systematic misnaming. Much more importantly, though, I hope to have suggested how the pursuit of unification may be threatening even the achievements it is supposed to crown. Indeed, if we convince ourselves that not advancing further along the path to "unity" is tantamount to failure, then we risk, so to speak, snatching failure from the jaws of success. For what has been done already to build liberal order in a large part of Europe is a very great success.

To consolidate that liberal order and to spread it across the whole continent is, I submit, both a more urgent and, in the light of history, a more realistic goal for European statesmanship at the beginning of the twenty-first century than the vain pursuit of unification in a part of it. Nor do I accept that liberal order is necessarily a less idealistic goal than unity. For unity is not a primary value in itself. It is a means to higher ends. Liberal order, by contrast, directly implies not one but two primary values: peace and freedom.

Culture and Society in Plato's Republic

M. F. BURNYEAT

THE TANNER LECTURES ON HUMAN VALUES

Delivered at

Harvard University
December 10–12, 1997

M. F. BURNYEAT is Senior Research Fellow in Philosophy at All Souls College, Oxford. He was educated at King's College, Cambridge, and the University College, London. He was for many years the Laurence Professor of Ancient Philosophy at Cambridge University, and has been a visiting professor at numerous universities, including Harvard, Cornell, Princeton, and the University of Chicago. He is a fellow of the British Academy, the Japan Society for the Promotion of Science, a member of the Institut International de Philosophie, and a foreign honorary member of the American Academy of Arts and Sciences. He is the author of nearly fifty published articles, has been editor or coeditor of such volumes as *Doubt and Dogmatism* (1980, edited with Malcolm Schofield and Jonathan Barnes); *The Skeptical Tradition* (1983); and *The Original Sceptics: A Controversy* (1997, edited with Michael Frede). He is also the author of *The Theaetetus of Plato* (1990).

In memoriam J. C. W. Reith (1889–1971)[1]

LECTURE I. COUCHES, SONG, AND CIVIC TRADITION

The Total Culture: Material, Moral, Musical

Imagine, if you please, a stormy night in the North Sea. It is around 3:00 A.M. The first lieutenant is on watch on the bridge, his jaw jutting out firmly to defy wind, rain, and sea. Midshipman Burnyeat, being wholly untrained in the arts of navigation and seamanship, has nothing to do but make cup after cup of the navy's peculiarly strong recipe for cocoa. There is time to think, between bouts of seasickness. For some reason my mind turns to the actor Jack Hawkins, hero of many postwar films about braving storms and the like. How accurately he portrayed the jaw-jutting stance of men like this. Then inspiration strikes. It is the other way round. Whether he is aware of it or not, the first lieutenant learned that stance by watching Jack Hawkins in the cinema.

Such was my earliest thought on the subject of these lectures, even though at the time I had not yet read a word of the *Republic*, where Plato offers a theory about how art affects the soul and forms character in ways that people are often not aware of. If you are designing an ideal society, as Plato does in the *Republic*, and contrasting it with the corruptions of existing societies, as he also does in the *Republic*, then you need to think about much more than political institutions in a narrow sense. You need to think about all the influences, all the ideas, images, and practices, that make up the culture of a society.

I do not mean "high culture," but culture in a more anthropological sense — the sense my dictionary defines as "the total of the

---

[1] John Reith was the first general manager of the BBC, then managing director, and finally director general (1920–38); chairman of the New Towns Committee (1946); chairman of a Labour Party Commission of Enquiry into Advertising (1962–65), which I had the honour of serving as secretary.

inherited ideas, beliefs, values, and knowledge, which constitute
the shared bases of social action." [2] Even this definition is not
broad enough, for it makes no mention of the material culture of
a society — its characteristic artefacts, its buildings, even the kinds
of landscape it creates. Plato did not forget the material culture.
Here, to get us going, is what he has to say about it.

We start with a general principle arising out of a long discussion of poetry: "Good speech [εὐλογία], good accord [εὐαρμοστία],
good grace [εὐσχημοσύνη], and good rhythm [εὐρυθμία] follow
upon goodness of character" (400de). [3] In other words, style —
style in all its manifestations — springs from, and expresses, the
character of a person's soul. This principle is now applied to material culture:

> "And must not our youth pursue these qualities everywhere if
> they are to carry out their proper task [τὸ αὑτῶν πράττειν]?" [4]
>
> "They must indeed."
>
> "Now painting and all crafts of that kind are full of them,
> I suppose, as are weaving, embroidery, architecture, the making
> of furniture and household utensils, [5] and so too is the natural

---

[2] *The Collins Dictionary of the English Language*, 2nd ed. (London and Glas-
gow, 1986) *sv.* One of innumerable descendants of the definition with which
E. B. Tylor, *Primitive Culture* (Boston, 1871), p. 1, founded anthropology as the
systematic, holistic study of human society: "Culture, or civilization, . . . is that
complex whole which includes knowledge, beliefs, art, morals, custom, and any other
capabilities and habits acquired by man as a member of society."

[3] Translations from the *Republic* are my own throughout, but I always start
from Paul Shorey's Loeb Classical Library edition (London and New York, 1930),
so his phrases are interweaved with mine; despite numerous competitors, Shorey's
translation is in my opinion still the best. For passages dealing with music, I have
borrowed freely from the excellent rendering (with explanatory notes) given by
Andrew Barker, *Greek Musical Writings*, vol. 1: *The Musician and His Art* (Cambridge, 1984), pp. 128–40.

[4] An allusion to the "one-man one job" principle which grounds the *Republic*'s
definition of justice in terms of "doing one's own" (374a ff., 433a ff.). The principle will be crucial to the rejection of tragedy and comedy in book III: see lecture II.

[5] The word σκεύη is standardly used for household equipment in contrast to
livestock: Liddell-Scott-Jones, *A Greek-English Lexicon*, 9th ed. (Oxford, 1940) *sv.*
(cited hereafter as LSJ).

form of our bodies and of other living things. In all these
there is grace or gracelessness. And gracelessness, bad rhythm,
and disaccord are sisters of bad speech and bad character,
whereas their opposites are sisters and imitations [μιμήματα]
of the opposite — a temperate and good character." [6]

"Entirely so," he said.

"Is it, then, only the poets that we must supervise and compel
to embody in their poems the image [εἰκόνα] of the good character, on pain of not writing poetry among us? Or must we
keep watch over the other craftsmen too and prevent them
from embodying the bad character just mentioned — licentious,
mean, and graceless — either in images of living things or in
buildings or in any other product of their craft, on penalty, if
they are unable to obey, of being forbidden to practise among
us?" (400e–401b)

Finally, Plato has Socrates describe the way grace and gracelessness
in the material culture affect the soul:

"Our aim is to prevent our Guards being reared among images
of vice — as it were in a pasturage of poisonous herbs where,
cropping and grazing in abundance every day, they *little by
little and all unawares* [κατὰ σμικρόν . . . λανθάνωσι] build up
one huge accumulation of evil in their soul. Rather, we must
seek out craftsmen with a talent for capturing what is lovely
and graceful, so that our young, dwelling as it were in a salu-
brious region, will receive benefit from everything about them.
Like a breeze bringing health from wholesome places, the impact of works of beauty on eye or ear will *imperceptibly*
[λανθάνῃ] from childhood on, guide them to likeness, to friendship, to concord with the beauty of reason." (401bd)

Since 1904 a number of new towns have been built in Britain
on this principle that it makes a difference to your soul what kind
of environment you grow up in. Ebenezer Howard's idea of the

---

[6] The word μιμήματα here is bound to evoke the preceding discussion of
μίμησις in musical poetry (392c ff.). I return to this extension from musical to
material culture in lecture II.

Garden City was to juxtapose industry, agriculture, and housing with gardens and greenery in a way that would be healthier for its inhabitants than the industrial slums. Healthier not just physically, but spiritually as well. Howard's vision of the future was also influential in the U.S.A. and Scandinavia. We can all celebrate a world in which

> parks and gardens, orchards and woods, are being planted in the midst of the busy life of the people, so that they may be enjoyed in the fullest measure; homes are being erected for those who have long lived in slums; work is found for the workless, land for the landless, and opportunities for the expenditure of long pent-up energy are presenting themselves at every turn. A new sense of freedom and joy is pervading the hearts of the people as their individual faculties are awakened, and they discover, in a social life which permits alike of the completest concerted action and of the fullest individual liberty, the long-sought-for means of reconciliation between order and freedom — between the well-being of the individual and of society.[7]

That was written in 1898. It is a more populist Utopia than Plato's, but it shares his belief that an environment which is "bright and fair, wholesome and beautiful"[8] will gradually, over time, have a good effect on everyone, without their necessarily noticing how and by what means it happens.

In Plato's advocacy of the idea, the key terms are gracefulness (εὐσχημοσύνη) and its opposite, gracelessness (ἀσχημοσύνη). Gracefulness can be seen both in inanimate things like buildings and furniture and in living things. In a person gracefulness can show in their physical movements, in their stance or the way they

---

[7] Ebenezer Howard, *Garden Cities of Tomorrow*, ed. F. J. Osborn (London, 1945; repr. of revised ed., 1902 [1st ed., under different title, 1898]), p. 151. For an enthusiastic appraisal of Howard's work and influence, see Lewis Mumford, *The City in History: Its Origins, Its Transformations, and Its Prospects* (London, 1961), pp. 514ff.

[8] Howard, *Garden Cities*, 111.

hold themselves, and also in their talk and how they think.[9] If you are sympathetic to the idea that the material environment has effects on the soul (particularly, but not only, when you are young), that over time it influences your character and outlook in all sorts of ways you are not aware of, then gracefulness is a good example of a quality that can be taken in from the material environment and internalized as a quality of mind and spirit.

Gracefulness is *attractive*. It is a quality we welcome and would like to have ourselves. Certainly, it can be faked, an outer garment disguising an unjust soul (366b 4: εὐσχημοσύνης κιβδήλου). But true grace is the reflection of virtue in a harmonious soul (554e). This not a sleight of hand on Plato's part, or merely verbal stipulation. It is a substantive thesis of the *Republic* that beauty and goodness always go together. But that thesis lies a long way ahead.[10] Meanwhile, consider negative descriptions like "a shabby house," "a cheerless room," "a desolate landscape," and how novelists like Dickens or Balzac use them to establish the moral atmosphere of a scene. To the extent that the moral overtones are brought alive for us, we sympathise with Plato's view that material culture and moral culture are continuous with each other.

The passage I was quoting from turns next to music:

> "And is it not for these reasons, Glaucon, that music is the most decisive factor in one's upbringing? It is above all rhythm and attunement [ἁρμονία] that sink deep into the soul and take strongest hold upon it, bringing grace, and making one graceful, if one is rightly reared — but if not, it has the opposite effect. Secondly, someone who has been reared in music as they should will be the sharpest at spotting defects in things that are badly crafted or badly grown. Rightly disgusted by them, they will praise things that are fine, delighting in them and

---

[9] Cf. 486d for a contrast between the grace of thought (εὔχαρις διάνοια) to be looked for in a potential philosopher and the misshapen nature (ἀσχήμων φύσις) of a nonstarter.

[10] Lecture III: "The Poet as Painter." I am indebted to Alexander Nehamas for discussion about the possibility of combining grace and evil.

welcoming them into their soul. With such nourishment they will grow up fine and good [καλός τε κἀγαθός] themselves. Ugly things, by contrast, they will rightly decry and hate while still young and as yet unable to understand the reason. But when reason comes, someone brought up this way will greet it as a friend with whom their rearing had made them long familiar." (401d–2a)

Music is decisive because of its influence on your sense of beauty — your taste, the eighteenth century called it — which in turn guides your response to other things in the environment. In this way, music is included in the same range as material and moral culture. And not only music in the narrow sense of rhythm and attunement. Plato's word μουσική covers music and poetry together, because in the ancient world you usually hear them together, as song. Those rhythms and attunements convey verbal messages to the soul, and Plato is as concerned about their content as about their musical form. In an ideal city, the whole culture must be as ideal as possible, because all of it influences the character of the citizens.

First Glance Ahead: The Divided Soul in Book X

The cultural factors I have introduced so far fall into two broad classes, corresponding to our two most impressionable distance senses: sight and hearing. Poetry and music appeal to our ears; painting, architecture and furniture to the eyes. To explain why this broad classification will be important throughout the *Republic*, let me anticipate some Platonic theory from book X. And to motivate the theory, let me tell you the outcome of a wholly un-Platonic experiment.

Each time I have given this lecture I ask members of the audience to raise their hands if (1) they *do not* believe in ghosts, but (2) they *do*, nevertheless, get anxious or afraid when listening to ghost stories. Each time, plenty of hands go up.[11] I take this

---

[11] The experiment was tried at meetings in Brandeis University, Bristol, Cambridge, Eton College, New Orleans, Oslo, Oxford, Philadelphia, and Pittsburgh, as

as evidence — evidence independent of any theory, ancient or modern, psychoanalytic or cultural — that we can be affected emotionally in ways that bypass our established beliefs and the normal processes of judgment. Any sound philosophy of mind will need to take account of this phenomenon and give a theoretical explanation of it. Plato did not shirk the task.

Already in *Republic* IV we meet the well-known division of the soul into three parts: reason, spirit, and appetite. This division is grounded on cases of *motivational* conflict, as when someone both wants a drink, because they are thirsty, and wants not to drink, because they know it is bad for their health. Plato makes Socrates argue that the persistence of opposed desires can only be explained by locating them in separate parts of the soul. The thirst which does not go away when you think about your health is due to appetite. The concern for your health which keeps you struggling against the temptation to drink is due to reason. *Republic* X (602c–5c) adds a new division, grounded on cases of *cognitive* conflict in which the reasoning part of the soul appears to be at variance with itself.[12]

Consider an oar half submerged in water, or a picture done in a shadowing technique (σκιαγραφία) that gives an impression of depth when the painting is viewed from a distance (Seurat's *pointillisme* will serve as an approximate modern analogue),[13] or

---

well as on the grand occasion at Harvard. Needless to say, I am grateful to these audiences for much more than their susceptibility to ghost-stories. Their discussion of earlier versions of these lectures helped to shape their final form; so did the reception of the very first version at the Courtauld Institute of Art in London.

[12] At 602e 4 τούτῳ must refer to the subject which did the measuring, which has already been identified as the reasoning part: it is *this* part that receives opposite appearances, hence this part that has to undergo division to avoid the contradiction. The same interpretation in Anthony Kenny, *The Anatomy of the Soul: Historical Essays in the Philosophy of Mind* (Oxford, 1973), p. 22; and Alexander Nehamas, "Plato on Imitation and Poetry in *Republic* X," in Julius Moravcsik and Philip Temko, eds., *Plato on Beauty, Wisdom, and the Arts* (Totowa, 1982), pp. 65–66.

[13] Shorey and others mistranslate σκιαγραφία at 602d as "scene-painting." The Greek for perspectival scene-painting is σκηνογραφία, which Plato never mentions. The pictorial technique referred to as σκιαγραφία seems to have been one which

a large object which appears small when seen far off. We know, if necessary by measuring the real size of the object seen at a distance, that it is not small, just as we know that the oar is not actually bent. But this does not stop it *looking* smaller than it is, any more than our knowledge stops the oar *looking* bent or the picture *seeming* to have depth. There is a cognitive conflict which Socrates explains as a conflict between two opposed judgments, each located in a different element of the soul. One element in us evaluates the character of an object by the results of measurement, counting, and weighing; the other goes by how the thing looks to the eye from a particular point of view.

This cognitive division is neither the same as, nor inconsistent with, the motivational division of book IV. The new division is an addition, meant to work alongside the earlier one. For the earlier division is brought back in book X to supply a part of the soul to which tragedy appeals, by analogy with painting's appeal to the cognitive part that goes by visual appearances. This time Socrates promises to complete the book IV account by explaining things he missed before (603be).[14] Thus book X has two divisions in play. Painting appeals to a cognitive part that goes by appearances, tragedy to an irrational motivational part which is best seen, I think, as an enlargement of book IV's appetitive part. For its nature is to desire (ἐπιθυμεῖν) its fill of tears, it *hungers* for a satisfying cry (606a). This is new, but the process of enlarg-

---

depended on contrasts between light and shade to create the appearance of form and volume: see Plato, *Parmenides* 165cd, *Theaetetus* 208e. Further information in Nancy Demand, "Plato and Painting," *Phoenix* 29 (1975): 1–20; Eva Keuls, "Plato on Painting," *American Journal of Philology* 95 (1978): 100–127. I agree with Keuls, against Demand and others, that Plato's frequent use of σκιαγραφία as an image of the merely apparent (e.g., a pretence of justice: 365c; cf. 583b, 586b) does not indicate disapproval of it as a technique in painting itself.

[14] N. R. Murphy, *The Interpretation of Plato's "Republic"* (Oxford, 1951), pp. 241–42, questions the legitimacy of the back-reference at 602e: "Did we not say that it is impossible for the same thing to make opposite judgements at the same time about the same thing?" True, it was not said in those words. But the examples subsumed under book IV's principle of opposites included assent and dissent (437b 1).

ing book IV's appetitive part beyond the basic desires for food, drink, and sex began already in book VIII. Among the numerous and varied appetites (ἐπιθυμίαι) to which the democratic man grants equal indulgence are an appetite to do some philosophy, for fun, and another to play a while at politics (561cd).[15]

To sum up: book X's new bipartite division puts reason and sight in parallel to reason and appetite in the book IV division, which returns with the appetitive part already enlarged. The first division explains our susceptibility to visual illusion, the second our susceptibility to the auditory images of poetry (603b). The parallel demands that the middle part be less prominent (though notice the role of shame as ally of reason at 604a, 605e, 606c). But this is no excuse for supposing that book X replaces the earlier three-part division by a vaguer bipartite one.[16] Still less should one adduce book X as evidence that Plato was not really serious about the tripartite division in book IV.[17]

However, as often with Plato, what begins as a parallel or analogy ends with one term dominating the other. The classic case is the analogy between city and soul. It begins in books II and IV as no more than a parallel. Once we know the social structure that makes a city wise or just, we can infer that a psychological realization of that same structure will give these virtues to the individual soul. But in *Republic* VIII–IX, where Socrates traces the decline of the ideal city through a series of worse and worse constitutions, in parallel to a series of worse and worse individual personalities,

---

[15] For a valuable discussion of how such desires can be appetites, not desires of reason, see John M. Cooper, "Plato's Theory of Human Motivation," *History of Philosophy Quarterly* (1984): 3–21.

[16] So, most recently, Stephen Halliwell, "The *Republic*'s Two Critiques of Poetry," in Ottfried Höffe, ed., *Platon: Politeia* (Berlin, 1997), pp. 329–30.

[17] So Terry Penner, "Thought and Desire in Plato," in Gregory Vlastos, ed., *Plato: A Collection of Critical Essays*, vol. 2: *Ethics, Politics, and Philosophy of Art and Religion* (Garden City, 1971), pp. 111–13. Penner makes much of 606d 1, where anger (θυμός) is treated as an appetite or very like one, not assigned to the middle part. But in context it is the desire to indulge anger or grief that Socrates is discussing, not anger and grief as such.

city and soul are increasingly fused. The city side of the analogy
takes over. The soul is depicted in ever more vividly political
terms, as if it were a city in which the three parts struggle for
dominance over each other. One example out of many is the image
of a mob of appetites seizing the "acropolis of the soul" (560b).
The climax of the process comes at the end of book IX, where
Socrates declares that what a philosopher must guard most carefully is the constitution (πολιτεία) of their soul (591e). That constitution is the psychological realization in the philosopher's soul
of the city laid out in the pages of the *Republic* (592ab).[18]

A similar move, on a smaller scale, fuses the two divisions of
the soul in book X. To explain how tragedy sets up a bad constitution in the soul, Socrates takes visual language appropriate for
the cognitive part to which painting appeals and applies it to the
motivational part to which tragedy appeals. In the presence of
images (εἴδωλα) fashioned by the poet, this part "is unable to distinguish the greater from the less, but calls the same thing now
greater, now less" (605bc). I shall have more to say later about
Plato's transferring the idea of perspectival illusion from visual
to tragic appearances.[19] At present it is enough to know that in
book X we will meet a Platonic theory according to which the
poetry and music of tragedy create their own kinds of cognitive
illusion, which are just like visual illusions in the way they persist
and maintain their hold on us despite the opposition of our better
judgment. Eyes and ears offer painter and poet an entry through
which their images can bypass our better judgment and infiltrate
the soul.

Already in *Republic* V (475d–76d) Socrates had contrasted
two types of thought (διάνοια). On the one side, there is the

---

[18] Compare Plato's *Cratylus*, where the name-tool analogy ends up defining
names as tools (for teaching), and *Statesman*, where the ruling-weaving analogy
ends in a conception of ruling as itself a kind of weaving. This heuristic device is
what *Statesman* 277a–79a labels "example" (παράδειγμα).

[19] Lecture III, "Back to the Divided Soul."

sense-based thinking cultivated by lovers of sights and sounds who enthusiastically rush around the countryside to view the plays put on at the Rural Dionysia, "as if they had farmed out their ears to listen to every chorus in the land" (475d); on the other side, the philosophical mode of thinking cultivated by those who are awake to the distinction between the many beautiful sights and sounds and the single Form, Beauty itself. When Socrates speaks of thought (διάνοια) in this passage, he clearly has in view not isolated, occurrent thoughts ("What a pretty picture that is!"), but a style of thinking which pervades one's life and structures one's outlook on the world.[20] Book X confirms what we should have suspected all along, that sense-based thinking is at work in each and every embodied soul. Hence Plato's concern to make sure that only graceful appearances meet our eyes, only the appropriate kinds of musical poetry come to our ears. He must make the whole culture ideal. Not only because, as I said just now, all of it influences character, but also because of the *way* it does this: by a gradual, often unnoticed accumulation of images that come in at a level below, and relatively independent of, reason's activities of judgment, evaluation, and belief-formation.

It is easy for a modern reader to misunderstand this, just as it is easy to mistake Plato's motivational division for the now familiar distinction between reason and desire. In the divided soul reason has desires and pleasures of its own, while appetite has conceptions of what is pleasurable and can reason how to get it; the middle, spirited part is devoted to honour and has a network of beliefs about what that requires.[21] What distinguishes reason from

[20] Note ζῆν 476c, 476d, and the διάνοια shaped by good character at 400e 3 (cf. 403d 7). For the philosopher's διάνοια, cf. also 486a, 486d, 500b. Tragedy threatens the philosopher's διάνοια because it appeals to a lower part or mode of διάνοια (595b, 603bc).

[21] Julia Annas, *An Introduction to Plato's "Republic"* (Oxford, 1981), pp. 125–31, is an excellent introduction to this topic — except that she finds only one division in book X, so that *appetite* "appears as the part which unreflectively accepts visual appearances" (p. 131). On my picture, reason is the superior part in both

the other motivational parts is its concern for the overall, long-term good in one's life; appetite just longs for that drink, regardless of consequences. Similarly, in the cognitive division, reason has no monopoly on judgment, evaluation, and belief-formation. Its specialty, as the part bent on knowing the truth of things in every sphere (581b), is to weigh up all the evidence, so that we are not ruled by misleading appearances (602d); it ensures that we are not often taken in by objects that look small far away. But for Plato the misleading appearance already involves judgment.[22] Throughout the *Republic* perception is treated as a judgment-maker independent of reason, but much less reflective.[23] A modern Idealist philosopher wrote: " 'Sense-perception' is a form of 'knowledge,' a 'cognizant experience,' in which the mind *thinks sensuously*. There is 'thought' in sense-perception, but not thought free and explicit — not 'thought' which the percipient controls, or of which he is even aware *as* 'thought.' " [24] With much of this Plato could agree. Especially the last clause.

A Tale of Two Cities

But let us stay a while longer with material culture. If there is a problem about ensuring it is graceful rather than ugly, the existence of such a problem is a kind of luxury. A society faced with a choice in the matter must have resources beyond those needed for survival. As Aristotle will put it (*Politics* I 1, 1252b 29–30), it is a society which, having come into existence for the sake of life, now exists for the sake of the good life. To mark this distinction Socrates describes two cities: the first confined to the economic

---

divisions, for it desires both truth and the good; the lower parts are different in the two cases, identified by the ways they differ from reason.

[22] Explicitly stated at 602e–3a and more formally theorized in Plato's *Sophist* (263d–64b).

[23] See especially 523a–25a.

[24] Harold H. Joachim, *Logical Studies* (Oxford 1948, from lectures given in 1927–35), p. 83 (italics mine). The context is an attack on the Empiricist search for a *datum* in sense-perception. The next page cites *Rep.* 523a–25a.

necessities of city life in the fifth century B.C.,²⁵ the second enjoying all the pleasant "extras" of ancient Greek civilization — including that wonderful architecture, which Socrates speaks of as
"houses and clothing beyond the requirements of necessity" (373a
5–6).²⁶ And to make the contrast vivid, he tells us (with a good
deal of irony) how in each city — the primitive city at subsistence
level and the "luxurious" city with a surplus — the citizens will
enjoy the high point of ancient social life, the feast or communal
meal.

We start with the uncouth simplicity of the first city:

> "For their nourishment they will prepare barley-meal and
> wheat flour: the latter to bake, the other to knead. The barley-
> cakes and wheaten loaves²⁷ they will throw on some rushes or
> fresh leaves and, reclining on beds [κατακλινέντες ἐπὶ στιβάδων]
> of strewn bryony and myrtle, they will feast [εὐωχήσονται]²⁸
> with their children. Afterwards, they will drink their wine with
> garlands on their head and sing hymns to the gods. They will
> enjoy sex with each other without begetting offspring beyond
> their means, lest they fall into poverty or war." (372bc)

So far the feasting has involved nothing more elevated than bread
and wine (drunk, as was customary in ancient Greece, *after* the

---

²⁵ For an illuminating analysis of the economic base, see Malcolm Schofield,
"Plato on the Economy," in Mogens Herman Hansen, ed., *The Ancient Greek City-
State*, Acts of the Copenhagen Polis Centre, vol. 1 (Copenhagen, 1993), pp. 183–96.

²⁶ I follow the construal in Shorey's note *ad loc.*

²⁷ The text alternates barley and wheat in a double chiasmus. For culinary
clarification I quote J. Adam's edition of the *Republic* (Cambridge, 1902), *ad loc.*:
"Only the wheaten meal was (as a rule) baked (πέσσειν or ὀπτᾶν) into loaves
(ἄρτοι): the barley-meal was kneaded into a simple dough (μάσσειν, whence μᾶζα),
dried in a mould, and moistened with water and eaten. . . . μᾶζαι made of barley
meal was the staple food of the common Greek: the wheaten loaf was a luxury."
Adam's notes will guide my translation in the sequel.

²⁸ This verb can be used of animals as well as humans; not so the verb
ἐστιάομαι, which Glaucon sniffily substitutes at 372c 3. εὐωχέομαι evokes the
quality consumed, ἐστιάομαι the sociability of the occasion. At 586a the noun
εὐωχίαι evokes gluttony and worse.

meal is over),[29] hymn-singing, and (responsible) sex. No details
are given to clarify the sexual arrangements, but if, as seems clear,
the children's mothers eat, drink, and then have sex with the men,
this does not reflect contemporary Greek practice at all. It looks
as though Socrates is sketching a primitive anticipation of the arrangements he will propose for the ideal city, where the family is
abolished in favour of communality of women and children, and
the breeding festivals (which include feasting and hymn-singing)
are carefully regulated to keep the size of the population steady
(459e–60a). No wonder Glaucon breaks in to complain:[30] " 'No
relishes [ὄψον] apparently,' he said, 'for the men you depict at
dinner [τοὺς ἄνδρας ἐστιωμένους]' " (372c).

What Glaucon wants is a proper, male-only dinner-party of the
kind he is used to, with meat or fish to accompany the bread.[31] But
Socrates keeps up his teasing:

> "True," I said, "I forgot that they will also have relishes —
> salt, of course, and olives and cheese, and country stews of roots
> and vegetables. And for dessert [τραγήματα][32] I suppose we
> will serve them figs and chickpeas and beans, and they will
> toast myrtle-berries and acorns at the fire, while they sip wine
> in moderate amounts. In this way, living out their life in peace
> and health, they will no doubt survive to old age and, on dying,
> bequeath a like life to their offspring." (372cd)

Glaucon is still not happy: "That's just the fodder you would provide, Socrates, if you were founding a city of pigs."

---

[29] That is the force of the prefix in ἐπιπίνοντες: Adam, *ad loc.* The practice
itself can be observed in Plato's *Symposium* (176a).

[30] In the *Republic*, a switch from Adeimantus to Glaucon typically marks a
move to a higher level of discussion: see my "First Words: A Valedictory Lecture,"
Proceedings of the Cambridge Philological Society 43 (1997): 13–14.

[31] ὄψον means anything to accompany the bread, but especially meat or fish;
Socrates will ironically insist on the wider meaning.

[32] τραγήματα (things chewed alongside the wine) are not part of the meal but
accompaniment to the drink.

Do not be misled here by thinking of pigs as greedy. This is our culture's stereotype. For the ancient Greeks, the pig was an emblem rather of ignorance (so *Rep.* 535e). "Any pig would know" was the saying.[33] What Glaucon means is, "You describe the feasting of people who do not know how to live. It is *uncivilized.*"

Socrates asks, "Then how shall I feed them?" Glaucon replies — and this is the motif I have been leading up to: " 'In the customary way [ἅπερ νομίζεται]: they must recline on couches [κλῖναι], if they are not to be uncomfortable,[34] and dine from tables,[35] with the relishes and desserts that people have nowadays' " (372de). The list of requirements for civilized feasting is soon enlarged, in terms that make it clear that in the second city the men have wives, whom in the usual Greek fashion they leave at home. There will be couches, tables, and other equipment (*sc.* for dining), unguents, incense, girls (ἑταῖραι, "courtesans"), and pastries — all sorts of them, plus painting (*sc.* to decorate the pottery and, for the rich, wall-paintings in the dining room), embroidery, gold and ivory, and similar adornments (373a). This list defines the "luxurious" or "inflamed" city (so called at 373e), which Socrates and his interlocutors will purify step by step (as becomes explicit at 399e). By removing objectionable features, like tragedy and comedy, the family and private property, they will gradually fashion the ideal city, where life will be moderately austere — as in the "city of pigs" — but civilized. Couches and tables are not removed.[36] They remain at the top of the list of equipment for civilized, cultured life.

---

[33] See Plato, *Laches* 196d and scholium *ad loc.*

[34] So Shorey, but Glaucon may intend ταλαιπωρεῖσθαι in its stronger meaning: "suffer distress or hardship."

[35] Note the τε . . . καί, which links couches and tables as the basic unit, so to speak, of civilization.

[36] The rule of commensality in Spartan-style ξυσσίτια (416e, 458c, 547d) implies couches and wine-drinking after the meal (see the quote from Alcman below). Glaucon's demand for ὄψον as is conducive to physical fitness (559ab — I owe thanks for this reference to Susan Sauvé). In general, austerity is preserved

HISTORICAL INTERLUDE: GREEK COUCHES

A bit of history is in order here, to establish the cultural reso-
nances on which Plato draws when he talks of the couch. It is not
a psychoanalyst's couch, let alone a casting couch; nor a chaise
longue in an elegant château. It is dining room furniture.

Both the word κλίνη and the practice of reclining[37] to feast are
unknown to Homer. Homeric heroes sit on chairs to feast, as gods
and goddesses continue to do in classical times. Reclining derives
from the Near East — for the Greeks, a place of luxury. The first
evidence of the practice there is in the Bible: a tirade by the prophet
Amos in the eighth century B.C. against luxurious feasting and
drinking (*Amos* 6, 4–7). The practice, and the word κλίνη, were
established in Greece by the seventh century.[38] The couch, and the
knowledge of how to use it, was a feature of "polite society," as
is clear from a scene in Aristophanes where Philocleon, an old man
from the plebeian classes, has difficulty learning how to recline
gracefully at an imaginary feast.[39]

> BDELYCLEON. No more of that: but lie down there, and learn
> To be convivial [ξυμποτικός] and companionable.
> PHILOCLEON. Yes; how lie down?
> BD.   In an elegant graceful way [εὐσχημόνως].
> PH. Like this, do you mean?

---

by a sensible diet (403e–4e, 416d), by not allowing the Guards to drink from silver
or gold cups (417a), and by not giving them money to pay for courtesans (420a).
Incidentally, 468e does not imply that they sit on chairs to dine and drink: the word
ἕδραις is part of a line from Homer (*Iliad* VIII 162 et al.), whom Socrates is keen
to follow in the matter of honouring the valiant (420cd), and Homeric heroes do
not recline to feast (see below).

[37] Our word "recline" is cognate with the Greek κλίνη.

[38] This is the standard view, based on the lines of Alcman quoted below. A
subtle argument for back-dating to the eighth century may be found in Oswyn
Murray, "Nestor's Cup and the Origins of the Greek *Symposion*," *Annali di Archeo-
logia e Storia Antica* n.s. 1 (1994): 47–54.

[39] *Cf.* Rep. 420e, where the image of the potters reclining on couches to feast
is meant to be as grotesque as that of farmers dressed up in finery and surrounded
by gold.

BD.   No, not in the least like that.

PH. How then?

BD.   Extend your knees, and let yourself
With practised ease subside along the cushions;
Then praise some piece of plate; inspect the ceiling;
Admire the woven hangings of the hall.
Ho! water for our hands! bring in the tables!
Dinner! after-wash! now the libation.

PH. Good heavens! then is it in a dream we are feasting?

(*Wasps* 1208–18; tr. Rogers)

All in all, couches and tables are items well chosen to mark the
transition from primitive to civilized social intercourse. They ini-
tiate the material culture of a society which no longer has to make
do with reclining on beds of leaves in the open air[40] to eat country
vegetables and roasted acorns together. It can *choose* not only its
menus, but also, more importantly, whether the evening's post-
prandial entertainment shall focus on singing-games, which Philocleon is made to practise, or some more improving pursuit.[41] We
shall see, indeed, that couches and tables are the setting for a *continuing* series of cultural choices, which do much to determine over
time the character and development of the culture of a society.
The social gathering with couches and tables is as good a place as
any to localize the overall choice which is the main theme of the
Republic, the choice between living well and living badly.[42]

---

[40] The phrase κατακλινέντες ἐπὶ στιβάδων (372b 5) in Socrates' description
of the primitive feast would suggest to ancient readers a picnic, with beds of leaves
(or mattresses stuffed with them) in place of couches.

[41] Compare, again, Plato's *Symposium* 176e.

[42] This is the point at which to acknowledge my debt to some of the fascinating literature which has grown up around issues of sympotic culture: J. M. Dentzer,
*Le motif du banquet couché dans le Proche-Orient et le monde grec du VIIe au IVe
siècle avant J.-C.* (Rome, 1982); E. L. Bowie, "Early Greek Elegy, Symposium, and
Public Festival," *Journal of Hellenic Studies* 106 (1986): 13–35; François Lissarague,
Un flot d'images: Une esthétique du banquet grec (Paris, 1987; Eng. trans. Princeton, 1990); Oswyn Murray, ed., *Sympotica: A Symposium on the Symposion* (Ox-

We have just looked ahead to the passage in book X where painting becomes the paradigm for understanding the perspectival illusions fostered by tragic poetry. The example chosen to start the book X discussion is a painted couch (596e). Book X also posits Platonic Forms of Couch and of Table (596b). But in these contexts scholars all too often translate κλίνη as "bed," an item which has a more restricted resonance than the couch.[43] Bed and table do not go together. Couch and table do — and together they promise poetry.

Κλίναι μὲν ἑπτὰ καὶ τόσαι τράπεσδαι, sang the seventh-century poet Alcman: "Seven couches and as many tables laden with poppy-seed loaves and linseed and sesame, and chrysocolla in (full?) bowls" [44] That was not a lullaby to bring on sleep, but a drinking song for Spartans reclining on bare wooden couches (without the coverings and cushions usual in other cities). It is also the first extant occurrence of the word κλίνη.

Again, Aristophanes in the fifth century has a herald announce a feast with a long list of attractions: "Κλίναι, τράπεζαι — couches, tables, cushions, covers, garlands, unguents, sweetmeats; the whores [πόρναι] are there; sponge-cakes, flat-cakes, sesame-cakes, wafer-cakes; and dancing girls — 'beloved of Harmodius' — lovely ones. Hurry, as fast as you can." (*Acharnians* 1090–94). I will explain the phrase "beloved of Harmodius" shortly. For the moment my point is that, if the couch is furniture for the dining room, a painted couch will be something you see in a picture of eating and drinking. And this is relevant to poetry in a way that beds are not, because feasting and symposia were typically occasions for poetry.

---

ford, 1990); William J. Slater, *Dining in a Classical Context* (Ann Arbor, 1991); Pauline Schmitt Pantel, *La cité au banquet: Histoire des repas publics dans les cités grecques* (Rome, 1992); Oswyn Murray and Manuela Tecuşan, eds., *In Vino Veritas* (Rome, 1995).

[43] But Shorey got the translation right long ago.

[44] Translation and text in David A. Campbell, *Greek Lyric*, Loeb Classical Library (Cambridge, Mass., and London, 1982), V 2: 410–11. Chrysocolla is a dish made of honey and linseed.

Beds are for sex and sleep, couches for food, drink, sex — and poetry. A Greek reader would find it entirely natural that in *Republic* II feasting is the prelude to a long discussion of poetry.

In the pious simplicity of the "city of pigs," they sang hymns to the gods. In the civilized Greek world reflected in our surviving literature, both epic and lyric poetry were regularly performed at social gatherings such as festivals, sacrifices, feasts, and symposia.[45] Aristophanes' phrase "beloved of Harmodius" is a joke rewriting of a drinking-song (σκόλιον) in praise of the famous lovers, Harmodius and Aristogeiton, who were celebrated in Athenian folk memory for slaying the tyrant.[46] The song began (in one of its versions), "I shall carry my sword in a spray of myrtle, like Harmodius and Aristogeiton when they killed the tyrant and made Athens a city of equal rights [ἰσονόμους]." The response was, "Beloved Harmodius, No, you cannot be dead . . ."[47] Without changing a letter of the Greek, Aristophanes rewrites "Beloved Harmodius, No" (φίλταθ' Ἀρνόδι', οὔ) to get "Beloved of Harmodius" (φίλταθ' Ἁρμοδίου), thereby suggesting that Harmodius loved girls!

Aristophanes, however, was having fun with something serious. The song celebrates Harmodius and Aristogeiton for making Athens a city of equal rights (ἰσονόμους). Ἰσονομία, equality before the law, was the buzzword of Athenian democracy. Symposia and feasts are among the most important places where the culture is transmitted from one generation to the next. Singing the Harmodius song is like singing the Marseillaise with its bloodthirsty chorus, "Aux armes, citoyens!" It is at once a celebration and a confirmation, each time it is sung, of a foundational civic tradi-

[45] Symposiasts might also recite speeches from tragedy: Aristophanes, *Clouds* 1353–76, has the symposiasts recite.

[46] Never mind that they killed Hipparchus, not his brother Hippias, who had succeeded their father, Peisistratus, as tyrant: every society needs its "noble lie." To honour Harmodius and Aristogeiton, the city gave their descendants the privilege Socrates demands at Plato, *Apology* 36de: free meals in the prytaneion.

[47] Translation and text in Campbell, *Greek Lyric*, 5: 284–87.

tion.[48] The symposium (like pubs and cafés today) is a prime setting for the young to be socialized into that tradition.[49] The songs
sung there become common currency.[50] At the symposium you hear
stories about the gods and heroes from the near or distant past and
acquire the group loyalties, values, beliefs, and knowledge which
constitute, as my dictionary says, the shared bases of social action.
And the main vehicle for this transmission is poetry, sung and performed after the food has been cleared from the tables and the
party is reclining comfortably on their couches.

SELF-REFLECTIONS IN THE CAVE

Now look at Figure 1. The picture is by the Brygos painter,
around 490 B.C.[51] We see two of the couches, two tables (no food
on them now) ; pipes and lyre for the music. We also see a cup of
the very same shape (termed kylix) as the cup the picture is
painted on. The picture of drinking is painted on a drinking cup.
Such self-referential scenes are very common on the cups and mix-
ing bowls used at symposia. So imagine yourself at a symposium
using this cup. What you see on it is, in a certain sense, yourself
and your companions.

Recall also Alcman's song, "Seven couches and as many
tables. . . ." The archaeological remains of ancient Greek buildings
confirm that seven was the minimum number of couches required

---

[48] It is the song the "demagogue" Cleon leads off with (in a different version)
in the singing-game at the imaginary symposium cited above from Aristophanes'
Wasps (1224–25).

[49] Reclining started at eighteen, but the vases show younger boys sitting or
standing by: see Alan Booth, "The Age for Reclining and Its Attendant Perils," in
Slater, *Dining*, 105–20; cf. Xenophon, *Symposium* 1.8. Aristotle, *Politics* VII 17,
1336b 20–23, uses "the age of reclining" as his criterion for when boys should be
allowed to watch comedy.

[50] Example: "I'm sure you've heard people at drinking parties singing that song
in which they count out as they sing that 'to enjoy good health is the best thing;
second is to have turned out good looking; and third . . . is to be honestly rich' "
(Plato, *Gorgias* 451e; tr. Zeyl).

[51] British Museum E 68 = ARV² 371.24.

FIGURE 1. Courtesy of the British Museum.

for a symposium.[52] Alcman's poem is a song to be sung at a symposium about the symposium it is sung at. As with the cups and vessels, self-reference of this kind is common in Greek lyric poetry. An example familiar to students of ancient philosophy is fragment 1 of the sixth-century poet-philosopher Xenophanes:

> For now the floor is clean, and everybody's hands
>   and cups; a servant garlands us with wreaths;
> another offers fragrant perfume from a dish;
>   the mixing bowl's set up, brimful of cheer,
> and further jars of wine stand ready, promising
>   never to fail — soft wine, that smells of flowers.
> The frankincense sends out its holy scent all round
>   the room; there's water, cool and clear and sweet;
> bread lies to hand, gold-brown; a splendid table, too,
>   with cheeses and thick honey loaded down.
> The altar in the middle's decked about with flowers;
>   festivity and song pervade the house.
> The first thing men of sense should do is sing of God
>   in words of holiness and purity,
> with a libation and a prayer for means to do
>   what's right [τὰ δίκαια]; that's more straightforward, after all,

---

[52] The alternatives were eleven or fifteen. A couch might be occupied by one person or two.

than crimes. Then drink what you can hold and still get home
   unaided (if, of course, you're not too old).
Applaud the man who proclaims noble deeds in his cups,
   so that there may be memory and striving for virtue:
don't be relating wars of Titans or of Giants
   or Centaurs, fictions of the men of old,
or strife and violence. There's no benefit in that.
No, always keep the gods duly in mind.[53]

Xenophanes sings about good order at the symposium (drink as
much wine as allows you to get home without a servant's assistance), and then he turns to appropriate subjects for the singing.
The right accompaniment to the wine is tales of noble deeds,
whose memory will inspire those present now to emulate their
ancestors by striving for virtue themselves. Then Xenophanes tells
the symposiasts, as Socrates will tell Adeimantus in *Republic* II,
not to sing about battles and disputes among the gods; such stories
are dangerous fictions ($\pi\lambda\acute{\alpha}\sigma\mu\alpha\tau\alpha$ in Xenophanes, line 22; $\mu\acute{\upsilon}\theta o\upsilon s$
$\pi\lambda\alpha o\theta\acute{\epsilon}\nu\tau\alpha s$ in *Rep.* 377b). Imagine yourself at a symposium where
this song is sung. In a certain sense, you are hearing about your-
self and your companions, and how you should spend the evening
together.

   In quite what sense you see or hear about yourself is a complicated question, to which I will return. Meanwhile, I should like
to connect these cups and poems with a significant detail in Plato's
famous image of the Cave in *Republic* VII. You will remember
that the prisoners are chained in such a way that they see only the
shadows cast by firelight on to the back of the cave by a variety
of objects carried along a low wall behind them. The wall is com-

---

[53] I follow the text of M. L. West, *Iambi et Elegi Graeci ante Alexandrum
Cantati*, 2nd ed. (Oxford, 1992), vol. 2, which is different in crucial respects from
that familiar to students of ancient philosophy from Hermann Diels and Walther
Kranz, *Die Fragmente der Vorsokratiker*, 6th ed., 3 vols. (Berlin, 1951–52); note,
for example, that West prints $\acute{\omega}s$ $\mathfrak{\^{\eta}}$ at the beginning of line 20. The translation is
borrowed from M. L. West, *Greek Lyric Poetry*, translated with introduction and
notes (Oxford, 1993), but with my own version of lines 19–20.

pared to the screen above which a showman displays his puppets, so the people manipulating the objects are rather like puppeteers. The first thing Socrates says about the chained prisoners is that they have seen nothing *of themselves or each other* save the shadows on the back of the cave (515a). What does that mean?[54]

The most literal approach would suppose that the shadows of themselves are cast by the prisoners' bodies, which must therefore (despite the wall) be within the light beam of the fire higher up in the cave. But consider: their bodies are immobile, chained since infancy at the neck and legs (514ab). Do the prisoners think of themselves and their companions as inactive and stationary in a world where everything else is moving? The shadows cast by the puppet like objects (models of people, animals, artefacts) carried along the wall certainly move. Some prisoners are honoured by the others for memorizing sequences of shadows so successfully that they can predict what will turn up next (516cd). If none of the prisoners move, predictions about shadows cast by the statuettes of humans (514c: ἀνδριάντας) will always concern *other* human beings, never the prisoners themselves. But who are these other human beings? Why, and in what sense, do the prisoners who are good at predicting their behaviour hold power over the rest (516d 4: ἐνδυναστεύοντας)?

Again, Socrates sums up the sorry state of the prisoners by saying that the only things they consider real are the shadows of the puppets (515c: τὰς τῶν σκευαστῶν σκιάς). Do they not count themselves as real too? If the shadows of themselves are cast by their own immobilized bodies, not by the statuettes of humans carried along the wall, they will get no closer to the truth about themselves when they are forced to turn round towards the wall and look at "the things whose shadows they saw before" (515cd).

---

[54] I owe deep thanks to Jacques Brunschwig for asking me this question, seldom discussed in the scholarly literature, and for subsequent debate about our conflicting answers. His answer, "Un détail négligé dans la Caverne de Platon," will appear in a *Festschrift* for Bernard Rousset.

They will only be looking at some of the things whose shadows they saw before. So literal an interpretation brings insuperable difficulties.

Let us start again. The Cave is introduced as an image for our condition in regard to παιδεία and its opposite, ἀπαιδευσία (514a–15a). The Greek word παιδεία means both education and culture, because culture is what educates and forms the soul. After describing the cave, prisoners, and puppets, Socrates adds that some of the puppeteers speak, their voices echoing back from the bottom of the cave in such a way that the prisoners suppose it is the shadows that speak the words; other puppeteers remain silent and produce visual effects alone (515ab). Just so, painters do not speak, but poets and dramatists do. I propose that among the shadows the prisoners are looking at and listening to are their culture's images of themselves and their companions — just like the drinker with the cup and the audience of sympotic poems. Both painters and poets are among the people who manage the show over the wall behind the prisoners to make the sights and sounds that flit before them. They play a key role in shaping the culture and educating the citizens.

On this interpretation, the Cave image shows the prisoners unaware that their values and ideas are uncritically absorbed from the surrounding culture. They are prisoners, as we all are to begin with, of their education and upbringing. When Socrates introduces the point that they have seen nothing of themselves and each other save the shadows on the back of the cave, he is explaining (515a 5: γάρ) what he means by saying the prisoners are "like us." He means they are like us in respect of the education and culture we were brought up in.

Imagine people listening to Xenophanes' poem or drinking from the Brygos painter's cup. They do not think, "That's me — Glaucon, son of Ariston." They think, "That's us, that's how we do or should behave; that's how to drink together." In the theatre they do not think, "That's Pericles," but "That's how a resourceful leader gets his way — he's the sort to vote for." It is the generic characterisations that matter to their conception of themselves and each other, not the actual details of each individual life. One of the very few scholars to comment on the shadows "of themselves and each other" has this to say:

> They have never observed the genuine facts of human nature in themselves or in others. They think that they have a clear idea of their own character and relation to their neighbours, but really the image which does duty in their mind for such an idea is a mere phantasm projected by a false light of sentiment or association.[55]

All I would add is that these sentiments and associations are fostered by poet and painter and any other puppeteers who make and manipulate the surrounding culture. It is the culture from which we derive our "self-image."

I am tempted to include orators on the list of culture-makers. As he develops the Cave simile, Socrates emphasises the difficulty a philosopher who has seen the Form of Justice will encounter when debating, in the lawcourts and elsewhere, about shadows and puppets of justice (517de). The orator who appears before juries, assemblies, and other large gatherings has a formative influence on people's sense of themselves and their companions. A famous example is Pericles' Funeral Oration in Thucydides, which could well be described as giving the Athenians a powerful image of themselves — an image that Plato took the trouble to satirize at length in the *Menexenus*.

Socrates opens the *Menexenus* by saying that funeral orations always make him feel great. By the time the speaker has finished praising the dead and their ancestors and all the glorious deeds they did (plus some they did not really do), he feels himself to be taller and nobler and more handsome than he has ever been, while the city he lives in seems even more wonderful than before

---

[55] Bernard Bosanquet, *A Companion to Plato's Republic* (London, 1895), *ad loc.*

(234b–35c). The speech he then recites (allegedly borrowed from Pericles' mistress, Aspasia) gives a radiant picture of Athenian history up to (and after) his own day. Even the civil war to oust the Thirty Tyrants comes across as the ideal civil war to have if you have to go through such a thing: the two sides were so kind to each other (243e).

This is not just flattery to boost the survivors' self-estem. The idea is that the audience will be inspired to greatness themselves, in emulation of their predecessors. For after the history come exhortations to valour and virtue (246d ff.). Never mind that Plato contrives to write a healthy dose of Socratic moral philosophy into this part of Aspasia's speech. She gives a fine illustration of what Xenophanes called for: "memory and striving for virtue."

But it is not just the prisoners' self-image that is constructed (as we now say) by the surrounding culture. It is also their image of the world around them. Besides the statuettes of human beings, there are puppets of animals and artefacts casting shadows from the wall. Of these too the prisoners have seen nothing but the shadows (515b 2).[56] In book X, where the puppeteer's art returns, alongside shadow-painting, as one of the creators of visual illusion (602d 3–4),[57] we will be told that the couches and cups in a pic-

---

[56] To read the antithesis πρῶτον μὲν ἑαυτῶν . . . τί δὲ τῶν παραφερομένων (515a 5–b 2) as contrasting the prisoners' immobilized bodies with the puppets generally would take us back to the difficulties of the literal approach. Better, therefore, to read it as a contrast between human statuettes and the others, between "ourselves" and "everything else"; similarly, outside the cave, reflections of people contrast with reflection of other things (516a 7). An alternative would be to take a subset of the human statues as the ones whose shadows the prisoners identify with and contrast them with other humans (foreigners, perhaps also women) as well as other things: Us vs. the Other.

[57] The word used for puppeteering, θαυματοποιία, can refer to all sorts of illusionistic performances, and in Plato's *Sophist* (235b; cf. 224ab) it appears as the genus which subsumes sophists as well as other image-makers. If I do not include sophists among the manipulators behind the wall in the cave, this is for two reasons. First, because in the *Republic*, the real sophist is the multitude; those who ask a fee for their teaching are small fry, who merely echo the opinions of that great beast (492a–93e). Second, the *Sophist* strikes me as designed to surprise and instruct by capturing the sophist in a network of ideas familiar to the reader from the *Republic*'s discussion of art and illusion; on this, see further Noboru Notomi, *The Appearances of the Sophist* (Cambridge, forthcoming).

ture of drinking are at third remove from the truth and reality of the Forms (597e). So too are the images put before us by Homer and the tragic poets (599d, 602c).[58] This matches exactly the status of the shadows in the Cave: they derive from the puppets carried along the wall, which are themselves likenesses of the real people, animals, and things outside the cave. The shadows are at third remove (Greeks count inclusively) from the real things outside, which represent the Forms. Book X gives a metaphysical restatement of the understanding of poet and painter I have proposed for the Cave.

True, it is only in retrospect that this interpretation is confirmed. Equally, it is only in retrospect that we learn that the Cave has to do with mathematics as well as cultural values (532bc). This is not the place to wonder how two things which seem so disparate can fit together in one simile.[59] I shall simply say that there are other passages in the *Republic* which gain further significance later, from a retrospective filling out of meaning. My next example is Socrates' account of the feasting in the "luxurious" city.

Two Types of Imitator

Besides couches and tables, luxurious feasting requires every available kind of hunter (because Glaucon insists on meat and fish), and many types of imitator (373b). Lots more skills are needed too: wet-nurses, chefs to prepare the relishes, beauticians, barbers, swineherds, and others (373c). But the extra that interests me here is the imitators (μιμηταί).

Imitators are people who make the likenesses by which the culture is transmitted. μίμησις or likeness-making will become the

[58] Detailed discussion of these claims must wait for lecture III.

[59] For some suggestions, see my "Platonism and Mathematics: A Prelude to Discussion," in Andreas Graeser, ed., *Mathematics and Metaphysics in Aristotle* (Bern and Stuttgart, 1987), 213–40, and "Plato on Why Mathematics Is Good for the Soul" (forthcoming).

key concept of Plato's critique of art in books III and X. In book II, where he first introduces the concept, Socrates confines himself to distinguishing two main types of imitator, corresponding (as already mentioned) to our two most impressionable distance senses, sight and hearing.

Some imitators make likenesses of things in shapes and colours; they will be visual artists such as painters, sculptors, embroiderers. Others are sound-artists, who make likenesses in music, where "music" covers the entire range of poetic or theatrical performance. The sound-artists mentioned are the poets, who composed the music (in our narrower sense of the word) as well as the verse, and their assistants — rhapsodes, actors, chorus-masters, contractors,[60] all of whom contribute to the performance on the day.

We have now moved from couches and tables to the theatre. But we have not changed the subject, only the size of the social gathering. Athenian tragedy and comedy happened at a civic and religious festival which brought the whole citizen body together. The tragedies usually enacted new versions of the citizens' shared religious and heroic myths; the comedies played with themes from their shared social and political life. This is cultural transmission at its most intense, with the whole society present (even if represented only by the males), with a parade of tribute from the empire, and the god Dionysus presiding — the god of community joy and wine, madness and violence. When Plato talks about the theatre, the question he is asking is still, How can the total culture be as ideal as possible?

So couches and tables are about a good deal more than appetites for food, drink, and sex.[61] Plato agrees with modern anthro-

---

[60] For an example of contractors (ἐργολάβοι), who were required to engage performers and provide for them during the festival, see the Euboean law quoted and discussed by Sir Arthur Pickard-Cambridge, *The Dramatic Festivals of Athens*, 2nd ed. revised by John Gould and D. M. Lewis (Oxford, 1968), 281–82, 306–8. Plato ends his list with a sneer at the intrusion of commerce.

[61] *Pace* Charles Griswold, "The Ideas and the Criticism of Poetry in Plato's *Republic*, Book 10," *Journal of the History of Philosophy* 19 (1981): 143–45, followed by Nehamas, "Imitation," 73, n. 32 (c).

pology that food, drink, and sex are as much part of the culture as song and dance. Hence the question how to use couches and tables in the ideal city is part of a larger question: How to shape the culture to have the best possible influence on the souls of its citizens, especially when they are young. The cave is not abolished in the ideal city, only purified. That is where the philosophers return to rule: to *"that* cave again," as Socrates will put it later (539e 3). All the young and most of the grown-up inhabitants of the ideal city spend their lives in the condition of the chained prisoners, accepting uncritically the values of their culture.[62] The ideal city is ideal because its entire culture — material, moral, and musical — is pervaded by the right values, thanks to the philosopher-rulers' understanding of the Forms, including the Forms of Couch and of Table. Book X's positing of these two Forms indicates that Plato wants to claim there is an objectively correct answer to the question how the city should make use of couches and tables and all the other apparatus of civilized gatherings.

SECOND GLANCE AHEAD: THE FORM
OF COUCH IN BOOK X

By an objectively correct answer I mean one that is rooted in human nature, so that in the ideal city human nature achieves the best cultural expression it can aspire to. A Platonic Form is in the first instance what is specified by an objectively correct definition. The definition of the Form of Couch would be an account of the couch as an instrument for the education and cultural fulfillment of human nature, in much the same way as Plato's *Cratylus* defines the Forms of Shuttle and Name. The shuttle is an instrument for

---

[62] The Cave as we read it contains an unmistakable allusion to the fate of Socrates, killed for trying to release prisoners from their chains by engaging them in dialectic (517a). This would not happen in the purified cave of the ideal city, for two reasons. First, conversion begins with mathematics (521d, 524d–25a, 526e) and dialectic is postponed until the age of thirty (537d–39d). Second, each stage of the curriculum is restricted to the select few who have proved their worth, both moral and intellectual, at the previous stage (537d, 540a).

weaving, the name of something is an instrument for teaching. The correct way to design and use a shuttle is determined by its function, to help turn thread into cloth. The correct way to design and use a couch is likewise determined by its function, to help turn the impressionable young into worthy citizens. There are constraints in both cases: you need a sound knowledge of the material you have to work with (the potential and limitations of woollen thread and human nature), and a clear understanding of the end-product you are aiming for (high-quality cloth, high-quality citizens). These constraints make it possible to give an objective account of what a shuttle or couch is and how best to use it. The long discussion of musical poetry in *Republic* II–III can be read as Plato's account of the objectively best way to use couches and tables for the education and cultural fulfillment of human nature. *Republic* X confirms that "the excellence, the beauty, the rightness of every implement, living thing, and action are determined solely by reference to the *use* for which each has been made or grown" (601d). The use of a couch is not just reclining. It is reclining to participate in a culturally intense social gathering.[63]

I said that a Platonic Form is *in the first instance* what is specified by an objectively correct definition. The second main feature of Platonic Forms is that they are eternal, uncreated, and independent of the sensible world. But in *Republic* X the Form of Couch is made by God (597b). This novelty has caused much knitting of scholarly brows. Many refuse to take the statement seriously. What I think it means is that Forms such as Couch, Shuttle, and Name have a rather different status from Forms like Beauty, Justice, and the Good. I have a speculation to offer about what that status is, but this will be a digression from the main line of my argument.

---

[63] One of the differences between Platonic and Aristotelian teleology is that Plato tends to go for the highest purpose a thing can achieve. Eyes are for astronomy, ears for harmonics (530d); both organs are given to us for the improvement of our intellectual understanding (cf. *Timaeus* 46e–48e). At a lower level, the human liver is for divination (*Tim.* 72b).

The clue I want to follow up is the agri-cultural imagery invoked to describe God's making of Couch. He made it grow: φυτεύειν, φύειν (597cd). He is the φυτουργός of Couch (597d), its Planter or Grower, and his product is repeatedly described as "the Couch in nature" (597b 6, c 2, d 3, e 3–4, 598a 1). Glaucon approves the title φυτουργός, saying, "At any rate, it was by means of nature [φύσει γε] that God made this [the Form of Couch] and everything else [*sc.* everything else he made]" (597d 7–8).[64] The remark should encourage us to think about Plato's view of nature.

The Greek word for nature, φύσις, which is the reason we call the study of nature "physics," originally meant "growth." Plato's physics is to be found in his discourse on nature, the *Timaeus*. In the *Timaeus*, the Divine Craftsman is directly or indirectly the source of good order in nature, or "growth," throughout the sensible world. The best part of human nature, the rational soul, is his own handiwork. The human body and the nonrational parts of the soul are produced at his command by the imperfect efforts of the lesser (created) gods, who are the Sun and other intelligent heavenly bodies responsible for seasonal growth and decline. By supplying the rational soul with a body and nonrational desires, the lesser gods set the arena of challenge and choice within which the embodied rational soul is enjoined by the Demiurge to achieve

---

[64] The puzzlement this sentence has provoked is evident from the variety of translations it has been subjected to: "by the natural process of creation He is the author of this and of all other things" (Jowett, 2nd ed., 1875), "it is by and in nature that he made this and all other things" (Shorey, 1930), "his making of this and all other things is nature's making of them" (Lindsay, 1935), "all his works constitute the real nature of things" (Cornford, 1941), "all his creations are ultimate realities" (Lee, 1955), "by nature he has made both this and everything else" (Bloom, 1968), "he made the true nature of this and everything else" (Grube, 1974), "he is by nature the maker of this and everything else" (Reeve, 1992), "it is by *nature* that he has made both this and all other things" (Halliwell, 2nd ed., 1993), "he has made this and everything else that exists in nature" (Murray, 1996). The older translators are clear that φύσει γε is an instrumental dative. Of the versions quoted which acknowledge this, some allow the reader to think it may be a reference to God's own nature; but that does not suit the reservation γε. My prize for the best rendering goes to Jowett.

justice, virtue, and salvation (41e–42d). On this picture, God sets the goal for which human nature is designed, and himself makes the part of our soul which is able — and duty-bound — to achieve it. Platonic physics is anything but value-neutral.[65] The moral end, and the agent who is to attain it, belong to the divinely arranged order of nature.[66] God is thereby responsible for there being objective standards of correctness for the agent's use of the instruments of salvation, among which couches and tables have an important role to play.[67]

The picture in the *Republic* is much less detailed, without the distinction between the Demiurge (mentioned at 530a) and the lesser gods, between direct and mediated creation. But one of the first things the young will be taught by the poetry they hear in the ideal city is that God is not responsible for everything in human life, good and bad, only for the good (379ac; cf. *Tim.* 42de, 68e). If God is ultimately responsible for the good in human life, then he is responsible for there being objective answers to the ques-

[65] Even in the section devoted to the "necessary" or automatic consequences of the Demiurge's construction of the four elements, 60a singles out wine, "which warms the soul together with the body" (this must be the natural fermentation, prior to human attempts to produce a pleasant drink), and 60e salt, "beloved of the gods." From the Demiurge's point of view, all these are "subservient causes" which help realize the goodness of his grand design (68e).

[66] It is perhaps worth mentioning that many of the created items in the *Timaeus* are kinds or forms of some sort, not individuals. The created individuals include the cosmos itself, the intelligent heavenly bodies (the lesser gods), and individual souls. But besides these we read of created γένη (e.g., the four elements: 53bc) and εἴδη (e.g., the nonrational soul: 69cd), and ἰδέαι (e.g., lungs and liver: 70c, 71a). Presumably, the Sun and the other lesser gods do not intervene to make Jones's liver one day, Smith's the next; rather, they make the course of nature run in such a way that, in general, humans are born with a liver. But this is not the place to explore the ontological implications of Plato's creation story.

[67] When Aristotle, *Metaphysics* XII 3, 1070a 18–19, reports Plato as saying there are Forms for (*sc.* and only for) such things as exist by nature, we should distinguish Aristotle's understanding of the thesis, in terms of his own contrast between nature and art, from the meaning Plato would have intended. For Aristotle, artefacts necessarily fall outside the realm of nature; for Plato, they do not. See *Sophist* 265e: "I will lay it down that the products of nature, as they are called, are works of divine art, as the things made out of them by man are works of human art" (tr. Cornford).

tion how this human nature he has devised can best fulfil itself — individually, socially, and culturally. Forms are involved, because the answers set standards which are independent of actual societies (past, present, or future). But unlike Beauty, Justice, and the Good, they are Forms that presuppose the existence of human life in the sensible world.[68] They are contingent upon God's sowing our souls (if I may borrow another agri-cultural image from the *Timaeus*: ἔσπειρε, 42c) into the flux of time, to pursue justice, virtue, and salvation on our own responsibility.

End of digression on the ontological status of the Forms of Couch and Table. For my main line of argument, it is enough that these Forms exist. That ensures, uncontroversially, that Plato believes there is an objective answer to the question before us: How can the total culture be made as ideal as possible? But before coming to Plato's answer, I would like to sketch some modern parallels to his question. For I believe that his question is of more lasting importance than his answer.

MODERN ANALOGIES

In our world, poetry and drama have become minority, often élite pursuits — although we should not forget the role of poetry, song, and story in transmitting a *counter*-culture in divided societies like Ireland, Communist Russia, Greece under the dictators. The visual arts now fall under the limiting rubric "high culture." The things Plato would focus on if he were asking his questions today — and here I take my lead from Julia Annas and Alexander Nehamas[69] — would be the recorded music (both popular and classical) with which we are surrounded at home and in public places; popular magazines; radio, film, and TV; and the images in

---

[68] *We* might think that Justice presupposed human life. Not so Plato, for whom Justice is an abstract order exemplified in the heavens as well as in cities and souls, and even healthy bodies: *Rep.* 592ab, *Tim.* 81e ff.

[69] Annas, *An Introduction to Plato's "Republic"* 94; Alexander Nehamas, "Plato and the Mass Media," *Monist* 71 (1988): 214–34.

advertisements. These are the universal media of cultural transmission today.

It is not surprising, then, that advertisements, film, and TV provoke in us the very same concern as Plato has in the *Republic*. Are their effects on the souls of the citizen body, especially when young, harmful or beneficial? Plato's question "Shall we banish Homer, tragedy, and comedy? is an ancient version of the question we would be asking if we stopped to wonder whether, if we had known or suspected at the outset what we now know or suspect about TV and its influence, we should have let it go ahead. Would life without TV, or without advertising, be spiritually better? But Plato's focus is interestingly different from ours.

First, sex and violence are less important to him than moral and religious values more generally. Take castration. When Socrates bans Hesiod's story of the violence done by Cronos to Ouranos and Zeus to Cronos, the reason he gives is that this is not how *gods* behave, and it sets a bad example to *sons* (377e–78b). Violence as such is not to the fore. When he objects to the story of Zeus, overcome with desire for Hera, wanting sex at once in the open air, he couples it with a quote from Odysseus about the enticements of food and wine. At such moments, neither Zeus nor Odysseus encourages the young to practise temperance and self-control (390ac); gluttony is as bad as sexual passion.

Another contrast with popular debate today about sex and violence on the screen is that our newspapers are obsessed with the idea of cause and effect, where cause and effect are understood in terms of individual events: the showing of a film on Tuesday, followed by a rape or murder on Wednesday. Does the first cause the second? Some conservatives would like to be able to say yes. The liberals protest that no causal link has been proved. Modern professional studies of media influence are of course more subtle than that.[70] So is Plato.

---

[70] For a useful evaluation of their results, see Sissela Bok, *Mayhem: Violence as Public Entertainment* (Reading, Mass., 1998).

In a famous passage, Socrates says he is convinced that innovations in music must not be allowed in the ideal city, because "the modes of music are never disturbed without unsettling of the most fundamental political and social conventions" (424c). Plato does not mean to say, "The Beatles and Mick Jagger sang — as a direct result, the sixties began." On his account the causal influence is more gradual — and more insidious:

> "Contravention of established custom [παρανομία] in this sphere [music]," [71] Adeimantus said, "all too easily insinuates itself *without people being aware* of what is happening [λανθάνει παραδυομένη]."
>
> "Yes," I said, "because it is taken to be nothing but a form of play, which does no harm to anyone."
>
> "Naturally enough," [72] he said, "because all it does is to make itself at home little by little [κατὰ σμικρόν], until it overflows ever so quietly [ἠρέμα ὑπορρεῖ] into people's character and pursuits. From these it emerges, grown larger, into their dealings and associations with one another,[73] and from dealings and associations it proceeds against laws and constitutions (so great, Socrates, by this stage is its insolence), till it ends up overthrowing everything in private and public life." [74] (424de)

We have already met the idea that music is the basic source of people's sensibility in other spheres, not least in morals. What this

---

[71] The word νόμος means both "law, convention" and, in music, "mode." Hence παρανομία is a pun: contravening the established musical modes is tantamount to contravening the established rules of life generally.

[72] οὐδὲ γάρ explains the supposition, not the thing supposed.

[73] "Dealings and associations" translates the single Greek word ξυμβόλαια, the range of which is illustrated at 333ad and 554c–55a.

[74] An unusually substantial contribution by Adeimantus, at which Socrates seems a bit surprised, for the text continues: " 'Well, well,' I said, 'Is that really so?' 'I think it is,' he said." Plato has already made Socrates acknowledge that the basic thesis about the drastic consequences of innovation in music is borrowed from Damon (424c). Adeimantus thereupon says that he too is one of those whom Damon has persuaded. I suspect that the further elaboration of Damon's thesis is put into the mouth of Adeimantus, rather than Socrates, because the whole thing is originally due to Damon. A rare case of Plato accepting someone else's theory without qualification or modification.

passage adds is a powerful description of the gradual, unnoticed way in which music infiltrates people's souls and affects their way of life.[75] Gradual, unnoticed influence was the theme of the passage I began from about gracefulness in the material environment. Gradual, unnoticed influence again is the reason for spotlighting couches and tables, where the shared symbols of society are confirmed evening after evening and passed on to successive generations. This seems to me a more convincing, less hysterical approach than we find in the newspapers today.

Let me illustrate with a visual parallel from our own world. Instead of the hotly disputed impact of explicitly pornographic magazines, think about the more subtle influence over time of the increasing levels of nudity and eroticism in contemporary advertising. This surrounds everyone everywhere, but causes much less anxious discussion than pornography at the corner store. Or consider the fashion magazines which lie around in the most respectable homes. The models in the clothes ads get thinner and thinner every year. On a recent visit to Ireland, I noticed that the models in the magazines there seemed almost portly; in my youth they would have looked elegantly slim. Question: do the advertisers' images of feminine beauty have an influence on men's attitudes to women and women's sense of themselves and their companions?[76] If they do — and various movements for the defence of larger women declare that it must be so — then it can only be in the way Plato describes, by a gradual, unnoticed infiltration of images into the soul. In which case, the best means of defence would seem to be by the same process. Put up posters from Rubens all over town.

Popular magazines are a good field in which to broach the complexities of the question I set aside earlier: In what sense are the

[75] A similar emphasis on the gradualness of music's influence at 411ae (concerned only with the individual): Socrates distinguishes the short-term and the long-term effects of letting too much soft music pour in through your ears, then the short-term and the longt-erm effects of exercising too much in the gym.

[76] An influential discussion of this issue is Naomi Wolf, *The Beauty Myth* (London, 1990).

shadows in front of the prisoners images of *themselves and their companions?* A straightforward example is the "embarrassment" column in a magazine called *Sugar*, read by girls aged nine to thirteen (though nominally marketed at older teenagers). You learn that other girls' parents do embarrassing things too. It is a comfort to know this, and it confirms the rightness of your own feelings. Very different from the pictures in fashion magazines, which do not show how you and your companions actually look, but how you might dream of looking. Men are vulnerable too: "To be on the cover of a muscle magazine," says a letter in *Muscle Media*, "was always one of my dreams, and now I've done it."

These examples illustrate two opposite extremes. At one end, images of what you are at your most mundane and embarrassing. At the other, images that focus hopes, aspirations, or fantasies — these two are part of what you and your companions are. In between there is room for a variety of relations between image and reader. Those fashion adverts also provide factual news about the clothes you will be able to buy in the stores this season. A *Sugar* story about one girl's promiscuity ("I slept with 40 boys . . .") prompted a question in Parliament, but my daughter said, "The girl didn't think it was a good idea." In their context, such stories prepare young girls for problems that await them in the future. Besides the kitchen of your dreams in the latest number of *House and Garden*, there is the kitchen you can realistically hope to have if you work hard and succeed. In general, advertisements offer information as well as temptation. They provide both a mirror of the present and a promise for the future. In other words, the appeal of popular magazines is as varied and complicated as the human soul. But some appeal to the soul there has to be. Magazines must sell, in fairly large numbers, to make money and survive. And this has implications for our understanding of gradual, unnoticed influence.

It cannot be a simple, one-way process of cause and effect. We should think rather of a continuing interaction over time, as in a marriage, where each party is influenced by the other. In ways neither need be aware of, each is gradually adjusting to the other's expectations while at the same time each is gradually changing what the other's expectations are. London and New York have adjusted to slimmer models than Dublin. Häagen-Dazs does not promote its ice-cream in Ireland by pictures of naked couples licking it off each other. The culture there is not ready to respond.

Marriage is a useful model also for appreciating that individual episodes of influence are connected with developments in the culture as a whole. Changes in the divorce rate show that any given couple's experience — whether wonderful, disastrous, or consolingly in between — belongs to a wider pattern, woven by historical and social factors they neither know nor can control. Similarly, no one magazine, no one film or TV programme, can be held responsible for the rise in teenage pregnancies, their lack of interest in ballroom dancing, the fashion for body piercing, or any of the other things that older generations deplore.

Plato saw this very clearly, I think. He is sometimes accused of siding with those who claim that advertising and TV implant in people desires and attitudes they would not otherwise have had. Aristotelian katharsis is hailed as the sane view, in contrast to Plato's so-called infection theory of art. The infection theory is as implausible as the opposite view that advertising and TV do no more than give the public what they (already) want; besides, many diseases are powerless without a patient who is run-down or otherwise susceptible already. But the famous passage just quoted, on the consequences of innovation in music, describes a long drawn-out *communal* process, in which everybody is involved. When the Beatles and Mick Jagger sang, change spread gradually in ever-widening ripples throughout the society (Plato's water imagery is most apt). We all took part, in different ways, without realizing it. We all share in the responsibility. That is why Plato put his question as one about making the *total* culture as ideal as possible. That is why for him the rulers' most important risk is to guard the culture against *unnoticed* change for the worse (424b 4: μὴ λάθῃ διαφθαρέν).[77]

We are now ready for Plato's answer.

LECTURE II. ART AND THE MENACE OF MIMESIS

PLATO'S PROGRAMME

Plato is famous for having banished poetry and poets from the ideal city of the *Republic*. But he did no such thing. On the contrary, poetry — the right sort of poetry — will be a pervasive presence in the life of the society he describes. Yes, he did banish Homer, Aeschylus, Sophocles, Euripides, and Aristophanes — the greatest names of Greek literature. But not because they were poets. He banished them because they produced the wrong sort of poetry. To rebut Plato's critique of poetry, what is needed is not a defence of poetry, but a defence of the freedom of poets to write as, and what, they wish.

No big problem, you may think. But suppose poetry was not the minority pursuit it has become in Britain and the U.S.A. today. Suppose it was the most popular form of entertainment available, the nearest equivalent to our mass media. As I explained in lecture I, that is not far from the truth about the world in which Plato wrote the *Republic*. The Athenian democracy, audience for much of the poetry Plato objected to, accepted that it was their responsibility to ensure the quality of the poetry funded by the state. In modern terms, they thought that democracy should care about whether the mass media encourage the right sorts of values. Do

[77] For a more psychoanalytic treatment of several themes of this lecture, compare Jonathan Lear, "Inside and Outside the *Republic*," *Phronesis* 37 (1992): 184–215. I would find it hard to say at which point in this very brilliant essay I begin to disagree, but I am suspicious of his handling of the process he calls "exteriorization," especially in books VIII–IX; we certainly disagree about the poets, whom I discuss in lecture II.

we want Rupert Murdoch to determine the overall quality of the culture? Should money decide everything? If not, what can we do about it?

Plato was no democrat, and had no qualms about proposing Soviet-style control from above, by those who know best. But democrats who reject such authoritarian solutions may still learn from Plato's disturbing presentation of the problem. What he is chiefly talking about is the words and music by which the culture is transmitted from one generation to the next. Tragedy and comedy were performed before a crowd of 14,000 people at the Great Dionysia and other civic festivals. We hear of 20,000 people attending a recital of Homer. Then there are hymns sung at religious ceremonies and songs at feasts or private symposia. Forget about reading T. S. Eliot to yourself in bed. Our subject is the words and music you hear at social gatherings, large and small. Think pubs and cafés, karaoki, football matches, the last night of the proms. Think morning service at the village church, carols from King's College Cambridge, Elton John singing to the nation from Westminster Abbey. Think popular music in general and, when Plato brings in a parallel from the visual arts, forget the Tate Gallery and recall the advertisements that surround us everywhere. Above all, think about the way all this is distributed to us by television, the omnipresent medium at work in every home. What Plato is discussing in the *Republic*, when he talks about poetry, is how to control the influences that shape the culture in which the young grow up. How to ensure that what he calls the ethos of society[1] is as ideal as possible. Even as adults, none of us is immune.

Books II-III of the *Republic* present Plato's proposals for reforming the culture in a carefully arranged sequence of stages.

---

[1] The English word "ethos" transliterates the Greek ἦθος, meaning "character." Plato holds that different societies have different ἤθη (435e 2, 545b 3–4), which derive (in complicated ways) from the character of individuals in those societies (435e–36a, 544de). More often, the *Republic* names the specific character traits of different cities, their virtues and vices.

The first stage concentrates on the content of musical poetry, the last on its material and social setting — with special reference (I will suggest) to the symposium or drinking party. In between come various other elements of poetic performance. The sequence of stages is not a sequence of independent topics. Each should be thought of as one layer among others in the analysis of a single cultural phenomenon: the performance of poetry with music (and sometimes dance as well).

From time to time the discussion touches on a nonmusical topic, be it nursery tales or the content of the visual arts. But the central thread is the performance of musical poetry at a social gathering.[2] This for Plato is the main vehicle of cultural transmission. This is what he is trying to get right when he designs a musical education for the warrior class in the ideal city — the Guards, as they are called[3] — from whose ranks a select few will go on to become philosopher-rulers. All else is subordinate.

One further preliminary. Plato is well aware that what he has to say will shock and appal his readers, then as now. His proposals for the ideal city amount to a complete reconstruction of Greek culture as it existed in his day. What motivates the proposals is his profound understanding of the many subtle ways in which the ethos of a society forms the souls who grow up in it. If you shudder at the authoritarianism of his programme, remember that shudder when the newspapers next debate whether bad behaviour

[2] One of the many merits of G. R. F. Ferrari's superb essay "Plato and Poetry," in George A. Kennedy, ed., *The Cambridge History of Literary Criticism* (Cambridge, 1989), pp. 92–148, is to have insisted more strongly than previous scholarship that Plato is talking about the performance of poetry, not reading it to oneself in private, in the schoolroom, or on a journey (as Dionysus reads Euripides' *Andromeda* to himself on deck in Aristophanes, *Frogs* 51–52).

[3] The standard translation of φύλακες as "Guardians" is too kindly. Socrates' jailor at *Crito* 43a is a φύλαξ, while the φύλακες of the ideal city are not just warriors for defence against enemies attacking from outside: they also have internal police duties, to stop anyone disobeying the law (415e, *Timaeus* 17d), especially in cultural matters (424bd, leading up to the passage about innovation in music quoted in lecture I). (I am indebted to Malcolm Schofield for opening my eyes to the error of the standard translation.)

in schools is the fault of parents or teachers. As if parents and teachers were anything but a tiny facet of the total culture of our time. Either grasp the nettle of devising democratic alternatives to Plato's authoritarianism, or stop bleating.

STAGE 1 OF THE REFORM: CONTENT

A performance of musical poetry is an act of communication between two parties, the performer(s) and the audience. At stage 1 of the reform Plato concentrates on the Guards as audience. What should be the content of the performances they hear? From Stage 2 onwards he concentrates (I will argue) on how Guards themselves perform, where performance includes writing and producing drama. How does such performance affect the soul? Only in book X does he come back to the effects of musical poetry on the audience.

Plato's first charge, and perhaps the most shocking to ancient readers, is that, from Homer onwards, poetry has been full of lies about the gods. The entire religious and mythological tradition stands condemned for blasphemy.[4] It is like someone today proposing to ban the Bible and all reference to biblical stories, on the grounds that the Bible presents a wrong picture of divinity. None of the stories of God's dealings with humankind can be true, and even if some of them were true, they are morally unsuitable for the ears of the young (cf. 378ab).

And what is unsuitable for ears is unsuitable for eyes as well. Stories it is wrong to sing, like the battle of gods and giants, must not be represented in embroidery (378c). This is no joke. Plato's readers would think at once of the colossal embroidered robe (πέπλος) carried in procession at the festival of the Panathenaea. The robe showed the battle of gods and giants, spotlighting the

---

[4] The verb βλασφημεῖν is used at 381e.

victory of Athena over the giant Enceladus.[5] A ban on such embroidery is a stake through the heart of Athenian religion and Athenian civic identity. Though Socrates does not stop to mention it, the censorship of embroidery will inevitably extend to painting and sculpture. The battle of gods and giants will be removed from the carved metopes of the Parthenon (currently on display in the British Museum). In the ideal city, the religious content of the visual arts will be as restricted as the religious content of poetry and music.

How much of the Greek literature you know would survive enforcement of the following norms ($\tau\acute{v}\pi o\iota$, $\nu\acute{o}\mu o\iota$)? (1) Divinity, being good, is not responsible for everything that occurs, only for the good. So gods never lead mortals into crime (379a–80c). (2) Divinity is simple, unchanging, and hates falsehood and deception. So gods never appear in disguise to mortals, never send misleading dreams or signs (380d–83a). (3) Hades is not the dreadful place the poets describe. So a good man finds no great cause for grief in the death of himself, his friend, or his son (386a–87c). (4) Heroes are admirable role-models for the young. So they never indulge in lamentation, mirth, or lying (save for high purposes of state), impertinence to their commanders or arrogance toward gods and men, sexual passion or rape, longing for food and drink, or greed for wealth; nor, *mutatis mutandis*, should any such thing be attributed to the gods (387c–91e). Finally, (5) the moral argument of the *Republic* itself, when completed, will prove that it is justice, not injustice, that makes one happy. So no poet may depict a happy villain or a virtuous person in misery (392ac). Under this regime very little of the Greek litera-

---

[5] Cf. Plato's *Euthyphro* 6ac, where the robe figures alongside representations of strife among the gods in poems and temple paintings; Socrates finds them all repellent (I am indebted to the notes *ad loc.* in Burnet's edition [Oxford, 1924]). For a detailed account of the Panathenaea, see H. W. Parke, *Festivals of the Athenians* (London, 1977), pp. 33–50.

ture we know would remain intact,[6] and much of the art would disappear.[7]

Nearly all the poetry cited in the *Republic* so far will be banned.[8] Many of the themes of the earlier discussion came from poetry, because poetry articulates the values and beliefs of the culture. In book I, Cephalus recounts how, when old age comes and death is near, one takes seriously, in a way the young do not, the stories (μῦθοι) about Hades and the terrors it holds for wrongdoers (330de). In a society with no Bible or canonical sacred text, the chief source for these stories is poetry. Conversely, it is poets like Pindar who hold out the rope of a nice afterlife for those who have lived in justice and piety (331a). On the other hand, a major theme of the speech of Adeimantus at the beginning of book II (362d ff.) is the way the poets instill in the young a wrong attitude towards justice, because they praise it for its contingent consequences rather than its intrinsic value. Justice, the poets say, is a real sweat in this life, much harder and less pleasant than injustice (provided you can get away with it). It is only in the very long run that justice pays: the poet Musaeus, for example, promises the righteous that their afterlife will be an unending symposium, as if the ultimate reward for virtue was eternal intoxication (363cd). But at the same time his teaching is that the wicked can always bribe the gods with sacrifices and festivals to let them off (364e–65a).[9] None of this is compatible with the norms that Socrates has now put before us.

[6] I have heard it suggested that the *Odyssey* would still be a good story after Platonic censorship. It is true that the bulk of the quotations in *Rep.* II–III are from the *Iliad*, but the *Odyssey* is not neglected (381d, 386d, 387a, 389d, 390b, 390c, 390d). If Plato's main target is the *Iliad*, this is in part because he is discussing the education of the warrior class. In any case, the narrative of the *Odyssey* is driven by the anger of Poseidon and by Athena's countervailing help for Odysseus, to whom she appears in several different disguises; none of that is admissible by Plato's norms. Note that Aristotle, *Poetics* 4, 1448b 38–49a 2, sees both *Iliad* and *Odyssey* as akin to tragedy.

[7] Example: vase-painters loved the story excised at 378d about Hephaestus being hurled from heaven.

[8] A point well observed by Halliwell, "Two Critiques," pp. 314–15.

[9] Cf. the remarks of Cephalus at 331b.

To begin with, however, Socrates speaks as if he is merely purging the culture of certain objectionable features. He asks Homer and the other poets not to be angry if he and Adeimantus expunge all the passages that breach the norms (387b). He takes the scissors to Aeschylus (380a, 381d, 383b, 391e), but implies that tragedy (cleaned up by himself) will still be performed (379a, 381d, 383c). At this stage, Plato is concerned only with the *content* of the arts, especially their religious content. Like many later (and earlier) religious reformers, he will have his new orthodoxy, utterly different from traditional Greek religion, rigorously enforced throughout the society. It is the next stage of the discussion, concerned with the *manner* of poetic performance, that will justify a total ban on tragedy and comedy (and ultimately, Homer too).

But already it is clear that the norms for art in the ideal city will reshape the whole culture. Students of Plato are sometimes told they need not be shocked by the censorship advocated in *Republic* II-III, because its target is the education of young Guards, and any responsible parent today keeps watch on the entertainment and reading-matter of young children.[10] Certainly, the proposals are made for the sake of the young. But Plato's insight is that if you are concerned about the souls of the young, it is no good simply laying down rules for parents and teachers, or agreeing to keep sex and violence off the TV screen until after 9:00 P.M. His conclusion: for the sake of the young, the entire culture must be purged.[11]

The text makes this quite plain. The stories which must not be told to very young children by nurses and mothers (377c; cf. 381e) should not be heard anywhere in the city (378b;

---

[10] Nehamas, "Imitation," pp. 50–53.

[11] So Halliwell, "Two Critiques," pp. 316–17. This is not quite the same as treating adults as though they too were children (paternalism as diagnosed by Annas, *Introduction*, pp. 85–86). Better to say (with Ferrari, "Plato and Poetry," pp. 113–14) that Plato is concerned for the childlike element that lives on in the adult soul.

cf. 378d) — or if at some ritual they have to be told, the audience should be kept as few as possible (378a).[12] Conversely, once we have the right kind of stories for the very young, we will compel the poets to tell them the same kind when they grow older (378d). The norms about the representation of divinity apply to all poetry, whether epic, lyric, or tragic (379a): epic and tragic metres are primarily used for public occasions, while lyric is for smaller group gatherings like the symposium. And things that must not be said in verse must not be said in prose either,[13] must not be said or heard by anyone in the city, young or old (380bc). They are not fit for the ears of boys *or men* (387b; cf. 390de). Such things are not merely false, but impious (378c, 380c, 381e, 391a), and therefore harmful for anyone to hear (391e). The one mention of schoolteachers is a sharp passage at the very end of book II, referring to some objectionable lines of Aeschylus: "When anyone says such things about the gods, we shall be angry with him, we will refuse him a chorus, and we will not allow teachers to use him for the education of the young" (383c). Nothing is to be put on in the theatre unless it is fit for classroom use afterwards. Plato's message is that culture (παιδεία) should be taken seriously for what it is: education.

Yet telling false, blasphemous, immoral, and passionate stories is not the worst thing a poet can do, in Plato's opinion. Such stories corrupt the young by filling their minds with wrong ideas about matters of great moment. But a more enlightened, grown-up mind, with the aid of philosophy, may come to reject the community's religious narratives, as Socrates does in the *Euthyphro*.[14] Stories as such are something a rational mind can resist, question, and reject. With visual images and likenesses in sound and music,

---

[12] I take the reference to ritual from Adam's note *ad loc.*

[13] For the combination "prose or verse," cf. also 390a, 392ab.

[14] Not just at 6ac, cited above in n. 5. The entire argument is a philosopher's critique of traditional religious ideas and (towards the end) practices: see my "The Impiety of Socrates," *Ancient Philosophy* 17 (1997): 1–12.

resistance is not so easy. The manner of poetic performance is more insidious than the content. Even the best philosophical minds are at risk (605c). To explain why, I must move on to the second stage of Plato's discussion of poetry and try to say what I think Plato means by mimesis.

STAGE 2 OF THE REFORM: MIMESIS AND THE MANNER OF PERFORMANCE

The advanced industrial countries of the West have fewer occasions for community singing than traditional societies, but one that survives is Christmas:

> Once in Royal David's city
> Stood a lowly cattle shed,
> Where a mother laid her baby,
> In a manger for his bed.
> Mary was that mother mild,
> Jesus Christ the little child.

This carol is third-person narrative, all the way through. Listeners *hear about* the birth of Jesus. But when someone reads the Lesson from the Gospel and their voice modulates to express kindness or anger in words that Jesus speaks in the first person or when Bach in his *St. Matthew Passion* has Jesus sing his words in recitative — then it is mimesis. We do not merely hear about the son of God. In a certain sense, we hear *him*. We hear him in the same sense as we see him on the cross in a picture of the Crucifixion.

I have already mentioned that in book X painting is the paradigm that Plato uses to explain the meaning, and the menace, of poetic mimesis. His example is a painted couch, and the point he emphasises is that the picture shows only how the couch appears when viewed from a particular angle — from the side, the front, or some other perspective (598ab). In Figure 2, a symposium by Douris,[15] the couches are seen in two such perspectives: sideways

---

[15] British Museum E49 = ARV² 432.52.

FIGURE 2. Courtesy of the British Museum.

and end-on . Of all the objects that turn up in ancient Greek paintings, it is probably couches (along with cups) that are most often seen from different angles, in a fixed perspective. Christ on the cross is also seen in a fixed perspective. But that does not stop us saying we see him there. Such language is equally appropriate for Douris's symposium.

Its date is 490–80 B.C., a good hundred years before the writing of the *Republic*. It is not particularly naturalistic, and it is certainly not *trompe-l'œil*. You would not, for example, see immediately that the tables have three legs, not four (less wobbly on rough floors). I do not agree with scholars who claim that Plato is concerned only with recent illusionistic painting of his own day.[16] For already at the beginning of the fifth century we encounter pictures — hundreds of pictures, by the Brygos painter, Douris, and many others — in which we see a couch and see it

---

[16] Annas, *Introduction*, pp. 336–40; *contra*, Nehamas, "Imitation," n. 60 (with references to the large literature on the topic); Ferrari, "Plato and Poetry," pp. 127–28.

from a particular point of view. We do not of course see a real couch. But anyone who looks at such a picture will be happy to say, "I see couches and tables, a group of people enjoying a party."

It is the task of the philosophy of art to explain what grounds this way of speaking, why it is not only possible but the correct thing to say in the presence of a wide range of representational painting. My interest here is in what happens when we transfer the same way of speaking to the likenesses of poetry and music.

Back to the *St. Matthew Passion.* As in a rhapsode's recital of Homer, there is a narrator (the Evangelist) to tell the story, and speeches sung in recitative by the different characters. There is also a Chorus, which plays two roles. It is both the jeering voice of the crowd hostile to Jesus and, in the Chorales, it is the voice of the Congregation reacting to the events with sorrow and repentance for what humanity did to the son of God. This dual role expresses rather well the idea I think is fundamental to mimesis, that the audience — in this case, the Congregation — is actually present, in a certain sense, at the events depicted. In a Greek tragedy the Chorus has a similar dual role, both participating in the drama and voicing the audience's reactions. The Athenians did not merely hear about Antigone's conflict with Creon. In a certain sense, they witnessed it.

We may find it easier to speak of seeing Jesus in a picture than of hearing him in Bach's music. Plato relies on the analogy with painting to make his point vivid. But he did not invent the analogy: "Painting is silent poetry, poetry painting that speaks" is a saying of the poet Simonides that Plutarch loved to cite (*Moralia* 17f, 58b, 346f, 748a). And no help is needed when we move to opera, which began as Monteverdi's and others' attempt to recreate the multimedia experience of ancient Greek tragedy, where speech (for the iambic verse) alternated with flute-accompanied recitative (παρακαταλογή) or lyric choruses sung and danced. In opera we do not merely hear the characters as we do in the *St. Matthew Passion.* We also see them. We see them moving, dancing, fighting, dying; not motionless as in painting and sculpture. Another contrast with the *St. Matthew Passion* is the absence of a narrator. Tchaikovsky's *Eugène Onegin* cuts out the narrator whose ironic commentary is crucial to Pushkin's poem, and shows us Tatiana herself in the intimacy of her bedroom, writing the fateful love-letter. Afterwards we see and hear Onegin crushing her hopes. At the end we see and hear Onegin declare his love — too late. It would be ridiculous to refuse to describe the opera-goer's experience in these terms; absurd to insist that all we see and hear are singers playing their parts. As Stanley Cavell said in reply to a parallel suggestion about film, "You might as well tell me that I do not see myself in the mirror but merely see a mirror image of myself." [17]

It is this sense of being present at the events enacted on stage, not merely at the theatrical event of enacting them, that Plato aims to capture, I believe, when he introduces the concept of mimesis. Mimesis is the production of visual and auditory likenesses which give us that sense of actual presence. Let me now display the textual basis for this interpretation.

For the second stage of the discussion of the Guards' musical education in *Republic* II–III (392c ff.), Socrates turns from the content of poetry to the manner of its performance.[18] He introduces a distinction, which at first Adeimantus is slow to grasp, between mimetic and nonmimetic storytelling. I take Adeimantus's initial slowness (392cd, 393d; cf. 394b) as Plato's signal to his readers that the distinction will be new to them. "Mimesis" is of course an ordinary Greek word, meaning "imitation," but the distinction between mimetic and nonmimetic storytelling cuts across

---

[17] Stanley Cavell, *The World Viewed: Reflections on the Ontology of Film*, enlarged ed. (Cambridge, Mass., 1979), p. 213. I borrow his words despite the fact that he is talking about how different film is from other arts.

[18] But the norms governing content are not to be forgotten. They are reaffirmed when the norms governing performance are joined onto them (398b), and when Socrates reaches the norms for attunement and rhythm (398d). The norms are built up layer upon layer, with those regulating content as the foundation.

the more familiar classification by poetic genres. The distinction is probably Plato's innovation.[19]

Nonmimetic storytelling is third-person narrative, as in "Once in Royal David's city" and ancient dithyrambic choral singing (394c).[20] The *Iliad* starts out that way, but at line 17 Chryses, the Trojan priest of Apollo, addresses Agamemnon, Menelaus, and the Greeks, imploring them to release his daughter. The address is in direct speech: "you" and "I" replace the pronouns "they" and "he" of the preceding narrative. Here is how Socrates describes the difference:

> You know then that up to these verses,
>   ". . . and he made prayer to all the Achaeans,
>   But especially to the two sons of Atreus, the marshallers of
> the host," the poet himself is the speaker. He makes no attempt
> to divert our mind into thinking that someone other than him-
> self is speaking. But the following verses he delivers as if he
> were himself Chryses, and he tries his best to make it seem that
> the person speaking is not Homer but the priest, an old man.
> (393ab)

Much more is packed into the concept of mimesis here than results from the change of pronouns. When I read the *Iliad* to my children at home and came to the words of prayer at line 17:

> "Sons of Atreus and the rest of you strong-greaved Achaeans,
> May the gods who dwell on Olympus grant
> That you sack the city of Priam and return safe to your homes;
> But release my dear daughter to me, and accept the ransom,
> Out of awe for Zeus's son Apollo, who strikes from afar"

---

[19] Contrast Adeimantus's familiarity with the work of Damon at 424c (lecture I, n. 74). Contrast also Plato's *Ion*, which does not call it mimesis when Homer speaks the lines of his characters (537ac, 538b, 538e–39b).

[20] [Aristotle], *Problems* XIX 15, 918b 13–29, speaks of dithyramb becoming mimetic at a later stage in its development. The change can be observed already in the fifth century (Bacchylides), yet Plato harks back to the purely narrative, original form. This confirms that he is not just targeting "degenerate" artistic developments of his own day.

I did not put on a quavering voice to make it seem an old man was
speaking. Evidently, Socrates has in view a performance of some
kind, not just reading aloud to an audience. A performance that
involves impersonating an old man or some other character-type.[21]

The performer Socrates talks about is Homer, the poet himself. But he is long dead. What Socrates and Adeimantus are
actually familiar with is rhapsodes reciting at the festival of the
Panathenaea from the official Athenian text, fixed a hundred years
earlier by order of the tyrant Peisistratus. The rhapsode Ion is
about to do just this in the dialogue Plato named after him (*Ion*
530b). But the message of that dialogue is that Ion is a mere
mouthpiece for the poet. The poet's voice speaks through his, as
the Muse speaks through the poet. There is a chain of inspiration,
which Socrates compares to a chain of iron rings suspended one
after another from a magnet, through which the divine power
pulls the audience's emotions this way or that (533d–35a, 535e–
36d). So when Ion speaks, it is the divinely inspired Homer
we hear.

From this point of view, while the rhapsode is not an actor on
stage, he is akin to one (cf. *Rep.* 395a, *Ion* 532d 7, 535e 9–36a 1).
In the *Ion* he is pictured in terms that bring to mind a modern
pop-singer: up on a dais in extravagant clothes before a festival
audience of over 20,000 people, he chants the verse, melodiously
and dramatically, with tears in his eyes during the sad bits (535ce).
The innovation in the *Republic* is Socrates' stress on the way
"Homer" modulates his voice or diction (λέξις) so that it becomes
like that of an old man praying (393c). The poet-performer
"hides himself" (393cd) and does everything he can, within the

---

[21] The emphasis at 393b 2 (πρεσβύτην ὄντα) makes it fairly clear that the
object of impersonation is an old man, or an old priest, not the individual Chryses,
whom the audience has never encountered. It is not only the manner of delivery that
changes when mimesis starts: so also does Homer's vocabulary and other aspects of
style, interestingly investigated by Jasper Griffin, "Homeric Words and Speakers,"
Journal of Hellenic Studies 106 (1986): 36–57.

constraints of the genre,[22] to make it seem that Chryses is present to your ears.

From this introductory example Socrates proceeds to a generalisation that covers visual as well as auditory likenesses. It is mimesis, Socrates says, if the poet likens himself to someone else *either* in voice *or* in ὄχημα (393c; cf. 397b). ὄχημα can refer to gesture, posture, or movements (393c; cf. 397b), including the movements of a dance.[23] This extends the concept of mimesis to the silent miming (as we still call it) of Jean-Louis Barrault in *Les enfants du paradis* or to the dance and music of modern ballet. For a case fulfilling both clauses of the disjunctive generalisation, imagine a performance where not only the rhapsode's voice, but also his gestures, posture, perhaps even some movements, are like those of an old man's supplication. He goes down on his knees (rather stiffly) and stretches out his hands.[24] Chryses seems to be present to our eyes as well as to our ears.

The generalisation still does not provide a definition of mimesis, only a sufficient condition. Socrates will not offer a general explanatory account of mimesis until book X.[25] We have to catch

---

[22] Epic is not the only genre to mix narrative with mimesis (394c). Lyric would be another.

[23] LSJ *sv.* Clear examples of the word extending to movement or action at Aristophanes, *Wasps* 1170–71; Xenophon, *Memorabilia* III 10.5; Plato, *Sophist* 267ac, *Laws* 815a. For dance movements, see *Wasps* 1485, *Laws* 654e ff. Note that σχῆμα is, and should be felt as, the base root of εὐσχημοσύνη.

[24] Difficult to do if he is accompanying himself on a lyre. But rhapsodes are also shown on vases with a staff instead of a lyre. See Hesiod, *Theogony* 30 with 95.

[25] Compare οὐ κατὰ ὅλον at 392d 9 with ὅλως at 595c 7. But book X's general account is a metaphysical explanation (597e: the imitator is the maker of a product at third remove from truth and reality), adding nothing to the conditions for mimesis. At *Sophist* 267a, discussed in lecture III, the conditions given here appear to be necessary as well as sufficient for poetic mimesis. This has interesting implications for the question whether Plato's own dialogues are mimetic. They have been regarded as mimetic since Aristotle, *Poetics* 1447b 11 (for discussion, see Proclus, *in Platonis rempublicam commentarii* 14.15–15.19, L. A. Kosman, "Silence and Imitation in the Platonic Dialogues," in *Oxford Studies in Ancient Philosophy*, supplementary vol. 1992: *Methods of Interpreting Plato and His Dialogues*, ed. James C. Clagge and Nicholas D. Smith, pp. 73–92). But they would meet 393c's criterion for mimesis only when read aloud in a way that made the individual speakers sound

on piecemeal as he adds in new types of example. Next comes
tragedy and comedy, which are entirely mimetic, without any narrative in the poet's own voice (394b). Yet he continues to speak
of the poet as the imitator. Just as Homer speaks through Ion, so
in drama it is the poet who tells the story — through his characters' speeches (394d, 397ab, 398ab; cf. 388c). It is as if the actors,
like the rhapsode, are mere conduits for the poet's own voice.
Euripides speaks the words of Medea, his voice modulating like a
ventriloquist's into that of the (male) actor playing the part.[26]

This way of thinking about actors as extensions of the poet is
taken further when Socrates goes on to say the Guards should not
imitate neighing horses, lowing bulls, the noise of rivers, the roar
of the sea, thunder, hail, axles and pulleys, trumpets, flutes, pan-
pipes, and every other instrument, or the cries of dogs, sheep, and
birds (396b, 397a). Is he talking about some crazy pantomime, in
which people mimic everything under the sun, including axles and
pulleys? Or about the dramatist's use of sound-effects? I suggest
the latter. In Aristophanes' *Frogs* the Chorus croak "Brekekekex,
koax, koax" — after all, they are a chorus of frogs. And in the
Laws (669d), Plato decries "programme" music that imitates the
sounds made by wild animals, *machinery*, and other things. If
the imitator is taken to be the poet-composer rather than the actors
or musicians, then it is Aristophanes himself who makes frog noises,
his voice that modulates into the accompanying music or rumblings
from the thunder-machine offstage.[27]

---

differently. They were so read at Roman symposia, according to Plutarch in a
passage (*Moralia* 711bc) bursting with allusions to *Rep.* III (e.g., ἀμουσίαν καὶ
ἀπειροκαλίαν echoes 403c). This implies that the plain text, unperformed, would
not be mimetic. I suspect the dialogues were written for the mind's eye, not for
physical ears. Would Plato wish to count himself a practitioner of the art of imitation (ἡ μιμητικὴ τέχνη), alongside painters, poets, and sophists? He is careful not
to say that of God (lecture III, n. 31). Certainly, a philosopher is one who imitates
(assimilates their thought to) the Forms (500c). But that is not done by exercising
an *art*.

[26] The same picture in book X, 605cd, quoted in lecture III.

[27] If you find it grotesque, this picture of the poet sprouting extensions of himself and his voice all over the theatre, Plato will be well pleased. By the grotesquery

This interpretation makes it easier to follow the argument. When the issue is raised whether in the ideal city poets should be allowed purely mimetic storytelling, as in tragedy and comedy, Socrates professes not to be sure; he will follow whichever way the argument takes him (394d). Then he asks whether the Guards themselves should be imitative (394e: μιμητικοί). This may sound like a digression away from tragedy and comedy into the Guards' daily life. But it is not a digression if Socrates, as I contend, means to ask whether it would be permissible for the Guards themselves to do what a dramatist does, imitate a multiplicity of characters, *in the way the dramatist does it.* This is not the question whether the Guards should indulge in mimicry at parties, but whether, when free of military duties, they should engage in the poetic "performance" of writing and producing tragedy or comedy, which would involve them in imitating many different characters with no narrative interludes (394e 8–9, 395b 5) in front of a large audience (397a).[28] No doubt Socrates also means that the Guards should not be mimics at a party, nor enjoy acting in plays. They should not imitate any unworthy character, let alone a whole variety of them (395c–96b); they should imitate only characters they wish to emulate in their own lives. But the primary focus of the argument is on the Guards as themselves mimetic storytellers, impersonating many characters both good and bad. Only later does Socrates raise the prospect of a professional dramatist arriving from abroad and seeking admittance (397c–98a).

This interpretation explains why the premise used to outlaw tragedy and comedy is the "one man–one job" principle. In the ideal city each man is to devote himself to the practice of one craft

---

is anticipated by Aristophanes, *Thesmophoriazusae* 130ff., where the tragic poet Agathon assumes in all seriousness the habit and the habits of the women he portrays; at line 156 he calls this mimesis. Note that the disjunctive generalisation has now been extended to cover imitating the sounds of nonhuman things, animate *or* inanimate; originally it meant imitating people, as is shown by the masculine pronoun at 393c 6.

[28] In ancient Athens the poet was also the producer, as we would call it — in Greek, the διδάσκαλος or teacher of it, because he trained the chorus.

only.[29] No craft or skill is needed to sit and watch a play. Some skill is needed for reciting a speech from Euripides. But much more is required to write and produce a play yourself. The Guards' sole job (395a 2: ἐπιτήδευμα), their special craft (395b 9: δημιουργία), is defending the freedom of the city (395bc). Hence they must not even to do what cultivated Athenians often did, *combine* their main pursuit with the writing of tragedies (395a 1–2).[30] (In real-life Athens, Sophocles did it the other way round: he served twice as general.) If it is true, as Socrates claims, that no one can successfully combine two imitative crafts, either as a poet of both tragedy and comedy or as an actor in both (395ab), *a fortiori* no one can successfully combine an imitative craft with a military career (395bc). The argument turns on the exclusive demands each craft makes on its practitioners. It is dramaturgy as a craft, much more than amateur theatricals, that Socrates wants the Guards to avoid, so that they concentrate on developing and practising the skills appropriate to their proper task.[31]

---

[29] But what makes a craft *one* craft rather than several? Some painters also made the pots they painted. Are they in breach of the "one man–one job" principle? It is a weakness of the *Republic* that this question is not addressed, even though the Guards' job is a novelty, not a profession already recognized in current nomenclature. The question is not taken up until the *Statesman*.

[30] Aristotle's *Poetics* was written for such people.

[31] The only scholar I know to have countenanced the possibility that dramaturgy is Socrates' primary target, rather than reciting, acting in, or watching plays, is H. Koller in his fascinating, yet frustrating, book *Der Mimesis in der Antike: Nachahmung, Darstellung, Ausdruck* (Bern, 1954), p. 17; in the end, he leaves the question open. Halliwell, "Two Critiques," pp. 321–22, asserts that 394de makes an abrupt transition from poet to audience. The objection is that nowhere in the *Republic* is it said or hinted that watching a play is or involves imitation. Even when book X speaks of the audience identifying with a character on stage, the imitator is the poet, not the audience (605cd, quoted in lecture III). Christopher Janaway, *Images of Excellence: Plato's Critique of the Arts* (Oxford, 1995), p. 96, wants it both ways: "You would take in Homer's depiction of Achilles either by seeing a rhapsode declaim the part on stage or by reciting and thereby enacting the part yourself." The objection still holds. A better view is that of Ferrari, "Plato and Poetry," p. 116: "The Guardians are to *perform* this poetry; imitation is as much what they do as it is what the poets do." My interpretation changes the emphasis. Imitation is first and foremost what the Guards would do *as dramatic poets*. Their reciting speeches from Euripides is of secondary importance, banned by implication rather than the main line of argument.

In itself, this is not an argument for banning tragedy and comedy altogether. There are lots of things the Guards must not do which, nevertheless, someone in the ideal city has to have the skill to do: pottery and painting, for example. But the "one man–one job" principle can be reapplied to block the suggestion that, provided he made tragedy or comedy (not both — 395ab) his specialty, a professional dramatist could be admitted into the city. The ideal city is like a symphony orchestra, in which each member plays just one instrument, so that together they create a beautiful whole called "Kallipolis" (527c). The dramatist is a walking-talking-singing-trumpeting-thundering subversion of the "one man–one job" principle responsible for this happy result. Not only must no Guard produce plays, but if a professional dramatist turns up at the city gate and asks to present his works, he will be treated as if he were a one-man band at the street corner asking to join the Berlin Philharmonic. It is not even lawful ($\theta\acute{\epsilon}\mu\iota\varsigma$) for such a multiplex personality to grow up within the ideal city, let alone for one to be let in (398a).

POETRY AND POLITICS

You may object that a professional dramatist does not really exhibit the multiple personality disorder Socrates ascribes to him. He only seems to do so. Plato knows this very well; in book X he will insist on it. But he also knows that "imitations, if continued from youth far into life, settle down into habits and [second] nature in one's body, voice, and thought" (395d). In John Banville's novel *The Untouchable*, a young recruit to the British Secret Service MI 5, out on his first assignment and moving in to detain the spy for questioning, "narrows his eyes as the thrillers had taught him to do";[32] by the time he retires, that eye-movement will be second nature to him (thereby proving the realism of the next generation of thrillers). Nothing is easier than to fall into the atti-

[32] John Banville, *The Untouchable* (London, 1997), p. 370.

tudes and outlook, even the accents, of one's friends and associates. Imitation may indeed have consequences. It is not a thing to take up lightly, still less to make a profession of. Some film stars have been said to lack a stable self of their own, to live only in the public appearance of a bundle of different roles. Given Plato's conceit of the actors as so many extensions of the poet, for him it is the dramatist who is like that. Not a person who will contribute to the austerely civilized life of Kallipolis.

At this stage, then, Plato's objection is to the dramatist rather than to the drama. His ban on dramaturgy (amateur or professional) is not primarily due to concern about what will happen to the souls of Guards who recite speeches from Euripides or act in his plays, nor to worries about Euripides' effect on the souls of his audience; this will be discussed in book X. In book III the decision is political. Euripides is an undesirable character to have around; so are politicians and military men who write plays in their spare time.[33] Plato here is like someone who would ban rock music not because of its heavy beat and racy words, but because of the singers' life-style. Or the French laws which until 1789 refused actors the right to legal marriage and burial in hallowed ground.[34] And beware of politicians (like Tony Blair and Bill Clinton) who play a musical instrument.

Contemporary readers would be sensitive to the political dimension of Plato's decision. Athenian tragedy and comedy were intensely democratic institutions, both in ways they were organized and in their physical presence. During the Great Dionysia, 1,200 citizens — 700 men plus 500 adolescents — took part in the choral singing and dancing of the various competitions (tragedy, comedy, dithyramb). Under Pericles' cheap ticket scheme, even the poorest of the rest could join the audience, which was further

---

[33] Plato's kinsman, the tyrant Critias, wrote tragedies.

[34] See M. Barras, *The Stage Controversy in France from Corneille to Rousseau* (New York, 1933), pp. 10, 174–85; wider vistas in Jonas Barish, *The Anti-Theatrical Prejudice* (Berkeley, Los Angeles, and London, 1981). The impropriety of acting is a major theme in Jane Austen's *Mansfield Park*.

swollen by visitors from the empire and abroad, reaching a total of between ten and fourteen thousand people. A big event, for which ultimate responsibility lay with the Assembly.[35] Only living poets could enter the competitions. But after the death of Aeschylus, the Assembly voted — it was an exceptional honour — to allow his plays to be produced, outside the competition, by anyone who wished. On a later occasion, the political advice in the "parabasis" of Aristophanes' *Frogs* of 405 B.C. so pleased the Athenians that the Assembly passed a decree of commendation, awarding him a wreath and instructing the archon to grant a chorus to anyone who wished to produce the play a second time.[36] This too was exceptional, but it is worth noting that the *Frogs* is itself the staging of a debate, before the assembled people of Athens, about whether Aeschylus or Euripides would benefit the city most if one of them could be brought back from Hades. It was only in the fourth century that the restaging of old, now "classic," plays became common, and that required a deliberate political decision to enlarge the festival.

Thus concern for the quality of poetry sponsored by the state was not a new and dastardly idea of Plato's. It was a concern shared by the Athenian democracy. And their decisions could be savage. When Phrynichus presented a tragedy about the Persian capture of Miletus in 494 B.C., the audience was so upset by this vivid reminder of the recent misfortunes of their friends that they fined the poet and forbade any future performance of his play (Herodotus VI 21). In oligarchic Sparta, on the other hand, there were choral festivals but no theatre. Plato would see this as the better political choice. If the link between theatre and democracy is not explicit in book III of the *Republic*, elsewhere the connection is loud and clear.

---

[35] A comprehensive account of the management of the various dramatic festivals may be found in Pickard-Cambridge, *Dramatic Festivals*, part II.

[36] For the evidence and its interpretation, see Kenneth Dover, *Aristophanes' Frogs*, edited with introduction and commentary (Oxford, 1993), pp. 73–75.

Book VI includes a discussion of what is likely to happen if, in a nonideal state like Athens, a truly philosophic nature is born, capable of becoming one of the philosopher-rulers of the ideal city. Would the young man escape the corrupting influence of the culture under which he grows up? The chances are small, says Socrates (492ad). Think of the impression made on a really talented soul by the applause and booing of mass gatherings in the Assembly, the courts (an Athenian jury was not twelve good men and true, but several hundred and one), *theatres*, or military camps. Is not the young man likely to end up accepting the values of the masses and becoming a character of the same sort as the people he is surrounded by? A democratic culture does not nurture reflective, philosophical understanding. Mass gatherings set the standards of goodness, justice, and beauty, in painting, in music (where "music" includes poetry and drama), and in politics (493bd). Plato knows all about democratic control of the general quality of the culture; in the *Laws* (701a) he will call it "theatrocracy." His vitriolic denunciation of the mass media of his age argues for rejecting democratic control in favour of his own, authoritarian alternative.

Even stronger is the claim at the end of the *Republic* VIII that tragedy both encourages and is encouraged by the two lowest types of constitution, democracy and tyranny (568ad). Note once again the interactive model of cultural change. As in a bad marriage, playwright and polity bring out the worst in each other. Each indulges the other's ways.

So what occasions for the performance of poetry will remain in the ideal city, after the dramatists have been turned away at the gate? The Guards' musical education will include dance (412b), which usually implies singing too. They will eat, as if they were permanently on campaign, in common messes;[37] this Spartan practice implies sympotic drinking after the meal and much singing of lyric poetry. The famous warning against innovation in music

---

[37] Lecture I, n. 36.

makes it clear that new songs are allowed, provided they are in the same old style (424bc).[38] Delphi will be invited to prescribe rules for religious ceremonies (founding temples, sacrifices, burials, etc.: 427bc, 540bc), all of which in the Greek world would involve singing hymns and other poetry. Hymns are an important element also in the ideal city's annual breeding festivals. "Our poets" will compose verse and music appropriate to the forthcoming unions (459e–60a). Again, at sacrifices and "all other such occasions" there will be hymns (i.e., songs of praise) to honour men and women who have distinguished themselves in battle (468de). Like Heroes of the Soviet Union, the good will be constantly extolled in public — to reward them and hold up models for everyone else.

This list is enough to show that poetry — the right sort of poetry — will be a pervasive presence in the life of the warrior class. *Republic* X sums it up as "nothing but hymns to the gods and encomia for the good" (607a), yet the occasions for these will be plentiful enough to keep the poets of the ideal city busy. In book II Adeimantus complained that no poet has yet sung adequately of justice as the greatest good a soul can have within it (366e). Perhaps the poets of the ideal city will manage better. Although it is often said that Plato banished poets and poetry altogether, this is simply not true.[39] For the most part, however, the list just given is merely a list, which I have put together from scattered remarks. No detail is given about how the various ceremonies will proceed, nor about their frequency (the Athenians had around 120 festival days a year).[40] Worse, phrases like "hymns to

---

[38] At least, I think it is clear, *pace* Nehamas, "Imitation," n. 21. Besides, encomia of the good (see below) will require new songs for the deeds of each generation.

[39] The reasoning behind this widespread view is countered in lecture III. Meanwhile, the references in the previous paragraph are enough to refute the claim of Nehamas, "Imitation," p. 53 with n. 22, that after books II–III there is no reference to poetry as a component in the life of the ideal city. Book III ends at 417b; my list extends into IV and V.

[40] A festival with animal sacrifice is the main occasion for eating meat, which the Guards must do (559ab, cited in lecture I, no. 36). This is a world without

the gods" may suggest the wrong sort of detail to a modern reader. The Greek ὕμνος covers a variety of forms more interesting than the hymns we are used to. The *Homeric Hymn to Hermes*, for example, is an engaging narrative, nearly 600 lines long, with lots of mimesis, about the birth and impudent tricks of the robber god. Equally, any Greek reader would expect "encomia of the good" to include tales of their noble deeds, as recommended by Xenophanes. Adventure stories will often be the order of the day.

One of the occasions for poetry does receive fuller treatment — the symposium.[41] Book III's discussion of poetry reaches its climax with a set of norms for the symposium. This has not been noticed, partly because Plato expects readers to recognize the familiar setting without being told. Another reason is that in the past scholars have preferred not to wonder why the discussion of poetry ends by imposing austere limits to homoerotic sex.

But of that, more shortly. We are still in the second stage of the discussion of poetry, dealing with the manner of poetic performance. Drama is not all the Guards are deprived of. Their epic recitals will be very unlike those the ancients were used to. No rhapsodic display, and much less speechifying than in the *Iliad* and *Odyssey*. The story will be mostly plain narrative,[42] interrupted by the occasional stretch of mimesis. The mimesis will be largely restricted to auditory and visual likenesses of a good person behaving steadfastly and sensibly (396cd: ἀσφαλῶς τε καὶ ἐμφρόνως).[43]

---

refrigerators: the whole animal is consumed immediately, by a large gathering of people.

[41] Hymns to a god are appropriate there too: Xenophanes, frag. 1 (quoted in lecture I), Plato, *Symposium* 176a.

[42] As illustrated by Socrates at 393d–94a. Being no poet, Socrates speaks in prose, but Dennis Feeney points out to me that Plato and his readers would recall Achilles' poetic version of the same narrative at *Iliad* I 365 ff. That is Homer imitating Achilles narrating. Socrates' narrative of the events, however, because it is prose, should not in my view (*pace* Ferrari, "Plato and Poetry," pp. 115–16; Kosman, "Silence," pp. 76–77) be read as Socrates imitating Homer. No one listening would say that Homer seemed to be present to their ears, as he is when narrating *in propria persona*.

[43] Note the disjunction "speech or action" (λέξιν τινὰ ἢ πρᾶξιν) at 396c 6.

The impressiveness of this steadfast, sensible behaviour will be reinforced by the speaker's even delivery (λέξις). There will be little variation in his voice, and the accompanying music will stick to a single mode and a single rhythm (397bc).[44] Even good people are struck down by disease, fall in love, or get drunk, but mimesis of such events is to be very sparing. The other side of the coin is that a villain may do the odd good deed: mimesis of that is admissible, but it is not likely to happen often. The final exception is that poets may imitate bad characters in jest, to scoff at them (396de).

Thus far, Chryses' prayer would survive, but not Agamemnon's angry, unrelenting response at line 26:

> Old man, let me not find you by the hollow ships,
> Either lingering now or coming back later —
> You may find that your staff and the god's ribbons will not
>   protect you.
> The girl I will not give up; sooner will old age come upon her
> In my house at Argos, far from her fatherland,
> Plying the loom and sharing my bed.
> Now go, don't rile me, and you will go more safely.

Already it seems that the *Iliad* will have to stop as soon as it has started. But Plato delays until book X the shocking news that Homer will be banished as well as the dramatists.

But remember that book II implies that a purged tragedy will still be allowed. Tragedy and comedy are not explicitly banned until book III. Plato deals out the pain in measured doses, allowing his readers to get used to one shock as preparation for the next.[45] No objections have been raised to mimesis or to poetry in themselves. There will in fact be lots of poetry in the ideal city,

---

[44] Plato here anticipates the third stage of the discussion of poetry: that is the stage where I shall comment on the meaning of "mode" in Greek music.

[45] Already at 394d 7 (quoted at the beginning of lecture III) Socrates drops a hint that more is at risk in the discussion of mimesis than tragedy and comedy.

some of it mimetic. The shock is, how little of it is to be mimetic; and how thoroughly edifying it all has to be.

STAGE 3 OF THE REFORM: MUSICAL TECHNIQUE

The third stage of the discussion deals with the nonvocal side of music: the modes, instruments, and rhythms which make the music in our narrower sense of the word. Socrates' norms in this department are as austere as the norms governing content and performance. Some Bach might scrape by; certainly not Beethoven, Mahler, or Stravinsky.

This is where Plato gives examples of the kinds of mimesis to be permitted. The examples remove all doubt about the answer to the question "What does Plato think is so bad about mimesis?" Nothing — *provided* it is mimesis of a good and temperate (σώφρων) character, the character (we later discover) of which gracefulness in architecture and bodily movement is also a likeness. On the contrary, mimesis has a formative educational role to play in the culture. What you imitate regularly is what you become, so from childhood on the Guards must imitate appropriate models of courage, temperance, and other virtues. These things must become second nature to them (395cd). Just as gracefulness in architecture and bodily movement has a gradual unnoticed influence on the soul of those who grow up in their presence, so too do the mimetic likenesses of the poetry Plato allows for the Guards. The examples to be quoted are designed to illustrate the permitted modes of music, but approriate words are taken for granted. In the songs sung at social and sacred gatherings, both music and verse will imitate the way persons of good character deal with the ups and downs of fortune; in book X we meet the contrasting case of bad mimesis, the way a tragic hero reacts to misfortune.

The musical modes (ἁρμονίαι) under discussion are the ancient alternative to our musical scales. A mode is an attunement — a way of tuning the instrument to certain intervals — which lends a certain character to the tunes that can be played with it. When

Socrates bans all but two modes, the Dorian and Phrygian (398d–99a; cf. 399c), it is somewhat as if he had said, "Scrap all the minor keys, but leave just two of the major keys." Here are Socrates' examples of good mimesis:[46]

> "Leave me that mode [ἁρμονία] which would fittingly imitate the tones and cadences of a brave man engaged unsuccessfully in warfare or any other enforced endeavour,[47] who meets wounds, death, or some other disaster but confronts it steadfastly with endurance, warding off the blows of fortune. And leave me another mode for a man engaged in unforced, voluntary activities of peace. He may be persuading someone of something or entreating them, either praying to a god or teaching and admonishing a human being. Or, contrariwise, he may himself be attending to another's entreaty, teaching, or attempt to change his opinion. In either case he does what he is minded to do without arrogance, acting throughout and accepting the outcome with temperance and moderation.[48] Just these two modes, the one enforced, the other voluntary, which will best imitate the tones of brave men in bad fortune and of temperate men in good — leave me these." (399ac)

If it was always these two types of song that we heard when we turned on the radio or went out to a social gathering, our culture would be very different. But not necessarily boring. Nothing stops a poet weaving the permitted types of mimetic display into a gripping third-person narrative, short or long; nothing stops a story including the imitation of more than one good character. A narrative of comradeship and dignified courage before death in a concentration camp could well satisfy Socrates' norms for what he calls "enforced endeavour." We might even be sympathetic to the

---

[46] My translation of the extraordinary syntax of the passage is guided by Adam's note *ad loc.*, especially on the chiasmus at the end.

[47] By "enforced," Socrates means that, unlike actual Greek states, the ideal city will not go to war unless it is necessary and unavoidable. The contrast "enforced"–"voluntary" reappears in Aristotle's discussion of the voluntary at *Eudemian Ethics* II 8.

[48] τε . . . καί shows that the adverbs modify both participles.

idea that it would be indecent to give the Nazis any significant speaking parts.

The second type of permitted mimesis is for "voluntary" activities. In Oliver Sachs's *Awakenings* a doctor persuades the hospital authorities to let him try a new treatment on patients sunk in a permanent catatonic trance. They are unable to react to people or the world around. This treatment brings the patients to life again, but only for a while. The doctor accepts the outcome with temperance and moderation. He did what he could; medical science made a modest advance. It is an engaging, sympathetic story. But if you want more action, Plato has nothing against adventure stories. Heroism in military and civil life is exactly what this education is designed to promote.

So do not think of the artistic culture of Plato's city as boring. Austere, yes; an even-toned, calm expressiveness prevails. Plato's word for it is "simplicity" (404be, 410a, 547e: ἁπλότης). Growing up in such a culture would be like growing up in the presence of sober people all of brave and temperate character.

STAGE 4 OF THE REFORM: THE MATERIAL AND SOCIAL SETTING

But the ideal city already ensures, so far as is humanly possible, that the young grow up in the presence of sober people all of good and temperate character. Why worry about likenesses, the cultural icons, if kids are already surrounded by the real thing in flesh and blood? Plato's answer is that, even in the ideal city, where the family and private property have been abolished, the people you know are only one part of the culture. When the influence of human role models is at odds with the predominant cultural icons, there is a risk of change. It is not just that multiplicity and variety are bad in themselves. That is indeed at the heart of Plato's objection to Homeric epic and Athenian drama, which revel in variety and the clash of different characters. But the main point is that change from the ideal is change for the worse (cf. 380e–81c). To avoid change as long as possible, the entire culture must be in harmony both with the people you meet in life and with those you know from poetry. That is why the discussion of musical poetry leads into the passage I began from about gracefulness in architecture, clothing, and everything that craftsmen make. A graceful material environment will ensure that the young are always and everywhere in the presence of likenesses (401a: μιμήματα) of the same good and temperate character as the human beings whose lives and stories they know.[49] The entire culture unites in harmonious expression of the best that human beings can be.

A musical education which forms a sensibility able to recognize gracefulness, and respond to it as an image of good and temperate character, also lets you recognize, and respond to, other images of good character — images of courage, liberality, high-mindedness (402ac).[50] A Guard so educated, and old enough to apprehend at least some of the reasons why these are images of goodness (cf. 402a),[51] is ready to fall in love. His education will ensure that the younger male comrade he favours has beauty of character to match the beauty of his physical appearance. Love (ἔρως) of such a person is the goal and consummation of musical education. Socrates' last word on poetry in book III is a summons to erotic desire: "Music should end in the love of the beautiful" (403c).[52]

---

[49] There is no need to suppose that the craftsmen who make the various artefacts are themselves persons of sobriety. They work to the orders of the rulers, who are the *users* (in the sense of book X, 601d) of the material culture. The rulers use everything to educate the young and maintain the ethos of the ideal society.

[50] High-mindedness (μεγαλοπρέπεια) in a young Guard prefigures the high-mindedness which distinguishes the thought (διάνοια) of the philosopher-ruler who contemplates all time and all being (486a; cf. 503c).

[51] The analogy at 402ab with learning one's letters implies that "the coming of reason" (402a) is a fairly low-level achievement, far removed from a philosophical understanding of the Forms; that only comes years later, to a select few. I agree with Ferrari, "Plato and Poetry," pp. 120–22, and others that the εἴδη of temperance, courage, etc., at 402c are not transcendent Platonic Forms.

[52] Curiously echoed in an etymology at Plato, *Cratylus* 406a: the Muses and music in general are so called from μῶσθαι (to desire, pursue) and search and philosophy.

Socrates has now moved from the material environment to the social setting for musical poetry. The symposium is not the only gathering where musical poetry is performed, but it is the one most relevant to love. Among the musical modes banned earlier, at stage 3 of the reform, were certain soft "sympotic" modes, which encourage drunkenness (398e); in the ideal city, as in Sparta, drunkenness is forbidden (403e). But the rule presupposes they will drink wine. No Greek equated sobriety with abstinence. After the meal in their Spartan-style common messes (ξυσσίτια), the Guards will drink in convivial moderation, like the inhabitants of the primitive city of book II. (We have actual figures for Spartan wine consumption: Sparta was famous for its sobriety, yet their daily ration was well over our driving limit.)[53] And the symposium is the main social occasion for dalliance: the couch is wide enough for two.[54] In the ideal city, the lover is permitted "to kiss and be with" his beloved, and "to touch him as if he were a son, for honourable ends, if he persuade him" — but nothing further, on pain of being stigmatized for being "unmusical and unable to enjoy beauty properly" (403bc). The combination of wine, music, and homoerotic love at the symposium was widely used in the Greek world (not only in Sparta) to forge bonds of loyalty and comradeship among those who fight for the city. Plato is adapting this institution to the austerely controlled ethic of Kallipolis.

Later, when readers have recovered from the shock of being told in book V that in this city women, too, are to be warriors and rulers, equally with men, they learn that those who distinguish themselves on campaign (which would include symposia in camp on beds of leaves)[55] will exchange kisses with everyone else. Indeed, they will have an unrefusable right to kiss anyone they

---

[53] Oswyn Murray, "War and the Symposium," in Slater, *Dining*, 91; his source is the amount the Athenians agreed to allow for supplying the Spartans trapped on Sphacteria during the Peloponnesian War (Thucydides IV 16).

[54] Cf. Plato, *Symposium* 175a–76a.

[55] Cf. lecture I, n. 40 on στιβάδες.

desire (ἐρῶν), male *or female*,[56] and they will be given more frequent opportunities to take part in the breeding festivals (468c).
The better you are, the more you can breed. Heterosexual desire,
like homosexual, is harnessed to the ends of the city.

RETROSPECT ON THE REFORM IN BOOKS II–III

Looking back over this long discussion of musical poetry, we
should be struck by how widely it ranged. Starting with religion,
ending with sex, taking in architecture and embroidery by the way,
Socrates has broached numerous issues that affect the ethos of society. All were woven around the central thread of musical poetry,
precisely because this for Plato is the main vehicle of cultural
transmission, the main determinant of the good or bad character
of the city.

In recent years, we have seen the ethos of British society go
through a quite dramatic change as a result of the Thatcher years.
The change was not planned in every detail from above. But there
was a deliberate, concerted effort by the Conservative government
to purge the prevailing values and substitute the values of "enterprise" and the spirit of the free market. In the political arena,
whether national or local (including universities), it became increasingly difficult to appeal to the idea that the better-off should
contribute to the welfare of the disadvantaged for the overall
good of the community. This attack on the values of community
was pursued in every area of life, even in areas (like universities)
where talk of "the market" is at best a metaphor. Metaphors and
images, as Plato knew better than anyone, are potent weapons,
especially in the wrong hands. If there are lessons for today in
Plato's discussion of musical poetry in books II–III, the unit of
comparison I would propose is not the details of censorship in the

[56] This extra rule is contributed by Glaucon, whose keen interest in homoerotic
relationships is remarked upon at 402e and 474d–75a. Another distinguishing feature of Glaucon is his knowledge of music (398e 1; cf. 548e 4–5). In the light of
403c, just quoted, we may see his being ἐρωτικός and his being μουσικός as connected: a compliment from Plato to his older brother.

carefully guarded, closed world of the ideal city, but Plato's concern for what he calls the ethos of society. Plato, like Mrs. Thatcher, saw this as a prime political responsibility. Democrats can only undo the damage done to our society by the excesses of market ideology if we find democratic alternatives for fostering a better ethos in society at large.

Most of us do not share Plato's confidence that objectively correct answers to these questions exist, and that, given the right education, men and women of talent can come to know what the answers are. Even if we did have that confidence, we would not think it right to impose our answers on everybody else. Democracy, both ancient and modern, puts a high value on individual choice and autonomy. That complicates the task. A further complication is that our culture values innovation and originality: after the initial shock, we welcome the new ways of seeing and hearing brought to us by a Picasso or Stravinsky; we enjoy the sparkle of sophisticated advertisements. But none of this relieves us of responsibility for thinking about what we can do to improve the world in which our children grow up.

LECTURE III. FAREWELL TO HOMER
AND THE HONEYED MUSE

The Reform Resumed in Book X:
Homer as the First Tragedian

"We must agree whether to let our poets imitate when they tell a story, or imitate for some parts of the story but not for others (in which case we must agree where they may imitate and where not), or whether we should not let them imitate at all.

"I divine," said Adeimantus, "that you are considering whether or not to admit tragedy and comedy into the city."

"Possibly," I said, "but possibly I have in mind even more than these. I don't myself know yet, but we must go wherever the wind of the argument blows us." (394d)

Already in book III Socrates hints that the discussion of mimesis may go beyond a ban on tragedy and comedy. There may be more pain to come.[1] But it is not until *Republic* X that Socrates braces himself[2] to denounce Homer openly as "the first teacher[3] and instigator of all these beauties of tragedy" (595bc). If Homer is the master of tragic mimesis, he too should be expelled.

Socrates is sorry the argument has carried him so far. He has loved and revered Homer since boyhood. But, he says, a man should not be honoured above the truth (595bc). This is often taken as a personal statement of regret by Plato.[4] I see it as Plato's warning that the most enlightened philosopher (Socrates) will still carry what Zeno, founder of Stoicism, called the "scars" of his upbringing in an ordinary, nonideal city.[5] He will feel the spell of Homer even after he has foresworn him for good (607ce). "Great is the struggle, dear Glaucon, greater than it seems" (608b). That struggle is enacted in the first half of book X,[6] where Socrates explains why in existing cities like Athens it is dangerous, even for the most morally secure individual, to attend the theatre, or Ion's performance of Homer at the Panathenaea. The mimesis you witness there is a threat to the constitution ($\pi o \lambda \iota \tau \epsilon \acute{\iota} a$) of your soul (605bc, 608ab).

The work we are reading is not a *Republic* in any antiroyalist sense of the word; still less is it the German *Die Staat*. The title

---

[1] Cf. Jowett and Campbell's edition (Oxford, 1894), *ad loc.*: "an anticipation of the condemnation of epic poetry in Book X." Adam's vehement denial of this view (*ad* 394d and 595a) is mere assertion. Shorey's comment is: "This seems to imply that Plato already had in mind the extension of the discussion in the tenth book to the whole question of the moral effect of poetry and art."

[2] Note the emphatic "I must speak out" (595b 9, repeated 595c 3: $\dot{\rho}\eta\tau\acute{\epsilon}o\nu$).

[3] Besides its ordinary connotation, "teacher" ($\delta\iota\delta\acute{a}\sigma\kappa a\lambda os$) is also used for the poet as producer of his play (lecture II, n. 28). Both meanings should be felt here.

[4] So Adam *ad loc.*, and numerous others.

[5] Seneca, *De Ira* I 16.7: "As Zeno says, the soul of the wise man too, even when the wound is healed, shows the scar. He will feel certain hints or shadows of emotion, but will be free of the emotions themselves."

[6] The first 13 Stephanus pages down to 608b. From 608c to the end is almost exactly another 13 pages.

πολιτεία means "constitution." An ancient reader would at first be put in mind of works like *The Constitution of the Spartans* by Plato's kinsman, the tyrant Critias. But Plato's πολιτεία is not the constitution *of* any people or any actual place. It is the ideal constitution, or better: constitutional order as such, which may be realized in souls as well as cities. This was not apparent when musical poetry was discussed in books II–III. It became apparent when the parallel between tripartite city and tripartite soul was developed in book IV. It was reinforced later by the fusion of city with soul in books VIII–IX.[7] In between came Sun, Line, and Cave, the grand epistemological and metaphysical theories of books V–VII. The structure of *Republic* II–X is, in broad outline, a ring composition: poetry/city and soul/Forms/city and soul/poetry.[8] This should help us see that book X does more than vindicate the earlier decision to ban tragedy and comedy (595a). By returning to discuss musical poetry in the light of the psychological, epistemological, and metaphysical theories introduced since book III, it shows that those theories have a practical significance even if the ideal city is not founded in our lifetime. They provide the antidote (595b: φάρμακον) or counter-charm (608a: ἐπῳδή) to mimesis. A proper understanding of what mimesis is, and what it does, can safeguard the constitution of a philosopher's soul. If Homer endangers the social order of the ideal city, he is no less of a threat to the psyche of an individual who aspires to virtue and wisdom.

Accordingly, my strategy with book X will be to read it as continuing book III's discussion at a higher level. Socrates in book X appears both as censor, adding more poetry to the proscription lists, and as a theoretician concerned to set the entire programme for reforming the culture in a higher, more philosophical perspec-

---

[7] On the fusion of soul with city, see lecture I: "First Glance Ahead: The Divided Soul in Book X.

[8] Here I am indebted to Reviel Netz. Book I stands outside the structure as "prelude" (357a) to the whole.

tive. But readers should be warned that this is a controversial approach.[9] It is often held that book X's treatment of mimesis is different from, even consistent with, book III's. Two main questions arise. Does book X ban more mimesis than book III? Is book X's concept of poetic mimesis different from book III's? Most scholars nowadays answer "Yes" to both questions. I shall answer "No." But I shall accept that book X bans more poetry than books II–III — more than is usually recognized. To defend these views, I shall need more scholarly exegesis than before, more wrestling with the text. Plato's discussion is so provocative that it can be hard to keep a cool head and read him accurately.

DOES BOOK X BAN MORE MIMESIS THAN BOOK III?

Banning Homer is obviously banning more poetry than book III. But, as just seen, the ban is the making explicit of a shocking proposal already prepared for there. Once Homer is cast as the first maestro of tragic mimesis, no further justification is needed. Socrates says (595ab) he will vindicate book III's decision by showing the damage ($\lambda \acute{\omega} \beta \eta$) that poetic mimesis does to the thought ($\delta \iota \acute{\alpha} \nu o \iota \alpha$) of its audience.[10] This promises a new and different justification from before.[11] But putting Homer under the same ban

[9] Annas, *Introduction*, 335, describes book X as "an excrescence . . . full of oddities"; Halliwell, "Two Critiques," p. 325, echoes earlier scholars' description of it as a "coda" or "appendix" to the main work. A tiny point of grammar confirms that book X was written to be read as part of the main body of the work: the very first line (595a 1) contains a pronoun, $\alpha \mathring{v} \tau \mathring{\eta} s$, whose reference lies in book IX. It has to be traced back via $\tau \alpha \acute{v} \tau \eta s \; \mu \acute{o} \nu \eta s$ (592b 4) $= \alpha \mathring{v} \tau \acute{\eta} \nu$ (592b 1) $=$ the city founded in this discussion (592a 10–11). Had book X been conceived as a distinct, appendix-like unit, Plato would surely have written $\pi \epsilon \rho \grave{\iota} \; \tau \mathring{\eta} s \; \pi \acute{o} \lambda \epsilon \omega s$, not $\pi \epsilon \rho \grave{\iota} \; \alpha \mathring{v} \tau \mathring{\eta} s$, which the next line clarifies as $\tau \mathring{\eta} \nu \; \pi \acute{o} \lambda \iota \nu$. We happen to have inherited the *Republic* in ten books, but an arrangement in six books is also recorded, and there is no ground for tracing either division back to Plato himself: see Henri Alline, *Histoire du Texte de Platon* (Paris, 1915), pp. 14–18.

[10] On the meaning of "thought" ($\delta \iota \acute{\alpha} \nu o \iota \alpha$), see lecture I: "First Glance Ahead: The Divided Soul in Book X."

[11] I argued in lecture II ("Poetry and Politics") that book III's ban on tragedy was not motivated by its effects on the audience.

(595bc) does not imply that any new *kind* of mimesis is proscribed. To give a different justification is not the same as justifying a different rule.

The question to ask is whether book III's good mimesis is still allowed — the imitation of a virtuous person behaving steadfastly and sensibly in good fortune or bad. Socrates reminds us of this when he brings back the contrast between enforced and voluntary endeavour (603c).[12] In book III he talked about imitating the right way to respond to good and bad fortune,[13] here he will discuss imitations of the wrong way to respond. If he has nothing further to say about good mimesis, the obvious explanation is that his view of it is unchanged. But scholars have seized on a single passage at the very beginning of book X, claiming that it bans all mimesis, even mimesis of good characters. Looking back on the long argument about justice and happiness, completed at the end of book IX, Socrates says:

> "There are a great many things about the city[14] which assure me that we gave it a sound foundation, and especially, I think, in the matter of poetry."
> "What do you have in mind?" said Glaucon.
> "Our refusing to admit such poetry as is imitative [ποιήσεως... ὅση μιμητική]. Now that we have distinguished the different parts of the soul, it has become even clearer that, quite definitely, it should not be admitted." (595a)

Book X goes further than book III if, *but only if*, the phrase "such poetry as is imitative" covers all *individual* mimetic utterances, including the good ones permitted before. In logical symbolism, Socrates' statement is of the form

(x) If x is poetry & x is mimetic, away with x!

[12] Reading, with Burnet, Ast's ἦν at 603c 7: "*Did* we find anything else but these?" (Shorey; many translators ignore the past tense).

[13] Lecture II: "Stage 3 of the Reform: Musical Technique."

[14] In context, just after the reference at the close of book IX to the philosopher founding in his own soul the city laid up in the heavens (592b), this means the city in that soul as well as the ideal city.

What is the range of the variable?

There are two ways to avoid concluding that the phrase covers every individual mimetic utterance. First, you can fix on the word "imitative" (μιμητικός) and say that in book III (394e–95a) it meant "multiply imitative." It applied to people who impersonate many different characters, good and bad—as Euripides and Homer do, but not an author who only goes in for good mimesis. On this understanding of μιμητικός, the passage bans nothing that was allowed in book III.[15]

Or you can fix on the range of the variable and say that the word "such" picks out kinds or species of poetry — poetic *genres*. In the divisions of the *Sophist* and *Statesman* one finds ὅσος (in the singular) used to mark off a particular part or species of some wider genus.[16] If "such poetry as is imitative" means "such *kinds* or *genres* as are imitative," the phrase fits precisely the poetry discussed and banned in book X: tragedy (now including Homer) and comedy. Lyric is not a mimetic kind, even though some songs are wholly mimetic[17] and others include mimetic passages. If book X's discussion of mimesis deals only with intrinsically mimetic genres, it is consistent with book III's allowing mimetic interludes in storytelling where the narrator imitates a good character.

Consistency is not just a desirable feature which the principle of charity directs us to seek. Plato himself keeps implying that book X is written to confirm, in the light of the psychology of book IV, the rightness of his earlier norms for poetry. There are numerous back-references: to the psychology of book IV (595a,

---

[15] So Elizabeth Belfiore, "A Theory of Imitation in Plato's *Republic*," *Transactions of the American Philological Society* 114 (1984): 126–27; Ferrari, "Plato and Poetry," pp. 115, 117, 125, followed by Nehamas, "Mass Media," p. 215 with nn. 3, 4.

[16] *Soph.* 219a, 10, 221e 6, 225b 13, *Polit.* 263e 9, 226a 1, 303e 10; cf. ἡ τῆς ποιήσεως μιμητική at *Rep.* 603c 1.

[17] How many of these you count depends on how often you take the pronoun "I" to introduce a voice other than that of the poet. Theognis 257, "I am a beautiful, prize-winning mare . . . ," is clearly mimetic. Some more subtle decisions in Bowie, "Early Greek Elegy," pp. 14–21.

602e–3a, 603d), to the norms governing poetic content (603e), to the banishment of drama in book III (595a, 605b, 607b), to the contrast between enforced and voluntary endeavour (603c). Plato is not usually so insistent on making his readers recall earlier parts of a discussion. Book III did not merely allow, it positively encouraged mimesis of good characters in enforced and voluntary endeavour; such performances, we are told, will be beneficial (398b). If this good mimesis has now become bad, the author of book X ought to alert us to the discrepancy and give some reason for the change. Yet he proceeds as if nothing had changed at all. The onus of proof is on those who would charge him with inconsistency.

There is in fact a perfect match in book III for the phrase ποιήσεως ... ὅση μιμητική: "such poetry as is imitative." At 394bc (referring back to 392d) Socrates said ποιήσεώς τε καί μυθολογίας ἡ μὲν διὰ μιμήσεως ὅλη ἐστίν: "Of poetry and storytelling one kind is entirely through mimesis." The contrast is with stories told in the narrative voice "of the poet himself" (e.g., dithyramb) and with stories told in the mixed style of epic and other genres. In the context ποιήσεως ... ἡ μὲν διὰ μιμήσεως refers specifically to tragedy and comedy. It seems reasonable to propose that book X's phrase ποιήσεως ... ὅση μιμητική picks up tragedy and comedy again by reference to the way they were characterized in the earlier three-part division.[18] There is no reason (yet) to suppose that book X bans more mimesis than book III.

UNDERSTANDING MIMESIS

I said that a proper understanding of what mimesis is, and what it does, can safeguard the constitution of a *philosopher's*

---

[18] For this suggestion I am indebted to Mary-Hannah Jones, "Tragedy and Book X of Plato's *Republic*" (unpublished); it fits well with my suggestion that the variable ranges over genres. She argues against the Ferrari solution that at 394e–95a μιμητικός was applied to *people* who are prone to imitation, not to types of poetry; but this becomes less of an objection if I was right (lecture II) to interpret that passage as about whether the Guards could be dramatists.

soul. Only a philosopher, or someone sympathetic to Platos' philosophy, can benefit from the antidote or counter-charm provided by the theories of books IV–IX. This suggests that the arguments before us will not be aimed at persuading everyone, no matter what opinions they bring to their reading of book X. The arguments aim to convince philosophers and people like Glaucon, who have been persuaded by everything Socrates has said since book II. Plato would be quite unmoved to learn that most readers are outraged by book X. That is what he would expect.

Throughout the *Republic*, Plato tailors his arguments and images to the type of soul they are meant to persuade, in accordance with the rules for a philosophical rhetoric laid down in the *Phaedrus* (271e–72b). Consider the two parallel deductions in book VI, one for Glaucon and one for Adeimantus, of the virtues that will make a philosopher the best person to rule the city. With Glaucon, Socrates proceeds from the high-level, definitional premise (first laid down in book V, 474b–75c) that a philosopher is someone whose passion (ἔρως) is to learn the truth about all unchanging being (485b–87a). Such a person will not care about wealth or other things that corrupt ordinary rulers. The more down-to-earth Adeimantus[19] interrupts to say that this lofty description hardly fits the philosophers we know, most of whom are cranks or rascals (487d). True enough, says Socrates: what you need is an image (εἰκών) — and he launches the image of the Ship of State (487e ff.) to show how different a genuine philosopher would be. That done, he repeats the argument for the virtues of the philosopher-ruler, in terms more suited to Adeimantus's understanding (489e–90e).

The same procedure is used to persuade the multitude to accept philosophic rule (499e–502a). There is hardly any metaphysics, just vague talk (with a suitably devout reference to Homer at 501b) of the philosopher as a semidivine figure, who like a painter will wipe clean the tablet of the city and its people and

---

[19] On the relative levels of Glaucon and Adeimantus, see lecture I, n. 30.

then sketch a new social order with his eye on a divine model.[20] Or take the well-known argument in book V to persuade the lovers of sights and sounds that their mode of thought (διάνοια) cannot be knowledge. It is carefully based on premises that even they will accept.[21] Most important of all, the main ethical argument about justice and happiness is addressed to Glaucon and Adeimantus as sympathetic critics who, unlike Thrasymachus in book I, would *like* to be persuaded that justice makes a better life than injustice (358d, 367b, 368ab).

Some arguments in the *Republic* are designed to persuade a philosophical soul. A good example is the argument in book VII to convince the philosophers that it is just for them to take their turn at ruling, because they owe a debt to the city which provided their privileged education (520ae). This will only work with someone who finds the requirements of justice compelling. So too, I suggest, the arguments about mimesis in book X are guided throughout by the Theory of Forms and will only work with a Platonic philosopher, or with someone like Glaucon who is sympathetic to his brother's philosophy. And for Socrates (whatever the case with Glaucon), the Theory of Forms is not just a set of premises. The Forms are the goal of a passionate desire for abstract, general knowledge. To a mind whose whole outlook and mode of thinking (διάνοια) is shaped by that craving for generality, the insubstantial images of poetry ought to seem an irrelevant distraction. If they still retain a certain allure, that is because Socrates and Glaucon contracted a rival passion (ἔρως) from the culture they grew up in.[22] Only philosophical theory can provide a counter-charm to the mimesis they adored and save them from slipping back into the childish loves of the multitude (607e–8a).

[20] Compare the more philosophical version of the painter analogy given to Glaucon at 484c.

[21] This was established by J. C. Gosling, "Δόξα and Δύναμις in Plato's Republic," *Phronesis* 13 (1968): 119–30.

[22] Mimetic poetry is imaged as a sex object at 603b 1 (ἑταίρα, courtesan) and 608a 5 (παιδικόν, boyfriend).

The other side of the coin is that philosophical theory will only help people like them, not anyone and everyone.

The Platonic Theory of Forms makes its first appearance in the *Republic* at 475e, prefaced by the remark that it would be difficult to explain to anyone but Glaucon. Fittingly, Glaucon is the interlocutor for the metaphysical discussion of poetry in book X, Adeimantus for the less theoretical discussion in books II-III (until Glaucon takes over at stage 3 for the more technical aspects of music). The two together form the intimate audience to whom Socrates addresses the argument of book X (595b: ὡς μὲν πρὸς ὑμᾶς εἰρῆσθαι); he is not trying to win over the type of person who would denounce him to the tragedians and other imitative poets. Glaucon will end by agreeing with everything Socrates has said about poetry; so would anyone — *provided* they accept the premises (608b: ἐξ ὧν διεληλύθαμεν).

Imagine telling book V's lovers of sights and sounds that what enraptures them is at third remove from the truth, because truth and reality reside in transcendent Forms. They will be bemused (cf. 476bc). So will anyone who has not devoted their time to dialectical discussion outside the cave. It is through dialectic that the conviction grows on one that Forms are more real than sensible things. Glaucon agrees: "That is how it would seem to those who are versed in this kind of reasoning" (597a). And if Forms are more real than sensible things, they are far more real than images of sensible things.

We are now ready for book X's account of mimesis:

(1) To imitate is to make something which is "third from the king and the truth." (597e 7)

This is Socrates' and Glaucon's agreed answer to the question "What is mimesis in general?" (595c 7, 597d 10), their definition (599d 3–4: ὡρισάμεθα). But who or what is "the king"?[23] The

---

[23] Solutions to the mystery are canvassed by Adam *ad loc.* with appendix I. The phrase confirms that this discussion is not designed to persuade all and sundry.

"third from nature" (597e 3–4) is not much easier. Only a philosopher familiar with lofty metaphysics could understand such a
definition. Only a philosopher well versed in "our customary
method" (596a) would believe it.

In context, as any reader can see, this definition results from a
survey of makers, each of whom is responsible for a product of
different metaphysical status (597de). God makes the Form of
Couch, the carpenter makes a particular wooden couch, so the
artist who paints a couch in a picture makes a product which is at
third remove (by the Greeks' inclusive reckoning) from the truth
and reality of the Form. If we set aside the Theory of Forms and
the difficult idea of God making the Form of Couch,[24] what remains of the definition is this:

(2) To imitate is to make a likeness or image of something.

(2) uses terms we can all understand to state conditions for anything to count as mimesis. What (1) adds to (2) is a metaphysical perspective on things that satisfy those conditions; it does not
strengthen the requirements for mimesis itself.[25]

(2) is more general than the disjunctive sufficient condition
we met in book III (393c): likening oneself to another in voice
or σχῆμα.[26] To do that is *one* way to make a likeness, turning your
body or voice into a likeness of some other person or thing. But
another way is to paint a picture of something. This parallel between poetry and painting will be crucial to the argument of
book X.

Is Book X's Concept of Mimesis Different from Book III's?

It is not new to treat the painter as an imitator alongside the
poet. That has been his status since he joined the "luxurious" city

---

[24] Discussed in lecture I.

[25] Cf. lecture II, n. 25.

[26] Lecture II, n. 23.

in book II (373b). The cultural norms of book III extend to painting and embroidery, sculpture and architecture, which must be full
of graceful likenesses (μιμήματα, εἰκόνες) of a good and temperate
character (400e–401d). But the analogy between such likenesses
and those of the poets is left unexplained. Book X explains in
detail, working from painter to poet.

The painter is introduced, somewhat mischievously, as a wizard
craftsman who can make anything and everything he chooses. He
is compared to a man who carries a mirror around to manufacture
the entire contents of heaven and earth. Just as this "craftsman"
is *in a way* the maker of everything, though in another way he is
not, so the painter is *in a way* the maker of a couch (596ce).
Glaucon is not deceived. He insists that, just as the people and
animals made by the mirror-carrier are only apparent, not real,
so all the painter makes is an apparent couch, not a real one
(596e 4, 11). Socrates seems to approve (596e 5). But the next
time Glaucon denies that the painter is the maker of a couch (that
role belongs to the carpenter), Socrates puts up the curiously
worded question, "Then what will you say he is of a couch?"
(597d 11–13). Answer: imitator of a couch. The painter is the
imitator of what the other two (God and carpenter) are makers of
(597e 2: μιμητὴς οὗ ἐκεῖνοι δημιουργοί). This is the cue for Socrates to introduce the idea that the painter's product is at third
remove from the truth.

It is also the cue for many scholars to conclude that Plato has
switched to a different concept of mimesis: mimesis as representation, which is different from book III's understanding of mimesis
as impersonation with one's voice or body.[27] Certainly, painting a
couch is not impersonating it. Yet both painter and dramatic poet
make a likeness of something. Both satisfy the conditions laid
down in (2).[28] Mimesis as impersonation by the poet is vividly
evoked later, when Socrates discusses our experience in the theatre

---

[27] The subtlest version of this claim is Janaway, *Images of Excellence*, chap. 5.

[28] Here I am indebted to discussion with Heda Segvic.

(605cd). My conclusion is that (2) identifies a generic concept which subsumes painting and dramatic poetry as coordinate species. In which case we have no reason (yet) to suppose that *poetic* mimesis is to be understood any differently from before.[29]

At the end of Plato's *Sophist* (265a–67b) we meet the following division:[30]

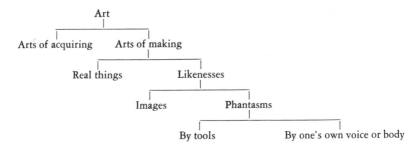

This is one portion of a huge division designed to discover what a sophist is, but with a bit of explanation it can be a useful guide to Plato's thinking about mimesis.

First, the art of making likenesses (εἰδωλοποιική): this is also called ἡ μιμητική, the art of imitation (235c 3, 236b 1, 264ab).[31] So everything in the division below "likenesses" comes under the heading of imitation. Second, the distinction between images and phantasms. Both are produced by artists, but when they make images (εἰκόνες) they reproduce the proportions of the original in all three dimensions, and its colours. When they make phantasms (φαντάσματα), they change the proportions so that from a particular perspective the imitation *seems* like the original (235d–36c). The example given is a colossal statue with its upper parts

---

[29] I shall argue later that 600e does not say, as commonly supposed, that all poetry whatsoever is mimetic. That *would* import a changed understanding of poetic mimesis.

[30] I omit, for simplicity's sake, God's making the real things of nature and their images (shadows, etc.), which complicates the division at 265c–66c.

[31] εἰδωλοποιική takes over once divine image-making is included; it would not sound right to attribute μιμητική to God (cf. lecture II, n. 26).

enlarged so that they look the right size to a viewer on the ground. Phantasms, then, are perspectival likenesses. Next, phantasms are further divided into two species, only the first of which (phantasms made by tools) is appropriate to painting and sculpture. The second species, parallel to the first, is our old friend from *Republic* III: impersonation, making a likeness by one's own voice or body. And this, we are told (267a 8), is the part of phantasm-making (and hence of imitation or μιμητική) which is especially or most typically called mimesis (μίμησις . . . μάλιστα κέκληται). Impersonation is mimesis *par excellence*, but the making of visual likenesses in paint or stone is a parallel species of the same imitative genus.[32]

One could hardly ask for a clearer analysis of the *Republic's* notion of mimesis. The parallel between poet and painter has been with us since book II. The generic concept identified in (2) fits both. Imitation is the art they both practice, one appealing to ears, the other to eyes. It may be helpful for some purposes to translate Plato's talk of imitation into the more modern idiom of "representation." But please do not call it a change of concept. Book X explains the concept that was left unexplained when the "imitators" (μιμηταί) first appeared.

Besides, if we let "representation" replace "imitation" altogether, we lose touch with the point that for Plato, in both *Republic* and *Sophist*, imitation is an art of *making*. To imitate a couch the painter makes a couch — not indeed a real couch, only an apparent one, a thing that looks like a couch when seen from the appropriate perspective. It is the couch we see in the picture that is "third from the king," not the wall or vase on which the picture is painted. That is an ordinary physical object. To imitate a couch is to make an imitation couch. Likewise, our word "poet" transliterates the Greek ποιητής, which means "maker." When Sopho-

---

[32] And has been since the earliest uses of the μίμησις family: compare the Homeric *Hymn to Apollo* 163 (auditory) with Aeschylus frag. 17.7 Mette (visual). Plato, *Cratylus* 430b, takes it as obvious that pictures are μιμήματα of things, but in a different way from words.

cles wrote and produced *Oedipus Rex*, for Plato that means
he made (himself into) a king and all the other characters we see
on stage. Consequently, when Socrates and Glaucon discuss the
question "What does the poet make? And what kind of knowledge goes into making it?" the answer "A play, or a poem, which
requires literary and musical skills" would be irrelevant. Not because it is untrue: Homer is the supreme literary artist (607a).
But this is beside the point if you are interested, as Plato is, in
what *nonliterary* knowledge the poet needs to make such phantasms as King Oedipus and King Agamemnon.[33] "What knowledge do you need to make an imitation *x*?" is not the same question as "What knowledge do you need to represent *x*?" The parallel
between poetry and painting is developed to answer the first question, not the second.

THE PAINTED CARPENTER

This interest in nonartistic knowledge explains why Socrates
abandons the painted couch and starts talking about a painted carpenter (598b). You can see him in Figure 3, shaping a beam with
his adze.[34] He could have been shown making a couch. In any
painting of a craftsman, we will see the product as well as the producer. If the painter shows the producer in action, that intensifies
the suggestion that he knows not only what the product is like, but
also what goes into making it. So the question becomes: "How
much knowledge of carpentry did the Carpenter Painter (as modern scholars call him) need to produce that picture?"

"Very little" is the expected reply. Analogy works by selecting
some well-known feature of a familiar object and projecting it

---

[33] The word φάντασμα, used at 598b 3 for the appearance imitated, is transferred to the imitation product at 599a 2. Noting this, Nehamas, "Imitation,"
pp. 62–63, speculates that Plato may be tempted to think of the painter as, in effect,
lifting the imitated appearance off the object and transferring it into his picture.
An engaging idea, but remember that the phrase "it looks like a couch" can be said
both of an actual couch and of the furniture in figure 2.

[34] British Museum E 23 = ARV² 179.1, dated 510–500 B.C.

onto the less-familiar thing we want to understand. (As the Sun analogy helps us to think about the Good in book VI.) People are convinced that poets must know a great deal about human life to make the wonderful phantasms they set before us (598e–99a). Novelists have a similar reputation in the modern world. It will take argument to dislodge that view. But Socrates offers no argument for his initial claim about painting: "A painter, we say, will paint us a leather-worker, a carpenter, other craftsmen, without himself having expertise in the craft of any of them" (598bc). No argument is given because none is needed. Those who protest at Plato's low esteem for painting miss the point. What Socrates puts forward here is not an adverse judgment on the painter, but an obvious, familiar truth. It is dramatic poets, not painters, who are up for judgment, and to judge them we must first understand the source of their creativity. Is it knowledge or not? It is certainly not expertise in woodworking that produced the delightful picture of a carpenter in figure 3. Or to make a modern point, the

FIGURE 3. Courtesy of the British Museum.

TV producer making a film of a heart-operation did not need to qualify as a surgeon before taking on the commission.

The sentence just quoted is part of a longer statement, which has been widely misunderstood:

> A painter, we say, will paint us a leather-worker, a carpenter, other craftsmen, without himself having expertise in the craft of any of them. But, nevertheless [ὅμως], if he was a good painter, he might have painted a carpenter which he displays at a distance, and he might deceive children and foolish persons by its seeming to be a real carpenter [τῷ δοκεῖν ὡς ἀληθῶς τέκτονα εἶναι]." (598bc)

The standard view, which gets written into the translations, is that these children and foolish persons are deceived into thinking that the painted carpenter is a real carpenter, from whom you could order a new set of couches for the dining room. Shorey's translation is typical:

> A painter, we say, will paint us a cobbler, a carpenter, and other craftsmen, though he himself has no expertness in any of these arts, but nevertheless if he were a good painter, by exhibiting at a distance his picture of a carpenter, he would deceive children and foolish men, and make them believe it to be a real carpenter.[35]

I offer three objections.

First, "nevertheless" (ὅμως) implies a contrast with what immediately precedes, to the effect that the *painter* (not that the painted carpenter) knows neither carpentry nor the other crafts he shows in action. If, nevertheless, children and foolish persons are deceived, this is what they should be deceived about. They should come to believe the contradictory of what has just been

---

[35] Janaway, *Images of Excellence*, pp. 133–34, is a rare case of someone struggling, within the standard view, to credit Plato with a sensible argument. More hostile critics do not mind leaving Plato looking as foolish as the people whose deception he describes.

said, mistakenly supposing that the *painter* (not the painted carpenter) does know carpentry. Why do they suppose this? Because the painted carpenter seems to be a real one, not in the sense that they think he *is* a real carpenter but in the sense that he *looks* to them just like a real carpenter looks: he is shown doing just what a carpenter in their (inadequate, superficial) experience would do to make a couch or shape a beam. Ergo, the painter knows what a carpenter needs to do to make a couch or shape a beam. On this reading, the clause "by its seeming to be a real carpenter" does not express the content of the deception, but the means by which it is effected: ". . . because it looks just like a real carpenter, he might deceive children and foolish persons [*sc.* into thinking he did know that craft]." [36]

Second, a closely similar passage in Plato's *Sophist* (234b) — so close that it amounts, in its context, to a reminiscence of the paragraph before us — expressly says that the painter's likenesses (μιμήματα), when displayed at a distance,[37] leave foolish young children with the impression that the painter could produce anything and everything *in full reality* (ἔργῳ), not just in the medium of imitation. In both dialogues the painter is someone who presents himself as an all-purpose producer (cf. the mirror analogy at *Rep.* 596ce): the picture we are to think of shows a couch, whether or not it also shows a carpenter. In both dialogues the painter is the visual analogue to someone whose deceptive likenesses come in through the ears: the tragic poet in the *Republic*, the sophist in

---

[36] Compare the back reference to our sentence at 600e 6–7: "As we said just now, the painter will make a leather-worker who seems to be a real one [σκυτοτόμον . . . δοκοῦντα εἶναι]." The grammar here offers no subject to cast as someone who thinks the object in the painting *is* a real leather-worker. The seeming leather-worker is better understood as *looking* like a real one.

[37] πόρρωθεν, as at *Rep.* 598c 3. But distance is relative: too far away and you will not see the detail clearly enough to be deceived about anything. Besides, most painting would have been indoors, where the size of the room limits your retreat. All that is meant is that if you step right up close, you lose the impression of depth and volume. This is hardly true of perspective painting (σκηνογραφία), but it was true of the Seurat-like σκιαγραφία technique mentioned later at 602d 2 (references at lecture I, n. 13).

the later dialogue (cf. διὰ τῶν ὤτων at *Soph.* 234c 5). Not that
sensible adults are deceived by the painter. On the contrary, it is
because they are not deceived that he is a useful analogue to show
up poets or sophists, by whom they are liable to be deceived. But
foolish young children might ask Van Gogh to make them a bedroom chair like the one in his picture.[38] That is rather more plausible than the idea of their putting this request to the man in
figure 3.

There is no suggestion, however, that the painter sets out to
deceive. If that was his purpose, he would be a sorry failure, since
the trick succeeds only with children and fools. No, like other
craftsmen he wants to earn his living. He presents completed work
to an audience, just as the tragedian produces on stage a play completed in time to be chosen at the first round of the competition.
The painter does not leave his picture on view in a gallery while
he turns to new work. He is with us here now, displaying his
"carpenter" and (at *Sophist* 234a) offering to sell it cheap.[39]

My third objection is based on the next paragraph (598cd),
which starts the transition from painter to tragic poet and is carefully written in terms that fit both.[40] Socrates envisages someone
announcing, in all seriousness, that they have come across a person who knows every craft as accurately as the individual craftsman know their own specialty. This simpleton (εὐήθης) has been
deceived (598d 3: ἐξηπατήθη). The content of the deception is
then specified: he has met an imitator and has been deceived into

---

[38] I am inclined to see the change from "children and foolish persons" to
"foolish young children" as a well-advised correction on Plato's part.

[39] Note the contrast between the present participle ἐπιδεικνύς and the past tense
of γράψας in the *Republic*, γεγραμμένα in the *Sophist*.

[40] The transition may also perhaps be felt verbally in the choice of the τέκτων,
rather than the leather-worker or other craftsmen mentioned at 598b 9: the poet is
imaged as a carpenter in Pindar, *Pythians* 3.113–14, Cratinus frag. 70, Democritus
frag. 21 (on Homer). At 600e the carpenter is replaced by the leather-worker to
prepare the transition to the section on user-knowledge, where it will be his job to
make reins for the horseman (601c); that is why we must translate σκυτοτόμος
"leather-worker," not "shoemaker" or "cobbler."

thinking *him* an all-round expert (πάσσοφος). That is what it is to be unable to tell the difference between knowledge and ignorant imitation. This surely confirms that, in the case of the painter, the deception was about the painter's competence in woodworking, not the competence of the painted carpenter.[41]

THE POET'S KNOWLEDGE

We now have a smooth lead into the all-important next section, on whether people are deceived about Homer and tragedy. Some people are deceived, Socrates argues, since they say that Homer and the tragedians know all the arts, including the arts most important to the city—generalship, legislation, educating the young. They know all about human virtue and vice. They are even knowledgeable about the gods (598de). On the interpretation of the painter just given, the content of the deception (598e 6: ἐξηπάτηνται) is exactly parallel: like the painter, Homer is an all-purpose expert. But this deception is dangerous, because sensible grownups, not just children and fools, are liable to regard Homer as the fount of wisdom in all things. Only genuine knowledge, they think, can explain his wonderful creations (598e).

The knowledge such people attribute to Homer is not of course philosophical knowledge of the Forms, but knowledge of practical arts and a deep understanding of human life. Homer, they say, has been the educator of Hellas. He is the leader to follow in the ordering and refinement (παιδεία) of human affairs. You should live all your life under his guidance (606e). But Socrates will argue that (nonliterary) knowledge is no more a prerequisite for Homer's mimesis than it is for the painter's. Poetic mimesis is the less obvious case to be illuminated by analogy with the obvious case of painting. The issue is whether to put Homer at second remove (599d 4: δεύτερος) from the truth of the Forms, rather than third, where Socrates would place him.

---

[41] Cf. the back-reference at 600e 6–7 again: the issue is whether the painter knows how to make leather goods, not whether the leather-worker in the picture does.

The notion of second-level knowledge needs clarification. Distinguish two questions: (1) Did the author of *Crime and Punishment* know as much about the criminal mind as a professor of criminology? (2) Did he have the very same body of knowledge as a professor has? Socrates argues strongly that if Homer really had the knowledge of the experts he brings into his stories — doctors, generals, educators — he would want to practise his expertise for real; even if he preferred writing to practice, other people would pester him to help in the real world (599a–600e). Imagine a supposedly brilliant surgeon who never performs an operation, preferring to write hospital dramas for TV. We surely would doubt his competence if he declined to help in a crisis. But is it really question (2)'s systematic, professional expertise that people have in mind when they speak of Homer's or Dostoyevsky's knowledge of life? Or some more imaginative, experiential understanding? Or do people fail to make the appropriate distinctions?

"My father," says a young man in Xenophon's *Symposium* (3.5), "being anxious for me to develop into a good man, made me get all of Homer by heart." The father was the famous general and politician Nicias, with whom Socrates discusses courage in Plato's *Laches*. Did Nicias seriously think that memorizing Homer would be enough to give his son the skills needed to win elections and battles? The son claims it was enough:

> "You know, doubtless, that Homer, the supremely wise, has written about practically every aspect of human affairs. If any of you wish to acquire the art of a householder, a political leader, a general, or to become like Achilles or Ajax or Nestor or Odysseus, then it is my favour you should seek. I know all these things." [42] (Xen. *Symp.* 4.6)

But this is a boasting competition at a party, not safe evidence for standard Greek attitudes toward Homer.[43] Socrates in the *Republic*

---

[42] ἐπίσταμαι here is neatly ambiguous between "I know them all" and "I know them all by heart" (for the latter use of the verb, see Plato, *Protagoras* 339a, *Republic* 392e).

[43] Though scholars often cite it as such, without regard for the comic context or for the intertextual relationship with Plato's *Ion*, where the same passage of the

is careful to limit his attack to what "some people" say (598d 8–e 1: τινων ἀκούομεν).⁴⁴ Perhaps exaggerated claims of this sort were believed, even without the encouragement of wine. Socrates' response is to pin them down to their literal meaning. If these people really think that Homer and the tragedians could not produce such wonderful images unless they had the very same knowledge as the generals and statesmen they imitate, that "inference to the best explanation" must apply to every expert a poet puts on stage. It is not enough for Sophocles to be a good general. He must be a good doctor as well, or he cannot write a part for Asclepius (cf. 599c). If the inference is sound, Homer must indeed know *all* the arts, so varied is the tapestry of his poems. But when Socrates and Glaucon look outside the poems for evidence of Homer's expertise, they find nothing to prove he knows *any* art save the literary art of imitation (601a 6). The inference, they conclude, is not sound.

This conclusion leaves open the possibility that poets have a more imaginative understanding of what it is like to carry the responsibilities of a general or statesman. Never mind that in book III Socrates insisted that it is better to avoid experiential or empathetic understanding of some characters and some actions; let the Guards learn *about* them, in a wholly external way (395e–96a, 409ae). The question is, why should not poetic imitation itself be, and convey, a certain kind of understanding, of good characters as well as bad? Sir Philip Sydney's reply to Plato was that it can:

> Anger, the Stoics say, was a short madness: let but Sophocles bring you Ajax on a stage, killing and whipping sheep and oxen, thinking them the army of Greeks, with their chieftains Agamemnon and Menelaus, and tell me if you have not a more

---

Iliad is quoted to illustrate the point that Homer often speaks of practical arts such as chariot-driving (*Ion* 537a with Xen. *Symp.* 4.6). Greek didactic poetry, such as Hesiod's *Works and Days*, did not hesitate to tackle practical arts — but of that, more shortly.

⁴⁴ They return as the hyperbolic encomiasts of Homer at 606e. But the son of Nicias, Niceravus by name, has been present throughout the discussion (327c).

familiar insight into anger than finding in the schoolmen his genus and difference. See whether wisdom and temperance in Ulysses and Diomedes, valour in Achilles, friendship in Nisus and Euryalus, even to an ignorant man carry not an apparent shining; and, contrarily, the remorse of conscience in Oedipus, the soon repenting pride of Agamemnon. . . .[45]

But could a Platonic philosopher accept imaginative understanding as knowledge worthy of the name, even at the second level where craftsmen can be relied on to get things right all or most of the time? Can a good poet's imagination be relied on to the same extent? And what counts as the poet getting it right? Does anything count except its *seeming* right to an audience ignorant of the truth (599a, 601a)? Socrates is one who would like say, adapting Wittgenstein, "Whatever is going to seem right to them is right. And that only means that here we can't talk about 'right.' "[46] In which case we can hardly talk about knowledge either.[47]

This discussion is vital to the *Republic*'s project for reforming the culture. If a poet like Homer is allowed to be an authority on any of the matters he sings about, he becomes a rival to the philosopher-rulers. The norms laid down for musical poetry in books II–III lose their justification. Socrates launched those norms with the observation that Homer, Hesiod, and other poets told

---

[45] *An Apology for Poetry* (1595), cited from the edition by Geoffrey Shepherd (Manchester, 1973), p. 108. On the idea of imitation as itself a kind of understanding, an excellent treatment in Ferrari, "Plato and Poetry," p. 120 and passim.

[46] Ludwig Wittgenstein, *Philosophical Investigations*, 2nd ed., translated by G. E. M. Anscombe (Oxford, 1958), § 258; the original has "to me," not "to them," because the context is Wittgenstein's famous argument against the possibility of a private language. Note Sydney's phrasing: "more familiar," "apparent shining."

[47] Aristotle's famous dictum that poetry is more philosophical and more serious than history because it speaks of "universals," what a certain *sort* of person is likely or bound to say or do (*Poetics* 9, 1451b 5–11), does not meet the difficulty: such universals can be false as well as true, as Aristotle concedes when he says that the poet, like the painter, must imitate things either as they were or are, or as they ought to be, *or as they are said or seem to be* (*Poet.* 25, 1460b 8–11, 1460b 32–61a 1, 1461b 9–15). For a salutary warning against the idea that the phrase "*more* philosophical" credits poetry with deep insights into the human condition, see Jonathan Lear, "Katharsis," *Phronesis* 33 (1988): 312–14.

false stories to people — and they are still telling them (377b). His first concern was the wrong picture of divinity these poets put into the minds of their audiences. Evidently, he agrees with the historian Herodotus (II 53) that it was Homer and Hesiod "who made a theogony for the Greeks and gave the gods their names, distributed to them their honours and skills, and indicated their outward appearance." But much more is at stake than religion. The norms for musical poetry touch every aspect of life and morality. They need to be comprehensive, because the issue is whose voice is to shape the culture: the poet's or the philosopher's? In ordinary Athenian education, as described by the sophist Protagoras in the dialogue named after him, the young are made to learn by heart poems in which they find "many admonitions, many narratives and eulogies and encomia of good men of old"; the aim is to get the boys longing to emulate (μίμεισθαι) these heroes of the past (*Protagoras* 325e–26a). Similarly, the ideal city will have "hymns to the gods and encomia for the good" (607a) — meaning gods and heroes conceived in accordance with the radically new norms of Kallipolis.[48] Plato adapts traditional methods to philosophically approved ends.

The Poet as Maker

At no point in the preceding argument has Socrates suggested that poets themselves claim the second-level knowledge he denies they have.[49] It is other people who wrongly infer they must have it, in a way they do not do for the painter. That mistake rebutted, Socrates can return to the analogy between poetry and painting:

"Shall we, then, lay it down (a) that all the poets [ποιητικούς], beginning with Homer, are imitators — they produce imitative

---

[48] See lecture II: "Stage 1 of the Reform: Content."

[49] Nor do the rhapsodes who perform Homer claim such knowledge on his behalf. Ion does not do so: what the *Ion* attacks is the rhapsode's belief that his art enables him to judge when Homer speaks correctly about the arts (536e ff.). Homer's followers in the rhapsodic guild known as the Homeridae do not mention any city that owes its laws to Homer as the Spartans owe theirs to Lycurgus (*Rep.* 599de).

images of virtue[50] and the other subjects of their making,[51] and do not get hold of the truth? Rather, we were saying just now, were we not, (b) that the painter will make a leather-worker who seems [looks] real in the judgment of[52] those who understand as little about leather-working as he does himself, but who go by the colours and shapes?"

"Yes indeed."

"Just so, I think, we will say (c) that the poet [ποιητικόν] too, understanding nothing but how to imitate, uses words and phrases to colour in the hues of each of the arts in such a fashion that, in the judgment of others equally ignorant, some-one[53] speaking in metre and rhythm and attunement seems to speak exceedingly well, whether it is about leather-working, generalship, or anything else. So powerful is the natural spell of these adornments." (600e–601b)

Unfortunately, part (a) of this passage is another misunderstood sentence of book X.

The standard view believes Socrates is saying here that all poetry whatsoever is mimetic. This connects with two ideas I have already rejected. First, if narrative and lyric poetry now count as mimetic, the concept of poetic mimesis must have changed from book III. Second, if all poetry is mimetic, all of it should fall to the ban on mimesis at the beginning of book X. This is not only

---

[50] Here I follow Lewis Campbell's construal (Jowett and Campbell *ad loc.*): μιμητὰς εἰδώλων is the nominalizion of μιμεῖσθαι εἴδωλον, where εἴδωλον is cognate accusative to the verb; cf. τοῦτο μιμήσεται at 602b 3–4, LSJ *sv.* μιμέομαι. Most translators have "All the poets are imitators of images of virtue," *vel sim.*, thereby making the image the object of imitation, instead of its vehicle as hitherto. That would seem to require the poet to produce an image of an image!

[51] Here I follow Bloom (1968); other translators have "the other things they write about," *vel sim.*, which encourages the thought that mimesis now covers narrative as well as impersonation. The περὶ construction goes back to 598e 3–5 (cf. 600c 4–5) and recurs at 602a 4, 8, 12.

[52] Here I follow Adam's construal of the dative.

[53] Translators vary in whether they treat τις as the poet or a character in the poem. The latter keeps a better parallel with the real-seeming leather-worker in a picture, but it makes little difference in the end, since the idea that the poet speaks the words of his characters is carried over from book III to book X (605cd).

inconsistent with book III, which allows narrative and good mimesis. It creates inconsistency within book X itself, which will soon welcome into the city "hymns to the gods and encomia for the good" (607a). No one should accept that Plato made such a mess of things without looking hard for an alternative interpretation.[54]

"All the poets are imitators." This is the climax of a long interrogation of the poets to determine whether they can make the originals they imitate as well as images of them (599a). The first question, which Socrates tactfully refrains from pressing, is about the poets' knowledge of medicine. Did you ever make a sick person healthy, or train them to be a doctor? Or are you no doctor yourself, *only* an imitator of doctors' speeches (599bc)? The question he does press is about Homer as educator. Did he really know how to make someone a better person, or was he capable *only* of imitating the process (600c)? I propose that, in context, the force of "All the poets are imitators" is that they are *only* imitators. They never make originals. For any value of x, what a poet makes is an imitation x, never a real x.

On this interpretation, part (a) of the passage is a straightforward generalization from earlier results. On the standard interpretation, it is a new thought, neither prepared for nor justified by what has gone before. Nor does the standard reading fit well with parts (b) and (c), which presuppose that the parallel is still between painter and poet as *makers*. Makers of mimetic images in the sense defined earlier. Narrative and lyric poets do not make anything in that sense, except when they change to another voice. So they are not under discussion. "All the poets" means all the poets we are talking about, the ones who make things at third remove from the truth.

---

[54] Nehamas, "Imitation," pp. 48–54, looks, but admits to not being able to rid book X of all inconsistency. Annas, *Introduction*, p. 344, takes a bolder line: "Whether he is aware of it or not, there is no real inconsistency here [*sc.* within book X], for Plato is enough of a creative artist himself to know that such productions [*sc.* hymns to the gods and encomia for the good] are not real poetry." So much for Pindar!

It may be significant that Plato avoids ποιητής, the normal word for "poet," here. The word he uses for the poets he is talking about is ποιητικός (600e 5, 601a 4), an adjectival form that means "productive, capable of making." It is as if Plato wants to revive in his readers' minds the original meaning of ποιητής itself: "maker." [55]

To test the interpretation I am proposing, let us look at the example of Hesiod, who is scrutinized with Homer to see whether either of them educated any of their contemporaries to virtue (600de).[56] Socrates no doubt has Hesiod's *Works and Days* in view. It is full of worthy precepts addressed to Perses, but did they make him a better person? The passage implies they did not. But is Hesiod a mimetic maker like Homer? Socrates does not explain, but we can look at the poem and see.

The *Iliad* and *Odyssey* have a narrative frame with lots of mimetic speeches in the story. The *Works and Days* does it the other way round: the stories of Pandora, the Five Ages of the World, and other narratives are set in a frame of direct speech. When Socrates pictures Hesiod rhapsodizing around Greece (600d 6), the performance he is imagining is a (public) display of advice to the poet's brother: "To you, foolish Perses, I will speak good sense" (286). The audience does not see Perses, except in their imagination. What they actually see and hear is the poet assuming the role of advisor on morals and hard work, farming, how to choose a wife, and much else besides. "Few know that the twenty-seventh of the month is the best day for opening a wine jar" (814–15). The poet presents himself as an all-round educator. A fair case of impersonation, as can be seen from his advice on taking to sea in a ship. Plato would be delighted if his readers recall it:

I will tell you the rules [μέτρα] of the loud-roaring sea,
Though I have no skill in sea-faring nor in ships. (648–49)

[55] This is confirmed by the phrase ὁ τοῦ εἰδώλου ποιητής, ὁ μιμητής (601b 9).

[56] The inclusion of Hesiod sets the context for the phrase "beginning with Homer" in part (a): the phrase means "Homer, Hesiod, and their successors."

At least Herman Melville had served in a whaler.

No doubt Hesiod is less mimetic than Homer and the tragedians, who are "imitative [μιμητικούς] in the highest possible degree" (602b 10). But his presence is not a sign that Socrates is now targeting all poetry whatsoever. The scope of the discussion here is just what it was at the beginning of book X: poetry which is mimetic in the sense of book III.

THE POET AS PAINTER

Now for parts (b) and (c) of the quoted passage. They start the fusion of poetry and painting I mentioned earlier.[57] The painter becomes the dominant paradigm: mimetic poetry is redescribed in terms of colours and shapes. Metre and music are the colours with which the poet paints pictures of each of the arts. Sensible adults do not attribute second-level knowledge to the painter. If they attribute such knowledge to someone they consider a good poet (598e 3), they are deceived. All the poet really knows is how to imitate the knowledge of others (601a 6). He may have an impressionistic flair for representing how experts talk and act, but he does not know, and does not need to know, what they know.

The next question is this. If what the poet makes is, as we have just seen, nothing but images of virtue, does he know, does he even have good reason to believe, that *virtue* is what they are images of? This question strikes much harder at Greek reverence for Homer. Even if we may doubt that many people looked on Homer as the authority on *practical* arts, it is clear that everyone found him a rich source of *ethical* ideas. When Socrates in book I (334ab) claims Homer's support for the paradoxical proposition that the just man is the best thief (a proposition he has derived from Polemarchus's definition of justice), he is mocking a common practice. On occasion, he takes Homer as a guide himself (468cd). Nonphilosophical readers will be outraged when in book X he

---

[57] Lecture I: "First Glance Ahead: The Divided Soul in Book X."

declares that imitative poets like Homer and the tragedians know nothing about values (602b).

The key premise is that "the excellence, the beauty, the rightness of every implement, every living thing, and every action are determined solely by the *use* for which each has been made or grown" (601d). This principle goes back to book V, where the conventional notion that it would be disgraceful for women to exercise naked like men is dismissed on the ground that "the fairest thing that is said or ever will be said is this, that what is useful is fair [beautiful], what is harmful foul [disgraceful]" (457b). The standard (σκοπός) we should set up for beauty is that of the good (452e).

Consider, then, a painter's judgment of the objects in his picture. Forget about what we call the (aesthetic) beauty of the picture itself. That is not even mentioned. The issue is whether the painter is any kind of authority on the "beauty" (in the strictly functional sense imposed by the premise), excellence, and rightness of the couches and tables, reins and bits, we see in his pictures.[58] Would we order a new kitchen table on the recommendation of the photographer who snapped it for the advertisement in *House and Garden*? Obviously not. But why not?

Well, even a carpenter who knows how to make tables has no idea what type of table we need or what would be the right size, shape, and height for our kitchen. It is the user who knows that (in an ordinary, second-level sense of "know"), the user who tells the carpenter when placing an order. The carpenetr takes it on trust that the user knows what they need; his expertise is in making a table to the given specification. Readers of the *Republic* have had it drummed into them since book V (479a ff.) that in the

---

[58] Note that the opposite of κάλλος (beauty) in this passage is πονηρία (badness), not αἶσχος (ugliness): 601e 8, 602a 9. We should also feel the kinship between χρῆσθαι and χρηστός. To those who are shocked by Plato's seeming indifference here to aesthetic value, I recommend the thoughtful defence offered by Stephen Halliwell, "The Importance of Plato and Aristotle for Aesthetics," *Proceedings of the Boston Area Colloquium in Ancient Philosophy* 5 (1989): 321–48.

sensible world where we live and prepare our meals, judgments of value are context-dependent. A table that is fine in one place, for one purpose, will be useless elsewhere for another. The photographer, however, *qua* photographer, has neither the user's knowledge of whether such and such a table will be good for its purpose, nor the carpenter's correct belief.

Equally, but less obviously, the poet has neither knowledge nor correct belief about the ways in which the characters in his story are good or bad. When he impersonates them, all he produces is words and deeds that "look fine" to the ignorant multitude (602b). He does not know (even in an ordinary, second-level sense), nor do they, whether it was a noble thing for Agamemnon to sacrifice his daughter for the Greek cause, or a useless crime. The poet's only knowledge is skill at imitating. So there is nothing worthwhile for us to learn from Homer and the tragedians, nothing they put before us that we should take seriously (602b).

Only a philosopher whose thought (διάνοια) was fixed on the truth and reality of the Forms could be satisfied with so simple an argument for such a shocking conclusion. This high-minded person is a "spectator of all time and all being," who has ceased to think human life is of great importance (486a), and who conceives the ordinary world we live in as itself a world of fluctuating appearances, where goodness is to be judged by referring each perspectival context to the unchanging Form of the Good (484cd, 520c, 534d). Without this reference to the Forms, the nonphilosopher's second-level knowledge of values is "knowledge" only by courtesy, better called opinion (δόξα). So how could philosophers expect to learn anything important from the *third*-level images of painter or poet? Certainly, they will make sure that the culture of the ideal city is full of beautiful images—that is, images which make an educationally useful appeal to eye and ear. But this does not mean they will take those images seriously themselves. Their minds are elsewhere. In more ways than one, book X speaks to us from the viewpoint of eternity. From a position of deep spiritual elitism.

At the end of the argument about the poet as musical painter, Socrates exclaims, "By Zeus, this business of imitation is about something at third remove from the truth, isn't it?" (602c). He reverts once more to the Theory of Forms. This is, to repeat, very much a philosopher's view of art. If we are disturbed by the simplicity of the argument, and shocked by its conclusion, what that shows is that we are not Platonic philosophers. The argument does not appeal to our type of soul.

THE HONEYED MUSE

I have argued that the shocking conclusion is reached without abandoning book III's concept of poetic mimesis, and without prohibiting more poetry than was explicitly (tragedy and comedy) or implicitly (Homer, Hesiod's *Works and Days*) banned before. But it appears that the reform is not yet complete. For after the long justification of book III's ban on drama (with Homer now explicitly included), Socrates says that no poetry is acceptable in the ideal city if it aims at pleasure for pleasure's sake. Otherwise pleasure and pain will reign in the city instead of law and consideration of the general good (607a). He extends this rule to lyric as well as epic metres (607a 5–6: ἐν μέλεσιν ἢ ἔπεσιν).

Socrates does not mention mimesis here. In principle, a lyric or epic poem could aim at pleasure for pleasure's sake even if it contains no mimesis, or only mimetic passages of the approved type. He condemns any poem, however enjoyable, which fails to be *beneficial* to constitutions[59] and human life in general (607de).

This new development comes with Socrates' final verdict on dramatic mimesis: even though Homer is the first and most poetic of the tragedians, it is wrong to hail him as the educator of Greece and take him as our guide in life (606e–7a). This conclusion is paired with [60] a positive ruling on what poetry is to be welcomed

---

[59] Including the constitution of the individual soul (608b 1). Likewise, "city" at 607a 5–6 should include the city founded in the philosopher's soul at the end of book IX. Cf. n. 14 above.

[60] Note the μέν . . . δέ construction.

into the ideal city: "nothing but hymns to the gods and encomia
for the good" (607a 3–5). The ruling is a fair summary of the
kinds of poetry explicitly allowed so far.[61] But it is, in fact, the
first time in the Republic that *Socrates* has specified the range of
permissible poetry in positive terms. Previously, his emphasis was
negative: this or that is *not* allowable. Now we know precisely
which genres will remain after the "luxurious" city has been
purged.

But we do not know *why*. Why only hymns and encomia? The
norms for content and performance, the banning of tragedy, comedy, and Homer, leave it unclear how much epic and lyric is left.
And these are the metres characteristic for hymns and encomia.[62]
The Homeric *Hymns* are in epic metre, but they frequently offend
against the norms for representing divinity. So does the nontragic
and minimally mimetic *Theogony* of Hesiod, in epic metre.
Book III subjected lyric to the norms governing content at 379a,
and took account of it in the discussion of mimesis at 394c. But
this still does not define clearly what nontragic epic or lyric may do
in the ideal city. To round off the reform of musical poetry, Plato
needs a general criterion to eliminate everything but praise of gods
and heroes — poetry whose beneficial subject-matter guarantees its
moral fitness.

This, I suggest, is why Socrates introduces the figure of the
honeyed Muse (607a 5: τὴν ἡδυσμένην Μοῦσαν) to represent poetry
that is oriented towards pleasure rather than benefit (607c: ἡ πρὸς
ἡδονὴν ποιητική). The greatest example is still Homer (607d 1),
the originator of the mimetic genres banished in book III. These
genres are still at the centre of attention. Socrates refers to them
as the honeyed Muse when he says, referring back to book III,
"it was reasonable for us to banish her then, such being her char-

---

[61] See lecture II: "Poetry and Politics."

[62] Iambic is firmly associated with tragedy: 380a (cf. 379a), 602b. If Plato
ignores the use of iambic in the lampooning invective of poets like Archilochus, this
may be because he considers it too awful to merit discussion.

acter" (607b 2–3).[63] The poetry we banished then was mimetic
drama, which we can now see is oriented towards pleasure rather
than benefit.[64] The same idea is conveyed by the phrase "poetic
imitation designed for pleasure" (607b 4–5: ἡ πρὸς ἡδονὴν ποιητικὴ
καὶ ἡ μίμησις).[65] But the contrast between pleasure and benefit
should in principle apply more widely. In which case book X goes
beyond book III to ban all poetry that is not beneficial.[66]

That is not at all the same as banishing poetry. On the contrary, the upshot of this discussion is that in the ideal city all musical poetry must be *beautiful*. This sounds simple, but to a nonphilosophical ear it is very strange. The strangeness comes from
taking usefulness as the criterion of beauty (601d); most people
would think that social utility and beauty are importantly different
values.[67] Only philosophers know that "the Good is the cause of
all things right and beautiful" (517c).

BACK TO THE DIVIDED SOUL

That completes my account of the various problems of interpretation that have made it hard to read book X as a continuation

---

[63] αὐτήν at 607b 2 refers to the honeyed Muse, not (as in most translations)
to poetry as such. Translate, with Shorey, "Let us, then, conclude our return to the
topic of poetry and our apology, and affirm that we really had good grounds then
for dismissing her from our city, since such was her character," and take "her" as
the honeyed Muse, who is the more dramatic antecedent. We did not banish all
poetry then and we are clearly not banishing all poetry now, for we have just admitted hymns to the gods and encomia for the good. τοιαύτην οὖσαν refers to the
grounds for banishing poetry that aims at pleasure: lest the city be governed by
pleasure and pain.

[64] I explain this claim in the next section.

[65] Halliwell's translation (1980); the singular αὐτήν in the next clause confirms
that the two noun phrases are in hendiadys.

[66] The lines abusing philosophers quoted at 607bc to illustrate "the ancient
quarrel between poetry and philosophy" are lyric. Their origin is unknown, but it
would be rash to insist they must all derive from comedy: see Adam *ad loc.*

[67] One such is the rhetorician Polus in Plato's *Gorgias* (474cd), who firmly
rejects Socrates' suggestion that the good (ἀγαθόν) and the beautiful/fine (καλόν)
are the same. In retrospect we can see this identity at work already in books II–III:
the fine/beautiful (καλόν) stories selected by the norms for content (377c, 378e)
coincide with those told by the "more austere and less pleasing" poet, whose performance will be beneficial (398ab: ὠφελίας ἕνεκα).

of the discussion in book III. Book X, I have argued, is designed to be consistent with book III and to give a retrospective, theoretical commentary on its major claims. We can now turn, at last, to see how Socrates fulfils the promise made at the start of book X, to demonstrate the mind-damaging effects of dramatic mimesis. The damage is worked through a slow poison: pleasure.

Socrates does not object to poetry giving pleasure. He would gladly welcome Homer back into the city if someone composed a defence that showed how his poetry benefits the audience as well as enchanting them (607ce). What Socrates fears is the long-term, unnoticed effect of the pleasure we take in mimesis of actions we would not, and should not, want to do ourselves. Of course poetry should be enjoyable. But not at the price of damaging the soul.

Recall that the problem with uncontrolled mimesis, as Plato sees it, is not just the kind of likenesses it brings into our presence. It is how those likenesses insinuate themselves into the soul through eyes and ears, without our being aware of it. Unlike narrative stories, which tell us *about* something, the seeming presence to our senses of the imitated characters has a way of bypassing reason's normal processes of judgment.[68] To account for this phenomenon we should return to the painted couch.

When we look at a painting, or to recall another of Plato's examples, when we look at an oar half submerged in water, we know perfectly well that the painting is flat with no depth to it, that the oar is straight. But knowing this does not stop the oar *looking* bent or the painting *seeming* to have depth. How is the persistence of the false appearance to be explained? Socrates argues that it can only be explained on the supposition that there is some part of us, some level of the soul, which believes, or is tempted by the thought, that the oar actually is bent, that the painting does have depth. *We* are not inclined to believe it, but something in us is — just as something in the most sceptical person may shiver at a ghost story. At a certain level, we entertain many

---

[68] Lecture I: "First Glance Ahead: The Divided Soul in Book X."

beliefs, thoughts, and fantasies that run counter to our better judgment.

Similarly, when we sit in the theatre and witness Oedipus discovering who he is, we know very well we do not hear Oedipus's own voice. Not because Oedipus is a fiction (for the ancient audience Oedipus is no more a fiction than Agamemnon or any of the other heroes of their drama),[69] but because Oedipus is not really there, only a likeness of him. Just as there is no couch there in the picture, only the likeness of one. Yet knowing this does not stop us being affected by the appearances before us. Oedipus still seems to be on the verge of his terrible discovery. Even though we know they are only images, the false appearances persist, and stir our feelings. It is as if eyes and ears offer painter and poet entry to a relatively independent cognitive apparatus, associated with the senses, through which mimetic images can bypass our knowledge and infiltrate the soul.

In modern discussions of the influence of the media, it is often said that a normal, healthy individual is not unduly influenced by images they know are unreal. For Plato, the audience's knowledge is the source of his deepest anxiety about mimesis. Since normal, healthy individuals are undoubtedly influenced, all the time and in ways they are mostly unaware of, by the images that pervade the culture, that shows that knowing the image is only an image is no protection at all. Schools used to give lessons to make the young more aware of the wily tricks of the advertising industry. The advertisers had no need to protest. They knew that Plato has the better of the argument. A sexy jeans ad invites the viewer to notice its brazen appeal — and then go shopping.

Similarly, in the theatre,

"Even the best of us, you know, when we listen to Homer or some other tragedian imitating one of the heroes in a state of

---

[69] See Plato, *Apology* 41bc, for testimony to this point: Socrates presupposes that his audience regard the Homeric narratives as in some sense a record of distant history.

grief, delivering a long speech of lamentation, or chanting and beating his breast with the chorus,[70] we enjoy it and give ourselves up to it. We follow it all with genuine sympathy for the hero. Then we praise as an excellent poet the one who most strongly affects us this way. . . . And yet when the sorrow is our own, you notice that we plume ourselves on the opposite response, if we manage to stay calm and endure. The idea is that this is the conduct of a man, whereas the sort of behaviour we praised in the theatre is womanish." (605cd)

In the theatre we enjoy, take pleasure in, emotions we would try to restrain in real life: grief, joy, pity, fear, erotic excitement, anger, scorn. (The point does not depend on our agreeing with Plato about when, and how far, or why such emotions should be restrained: anyone will accept that there are times when emotion should be restrained.) Worse, we deliberately allow ourselves to indulge these feelings. As Socrates puts it, in the theatre reason relaxes the guard it would maintain in real life (606a). There are two rather different ways, I think, in which the guard is relaxed.

One is what we now call suspension of disbelief. We do not keep reminding ourselves of what we know perfectly well, that the events on stage are not really happening there now. They may have happened in the past: compare Shakespeare's history plays and medieval mystery plays. But the events are not actually unfolding before our eyes and ears. We would be upset if we turned on the television one evening, watched what we took to be the end of a rather violent film, and then the announcer came on to say, "That's the end of the news." The jolt would be vivid proof of how completely we had suspended our everyday processes of judgment about what is apparently taking place. Conversely, I recall a news commentator during the Los Angeles riots exclaiming in disbelief, "This is not a film; this is for real."

But Plato worries more about our suspending *moral* judgment about what is apparently taking place. When we sympathize with

---

[70] On the switch from singular to plural, see Jowett and Campbell *ad loc*.

a grieving hero, we not only allow ourselves to share feelings we would wish to restrain in real life. We also allow ourselves, as part of that emotional bonding, to share a while, at some level of our soul, the hero's belief that a great misfortune has happened. And here the mistake is not that no such event has happened, it is only a play. The mistake in Plato's eyes is allowing yourself to believe, even vicariously and for a short while, that an event like the death of your child would be a terrible loss, a great misfortune, if it really happened. The law in the ideal city is stern:

> "The law declares, does it not, that it is best to keep as calm as possible in calamity and not get upset, (i) because we cannot tell what is really good and bad in such things, (ii) because it will do us no good in the future to take them hard, (iii) because nothing in human affairs is worthy of deep concern,[71] (iv) because grief will block us from taking the necessary measures to cope with the situation." (604bc)

The whole culture is set up to reinforce this law — remember the songs about calm endurance in adversity.[72] The mimetic genres of poetry — Homeric epic, tragedy, and comedy — encourage people to suspend the moral principles they try to live by, so as to enter into the viewpoint of emotions which their better judgment, if it were active, would not approve. This is how the analogy with visual perspective carries over to the theatre. When we share an emotion with a character on stage, we enter (despite our better judgment) the moral outlook from which the emotion springs. The images created by theatrical mimesis are so sensuously present to eyes and ears that they lock the audience into a distorted moral

---

[71] Believing this is a crucial part of the mind-set (διάνοια) of a Platonic philosopher (486a). I am inclined to think that *not* believing it is a crucial precondition for valuing the theory (or experience) of Aristotelian katharsis, which requires us to accept, outside as well as inside the theatre, that the loss of one's child would be a truly serious misfortune (see Lear, "Katharsis"). If this is correct, Aristotle's *Poetics* would fail to convince Plato that Homer could be safely welcomed back into the city.

[72] Lecture II: "Stage 3 of the Reform: Musical Technique."

perspective. Epic and drama encourage us to feel, and to some extent believe, against our better judgment, that the ups and downs of fortune are much, much more significant than they really are.

This is not the argument that showing a violent film on Tuesday brings about a rape on Wednesday. It is a more interesting claim about the longer-term influence of mimesis. By encouraging us to enter into the perspective of strong emotions, epic and drama will gradually erode the ideals we are attached to and still hope to maintain. Here is Socrates on comedy, claiming we will not notice the change:

> "When you take intense pleasure in hearing things laughed at in comic mimesis, or for that matter in a private gathering — things you would be ashamed to joke about yourself — and you do not just detest the behaviour as bad, you are doing the same as when you pity a grieving hero. You let free the element in yourself you restrained, with the help of reason, from indulging its wish to scoff, for fear of a reputation for buffoonery. And once you allow it to turn into a cheeky youth, you won't notice [ἔλαθες] how often you get carried away into being a scoffer [literally: a comic poet] in your own life." [73] (606c)

It is the *enjoyment* of other people's scornful laughter that does the damage, just as the sympathetic enjoyment (ἀπολαύειν) of other people's grieving in tragedy makes it harder to restrain grief in one's own life (606b). [74] The pleasure you allow yourself to feel in the theatre, thinking it harmless, reinforces aspects of your personality you would prefer to keep down.

This argument does not depend on the stern, other-worldly morality on which Plato's ideal city is founded. Let the prevailing

---

[73] Plato thinks of comedy as laughing *at*: in a lengthy analysis of the genre at *Philebus* 48a–50b, he explains that comedy appeals to the malice of its audience and invites them to enjoy the spectacle of people weaker than they are being brought to grief by their ignorance of their own failings. In the *Republic*, the failings it is appropriate to laugh at are those of people ignorant and bad (396de, 452d).

[74] The verb ἀπολαύειν connotes taking something in with enjoyment. At 395d 1 Socrates says the Guards should not imitate anything shameful, lest imitation be imbibed as reality (ἵνα μὴ ἐκ τῆς μιμήσεως τοῦ εἶναι ἀπολαύσωσιν).

morality be more relaxed, more humanistic: it will still include ideals we think we should live up to, and Plato will still caution us about mimesis. It is dangerous to enter feelingly and uncritically into viewpoints that our better judgment, if it were active, would not approve. That is why he would banish Homer, tragedy, comedy, and their modern equivalents.

Some writers have naively supposed they could defend Homer and imaginative literature generally against Plato's critique by claiming that literature enlarges the sensibility and makes us more feeling people, because it fosters empathetic understanding of all sorts of different characters, both good and bad. As if Plato did not know that. "Yes," he would reply, "That is what we need to prevent." Opposite conclusions are drawn from the same premise. What you cannot do, it seems to me, is accept that mimesis has the effects on which Plato and these critics are agreed and then argue that anything and everything can be allowed. If we agree with Plato about the power of mimesis (ancient or modern, epic and drama or advertising, film, and TV), but reject his authoritarian solution, then democratic politics has to take responsibility for the general ethos of society. Plato's problem is still with us. It needs a modern solution.[75]

[75] Besides the audiences thanked at lecture I, n. 11, I want to thank Julia Annas and Alexander Nehamas for acting as commentators: their challenging criticism, so gracefully delivered, has led to much rethinking and (I hope) improvement. Useful suggestions came from Jerome A. Barron, Ed Floyd, Penny Murray, Amélie Rorty, Malcolm Schofield, and others who are thanked in the relevant note. Christoph Harbsmeier showed me interesting discussions of music, morals, and the social order in Chinese thought: would that I was competent to make use of them here. Finally, I am grateful to Ruth Padel for constant advice on style and content.

The Idol of Stability

STEPHEN TOULMIN

THE TANNER LECTURES ON HUMAN VALUES

Delivered at

University of Southern California
February 9–11, 1998

STEPHEN TOULMIN is Henry R. Luce Professor at the Center for Multiethnic and Transnational Studies at the University of Southern California. He read mathematics and physics at Cambridge prior to World War II, when he did radar research and development for the Royal Air Force. Following the war, he returned to Cambridge where he studied philosophy with Ludwig Wittgenstein, and received his Ph.D. in 1948. Shortly thereafter he moved to Oxford as University Lecturer in Philosophy of Science. He has also been a professor at Brandeis, Michigan State, the University of California at Santa Cruz, the University of Chicago, and held the Avalon Foundation Chair in the Humanities at Northwestern University until he retired in 1992. He is the author of many books, including *The Inner Life, The Outer Mind* (1985); *The Return to Cosmology* (1982); *Knowing and Acting* (1976); *The Uses of Argument* (1958); and *The Place of Reason in Ethics* (1949). *Cosmopolis: The Hidden Agenda of Modernity* (1989), won the 1992 Book of the Year Prize from the International Society for Social Philosophy.

1

Twenty years ago Hans Küng, the German theologian, gave an evening lecture in the University of Chicago's Rockefeller Chapel: its title was *Science and the Problem of God*. Some of his hearers were surprised that a man of the cloth chose a title implying that the nature of God was problematic, while the nature of science was not. Might one not expect him to prefer, as his title, *God and the Problem of Science?* Yet a similar difficulty arises if we ask about the nature and standing of human values. On the one hand, the concept of *values* is in practice as little open to question among Europeans or Americans today as was that of *God* in Medieval Europe. We may disagree about cases; but we understand claims about the value of saving life, or building happy families, or respecting personal autonomy. All of these claims have clearly recognizable meanings. On the other hand, if we look at concepts and theories in the human sciences — whether concerned with individual behavior or with institutions and social relations — we find great weight placed on the need to confine ourselves to the *facts* and steer clear of *values*, which must (it is said) introduce damaging biases into our inquiries. Human scientists, as much as natural scientists, are exhorted to treat the difference between facts and values, not just as a *distinction*, but as a downright *separation*. How, then, can we do "factual" work in our scientific theorizing, while we continue to recognize "values" in all our practical activities and relations? That is the central issue for this Tanner Lecture.

For a start, I shall avoid debating the fact/value contrast as an issue in epistemology: we can return to this later. Instead, I shall examine the historical situation in which the founders of the human sciences became convinced of a need to frame their inquiries in "factual" and "value-free" terms. This will point us to the tasks we must tackle, if we are to reconcile the demands of thought and practice — theoretical and practical life — and rescue our everyday understanding of human values from the critiques of the behavioral and social sciences. Where, then, are we to begin? As so often, one good starting point is to look at the things that "went without saying" during the Scientific Revolution . In his *Essay on Metaphysics*, R. G. Collingwood showed us, first and lucidly, that the thought of any place and age rests on certain beliefs that are so basic and familiar that the people of the time have no occasion to articulate them: assumptions that are so unquestioned that they may go without saying. Collingwood called these "absolute" presuppositions, in contrast to the "relative" ideas and hypotheses of everyday science. (This was before all Kuhnian "paradigms" or *mentalités*.) So let us start by asking what "absolute presuppositions" underlay the image of nature and science on which the founders of the human sciences relied. When they set out to build up these novel sciences, what questions did they *not* ask?[1]

My initial question, then, will be one that teases me whenever I leave the evolution of the natural sciences for the methodology of the human sciences: namely, "Why was the type example of serious Science — to be emulated by economists, sociologists and psychologists no less than by physiologists and biochemists — Newtonian Dynamics? Why were the first human scientists so determined to be the *Newtons* of social theory?" Surely, the activities of human beings are not like the motions of planets in their orbits, or rigid spheres rolling down inclined planes? Surely, they are far more like the behaviors of living creatures? So why did the initial creators of the human sciences not rely on models from biology in their theory-building, rather than on implausible analogies with physics? No work in the natural sciences had greater influence on the idea of "theory" in the social sciences than Isaac Newton's *Principia* — at least as these are interpreted in our universities — yet no work (I shall argue here) has been more deeply misunderstood.

---

[1] R. G. Collingwood, *An Essay on Metaphysics* (Oxford, 1940), esp. chaps. 4 and 5.

2

Newtonian physics came to be seen as a model for the truly "hard" sciences, not least, because of its supposed success as an instrument of prediction and control. Yet those who hold dynamics up as an example to the human sciences in this respect have (I shall claim) failed to study carefully enough the conditions on which it played this role *even in physics*. Pierre-Simon de Laplace dreamed of an Omnipotent Calculator who, given the positions and velocities of every atom in the universe at Creation, could use Newton's equations to compute the entire subsequent history of physical nature. This (as I shall argue here) was never more than a fantasy *even at the outset*; and, if we ask how this fantasy reflected the original claims for theoretical physics, we shall find that the human sciences — not least theoretical economics — based their research programs, not on realistic ideas about the *actual* methods of Physics, but on their vision of a physics that never was.

So much for my agenda: How can I back up these claims? I shall focus on the aspects of Newtonian dynamics that led Gottfried Wilhelm Leibniz to dismiss Newton's *Principia* as metaphysically impossible: in particular, the puzzle mathematicians have called the *Three-Body Problem*. This is the subject of a monograph published by Henri Poincaré in 1889, deploying all the resources of nineteenth-century mathematics to resolve this problem without success. Now, a century later, Poincaré's monograph — instead of rescuing the solar system from the threat of instability — serves, instead, as a starting point for today's chaos theory.

Notice my phrase "rescuing the solar system from the threat of instability": it brings to the surface an assumption that "went without saying" from the early seventeenth century up to the first years of the twentieth century. From Hugo Grotius and René Descartes until the First World War, the ideals of intellectual order and rational intelligibility current among European intellectuals emphasized *regularity*, *uniformity*, and above all *stability*. From this standpoint, the merit of Newton's *Principia* was to show that the solar system of which the earth is a member is a "demonstration" — a *paradeigma*, in the Classical Greek — of an *intrinsically stable* system. This assumed success for Newton's theory convinced the "Mathematical and Experimental Natural Philosophers" (the theoretical physicists of the seventeenth century who took a lead from Galileo Galilei, Johannes Keplar, and Descartes) that their use of Euclid's *Elements of Geometry* as a model for a new physics — or, for Thomas Hobbes, a political theory — was not a dream born of Platonist epistemology alone, but a realistic program for scientific research.

In the 1630s, Descartes's *Discourse* set out philosophical reasons for seeing Euclid's *Geometry* as an intellectual model for theories in other areas of inquiry. Fifty years later, Newton showed that this model was not just formally rigorous, but empirically powerful: i.e., it resolved problems that had plagued European thinkers ever since the publication of Nicolaus Copernicus's *de Revolutionibus* (1543). If this could be done in astronomy, they asked, was the same not possible in other fields, too? Once taken up, this challenge engaged the intellectual imaginations of talented mathematicians and scholars for more than 200 years. This was the change that most recommended the Newtonian model of a "hard science" to the intellectuals of Europe, and its fiercest opponent was Newton's old enemy, Leibniz.

What exactly, then, "went without saying" in planetary theory in Newton's last years? And what continued to go without saying in philosophy and social science for much longer, even until after the First World War? At the heart of an answer lay this belief that the solar system is the prime example of a "rationally intelligible" system in nature; but we must take great care just how we state this belief. It was not just the *geometrical* move from the Ptolemaic to the Copernican picture of the solar system that was at issue: rather, it was a deeper assumption, about the *dynamic stability* of the whole system.

As Newton declared in a Scholium to the second edition of the *Principia*, the Stability of the Sun and Planets shows that the World of Nature displays the Creator's Rationality. This belief was consistent with any geometrical or dynamical account of the solar system. Tycho Brahe took the *stability* of the solar system for granted as surely as Copernicus or Galileo did; nor did it matter whether Descartes's "vortices" or Newton's "gravitation" were used to explain its operation; finally, it was compatible with all current ideas about *how far* and *in just what respects* the system was "rationally intelligible." At this point, then, we must make a more careful study of the things in Newton's theory that Leibniz found offensive. For here begins a bifurcation in physics and philosophy that shows up for 150 years in the budding human sciences, too — not least, in economic theory.

The central issue dividing Leibniz and Newton was the question "How is the Rationality of the Creation — more specifically, the Rational Design of the Solar System — to be *demonstrated?*" Newton was content to explain the regularities Kepler had found in the planetary orbits *empirically*, by appeal to his inverse-square Law of Universal Gravitation: in this way — he argued — they displayed just the kind of mathematical pattern a rational Creator might be expected to prefer. Leibniz, by contrast, was not content with an empirical demonstration: he would not accept anything but a *formal proof* that the planetary system *must* display the regularities we do in fact observe. By that measure — Leizniz argued — Newton had failed. And when Samuel Clarke, as Newton's amanuensis, replied, "Evidently, this is how God *chose* to create it," [2] that only sharpened the antagonism. To show what God *in fact* chose was not enough: you must also show that it was *right and just* for God to have chosen as He did. For Leibniz, Newton's theory was incomplete, because it included no Theodicy: no demonstration that the way in fact things *are* in God's World is also *for*

[2] Cf. *The Leibniz-Clarke Correspondence*, ed. H. G. Alexander (Manchester, 1956).

the best. So, Leibniz provided the model for Dr. Pangloss in Voltaire's *Candide*, who could continue to argue that "Everything Is for the Best in the Best of All Possible Worlds," even after the catastrophic Lisbon Earthquake of 1755.

When it came to a formal proof of the Divine Rationality, the Three-Body Problem was (to Leibniz) a fatal blow to Newton's theory. The theorems in dynamics that Newton relied on to explain the elliptical forms of the planets' orbits, or their speeds of motion round the orbits — both established empirically by Kepler — were highly *oversimplified*: they showed only that the Law of Gravitation fitted the motions of one small planet at a time around a much more massive center of gravitational attraction, viz. the sun. On this simplification, the equations of motion for a single planet were easily solved, and we could obtain general solutions having the same forms as Kepler's empirical laws. But as soon as we introduced any third body into the case (e.g., a second planet), the equations were no longer soluble in algebraic terms: the best a Newtonian can do is to calculate the third body's influence from moment to moment, arithmetically, as a "perturbation" of the simplified orbit.

How can one react to this discovery? In practical terms, it may be enough to improve our methods of computation bit by bit, so that the numerical match between the results and the planetary motions recorded by astronomers is increasingly exact: that was the agenda for the eighteenth century, progressively cutting down the "perturbations" in ways that led up to Laplace's *Système du monde*. Laplace was content to show that these perturbations were on a scale explicable by refined Newtonian calculations; so he rejected Newton's hint that God might intervene in the system from time to time, so as to remove all irregularities and so restore the stability of the system ("Je n'avais pas besoin de cette hypothèse").[3] But Leibniz could not take this step: for him, an acceptable theory *must* yield general algebraic solutions for any set of bodies whatever,

---

[3] See Leibniz's first letter in the *Correspondence* with Clarke.

however multiple or complex — not merely two at a time. Once he recognized that Newton's *Principia* did not provide such solutions, he set it aside as metaphysically inadequate; and it is hard to find evidence in his writings that he read more than the first thirty or so pages of the *Principia*.

From the death of Leizniz in 1715 to the last twenty years of the nineteenth century, then, we find a basic division in the philosophy of physics. On the one hand, starting with Leibniz himself and continuing *via* Leonhard Euler (and Laplace in metaphysical moments) to Pierre Duhem, there is a Continental tradition of *rationalism*: on the other hand, starting with Newton and continuing *via* John Dalton and William Herschel (and Laplace in practical moments) up to James Maxwell and Ernest Rutherford there is a British tradition of *empiricism*. Empiricists saw *any* regularities in the observed phenomena as evidence of God's Rational Order: rationalists still looked for comprehensive mathematical theories, having the full rigor of Euclid's *Elements*.[4] Only Immanuel Kant — keeping to the sidelines in natural philosophy as he did in epistemology and metaphysics — took neither side in the dispute. In the *Allgemeine Naturgeschichte und Theorie des Himmels* (1755), his intellectual imagination reached out beyond the previous limits of the Newtonian system, to hint at a cosmology with an evolutionary history barely glimpsed by his predecessors.

Working physicists — especially in Britain — took the empiricist line: it was enough to balance the books by fitting computations and observations. After 1810, the Three-Body Problem faded into the background and was seen as a metaphysical rather than a scientific issue. By the 1870s, however, the tide had turned. From Charles Lyell's *Principles of Geology* on, the history of the earth was a scientific preoccupation: the debate triggered by Charles Darwin's *Origin of Species* made a historical reinterpretation of

---

[4] Cf. Pierre Duhem, *La théorie physique: Son but, sa structure* (Paris, 1903), Eng. trans. by P. P. Wiener (Princeton, 1954), chap. 4, "Abstract Theories and Mechanical Models."

the order of nature only the more urgent. The scale of the universe — in both space and time — proved far vaster than was earlier assumed and provoked the anxiety exemplified in Alfred, Lord Tennyson's widely read poem *In Memoriam*. Soon, the debate about the history of nature became the focus of religious and intellectual discussion, and it is the background against which we can look at Poincaré's monograph "Sur le problème des trois corps et les équations de la dynamique." [5]

The circumstances of this monograph are themselves of some interest. It appeared as a special supplement to *Acta Mathematica*, one of the leading journels of pure mathematics. From 1882 on, this was edited by the Swedish mathematician Göran Mittag-Loeffler of Uppsala, with an editorial board that included two of the finest mathematicians in Europe, Karl Wilhelm Theodor Weierstrass from Germany and Charles Hermite from France. (Poincaré was one of Hermite's most talented pupils.) From the start, *Acta Mathematica* concentrated on "pure mathematics," as that subject was then understood. Georg Cantor, Heinrich Hertz, and David Hilbert all published in it, and in 1885 King Oscar II of Sweden lent his name to a competition for the best essay on a subject in pure mathematics.

In announcing the competition, Weierstrass, Hermite, and Mittag-Loeffler chose four areas for special attention. Three of the problem areas lay in theory of functions or other subjects still recognized today as belonging to "pure" mathematics; but the first topic was *la stabilité de nôtre système planetaire* (the stability of "our" planetary system). For a question in pure mathematics, this porblem was framed in oddly singular terms. It was not stated as having to do with general "stability conditions" for *any* planetary system: instead, it referred precisely to *our particular* planetary system. Shortly before his death in 1859 — it was said — Gustav L. Dirichlet claimed to found a proof of this stability; but he never explained it, and entrants to the competition were invited to recon-

[5] *Acta Mathematica*, vol. 13 (1889), pp. 1–270.

struct his feat. They were to send entries to Sweden, marked with an epigraph, their names given only in sealed envelopes bearing the same epigraph, to ensure that the judging was anonymous. Twelve entries arrived, and five of these tackled the stability problem. Two prizes were awarded, one for a monograph bearing the epigraph *Nunquam praescriptos transibunt sidera fines*: "Never will heavenly bodies transgress their prescribed bounds." This was Poincaré's meticulous reanalysis of the Three-Body Problem, set out in 23 chapters and 270 pages.[6]

Poincaré's epigraph recalls the antiquity of the belief in celestial stability; but the choice was also ironical, since the question "Do planetary motions have any 'prescribed limits'? Can one *prove* that the planetary system must in fact be stable?" was just the point at issue. By the time one reached the last page of Poincaré's monograph, there was clearly no more hope in 1889 than in 1715 of finding general methods of solving the equations of motion for two or more planets moving round the sun at the same time. Another result was even more damaging for philosophical debate: by the end of Poincaré's analysis it appeared that, when numerous objects move freely under mutual gravitational attraction, critical collisions (*chocs*) may take place whose outcomes are radically unpredictable. Instead of Laplace's dream of a world whose history was computable in Newtonian terms, a new picture began to enemge of a world in which — aside from the artificial case of the sun and a single planet — complete predictability was out of the question.

The world of physical determinism that was a nightmare for nineteenth-century thinkers thus gave way to the world we know today as the world of chaos. Far from proving that "our" planetary system is dynamically stable, Poincaré ended by laying a basis for chaos theory. True, he did not at once appreciate the full effects of his work. In the 1880s, his painful analysis of the Three-Body Problem only ended by reinforcing the difficulty and gave us no

---

[6] See n. 5, above.

new way of solving the equations of motion for three bodies or more: without some radically new kind of mathematics (e.g., our "nonlinear" mathematics) there seemed no prospect of overcoming the difficulty. In the 1890s, Poincaré developed a three-volume book on *New Methods in Celestial Mechanics*, with different conclusions from Laplace's. Only in his philosophical essays at the turn of the century did he open up clearly the issues of chaos and complexity that preoccupy physical scientists today.[7]

Poincaré's interest in the Three-Body Problem was never purely personal. Questions in many-body dynamics still fascinated mathematicians, from Sweden to Italy, Germany to North America: these questions crop up in *Acta Mathematica* throughout the 1880s and 1890s, up to 1906. Nor was this a purely technical issue for mathematicians: the year 1906 saw publication of H. G. Wells's novel *In the Days of the Comet*, in which the earth faces annihilation by a massive comet, and humans are moved to reorder their affairs. Even in the 1990s, the dynamics of our planetary system are a matter of public concern. In 1994, there occurred "by far the most spectacular event in the Solar System ever witnessed by the human race": a collision with the planet Jupiter of fragments of Comet Shoemaker-Levy 9. In mid-March 1998, again, astronomers foretold, for October 26, 2028, the possible impact of an asteroid on the earth violent enough to be a catastrophe for the human species, as an earlier one apparently destroyed the dinosaurs.

Far from the Euclidean model being the standard pattern for any "hard" science, then, physics itself never fully exemplified that form. Leibniz had been right: the Three-Body Problem raised insuperable difficulties for any strict reading of Newtonian theory, if not for a purelry pragmatic reading of his theories. From the outset, a strong case might have been made for radical unpredictability and complexity, chaos theory and nonlinear mathematics: failing that, the model that for so long held center stage as the

---

[7] Notably *La science et l'hypothèse* (Paris, 1902) and *Science et méthode* (Paris, 1908).

ideal form of theory in any would-be science was the model of a physics that never was.

3

What did this episode in the history of physics have to do with the actual development of the human sciences? Was the goal of eighteenth-century social theorists to be the Newton of the human sciences any more than agreeable rhetoric? In order to recognize the influence of this assumption about the stability of the planetary system on human thought and practice, we must look more closely at the people who laid the foundations of the social sciences. For this purpose, let us focus directly on those who tried hardest to model their work on mathematical physics: the creators of mathematical economics. Of all human scientists, the ones most confident of the rigor of their methods and the superiority of their results are the economists who develop abstract, universal mathematical systems. The formality of their arguments carries an air of theoretical rigor; the generality of their concepts gives them the apperaance of practical universality; and, as a result, the ideas of "neo-classical equilibrium analysis" have a special prestige among academic economists.

There are two ways to write a history of economic theory. We can start where we are now and look back at earlier writers who already used mathematical methods of analysis like those used by academic economists today: in this way, we can establish an honor roll of the *precursors* of modern economics. (This is a recipe for surprise and disappointment: surprise at the foresight of a few imaginative individuals, disappointment that their example took so long to be followed up.) Or we can begin at the beginning: asking what personal projects these creative individuals were engaged in and how their mathematical excursions into economics contributed to those projects. Depending which of the two roads we take, we end with a different story about the birth of economic theory. On the first, the creation of economic theory was delayed by the failure of readers to pursue the lines of argument of their creative precursors: on the second, theoretical economics — as we know it today — is a product of conceptual abstractions that became available only during the twentieth century, and the work of the "precursors" reflects quite different intellectual ideas and ambitions.

Until recently, most historians of economic theory chose the first road. For instance, the classic *History of Economic Analysis* assembled after his death from the *Nachlass* of J. A. Schumpeter took as heroes Adam Smith (1723–90) and Antoine Augustin Cournot (1801–77), William Stanley Jevons (1835–82) and Léon Walras (1834–1910). All of these writers were concerned in their own ways with connections between economics and physics: taking them in turn, we find close parallels between their ideas about *equilibrium* in economics and Newtonian ideas about the dynamics of the planetary system.

All biographers of Adam Smith remark on the unusual scope of his writings: from the uses of rhetoric to the theory of the moral sentiments, from the wealth of nations to the history of astronomy. His intellectual versatility they put down, in part, to the range of academic discussion and education in the eighteenth-century Scottish Enlightenment, in part, to the variety of his own interests and the width of reading he had accumulated in the course of his bachelor life. Yet it is evident that, for many years, his own personal project was to develop an overall vision of the universe—we might even call it a "cosmology" — of which he fully completed only this history of astronomy, and he abandoned this ambition only when he saw that it was too vast to finish in his lifetime. The essay on astronomy stands as testimony to his ideas about the proper method for any intellectual system; but he never pursued the parallels between economics and physics into more substantial fields.

In Britain, then, we find an empirical tradition in economics — linking Adam Smith and David Ricardo, by way of James Mill and John Stuart Mill, to Alfred Marshall — that parallels the empiricist tradition in physics, from Newton to Maxwell and Rutherford. In Continental Europe, by contrast, we find in the precursors of economic theory a rationalist tradition like that in natural philosophers from Leizniz to Duhem. At times, this analogy was stronger. Augustin Cournot's use of mathematics in his *Recherches sur les principes mathématiques de la théorie des richesses* (1838) was somewhat elementary, and for most of his career he set aside economics for broader issues in cosmology and epistemology: to judge the place of economics in his personal enterprise, we may look at the *Traite de l'enchainement des idées fondamentales dans les sciences et dans l'histoire* (1861). Of the 707 pages of this, his major work, only 28 are devoted to topics in economics.

The rationalist thrust of Cournot's cosmology is clear in his own intellectual evolution, as recorded in his *Souvenirs*. He came from a conservative royalist family and did not at first go to the university, but spent four "largely wasted" years in a law office. However, he read widely, and four authors specially caught his imagination: Bernard de Fontenelle's *Eloges* and *Pluralité des mondes*, Laplace's *Système du monde*, the Port-Royal *Logic*, and — of all things — the *Leibniz-Clarke Correspondence*. This last work had defined the rival, empiricist and rationalist, methodologies for physics, and Cournot's loyalties are clear. In his *Considérations sur la marche des idées* (1872), he comments that the true successors to Newton were not British empiricists, but Continental mathematicians like the Bernouillis, Euler and Johann Heinrich Lambert, Alexis-Claude Clairaut and Jean d'Alembert. The final pages of his *Revue sommaire des doctrines économiques* (1877) are pure epistemology: they discuss the proper method for any theory of human transactions and compare this to the theories of planetary astronomy. In both fields — he concludes — we must distinguish the general laws that define the *essential* form of the phenomena involved from "perturbations" arising from the *accidental* influence of other intervening bodies or agents. At the very end of Cournot's life, the power of the astronomical model was thus undiminished.

Jevons, too, is given a historical role among the precursors of economic theory that too easily exaggerates the centrality of economics to his thinking. Invited to speak to the British Association for the Advancement of Science in 1862, he prepared a "brief account of a general mathematical theory of political economy," followed by a book on *The Theory of Political Economy* (1871); but most of his papers on economics were edited only after his death.[8] Taken in isolation, these works may give us the impression of a writer for whom economics was a topic of central importance; yet Jevons's total *oeuvre* belies this. Increasingly, his concern was with the power of logic as an instrument in scientific theory of any kind; so, when he brought his general ideas together for publication in his 600-page *Principles of Science*, he did not give one page to economics, and the word "economics" is not in the index. His excursions into mathematical economics seem, as much as anything, to be making a methodological point.[9]

The most revealing case is that of Léon Walras, a French academic who (to his regret) spent his career at Lausanne in Switzerland, where his colleagues included Vilfredo Pareto. Walras was a more single-minded economist than Cournot or Jevons; yet, like them, he is preoccupied with *method*, notably with analogies between "equilibrium" in planetary theory and economic affairs. During his last ten years, he kept writing to Poincaré, hoping to win the great mathematician's approval for a parallel he thought he had established, between the laws of economic equilibrium and those that supposedly ensured the stability of the planets: Walras's last paper, in fact, was entitled *Economique et mecanique*. By this time, Poincaré himself, of course, no longer believed that the planetary orbits had any essential stability — let alone that Newtonian

[8] *Journal of the Royal Statistical Society* (London), 29 (June 1866): 282–87. For a more detailed and sympathetic view of Jevons as an economist as well as logician, see Margaret Schabas, *A World Ruled by Number: William Stanley Jevons and the Rise of Mathematical Economics* (Princeton, 1990).

[9] *The Principles of Science: A Treatise on Logic and Scientific Method* (New York, 1892, repr. with a preface by Ernest Nagel, New York, 1958).

dynamics give a mechanical guarantee of that stability — so it was embarrassing for Poincaré to answer Walras's pressing letters candidly, and the letter that is printed as an annex to Walras's paper reads, in retrospect, more like a diplomatic brushoff than an endorsement.[10]

Even after dreams of equilibrium and stability faded within physics itself, then, they remained alive in economics; and to this day many economists' ideal of a theory still rests on parallels with Newton's *Principia*. As attention in physics itself shifted to the relativity and quantum theory, however, the debate in economics began to change its tone. In his *History*, for instance, Joseph Schumpeter captured this shift in a footnote on the work of the founder of the Cambridge school of economics, Alfred Marshall: "The truth that economic theory is nothing but an engine of analysis was little understood all along, and the theorists themselves, then as now, obscured it by dilettantic excursions into the realm of practical questions. But it was emphasized by Marshall who, in his inaugural lecture at Cambridge [1885], coined the famous phrase that economic theory is not universal truth, but 'machinery of universal application in the discovery of a certain class of truths.' "[11] Two phrases shine out from this comment — Schumpeter's judgment on economists who apply theories to practical issues as "dilettantic"; and Marshall's argument that economic analysis may still have "universal application," even if it has abandoned all pretensions to "universal truth." For Marshall, concepts like "equilibrium" thus remained of universal *relevance*, even if we stopped reading them as accounts of *reality*.

[10] Walras's paper is in the *Bulletin de la Société Vaudoise des Sciences Naturelles (5e série)*, 45, no. 166 (June 1909): 1–15: for Poincaré's letter, see pp. 14–15. As to the other correspondence between the two men, cf. *Correspondence of Léon Walras and Related Papers*, vol. 3 (1898–1909), ed. W. Jaffé, esp. letters 1492 and 1495.

[11] Joseph A. Schumpeter, *History of Economic Analysis* (New York, 1954), part IV, chap. 7, p. 954, n. 2.

4

We live today in a time when public life is dominated by applications of economics to "the realm of the practical"; and we need to ask both how these applications can escape Schumpeter's charge of dilettantism and how far Marshall's claims of "universality" still hold good. My aim is to question the "universal" relevance of neoclassical theory. So let me here change gear and report two practical examples. In the first, Marshall's assurance of the "universal applicability" of abstract economic theory had disastrous consequences: in the second, admirable results flowed from abandoning that assurance. In practical cases, then, the distortions introduced by this assumption may be more serious than is commonly admitted, and we can escape them only if we "de-universalize" the application of economic analysis to practical problems — treating these as specific aspects of the actual social, cultural, and historical situations in which they arise.

My first vignette combines several of the difficulties that afflict contemporary economic analysis.[12]

*I have an anthropologist friend, with a Dutch wife, who does field work on Bali. His research has been on the system of "water temples" whose priests — by tradition — controlled the schedule by which irrigation water was shared between the rice fields of different farmers or communes. For 800 years, these temples were a central feature of Balinese society; yet the central government of Indonesia — the former Dutch colonial administration as much as the Indonesian government today — treated the water temples as "cultural monuments" and never saw them as having any **economic** significance.*

[12] J. Stephen Lansing, *Priests and Programmers: Technologies of Power in the Engineered Landscape of Bali* (Princeton, N.J., 1991), pp. 113–15. See also the report by Lucas Horst (Wageningen Agricultural University), "Intervention in Irrigation Water Division in Bali, Indonesia." Dr. Horst gives a very fair picture of the mistakes made in the Bali Irrigation Project. Notice Horst's comment, "The Italian and Korean consultants had no or little knowledge of the specific Bali-Subak irrigation" — even describing the traditional procedures as making an *arbitrary* allocation of water to the farmers!

*In the late 1960s and early 1970s, the Indonesian national gov-
ernment decided to introduce to Bali, on a massive scale, the new
strains of "miracle rice" developed at the International Rice Research Institute in the Philippines. So — my friend points out —
"Balinese farmers were forbidden to plant native varieties . . . Instead, double-cropping or triple-cropping of IR-36 [or similar varie-
ties] was legally mandated. Farmers were instructed to abandon
the traditional cropping patterns and to plant high-yielding varieties as often as possible." With this policy went an engineering
project launched by the Asian Development Bank in 1979, based
on a report from consultants in Milan, Italy, and Seoul, South
Korea. From a purely technical and economic point of view, this
project was a strictly rational recipe to increase rice production and
help make Indonesia self-sufficient in rice, which was the central
aim of the government policy.*

*What happened? For two or three years the policy succeeded
as forecast: the rice crop soared and farmers put money in the
bank. But, in the 1980s, the local authorities recorded "explo-
sions" of insect pests and infestations of funguses, both old and
new. Soon, all the biblical plagues of Egypt were afflicting the
farmers of Bali: "By the mid-1980s, Balinese farmers had become
locked into a struggle to stay one step ahead of the next rice pest
by planting the latest resistant variety of Green Revolution rice.
Despite the cash profits from the new rice, many farmers were
pressing for a return to irrigation scheduling by the water temples,
to bring down the pest populations. Foreign consultants at the
Irrigation Project interpreted any proposal to return control of
irrigation to the water temples as a sign of religious conservatism
and resistance to change. The answer to pests was pesticide, not
the prayers of priests. Or as one frustrated American irrigation
engineer said, 'These people don't need a high priest, they need a
hydrologist!' " Until matters reached crisis point, economists at the
Asian Development Bank found it hard to admit that the traditional irrigation schedules operated by the water temples were*

functional: what "worked" was not prayers of priests, but the centuries of experience embodied in the schedules. As they saw it, as
"religious" institutions, temples **must be** economically irrelevant;
so this was a hard lesson to learn.

Don't misunderstand me. I tell this story not out of a dislike
for technology — I am not a machine breaker — but to illustrate
another point. We too easily assume that economic and technical
issues can be *abstracted from* a situation: that economists and engineers can know in advance what things are or are not economically
or technically relevant to our decisions. If engineering and economics are *scientific* (we assume) their principles *must be* universal; so that the theoretical view from Milan, Italy, or Seoul, South
Korea, may be not less but more clear-sighted than the view on the
ground, in Bali itself.

The decision, prompted by the Asian Development Bank, to
replace traditional planting and irrigation schedules by uncoordi-
nated multiple cropping had the effect of destroying, at a stroke,
both the *material* infrastructure of Balinese *culture* — waterways
and practices developed through the history of the island, to minimize the exposure of crops to insects, diseases, drought, flood, and
other natural enemies — and the *moral* infrastructure of local
society — the institutions that embodied the people's respect for
the traditional procedures. At the same time that the crops were
blasted, the loyalties of the people were undermined.

My other example shows how economic analysis, applied more
perceptively, can have equally constructive results. Let us leave
Bali for Bangladesh.[13]

*The key figure in this story is a young graduate student called
Muhammad Yunus, who took a Ph.D. in economics at Vanderbilt
University, in Nashville, Tennessee. There he was taught the eco-
nomic principles of banking and finance, in a form that supposedly*

---

[13] The work of Dr. Yunus and the Grameen Bank has recently been widely discussed in the *Economist* and elsewhere, notably in connection with the Microcredit
Summit at Washington, D.C., in February 1997.

*applied in the same way in all countries. Returning home to Chittagong, he ran into difficulties. In class he handed on the "laws of the market" as he had been taught at Vanderbilt; but every day after class he walked home **via** the local market, and found it hard to square the transactions going on there with the theoretical principles he had just been teaching.*

Stopping at a stall where a poor woman made sandals, he asked how she ran her business. She bought raw material for the sandals (she said) from a moneylender, who lent her the cost of the materials and took her output at a price he himself set. Having nothing to offer as "collateral" for the initial loan — no house or car, nor even a sewing machine — she could not build up a surplus, but was trapped in dependence on the moneylender.

*Young Muhammad Yunus gave her a very small loan — $15, I think it was — so that she could sell sandals to the public at her own price, and at a profit. Then he went home and asked how the concept of **collateral** might be extended, to cover productive loans to the poorest of the poor. Instead of material collateral (he decided) one might experiment with a kind of "social" collateral, by which a group of individuals together ensured repayment of a small loan to their poorest member, on the understanding that this would qualify the other members for loans, in turn.*

Three years later, Yunus started his own Grameen Bank, which now operates in 50,000 Bangladeshi villages, making loan to local groups, chiefly of women, who keep up a repayment rate of 97 or 98 percent — any commercial bank would of course be very happy with such a rate — and, by now, similar "microcredit" schemes are to be found in more than fifty countries across the globe — even in the United States itself.

To repeat: I am not attacking economics: I argue only that, in real life, economic analysis yields just or fruitful human outcomes *only* if economists take into account all the relevant social, cultural, and historical features of a human situation. Muhammad Yunus understood the culture of his homeland well enough to see that it is no good equating a local market in Chittagong with the idealized "market" of economic theory. The lack of material collaterial of kinds familiar in mature economies was not a reason to penalize the poor even further: rather, it was a call to extend the application of the term "collateral" to fit the local culture and society better. Economic theories of universalistic kinds had too often led economists to overlook social, cultural, or historical factors that seemed to them "noneconomic"; so the new kind of "social collateral" had to be recognized, if you were to match the theories of banking and finance to the actual situation on the ground.

A briefer vignette underlines this point. It has to do with an anthropologist from San Francisco who went to work in Japan.

Why did he go to Japan, and what did he do there? He went because one of the top Japanese auto makers wanted to break into the California market and invited him to run their strategic planning unit.

That's the whole story. Someone at the headquarters recognized that all *economic* problems are, in practice, *cultural and social* problems, too, and that strategic planning that fails to take this fact into account is likely to prove shortsighted and unproductive.

I speak here about economics, but I might equally well have chosen other disciplines. A Japanese colleague of mine in civil engineering, Yoichi Arai, supervised construction of an artificial island in Osaka Bay for Kansai International Airport, to serve central Japan. He was impressed by the range of questions arising during construction that he could not answer by straightforward technical calculations: even questions about the effects of the new island on the fish population of the bay. So now he argues for a radical revision of the syllabus for educating engineers and technologists. What he calls for is a "humanized" technology, in which mathematical methods are taught always with an eye to their practical application in particular human situations.[14]

It is a far cry from the time when the U.S. Army Corps of Engineers could set in train construction of large-scale dams or

[14] See, e.g., the introduction to Y. Arai, *The World Airports* (Tokyo, 1996).

canals, without considering the interests of the people in the valleys inundated by their work. It is a far cry, too, from the time when nuclear power stations were built, without even a public inquiry into the effects of their construction on the neighborhood. Nor is it only the Japanese who react in this way: similar discussions about the education of engineers are going on, to my personal knowledge, in Sweden and the Netherlands. All over the world, the political debates about the human consequences and environmental impact of large-scale engineering works are, thus, reflecting back on the discussion of technical disciplines.

If real life problems in economics and engineering are historical, cultural, and social problems, too, the same is true of human problems more generally. None of the issues that affect the practical interests of human beings can be fully resolved in abstract, theoretical terms alone. This is not to question the intellectual value of well-established theories, or to deny their practical fruitfulness as applied to the human needs evident in real-life situations. It is only to comment on a tendency in Western thought, to focus on the core concepts or techniques of one single, abstractly defined discipline at a time, while failing to consider in concretely described terms the human effects of putting those same concepts and techniques to work in particular practical cases.

If we renounce that tendency, one immediate outcome is to challenge those dreams of universality and timeliness — what I called the *Idol of Stability* — that played a central part in the history of the human sciences in general, particularly of social and economic theory. We live in a world of flux as much as fixity, specificity as much as generality, particularity as much as universality. Nothing in human affairs is in total flux, let alone in total chaos. There are general similarities to be explored among human societies and organizations, as well as among the thoughts and feelings of different individuals. But, if we assume from the outset that all these things are governed by universal timeless laws, we lay up trouble for ourselves; and we do better to set the dreams of stability and equilibrium aside.[15]

<h1 style="text-align:center">5</h1>

At this point my road is at a fork, and there are two alternative ways ahead. On the one hand, we can stay in the world of theory and reformulate our ideas for the human sciences in subtler, less simplified terms, paralleling the newer physics that was made possible by twentieth-century critiques of Newtonian ideas. On the other hand, we can question the primacy claimed for theory in the modern era and reconsider the merits of a practical (even clinical) view of these subjects. May it not be better to view the social sciences as concerned, not with "value-free" facts, but *precisely* with human values and practices: with coming to understand how human lives go *well or badly, better or worse*, and how we can help them to fulfil their potential? That, of course, will mean turning our backs not just on the Idol of Stability but on the "fact/value dichotomy" as well.

To begin with, notice how the grip of equilibrium analysis is starting to loosen, even in economic theory itself. Analysing "increasing returns and path dependence" in economics, for instance, W. Brian Arthur quotes Schumpeter's *History*:[16] "Multiple equilibria are not necessarily useless, but from the standpoint of *any* exact science the existence of a uniquely determined equilibrium is,

---

[15] For detailed studies demonstrating the need to treat equilibrium theories with caution, see such recent books as *Range Ecology at Disequilibrium*, ed. R. H. Behnke, Jr., Ian Scoones, and Carol Kerven (London, 1993), and *Sustaining the Soil*, ed. Chris Reij, Ian Scoones, and Camilla Toulmin (London, 1996).

[16] W. Brian Arthur, *Increasing Returns and Path Dependence in the Economy* (Ann Arbor, 1994), p. 4. Arthur writes of this passage as having been *written* by Schumpeter in 1954, but by then Schumpeter had been dead for four years. The words quoted must in fact have been written half a dozen years earlier. Note also a comment Arthur quotes from J. R. Hicks about the danger of taking increasing returns seriously: "The threatened wreckage is that of the greater part of economic theory." On the use of equilibrium theories in economics, see Bruna Ingrao and Giorgio Israel, *The Invisible Hand: Economic Equilibrium in the History of Science* (Cambridge, Mass., 1990).

of course, of the utmost importance . . . without any possibility of proving the existence of [a] uniquely determined equilibrium — or at all events, of a small number of possible equilibria — . . . a field of phenomena is really a chaos that is not under analytical control."[17]   Writing in the late 1940s, Schumpeter was not (of course) using the term "chaos" in the new, "chaos theory" sense. But the idea of *equilibria* was still in his view indispensable, if any economic theory was to have analytical control over its subject matter. So understood, his ideas about the nature of any "exact science" retain a *universality* familiar from the writings of the Vienna Circle philosophers.

By contrast, Brian Arthur argues that economists must look carefully at the historical situation in which any economic fact occurs, since it may make that fact an exception to the hitherto universal rules. Familiar examples are the commercial success of the VHS video system, despite the technical superiority of the Betamax system; the success of gasoline-powered automobiles, despite the absence of pollution from steam-powered cars; and the general adoption of the *qwertyuiop* keyboard in typewriters. In each case, the success of an inferior product was "locked in" because it won its market position before there was any direct competition with its rivals.

Arthur's work extends the reach of economics, but stays clearly on the side of theory rather than practice. If he writes about cars, videotapes, and typewriter keyboards, it is to explain the general phenomenon of historical lock-in, not to promote the less successful rival products as objects of practical concern. It is as though Muhammad Yunus thought up "social collateral" simply to improve the economic theory of banking and finance, not to help the poorest of the Bangladeshi poor. That would certainly have been an advance in economic theory; but Yunus's later pursuit of other ways to tackle poverty and destitution in his home country showed that his core concern was practice, rather than theory.

[17] Schumpeter, *History*, p. 969.

Consider the alternative: I call this not just *practical* but *clinical* for a reason. Fifteen years with physicians, studying the practice of clinical medicine, have taught me to ignore any claim that medicine is merely "applied" scientific biology: that is a twentieth-century view, fostered to win support for better scientific training of doctors.[18] Advances in the natural sciences of physiology and biochemistry certainly contribute to our inventory of clinical procedures, but the day-to-day art of handling the problems of patients is both closer to the heart of medicine and also older than any of the natural sciences.

Early in the *Nicomachean Ethics*, Aristotle refers to the "timeliness" of all our practical understanding: the need to recognize how the changing "occasions" on which problems confront us affect our ways of handling them. He cites two activities in particular as timely and circumstantial — helmsmanship and medicine. As he himself was a doctor, and the son of a doctor, Aristotle well understood how medical problems arise and run their course, and how a doctor's actions are adapted to changes in that course. A doctor (we may say) "steers a way" through the shoals of illness and changes the direction of treatment as a patient's condition develops: if something unexpected comes up, the doctor may have to go off on a new tack. Increasingly, the range of diagnoses and treatments available may be supplemented by new scientific work; but the demands of practice still rule, and the value of scientific theory to clinical medicine must still be measured against those demands.[19]

There is a moment in medical training when a young student faces for the first time a key task of clinical practice: *taking a patient's history.* "How far is the patient's condition explained by his or her earlier life, diseases, and experience? And where in that condition are the pointers we require to see what is wrong now,

[18] The key document in this campaign was the Flexner Report of 1913.

[19] Aristotle, *Nicomachean Ethics*, bk. II, ch. ii, 1104a 4–5.

and how can it best be remedied?" These are the crucial questions for what I am here calling *clinical knowledge*.

If I am right, "clinical" understanding plays a part in all the problems of life, moral and technical alike. When Muhammad Yunus invented *social* collaterial as a method of securing loans, and founded the Grameen Bank to put this idea to work, his insight was to see that the general theory of banking could be applied to the particular local market in Chittagong only if you made allowances for the social situation in Bangladesh, where there were not enough *material* possessions as the collateral for small business loans. Correspondingly, when economists from the Asian Development Bank ignored traditional irrigation methods in Bali, what was wrong was their failure to understand how these methods fit into the social, cultural, and historical fabric of Bali. Bangladesh was a success, and Bali a failure, in *clinical* economics, and it is no accident that development economists are the ones who best understand the "clinical" aspects of their discipline.[20] Similarly, if my engineer friend in Japan calls for a *humanized* technology, and argues that students of engineering should be taught to judge the human effects of their projects, he too is offering a "clinical" view of engineering in which all *general* computations of structural stresses, quantities, margins of safety, and the rest are evaluated by their effect on the *particular* humans and other living creatures affected by the projects concerned.

This view of practice holds for all the human sciences. The attempt by the behavioral scientists in the academy to keep the human sciences "factual" and "value free" rested all along on misplaced analogies with physics rather than biology. Issues of human value (no doubt) raise methodological problems, but the human sciences are no less *scientific* for all that. The great nineteenth-century physiologist Claude Bernard called his work "experimental medicine": the topic for physiology was the difference between

---

[20] I have in mind (e.g.) Partha Dasgupta and Amartya Sen. See, especially, Partha Dasgupta, *An Inquiry into Well-being and Destitution* (Oxford, 1993).

(e.g.) a *well* functioning and a *mal*functioning heart; and, if that is not a "value" difference, it is hard to say what is! Rather than view sociology or psychology as narrowly factual, value-free disciplines, we may therefore think of them as asking, "On what conditions — social or cultural, intellectual or emotional, collective or individual — do we find human affairs going *well or badly* in practice? And how can we intervene in those conditions to help them go *better rather than worse?*" This suggestion can in no way be condemned as *unscientific*; so human scientists need no longer be shy about discussing the difference between *well* functioning and *mal*functioning societies and cultures, organizations, and personalities. Indeed, that is just what the rest of us can legitimately ask them to do.

Two postscripts are in order. The first has to do with the contrast between rationality and reasonableness — between the "rational" methods of the *explanatory* sciences and the "reasonable" decisions of *clinical* scientists. Not that an Aristotelian ("clinical") approach requires us to abandon all hope of establishing "universal" truths: on the contrary, the term "universal" won a place in philosophical usage in an Aristotelian context; however, the force of the term, in that context, reflects its etymology. A "universal" was *katholou* — or rather, *kat' holou* — and in Classical Greek *kat' holou* meant the same as the corresponding English phrase "on the whole" (or "generally"), and still means this on the streets of Athens today. It would be odd for a doctor like Aristotle to argue that universals and universal truths are what they are "invariably and without possible exception": in many situations, a universal is what holds good generally *as distinct from* quite invariably. In the human sciences as in medicine, then, we should keep in mind the difference between the formal deductions that figure "rationally" in mathematical theories and the factual assumptions that "reasonably" underlie medical and other practical arguments.

My other postscript concerns the history of the contrast between an Aristotelean and a Platonist approach to epistemology or philosophy of science. Professional philosophers may argue in principle that the validity of philosophical theories does not depend on the life stories of their supporters; but it can do more harm than good to emphasize this principle without allowing any exceptions. Aristotle (I said) was a doctor and the son of a doctor; and I used this fact to expound the difference between clinical and explanatory disciplines, implying that his firsthand experience of the nitty-gritty timeliness of medical judgments saved him from looking for universality or timelessness — let alone abstraction — where it was not to be found. Plato, by contrast, was preoccupied with fields like geometry and planetary astronomy, where mathematical abstractions had more part to play; so his "ideas" could be conceived apart from all down-to-earth instances, in a way neither Aristotle's interests in botany and zoology nor his concern for medical problems admitted.

Since seventeenth- and eighteenth-century natural philosophers took their Platonist ambitions from Galileo and Descartes, it is understandable that the role of universal, timeless mathematical theories could be exaggerated in all disciplines. From the start, formal systems modeled on Euclid had a charm that carried people's imagination over into fresh fields: if the world of nature exemplified in Newton's dynamics had a timeless order, this could presumably be extended to the world of humanity as well — hence, their readiness to use Newtonian physics as a source of analogies for human affairs. Very soon, indeed, in the Battle of the Ancients and Moderns, the name of Aristotle came to be equated with highly conservative — chiefly medieval — modes of thought. Among academic philosophers, the clinical nature of practical thinking dropped out of sight, and the resulting hostility to Aristotelianism and Aristotle himself lasted up to John Dewey's time. Formal logic put rhetoric in the shade, philosophically significant theories were expected to make timeless, universal claims, and the contingent world of experience lost prestige, as compared with the eternal truths of abstract reflection. So what other direction could the human sciences initially take?

At the end of the twentieth century, our own position is very different. Rather than jumping from the exact inferences of abstract economic theory (say) to practical recipes for solving concrete, real-life problems, we must keep in mind all the interpretative steps involved in applying any formal theorem to a specific social, cultural, or historical occasion. When he criticized economists' "diletanttic excursions into the realm of practical questions," Joseph Schumpeter had a point. It may be *rational* for us to have intellectual trust in the results of mathematical deductions; but it is *reasonable* to put our trust in the substantive recipes of a clinical science only if these rest on an understanding of the whole situation to which they are meant to apply. In the end, that is how the consideration of human values will most effectively be reintroduced into the practical work of the human sciences.

Experience and Its Moral Modes: Culture, Human Conditions, and Disorder

ARTHUR KLEINMAN

THE TANNER LECTURES ON HUMAN VALUES

Delivered at

Stanford University
April 13–16, 1998

ARTHUR KLEINMAN is Maude and Lillian Presley Professor of Medical Anthropology and Chair of the Department of Social Medicine at Harvard Medical School. He is also Professor of Anthropology at Harvard University. He was educated at both Stanford and Harvard, and received his M.D. from Stanford in 1967. He is a fellow of the American Association for the Advancement of Science, the American Psychiatric Association, the American Academy of Arts and Sciences, and the Royal Anthropological Institute. He has been a Guggenheim Fellow and fellow of the Center for Advanced Study in the Behavioral Science. He directed the *World Mental Health Report*. In addition to many published articles, he is the author of numerous books, including *Writing at the Margin* (1995); *Rethinking Psychiatry* (1998); *Social Origins of Distress and Disease* (1986); and *Patients and Healers in the Context of Culture* (1980), which was awarded the Wellcome Medal for Medical Anthropology by the Royal Anthropological Institute.

PROLOGUE TO THE LECTURES

What I seek to accomplish here is to bring the perspectives of medical anthropology, cultural psychiatry, and social medicine to bear on moral theory. I will draw on my knowledge of these disciplines along with my field research and clinical work in Chinese society and in North America to examine moral issues concerned with our era's great transformation of suffering and medicine and social life more generally. I will describe the profound implications of the truly dangerous burden of social suffering. In response to these human tragedies, neither the cultural resources of the programs of tradition nor those of the programs of modernity seem at all adequate. Indeed they all-too-regularly add to the sense and substance of disorder. Subjectivity itself is undergoing an epochal

I am deeply grateful for the opportunity to present these ideas that the Tanner Lectures afforded. I wish to thank the three official commentators on these lectures, Allan Werthheimer, Hazel Markus, and especially Veena Das for their reflections and for the tonic of lively intellectual colloquy. I also wish to thank Sylvia Yanagisako, Carol Delaney, Barbara Koenig, David Spiegel, and other friends and interlocutors at Stanford, including those in the Program of Values and Society, for their responses. And I extend the appreciation to my colleagues Michael Herzfeld and Amartya Sen for their thoughts regarding various parts of the argument I have presented. I have also benefited from the responses of Robert Hefner, Charles Rosenberg, Stanley Tambiah, and Don Seeman. Without the acutely critical sensibility of Joan Kleinman and the assistance of Mathew McGuire and the tremendous effort of getting it all into (and out of) the computer by Joan Gillespie there would be no published version at all.

I acknowledge Michael Oakshott's *Experience and Its Modes* (Cambridge and New York: Cambridge University Press, 1985 [1933]) as the source of the title of the lectures. I am not seeking to work out Oakshott's ideas here, but I find resonant these few: " 'Experience' stands for the concrete whole which analysis divides into 'experiencing' and 'what is experienced' " (p. 9); "practical activity is a form of experience" (p. 249); "a specific world of experience is the world of value" (p. 285); and "the practical comprises all that we mean by a moral life" (p. 296). These ideas, of course, are derivative of European philosophy, especially phenomenology, over the last century, and together with certain Chinese formulations, the writings of William James, and contemporary anthropological theory are the intellectual streams that build up into the source of what I have tried to develop in these lectures.

change. It may represent a deep and most dangerous transformation. Once I have described what I take to be the fundamental challenge, I will then try to indicate a possible direction for human engagement with it. So daunting is my subject, so limited my skills, that I must beg your indulgence with my overreaching. I do so not to amuse you with a display of my pretensions, but because of a keen sense that there is in this subject so much that matters for all of us. The perspectives and research I will present deal with moral processes at the local level of lived experience. Hence I need to begin first with an ethnographic orientation to *experience*.

Experience I will define, following many others, as the felt flow of *interpersonal* communication and engagements.[1] Those lived engagements take place in a local world.[2] Experience is thoroughly *intersubjective*.[3] It involves practices, negotiations, con-

---

[1] For an extended account of the theory of experience developed here, see Arthur Kleinman and Joan Kleinman, "Suffering and Its Professional Transformation: Toward an Ethnography of Interpersonal Experience," *Culture, Medicine and Psychiatry* 15, no. 3 (1991): 275–301; reprinted as chapter 5 in Arthur Kleinman, *Writing at the Margin: Discourse between Anthropology and Medicine* (Berkeley and Los Angeles: University of California Press, 1995), pp. 95–119. William James, in his Hibbert Lectures at Oxford in spring 1908, observed: "Reality, life, experience, concreteness, immediacy, use what word you will . . . by reality here I mean where things *happen*" (Linda Simon, *Genuine Reality: A Life of William James* [New York: Harcourt Brace, 1998], p. 359).

[2] The concept of local worlds is developed further in Arthur Kleinman, "Pain and Resistance: The Delegitimation and Relegitimation of Local Worlds," in *Pain as Human Experience: An Anthropological Perspective*, ed. M. J. Good, P. Brodwin, B. Good, and A. Kleinman (Berkeley and Los Angeles: University of California Press, 1992); and for the Chinese setting in Arthur Kleinman and Joan Kleinman, "Moral Transformations of Health and Suffering in Chinese Society," in *Morality and Health*, ed. A. Brandt and P. Rozin (New York and London: Routledge, 1997), pp. 101–18. As used in this paper "local worlds" is meant to emphasize the fact that ethnographic descriptions focus on micro-contexts of experience in villages, urban neighborhoods, work settings, households, and networks of bounded relationships in communities where everyday life is enacted and transacted.

[3] The idea of the intersubjectivity of experience can be found in the Western phenomenological and pragmatist traditions; see John Dewey, *Human Nature and Conduct* (New York: Modern Library, 1957 [1922]); William James, "The Consciousness of Self," in *The Principles of Psychology* (Cambridge: Harvard University Press, 1981); Alfred Schutz: *The Phenomenology of the Social World* (Evanston: Northwestern University Press, 1969); Max Scheler, *Man's Place in Nature*

testations among others with whom we are connected. It is a medium in which collective and subjective processes interfuse. We are born into the flow of palpable experience. Within its symbolic meanings and social interactions our senses form into a patterned sensibility, our movements meet resistance and find directions, and our subjectivity emerges, takes shape, and reflexively shapes our local world.[4] By local world I mean the ethnographer's village, neighborhood, networks, family, and other institutions. Even in a vast sea of globalization, in which we are more acutely aware that local worlds have permeable boundaries, undergo frequent change, and that their members may belong to several different networks at the same time — even with these qualifications the local perdures as the grounds of social life.[5] But I shall suggest that in local worlds we can also speak of local biologies with particular moral-

---

(New York: Noonday Press, 1971 [1938]); among such French thinkers as H. Bergson, *Les données immédiates de la conscience* (Paris: Alcans, 1889); Pierre Bourdieu, *The Practice of Theory: An Introduction to the Work of Pierre Bourdieu* (New York: Macmillan, 1990); Marc Auge: *"Théorie des pouvoirs et idéologie": Etude Cas en Cote-d 'Ivoire* (Paris: Hermann, 1975); and among the Chinese social scientists who developed the movement to sinicize social science (e.g., K. K. Hwang: "Face and Favor: The Chinese Power Game," *American Journal of Sociology* 92, no. 4 (1987): 944–74; Ambrose King, "Kuan-his and Network Building" *Daedalus* 120, no. 2 (1991): 63–84; K. S. Yang: "The Chinese People in Change," in his *Collected Works on the Chinese People* (Taipei: Kuei Kwan Book Co., 1987; in Chinese). In this paper, I elaborate the latter especially into a position that claims cross-cultural validity.

[4] On the emergence of subjectivity in interpersonal relations, language, and other symbolic mediators, see George Herbert Mead, *Mind, Self, and Society: From the Standpoint of a Social Behaviorist* (Chicago: University of Chicago Press, 1972 [1934]); Alfred Schutz, *The Phenomenology of the Social World* (Evanston: Northwestern University Press, 1967); Yang: "The Chinese People in Change."

[5] There is an extensive anthropological literature on the relation of the local and the global (see, for example, Ulf Hannerz, *Transnational Connections: Culture, People, Places* [New York: Routledge, 1996]). An unusual example is to be found in a collection of research studies of how McDonald's Restaurants have been a source of both globalization and indigenization in East Asia (see James L. Watson, ed., *Golden Arches East: McDonald's in East Asia* [Stanford: Stanford University Press, 1997]). It is difficult to sum up this literature, but on the whole it would seem to suggest that globalization has led to transformations in cultural, economic, political, and psychological processes, yet there is still considerable evidence of the power of local social processes to resist or reshape these influences.

bodily connections, connections that express and constitute the mundane and the supramundane.[6]

Experience is characterized by an orientation of overwhelming practicality.[7] What so thoroughly absorbs the attention of participants in a local world is that certain things matter, matter greatly, even desperately[8]. What exactly is at stake, across local worlds and historical epochs, varies, sometimes extravagantly so.[9] The

---

[6] The idea of local biologies has been developed by both social and biological anthropologists. Whereas some mean by this term that biology is represented differently in local knowledge (see Atwood Gaines, ed., *Ethnopsychiatry* [Albany: State University of New York Press, 1992], as, for example, in the case of anatomy in the Chinese medical tradition vis-à-vis its representation in biomedicine; others convey the idea that biological processes defined and measured in biomedical terms are transformed by social processes (see Margaret Lock, *Encounters with Aging: Mythologies of Menopause in Japan and North America* [Berkeley and Los Angeles: University of California Press, 1993]). It is in this second sense that I use the term in this lecture. (See also Peter Ellison's "Reproductive Ecology and 'Local Biologies,'" paper presented at the panel "The Body and the Cultural and Biological Divide," Annual Meeting, American Anthropological Association, Washington, D.C., 1996.)

[7] See, for example, Dewey (*Human Nature*), James ("Consciousness of Self"), and Schutz (*Phenomenology*). Among anthropologists, the most convincing ethnographic presentations are those of Michael Jackson, *Paths toward a Clearing: Radical Empiricism and Ethnographic Inquiry* (Bloomington: University of Indiana Press, 1989); Unni Wikan, "Public Grace and Private Fears: Gaiety, Offense, and Sorcery in Northern Bali," *Ethos* 15 (1987): 337–65; Veena Das, *Critical Events: An Anthropological Perspective on Contemporary India* (Delhi: University Press, 1994); Renato Rosaldo, "Grief and a Headhunter's Rage: On the Cultural Force of Emotion, in *Proceedings, American Ethnological Society, Washington D.C., 1983*, pp. 178–95. See also Kirsten Hastrup and Peter Hervils, eds., *Social Experience and Anthropological Knowledge* (London and New York: Routledge, 1994). Robert Desjarlais (*Shelter Blues: Sanity and Selfhood among the Homeless* (Philadelphia: University of Pennsylvania Press, 1997) provides a critical reflection on experience as an ethnographic category that is part of his study of the homeless mentally ill in Boston. That experience is characterized by overwhelming practicality does not diminish the importance of cosmologies, myths, rituals, or collective and individual theorizing in religious or secular contexts. It only clarifies that these crucial processes need to be seen as aspects of practical rationality and local practices.

[8] Arthur Kleinman ("Everything That Really Matters: Social Suffering, Subjectivity, and the Remaking of Human Experience in a Disordering World," *Harvard Theological Review* 90, no. 3 [1992]: 315–16) develops this point and illustrates it with interview materials from North America and China.

[9] The pertinent ethnographic and historical literature on cultural difference is by now simply immense. A few examples are Talal Asad, *Genealogies of Religion: Discipline and Reasons of Power in Christianity and Islam* (Baltimore: Johns Hopkins Press, 1993); John Bossy, *Christianity in the West, 1400–1700* (Oxford: Ox-

symbolic apparatuses of culture elaborate these meanings and constrain how individuals remember and act upon them so that local
worlds can be (and often are) greatly different cultural spaces.[10]
Even in the same world, there can be (and often are) conflicts

ford University Press, 1985); Clifford Geertz, *Local Knowledge and Further Essays
in Interpretive Anthropology* (New York: Basic Books, 1983); Catherine Lutz, *Unnatural Emotions: Everyday Sentiments on a Micronesian Atoll and Their Challenge
to Western Theory* (Chicago: University of Chicago Press, 1988); Ganneth Obeye-
sekere, *The Cult of the Goddess Pattini* (Chicago: University of Chicago Press,
1985); Michelle Rosaldo, *Knowledge and Passion: Ilongot Notions of Self and
Social Life* (Cambridge: Cambridge University Press, 1980); Bruno Snell, *The Discovery of the Mind (in Greek Philosophy and Literature): The Greek Origins of
European Thought* (Oxford: Blackwell, 1953); Unni Wikan, *Managing Turbulent
Hearts: A Balinese Formula for Living* (Chicago: University of Chicago Press,
1990). See also Jean Delumeau, *"Sin and Fear": The Emergence of a Western
Guilt Culture in the Thirteenth–Eighteenth Centuries*, trans. Eric Nicholson (New
York: St. Martin's Press, 1990); Peter Gay, *The Naked Heart* (New York: Norton,
1995); Carlo Ginzburg, *The Cheese and the Worms: The Cosmos of a Sixteenth-
Century Writer* (New York: Penguin Books, 1982); Irving Hallowell, *Culture and
Experience* (Philadelphia: University of Pennsylvania Press, 1967); Jackson (*Paths*);
Fred Myers: *Pintupi Country, Pintupi Self* (Washington, D.C.: Smithsonian Institu-
tion Press, 1986); E. Schieffelin, *The Sorrow of the Lonely and the Burning of the
Dancers* (New York: St. Martin's Press, 1976).

[10] The concept of culture has been used in different ways and is hotly debated
in the 1990s both within and without anthropology. Susan Wright ("The Politiciza-
tion of Culture," *Anthropology Today* 14, no. 1 [1998]: 7–15), writing in the
official publication of the Royal Anthropological Institute of Great Britain and Ireland, puts it: older views of culture emphasized its boundedness, defined characteristics, unchanging, shared, and homogenous elements, while newer views emphasize that culture is an active process of meaning making, is contested, involves
individuals who are differently socially positioned, has local, national, and global connections, is not closed or coherent, and can be used hegemonically. The appropriations of the idea of "culture" in politics, commercial practices, and international
development programs show that its uses are salient as its content. In this lecture,
I draw upon elements of both newer and older definitions, as will soon become apparent to the reader; but at both local and global levels I use "culture" to mean
symbolic apparatuses of meaning making, representation, and transmission. Culture
is closely connected with political and economic processes and changes in relation to
them; it is both shared and contested; it is differentially distributed across the divisions of class, ethnicity, religion, gender, and age cohort; it is realized in local
worlds yet extends beyond them; and it contains coherences and incoherences. The
idea of culture's appropriation as part of political and economic processes that are
historically shaped and consequential for human futures is one I am particularly
interested in and seek to develop in this lecture. Indeed, although treated as a
strawman in the guise of "cultural relativism" in moral theory in the 1980s and
earlier, in the 1990s culture has been taken up in moral debates, but more often in
a manner that strips it of its economic, political, and historical aspects. (See Arthur
Kleinman, "The Anthropology of Bioethics," chapter 3 in *Writing at the Margin*,
pp. 41–67.)

owing to differences of class, ethnicity, political faction, gender, and individuality.[11] So that heterogeneity and complexity define most social spaces. Culture in the form of local knowledge and practices is as much about what is not shared as it is about what is shared. But that some things do matter, matter greatly — such as status, relationships, resources, ultimate meanings, one's being-in-the-world and one's being-unto-death and transcendence, among many other things — and that what matters has a collective as well as a personal significance is what provides experience everywhere with its moral mode. Experience is *moral*, as I define it, because it is the medium of engagement in everyday life in which things are at stake and in which ordinary people are deeply engaged stake-holders who have important things to lose, to gain, and to preserve.

Among the things that order the course of the moral processes I will describe are dangers, dangers that are perceived to exist in the world and that represent serious threats to other things that are at stake as well. The dangers of social experience are multifarious. They occupy our attention because they can threaten our categories, our relationships, our projects, even our survival. In these lectures I will examine one type of danger: the sources, forms, and consequences of *social suffering*: a topic that I will develop at length later.[12] I select this subject for emphasis because,

---

[11] The ethnographic literature of the 1980s and 1990s is filled with examples of such differences from communities worldwide: e.g., James Clifford and George Marcus, *Writing Culture: The Poetics and Politics of Ethnography* (Berkeley: University of California Press, 1986); James Clifford, *The Predicament of Culture: Twentieth-Century Ethnography, Literature and Art* (Cambridge, Mass.: Harvard University Press, 1988); George Marcus and Michael Fisher, *Anthropology as Cultural Critique: An Experimental Moment in the Human Sciences* (Chicago: University of Chicago Press 1986); Mary Steedly, *Hanging without a Rope: Narrative Experience in Colonial and Postcolonial Karoland* (Princeton: Princeton University Press, 1993); Anna Lowenhaupt Tsing, *In the Realm of the Diamond Queen: Marginality in an Out-of-the-Way Place* (Princeton: Princeton University Press, 1993).

[12] See, for example, Arthur Kleinman, Veena Das, and Margaret Lock, eds., *Social Suffering* (Berkeley and Los Angeles: University of California Press, 1997). The Australian sociologist Bryan Turner, in a theoretical framing I only became aware of after writing these lectures, distinguishes between the "ontological fra-

as we will see, it is so consequential for human conditions globally.

This picture of social life may seem overly serious, even oppressive. Joy and humor and imagination can lighten experience and describe the mundane (and supramundane) in ways that are just as crucial. But here, to counterbalance our society's famous romance with progress and sentimentality, I seek to emphasize suffering and danger.

Seen in this light, moral processes differ in a fundamental way from ethical discourse. The latter is an abstract articulation and debate over codified values. It is conducted by elites, both global and local. Ethical discourse is usually principle-based, with meta-theoretical commentary on the authorization and implication of those principles. (In bioethics, the chief principles are autonomy, beneficence, and justice; they in turn privilege informed consent and confidentiality.) Ethical discourse is reflective and intellectualist, emphasizing cognition (more precisely, in today's jargon, rational choice) over affect or behavior and coherence over the sense of incompleteness and unknowability and uncontrollability that is so prevalent in ordinary life. Or at least this is its canonical form in the Western tradition. In the Western tradition it often includes strong emphasis on individual rights, what has been called "autonomy unbounded," and a search for an acontextual objectivity: a view from nowhere.[13] The result is a lack of emphasis, in medical ethics for instance, on solidarity with those who are disadvantaged and underserved in Euro-American communities and

---

gility" of ordinary men and women's being-unto-death, which human commonality he suggests is responsible for much of sociality, and the "social precariousness" that is the condition of societies. The latter, in turn, induces powerful responses from the state and its institutions that deepen precariousness. Medicalization, for example, is a response to ontological frailty and social precariousness that worsens the latter. Turner uses this approach to criticize much sociology as "ornamental" and to argue for a sharedness in experience that results from these elements of sociality as well as from the interpenetration of worlds and their hybridity (Bryan Turner, personal communication, University of Deakin, Melbourne, Australia, March 25, 1998).

[13] This analysis of the anthropology of ethics draws upon an extended review in Arthur Kleinman, "The Anthropology of Bioethics," pp. 41–67.

the poorest non-Western societies.[14] Indigenous ethical discourses elsewhere do not always share these goals; and, as in the Chinese tradition, they may emphasize the right conduct of the ethically cultivated person — a character trait, albeit a cultural-psychological one — over principle-guided decisions. But they, like the canonical Western tradition, aim to be normative, to offer a "should" and a generalizable "must" about practices. Concern for respecting cultural difference has repeatedly pointed up the need for ethical discourse to project local indigenous alternatives — which anthropologists call ethnoethical formulations — into global framings (and vice versa), but there is still great unclarity about how this is to be accomplished.[15]

[14] This point is made by Renee Fox, "More Than Bioethics Alone: Critical Reflections on the Relationship between Medicine, Ethics and Social Science in the Education of Medical Students," First W. H. R. Rivers Distinguished Lecture in Social Medicine, Harvard Medical School, March 10, 1998.

[15] Arthur Kleinman, "Bioethics." Certain moral theorists have been particularly sensitive to the issue of moral particularism and cultural differences: see, for example, Stuart Hampshire, *Morality and Conflict* (Cambridge, Mass.: Harvard University Press, 1983); as well as Amy Gutmann, "The Challenge of Multiculturalism in Political Ethics," *Philosophy and Public Affairs* 22 (1993): 171–206. But Gutmann's piece is also an example of the way moral theorists construct ethical relativism as a strawman that is used to limit the seriousness of cultural difference for moral enquiry. A more impressive engagement of moral theory with cultural difference and cross-cultural disagreements concerning lived values is to be found in Michele Moody-Adams, *Fieldwork in Familiar Places: Morality, Culture and Philosophy* (Cambridge, Mass.: Harvard University Press, 1997). Moody-Adams remarks: "Although inhabitants of different cultures admittedly have different experiences, they can nonetheless contribute to a cross-cultural moral conversation." She also insists that "philosophy must give up its claims to moral objectivity or a special knowledge and must see itself and become part of everyday moral inquiry about 'the life worth living and how human beings might attain it' " (p. 12). Moody-Adams also notes that "moral philosophy always presupposes a kind of interpretive ethnography" (p. 169) and that "no philosophical interpretation of the structure of moral experience — not even a systematic moral theory — can solve moral problems, but it can influence the decisions and actions of human beings who contemplate the implications, principally by virtue of its tendency to encourage self-scrutiny" (p. 170). All of this sounds congenial for an anthropological approach to moral theory. Indeed, this anthropologically informed philosopher goes so far as to recommend "thick description" as a "suitable appreciation of the contexts and processes of moral inquiry, and of the means by which moral inquiry helps state the . . . claims and practices claimed to constitute morality" (p. 189). And yet while rejecting standard Anglo-American moral philosophy accounts, Moody-Adams castigates cultural relativism. Still, her notion of engaged moral inquiry as moral experience comes close to what I advocate in the last section of the lecture.

In contrast to ethical discourse, moral experience is always about practical engagements in a particular local world, a social space that carries cultural, political, and economic specificity. It is about positioned views and practices: a view from somewhere and an action that becomes partisan. As local worlds become heavily infiltrated by *globalization* of the media, of political economy, and of folk and professional culture, so that the global discourse on ethics, for example, becomes hegemonic about such issues as human rights, under globalization moral experience is nonetheless still about the actualities of specific events and situated relationships. At the level of moral processes, accommodation and betrayal may seem to be different empirical options, but they are often made indistinguishable by ongoing compromises and negotiations. Local power relationships refract the force of economic and political pressure so that some persons are protected while others are more routinely and thoroughly exposed to the social violences that everywhere organize everyday life. Actions may not be coherent. Relations may be besotted. The sociologic of social roles and obligations and the exigency of situations and sheer personal cussedness may override choice, at least when it is modeled as an individual's rational decision making. The infrapolitics of interpersonal interactions may create conformity, confuse options, and encourage paralyzing perceptions of powerlessness. Irony, paradox, uncertainty, and change are the very stuff of moral experience. But like power, which thrusts particular people to the edge of social life and nullifies alternatives, these frustrating complexities are rarely taken up in ethical framings. Nor are the protagonists of ethical discourse and their ethical arguments understood as grounded in particular moral places and processes. But, of course, they are. And, to be sure, what is at stake in a local world may involve a moral economy of systematic injustice, bad faith, and even horror. Yes; from an ethnographic perspective what is at stake, what morally defines a local world, may be, when viewed in comparative perspective, corrupt, grotesque, even downright inhuman.[16] That is to say, the moral may be unethical, just as the ethical may be irrelevant to moral experience.

For this reason, consideration of values in society requires both approaches as necessarily complementary. Contributors to ethical discourse are working harder, it now seems to me, to engage the descriptive ethnographies and social historical materials that make up moral processes, as can be seen in the development of situational and processual ethics, which clearly have tried to take concrete local problems into account. And, like most dichotomies concerning the social world, this one blurs when we consider the influence that ethical discourse (local and global) has in informing moral experience. Indeed, the incoherences and fragmentations that the hybridity, interpenetrations, and uncertainty of experience so regularly create are made more coherent and interpretable through ethical discourse. Social suffering, as we will soon see, emerges from the remakes local worlds that need more, not less, ethical deliberation. My point is not to disparage ethics on behalf of the moral processes of experience, but rather to contribute to a more inclusive and availing engagement across these related yet distinctive domains.

Inclusiveness here must mean broadening the global discourse so that it considers other traditions beyond the canonical Western one and actively engages the local ethical discourse of participants in a local world.[17] And, of course, nothing that I have said or will

---

[16] Examples might include those described in Christopher Browning, *Ordinary Men: Reserve Police Battalion 101 and the Final Solution in Poland* (New York: HarperCollins, 1992); Primo Levy, *Survival in Auschwitz* (New York: Simon and Schuster, 1993); Rezak Hukanovic, *The Tenth Circle of Hell: A Memoir of Life in the Death Camps of Bosnia* (New York: Basic Books, 1997); E. Valentine Daniel, *Charred Lullabies: Chapters in an Anthropography of Violence* (Princeton: Princeton University Press, 1997); Nancy Scheper-Hughes, *Death without Weeping: The Violence of Everyday Life in Brazil* (Berkeley and Los Angeles: University of California Press, 1992).

[17] For examples of what I have in mind with respect to engaging distinctive cultural traditions and local ethical discourses, see Kleinman and Kleinman, "Moral Transformations"; Kleinman, "Bioethics"; Veena Das, "Moral Orientations to Suffering," in *Health and Social Change: An International Perspective*, ed. L. C. Chen,

say about suffering and moral disorder is meant to deny that moral processes also involve remorse, regret, endurance, aspiration, courage, transcendence, and other responses that have an ethical and religious significance.[18]

An idea of "human nature" often underpins ethical discourse, and not just in the Western tradition, inasmuch as it naturalizes and universalizes ethical decision making. Behind the excruciating diversity of cultural contexts and the bewildering inexpediences of social situations, the claim can be made that human nature provides a universal basis for ethical standards and actions.[19]

Jean de La Bruyère, writing in the seventeenth century, observed: "In short, Men's souls and passions change not, they are yet the same still as they were. . . ." Denis Diderot, like the other Encyclopedists, claimed: "Human nature is the same everywhere; it determines everything that matters in human behavior; science is the best way to know human nature; science must therefore govern ethics and politics." And reflecting on human nature from a comparative cross-cultural perspective that capaciously encompasses both Brazilian aboriginal shamans and Parisian academic mandarins, Claude Lévi-Strauss insists: "the outer differences conceal a basic unity."[20] In psychology, in economics, in medicine,

---

A. Kleinman, and N. Ware (Cambridge, Mass.: Harvard University Press, 1994); Talal Asad, "On Torture, or Cruel, Inhuman, and Degrading Treatment," in Kleinman et al., *Social Suffering*, pp. 285–308; J. W. Bowker, *Problems of Suffering in the Religions of the World* (Cambridge: Cambridge University Press, 1970); and Wei Ming Tu, ed., *The Living Tree: The Changing Meaning of Being Chinese Today* (Stanford: Stanford University Press, 1994).

[18] Kleinman, "Everything That Really Matters."

[19] It is not my purpose here to comprehensively review the idea of human nature. It has, of course, an ancient provenance, even if Michel Foucault claimed that in its eighteenth-century form of human nature underwriting the rights of man it is a historically recent arrival. During the nineteenth century especially it got caught up with the ramifying cultural discourse on natural history, which increasingly lent to it a biological significance, as in the natural history of plants, animals, and diseases (see N. Jardine, J. Secord, E. Sparry, eds., *Culture of Natural History* [Cambridge and New York: Cambridge University Press, 1996]).

[20] The quotations from La Bruyère, Diderot, and Lévi-Strauss are cited in Tzvetan Todorov, *On Human Diversity in French Thought* (Cambridge, Mass.: Harvard University Press, 1993), pp. 3, 24, 61, respectively.

and in other fields the idea of human nature is appropriated as an essentialized rationale for universals, including universal ethical standards. In a rather typical statement from bioethics, the physician–moral theorist Leon Kass writes that medical practice in its engagement with the existential questions of life and death, suffering, and solace "is a matter not only of mind and hand but also of the heart, not only of intellect and skill but also of character. . . . It is rooted in our moral nature." [21] The cultural psychologist Richard Shweder and his colleagues, in a controversial essay whose conclusion many anthropologists are likely to contest, argue from a review of the cross-cultural record that moral concerns with autonomy, community, and divinity are rooted in human (or moral) nature.[22] But Shweder et al. understand that "nature" not simply as a psychobiological universal, but rather as the coming together of "psychology, experience, and society" to create a pan-human moral orientation. Putative universals in cross-cultural perceptions of colors, preferences in life style, and other psychological processes have been used by sociobiologists to argue for a biological basis to human nature and even to claim an evolutionary source to ethical commitments. Thus, E. O. Wilson, the ever expansive entomologist, writing popularly about "the biological basis of morality," claims that "causal explanations of brain activity and evolution, while imperfect, already cover most facts known about behavior we term 'moral.' " [23]

Beyond the Western tradition, one can find uses of the idea of human nature in ways that are similar to these statements from the

[21] Leon Kass, " 'I Will Give No Deadly Drug': Why Doctors Must Not Kill," *Bulletin of the American College of Surgeons* 77, no. 3 (1992): 6–17.

[22] Richard Shweder, Nancy C. Much, Manamohan Mahapatra, and Lawrence Park, " 'The Big Three' of Morality (Autonomy, Community, Divinity) and the 'Big Three' Explanations of Suffering," in A. Brandt and P. Rozin, eds., *Morality and Health* (New York: Routledge, 1997), pp. 101–18.

[23] See E. O. Wilson, "The Biological Basis of Morality," *Atlantic Monthly* 28, no. 4 (1998): 53–70. Wilson's polemical statement is based upon the idea of a biological basis of human nature, which itself is viewed as the product of gene-culture co-evolution. See also "From Ants to Ethics: A Biologist Dreams of Unity of Knowledge," *New York Times*, May 12, 1998, p. C1.

West. Thus, one reads in the Chinese philosophical tradition: "only those who are rash in their argument would say that human nature today isn't what it was in the past" or "the passions of a thousand men, of ten thousand men, are ever the same as the passions of any one man" (*Xunzi*, chapters 3, 5). Mencius, whose disagreement with Xunzi over whether human nature is inherently good or not is fundamental, nonetheless also remarks that all persons possess a number of qualities of human nature and that all must obey the same laws in moral life. Thus, it was characteristic of a major stream of the Chinese tradition to relate *xing* (physical nature) with *qing* (emotions) and the moral order.[24]

Yet biology, once invoked as the source of that unifying human nature, appears to exert such a thin influence in the complexity of human affairs that most of the time it cannot be shown to be immediately consequential. The coarse-grained sentiments of the newborn and toddler may tell us a good deal about psychobiological physiology and its genetic bases, but the complex emotions of social life, such as remorse and regret, are the consequences of crisscrossing meanings, relationships, and subjectivities reworking biology to such an extent that the situation of adults is another case entirely. The front page of the *New York Times* of Tuesday, March 10, 1998, offers an impressive illustration of the immense disjuncture between the claims made for what is supposedly known about the biological bases of human nature and what is actually known about human conditions (Figure 1). The upper lefthand columns contain a picture of a flood in Elba, Alabama; the middle columns contain an article on a "gruesome" Serbian atrocity in Kosovo. The righthand column tells a tale about Trent Lott, the Republican leader of the U.S. Senate, who is trying to shift blame from Kenneth Starr, the Whitewater independent counsel, whose investigations of Monica Lewinsky's allegations

[24] For a review of these arguments, see D. C. Lau, trans., *Mencius Vol. 1 (xiii–xxvii)*. (Hong Kong: Chinese University Press, Hong Kong, 1970), as well Siu-Kit Wong, "Ching in Chinese Literary Criticism," Ph.D. dissertation, University College, Oxford, 1969.

"All the News That's Fit to Print"

The New York Times

New England Final
Boston: Variable clouds, becoming windy and colder. High in the 40's. Tonight, clearing and colder. Low near 20. Tomorrow, bright skies and frigid. High in the 30's. Details, page A20

VOL. CXLVII . . . . No. 51,092 — Copyright © 1998 The New York Times — TUESDAY, MARCH 10, 1998 — ONE DOLLAR

A storm system that pounded the Southeast and Midwest over the weekend left 5 feet of water surrounding the Coffee County Courthouse in Elba, Ala. The flooding Pea River forced 2,000 residents to evacuate.

On a Garage Floor in Kosovo, A Gruesome Serbian Harvest

By CHRIS HEDGES

SRBICA, Serbia, March 9 — The bodies of 51 ethnic Albanians, their lower torsos wrapped in white sheets, lay stretched out in two rows on the cement floor of an old garage today as a steady drizzle pelted the tiled roof.

The bodies, a few burned beyond recognition, included 25 women and small children. Most bore the small, dark red holes of bullet wounds. The skulls of some of them were shattered, and one was decapitated.

The release of the bodies brings the number of ethnic Albanians known to have been killed in the fighting in the last week to 77, and dozens more remain missing. The victims, almost all from the village of Prekaz, a stronghold of the outlawed Kosovo Liberation Army, included the rebel commander, Adem Jashari — his head tilted back and his throat slit by a bloody gash.

The Jashari family dominates the village, and more than 20 family members were killed in the last few days of violence. Heavily armed Serbian police and paramilitary units, backed up by armored personel carriers and helicopter gunships, cordoned off the region to keep outsiders away, then attacked the Albanian separatists with bullets and shells. The Albanians are fighting for a separate state in Serbia's southernmost province, where 90 percent of the population is Albanian.

"The police brought the bodies from the morgue in Pristina in two trucks," said Adem Meta, a community leader, "and told us we could do what we wanted to with them because the police had finished their work. They said that if we did not bury the bodies by tonight they would dump them in a mass grave."

"We do not want to bury them without families being able to come and identify the victims," he said. "But no one dares to come here now. It is too dangerous."

Serbian officials contend that the women and children who died were killed by armed rebels who refused to let them surrender. But there is mounting evidence that although many of the Jashari clan in Prekaz were armed and fired back on police units, unarmed civilians, and apparently all males detained by the police, were executed, often in front of their wives and children.

Bosko Drobnjak, the Serbian official in charge of information, said Adem Jashari had killed his own wife and nephew.

Those who fled the village, including 20 members of the Jashari clan, said the police had forced men to lie on the ground in front of their families and then had fired automatic rounds into their bodies.

Nazmi Jashari was helping his elderly mother out the back of

Continued on Page A10

Croatia — Danube — Romania — Sava R. — Belgrade — Bosnia and Herzegovina — Yugoslavia — Serbia — Sarajevo — Kosovo — Mitrovica — Montenegro — Srbica — Pristina — Prekaz — Adriatic Sea — Albania — Macedonia — The New York Times

Most of the dead were from Prekaz, a rebel stronghold.

Sanctions on Yugoslavia

The United States and its Western allies agreed in an emergency meeting to impose modest sanctions on Yugoslavia over its use of force against the ethnic Albanian majority in Kosovo. Page A10.

LOTT SHIFTS BLAME ON INQUIRY'S PACE TO THE PRESIDENT

BACK INTO THE G.O.P. FOLD

After Pressing Starr to 'Show Cards,' He Tells Clinton to Tell 'the Whole Truth'

By ALISON MITCHELL

WASHINGTON, March 9 — Recalibrating his views on the inquiry into President Clinton, Senator Trent Lott today called for the President to come forward and tell "the whole truth" about his relationship with a former White House intern. He said the issue "is beginning to have an impact on his Presidency."

Senator Lott's remarks, at a news conference, put the blame for the pace of the investigation into the President's relationship with the intern, Monica S. Lewinsky, on the White House instead of on the Whitewater independent counsel, Kenneth W. Starr.

That brought Mr. Lott, the Senate majority leader, back into the Republican fold after he had unintentionally whipped up a storm over the weekend by saying on the CNN program "Evans and Novak" that Mr. Starr had "had enough time and it's time to show his cards."

His news conference today sought to focus attention back on Mr. Clinton. But it was just another sign of the Republicans' predicament as they search for ways to capitalize on Mr. Clinton's latest embarrassment without being seen as unduly partisan — something they were accused of during the Whitewater and campaign finance hearings.

Worse, some Republicans fear a voter backlash in an election year if they are asked to begin impeachment proceedings against a President with high popularity ratings.

Today Mr. Lott said that to complete his work, Mr. Starr needed cooperation from the President. "Instead," Mr. Lott said, "what he has been getting is stonewalling and smear tactics and attack methods" from Mr. Clinton's allies.

"I today call on the President to come forward, tell the American people what has happened in these cases, particularly the Lewinsky case," Mr. Lott said. "What is the whole truth? Tell that to the independent counsel, call off his attack dogs, get this behind us so that we can go on with the people's business."

The grand jury hearing testimony in Mr. Starr's investigation is to resume Tuesday with an appearance by Bayani Nelvis, a White House steward who has testified twice before, officials involved in the investigation said. Mr. Nelvis works in and around the Oval Office and is in a position to observe the President meeting privately with visitors.

In another dramatic change of direction, David Brock, the conservative writer whose 1993 article in The American Spectator led Paula Cor-

Continued on Page A16

2 Arms Makers Suddenly Face Antitrust Snag

By ANDREW POLLACK

LOS ANGELES, March 9 — The Lockheed Martin Corporation said today that the Government "fundamentally opposed" its planned purchase of the Northrop Grumman Corporation, suggesting that Federal regulators may believe that the consolidation among military suppliers has gone too far to maintain competition.

The Defense Department and the Justice Department, which are reviewing the agreement, characterized their positions slightly differently, saying only that they had serious concerns about the deal and were talking with the companies about it. But if the Government tried to block the acquisition, which is possible, it would be a reversal from the Pentagon's recent policy of encouraging such mergers to help cut costs amid the fall in military spending since the end of the cold war.

Until now, the mergers have sailed through their required antitrust clearance with only minor divestitures required in some cases as the number of major military contractors has shrunk to three.

"This is a statement by Justice that future defense mergers will be held to a different standard," said Wolfgang Demisch, aerospace analyst with BT Alex. Brown.

The news of the Government's concern, eight months after the purchase was announced, surprised the industry and Wall Street. "It's awfully strange to wait this long without anyone knowing," said Paul Nisbet, aerospace analyst at JSA Research Inc. in Newport, R.I.

Lockheed and Northrop shareholders had approved the transaction on Feb. 26, and their executives had been speaking confidently of winning approval. Lockheed has spearheaded the consolidation trend and has gone

Continued on Page D2

Snow, Floods and Bitter Cold: Storm Rakes Much of Nation

By SHIRLEY CHRISTIAN

A vast storm system over the weekend caused deadly flooding in the South and heavy rain and high winds in the New York region, and hurled a bitter onslaught of snow, ice and frigid temperatures from Wisconsin through Nebraska that blasted Midwesterners out of their smugness over a winter that almost wasn't.

The toll was worst in the South, where thunderstorms and floods were blamed for nine deaths, five of them in southern Alabama, where Gov. Fob James Jr. declared a state of emergency. The town of Elba, Ala., was under more than six feet of water after the Pea River broke through its levee, forcing the evacuation of 2,000 people — half of all the residents.

It was a repeat of a 1990 flood, when a different part of the levee broke and sent floodwaters rising more than 12 feet across downtown.

"I'm not going through this again," Charles Lee Marler, [illegible], was quoted by The Associated Press as saying. "When you lose everything you have, two, three, four times, that's enough."

Rain was also causing havoc in southeast Georgia, which got 5 inches of rain in 24 hours Sunday and through much of Florida, still recovering from the twisters last month that killed 42 people.

In the Midwest, the snow and generally miserable weather descended on crocuses that had been blooming for weeks in some areas, tulips several inches tall and wisteria trying to blossom. It shocked people who had been practicing golf swings and those who had set out on weekend trips thinking that spring was virtually here.

"I want spring back, right now," bemoaned Kerrie Raggett after she slept late with a headache in a St. Joseph, Mo., motel room. Like many others, she and her husband and four-year-old daughter took shelter there Sunday night after encountering a closed interstate highway on the way to their home in Council Bluffs, Iowa.

They were among the luckier ones. Many people were stranded in their cars along highways in Kansas and Nebraska, unable to see to stay on the road in blizzard conditions yesterday morning. The storm was blamed for two deaths on Kansas highways and one in Wisconsin. Near Kansas City a woman drowned when her car went off a bridge into the Little Blue River on Sunday.

The startled reception to the snow in the Midwest and the soggy misery in the South confirmed an announcement yesterday by the National

Continued on Page A12

Seoul Leader, Ex-Inmate Himself, Is Slow to Free Political Prisoners

By NICHOLAS D. KRISTOF

SEOUL, South Korea — The world of Prisoner No. 3514 is a closet-size space with three brick walls and one solid steel door with a flap that opens to deliver his meals. His only "furniture" is one blanket that he lays on the floor as a mattress and another that he wraps around himself to fight the winter cold.

Possibly the longest-serving political prisoner in the world today, Prisoner No. 3514 has spent the last 39 years and seven months in prison. Others who have been released say that he is partly paralyzed from a stroke and that his teeth are all gone because of decades of torture.

In 1958 the prisoner, Woo Yong Gak, was the head of an eight-member North Korean military reconnaissance team whose boat was seized when it entered South Korean waters. Human rights specialists in South Korea and abroad say he is being kept in prison long after others accused of being spies were freed because he will not renounce his belief in Communism.

This short, balding, 60-year-old man seems a monument to the dark, dictatorial days of Korea past, and yet he and hundreds like him remain imprisoned in the democracy that is Korea present.

While some of the prisoners, like Mr. Woo, were imprisoned on charges of espionage, others are South Korean labor activists and leftists who were convicted of distributing North Korean propaganda or of burning incense to mourn the death of President Kim Il Sung of North Korea in 1994.

Now another former political prisoner, Kim Dae Jung, has just taken office as President, but South Korea remains profoundly suspicious of Communists like Mr. Woo, and President Kim is reluctant to expend his political capital by rapidly releasing the country's political prisoners.

"The time is not yet ripe for the release of all prisoners of con-

Continued on Page A6

Bilingual Education Facing Toughest Test

By DON TERRY

LA HABRA, Calif. — Rosa Espinoza and Alice Callaghan spend much of their lives nurturing the American Dreams of poor and working class Latino immigrant children by tutoring them after school in English, math and faith in themselves and in their new country.

The two women have never met, but they agree that if the children they care about so deeply are to do better than working in a sweatshop, the way many of their parents do, then the key is for them to learn how to read, write and speak English as quickly as possible. Still, when it comes to the best way for the public schools to teach those make-or-break lessons, Mrs. Espinoza and Ms. Callaghan are on opposite sides of a bitter debate.

Ms. Callaghan supports a California ballot initiative that could virtually wipe out bilingual education in the country's most populous and diverse state. Mrs. Espinoza opposes it.

It is called Proposition 227, or the English for the Children initiative, or simply the Unz initiative after its author and chief financial backer, Ron K. Unz, a Silicon Valley millionaire and conservative Republican who has no children or background in education and has never set foot in a bilingual education class. But Mr. Unz, who is 36 and a former candidate for governor, said he had been interested in the issue for more than a decade and had come to an unwavering conclusion: "The system seems completely nuts. It's time for a change."

Proponents of 227 assert that the bilingual program has been a failure, turning out students with little knowledge of English and condemning them to a life of menial jobs.

If 227 passes on June 2, as polls suggest that it will, the tremors will be felt far beyond California's borders. The battle here is being carefully watched by educators and politicians across the country. In essence, voters will decide whether to end an era of pedagogy first ushered into the state's school houses in 1967 when Gov. Ronald Reagan signed a bill eliminating the state's English-only instructional mandate and allowing bilingual education. In its place, the Unz initiative calls for one year of courses taught in English, with an emphasis on learning the language — a system that many fear is a return to a past when children were sometimes punished for speaking Spanish, but that others say is a return to sanity.

Supporters of 227 blame bilingual education for a variety of

Continued on Page A15

Edward Carreon for The New York Times

Alice Callaghan, an Episcopal priest who opposes California's bilingual education program, tutoring her Latino students.

Mapping the Codes That Define Humans

A team of about 200 people is working 19 hours a day in pursuit of the ultimate self-knowledge, an effort to sequence the human genome by 2005. The odds of success at this point are not overwhelming.

At the end of this month the project will be halfway through its planned 15-year course, yet only 3 percent of the genome has been completed.

The goal of sequencing the entire three billion letters of human DNA is not just technically ambitious. The coiled double ribbon of DNA holds the genetic instructions to make and operate the human organism.

Article, page C1.

In Plea Deal, Youth Promises to Testify About Baby's Death

By ROBERT HANLEY

WILMINGTON, Del., March 9 — Breaking his long silence on charges that he helped his sweetheart kill their newborn son in a Delaware motel 16 months ago, Brian C. Peterson pleaded guilty to manslaughter today and agreed to become a central witness against his former girlfriend in her murder trial.

A lawyer for Mr. Peterson, who is 19, told the judge that Mr. Peterson regretted that he did not seek medical help for the baby or try to get confirmation for his belief that the baby was born dead.

The lawyer, Russell M. Gioiella, said Mr. Peterson had no intention of harming the infant and said he disposed of the baby in a trash bin behind the Newark motel at the insistence of his girlfriend, Amy S. Grossberg, minutes after she gave birth. "During that extremely emotional and trying time, Amy was telling Brian, 'Get rid of it, get rid of it,'" Mr. Gioiella said.

Under the plea agreement, Mr. Peterson now faces a maximum prison term of 10 years. He could have received the death penalty if convicted.

Mr. Peterson's decision to testify against his former girlfriend, also 19, completed a sharp recasting of the emotions and images of a widely publicized and highly charged case

Continued on Page A20

INSIDE

Iraq Inspections Set

The United Nations Secretary General forged another direct link with Iraq by outlining new procedures for weapons inspections there. A3

'Gray Market' Upheld

A Supreme Court decision virtually insures a multibillion-dollar "gray market" in sales not authorized by companies will continue. Page D1.

News Summary	A2
Arts	B1-8
Business Day	D1-21
Editorial, Op-Ed	A22-23
International	A3-11
National	A12-16, 19-20
New York	A17-18
Science Times	C1-8
SportsTuesday	D23-26
Fashion	A21
Health	C7
Obituaries	D22
Weather	A20
Classified Ads	[illegible]
Auto Exchange	[illegible]

On the Internet: www.nytimes.com

FIGURE 1. Front Page, *New York Times*, March 10, 1998.

Lott had earlier decried as too slow, to President Bill Clinton, who Lott demands should now tell "the whole truth." Other stories on page one's layout include an account of political prisoners in Korea, an article on snow and bitter cold in the American Middle West and their effects on everyday life, the details of an antitrust case, and also plea bargaining in the killing of a baby by its teenage parents, as well as an essay on the challenges faced by bilingual education in America's increasingly diverse public schools. Taking up a small space in the lower left column, almost like the bottom line "sum" on a restaurant bill, is a headline about the current status of the human genome project that carries, in light of the other articles, the astonishing title "Mapping the Codes That Define Humans."

The irony is extreme. Do political violence in the Balkans, the politics of a presidential scandal, natural disasters and their traumatic consequences, multiculturalism, American business, Korean prisons, and teenage pregnancy and infanticide receive their explanation from what the human genome project's proponents define as the genetic basis of human identity? I find the claim immodest and even ludicrous. Genes would seem to have precious little to do with the major political, economic, moral, and social issues discussed in the other stories, yet these issues are the very stuff of what it means to be "human."

Viewed from the decidedly ordinary practices of everyday experience, human conditions certainly have a biology, but they have a history, a politics, an economics, and they reflect cultural and subjective differences. Indeed affective processes — understood in these social psychological terms — turn out to be even more consequential for moral processes than cognitive ones — a point made by the great Finnish anthropologist Edvard Westermarck, three-quarters of a century ago. "Moral values," wrote Westermarck, "are not abstract but relative to the emotions they express." [25]

[25] Edvard Westermarck, *Ethical Relativity* (London: K. Paul Trench, Trubner and Co., 1932), p. 289.

"The emotional constitution . . . does not present the same uniformity as the human intellect," he opined after a review of a then
large cross-cultural literature that today is too vast to review comprehensively. Affect and its biology, we might say in the way of
an update, however, contribute more to difference than to same-
ness.[26] In other words, moral processes are simultaneously social
and subjective, or as I put it earlier, *intersubjective*, not *natural*.
In place of a single "human nature," the moral modes of experience are more appropriately described by a large variety of "human conditions," particular conditions of social life and personal
positioning that contain elements that are shared as well as many,
many others that are quite distinctive. Psychobiology, once taken
up in language, in symbolic codes, in narratives, in social relationships, and in collective and personal memories, does not specify a
universal human nature, then, but rather local mind-body processes
that are so open to the social world that human conditions are different, even greatly so, and change as local worlds and our places
in them change.[27] Biology is important, but in a rather different
way than it is customarily invoked by those who appropriate it as
the grounds for a universal human nature.

My purpose here is to draw critical attention to the uses of the
idea of "human nature" in ethics. There it often seems to be a
means of begging difficult questions. (The Australian philosopher
C. A. J. Coady is skeptical as to whether any authoritative testimony can be given at all about human nature.)[28] It just as often
seeks to authorize the idea of an autonomous naturalized realm of
universals that can be objectively assessed independent of culture,

[26] This is a rather large subject, which I have reviewed elsewhere, that would
take too extensive a digression to develop here: see Arthur Kleinman, *Rethinking
Psychiatry* (New York: Free Press, 1988).

[27] Ellison, "Reproductive Ecology"; Lock, *Encounters*; Arthur Kleinman and
Anne Becker, "Introduction," in *"Sociosomatics": Psychosomatic Medicine* (in press).

[28] C. A. J. Coady, *Testimony: A Philosophical Study* (Oxford: Clarendon Press,
1992).

politics, or economics.²⁹ That asocial abstraction, which is so helpful to those who would restrict the idea of justice, for instance, to
talk about the intentions of policy makers and the legal language
of programs, rather than the unjust distribution of human problems and resources, is an impossibility when we use the socially
grounded concept of actual "human conditions."

Because I find that concern with ethical discourse far predomi-
nates over an orientation to moral experience in programs in
values and society, and because my own professional positioning
prepares me to do so, in these lectures I take my responsibility to
develop the case for *experience*. One thing that a focus on experience entails is concern for change. For the ethnographer like the
social historian, in order to specify a local world and its transformations, it is crucial to understand how moral experience changes
under the interactions between *cultural representations, collective
processes*, and *subjectivity*, interactions that are in turn shaped by
large-scale changes in political economy, politics, and culture.
Moral experience, then, possesses a genealogy just as it does a
locality.

Ours clearly is an era of the most pronounced transnational
changes, changes that are remaking both the global and the local.
The latest phase of finance capitalism has created unprecedented
space and time compression, dissolved established value systems
and social organizations, fostered the corporatization of professional work and the infiltration of technical rationality into all
aspects of domestic lifeworlds, accelerated commodification of cultural processes, authorized entirely new aesthetics, and intensified
"volatility" and "ephemerality" of style, products, technology, relationships, and lifestyles.³⁰ As a result, local worlds have been dis-

²⁹ On the contested issue of objectivity and measurements of attitudes and
values relating to an autonomous realm of nature, see the different positions of
Amartya Sen and myself in Chen et al., *Health and Social Changes*. On the question
of the cultural history of nature, see Jardine et al., *Culture of Natural History*.

³⁰ The most impressive case for these effects is found in David Harvey, *The
Condition of Postmodernity* (Cambridge: Blackwell, 1990). See also the chapters

mantled, remade, marginalized, and brought under enormous global, especially financial and marketing, influence. For example, to understand the changing forms of suffering and responses to them, both the three-sided set of local interactions among representations, collective processes, and subjectivity and the influence on it of the broader social forces I have described must be taken into account. Out of those interactions, as we will soon see, suffering mutates as do our responses to it.

Indeed, among the dangers that absorb the practical attention of ordinary men and women toward social experience are the varieties of human suffering. Social suffering has always been a disquieting part of human conditions, but we are today — thanks to global media coverage — made more intensely and regularly aware of the anguish and destruction of war, genocide, structural violence, and the immense disparity of the life ways of the well-to-do and the truly poor. You no longer need to be an expert in public health or social development to know that disease and death are unequally and unjustly distributed in communities, so that those in extreme poverty—approximately 20 percent of the world's population — bear much higher rates of sickness, disability, and premature death. That there are 200 million enslaved people in the world — mostly children forced to work in awful sweatshops, but also millions of young Asian, African, and Eastern European women sold into prostitution — as astonishing a figure as it is — may not mean that much on a day-to-day basis in a North American suburb, but high rates of domestic violence, crime, substance abuse, suicide, sexually transmitted diseases, and runaway adolescents and broken families do.[31] There is also better understanding

---

on social and cultural change in Eric Hobsbawn, *The Age of Extremes* (New York: Vintage, 1994); as well as Saskia Sassen, *The Global City* (Princeton: Princeton University Press, 1991). Recent illustration of an extreme kind is given in a special issue of the *New York Times Magazine* (March 8, 1998) on "Business Class as a Way of Life."

[31] Robert Desjarlais et al., eds. *World Mental Health* (New York and Oxford: Oxford University Press, 1995).

that policies and programs aimed at controlling these problems can contribute to and even intensify the misery.[32] And there is vague if widely held recognition that commercialism contributes to the sordidness. The frightening implications of a huge number of inner city youth (many of them African American and Hispanic) incarcerated in prisons is but one example, along with failed public housing, welfare, teenage pregnancy, drug enforcement, and immigrant and refugee programs, of the contemporary sensibility that social policies and programs are part of social suffering. Add to this the fear of downward social mobility, of ending up in a dead-end job without benefits, of being let go before a retirement pension becomes operative, of being uninsured or underinsured for health problems and injuries, of being unable to make a go of it as a single working mother or a retired widow, or for that matter as anyone marginal to the information technology that is the leading edge of economic opportunity, and the danger social suffering poses to ordinary human conditions, even in an era of self-pronounced material prosperity, becomes all too real.

Among the varieties of suffering that will concern us, illness and injury are also important, because they are among the most frequent and widespread of contingent misfortunes. Read through a list of serious acute and chronic disorders from life-threatening infectious diseases to heart disease, cancers, diabetes, depression, emphysema, Parkinson's disease, stroke, dementia, and the hundreds of other common chronic illnesses from arthritis to psoriasis, add the threat of particular risk factors from moles to cholesterol levels, throw in the congenital and acquired disabilities and the fear of peculiar genetic vulnerability to diseases that cluster in families, add injury and trauma from vehicular collisions and from work and household accidents, and fear of impotence and of iatrogenesis, and also the stark reality of end-of-life care, and you have illustration enough from just this one realm of misfortune of why

[32] Arthur Kleinman, Veena Das, and Margaret Lock, "Introduction," in *Social Sufferings*.

social experience — for all our use of euphemisms, statistical and metaphoric — carries a sense of danger; and perhaps also of why that sense is so troubling that it is routinely disguised and denied.[33]

Here then is the social terrain where I will lodge these lectures. We stand in the thick of human experience, in the space of human problems, in the real-life local places where people live in the face of dangers, grave and minor, real and imagined. Here is where fear and aspiration, desire and obligation, mesh in the close encounters of ordinary men and women with pain and disaster and with the infrapolitics of power that apportion those threats unequally and distribute responses to them unfairly across the social fault lines in actual worlds.

LECTURE I. THE DANGER OF SOCIAL EXPERIENCE: SUFFERING IN LOCAL AND GLOBAL PERSPECTIVES

> You grow up in our [American] society and you kind of get lulled into the view that you are protected, things are easy. You can take life easy. Then something happens, and . . . and you come to see just how dangerous things are. I've had it happen several times in my life so I should be prepared. But the only preparation is to be wary . . . all the time. That's why over time you stay very attentive to things at work, in the neighborhood, even in the family. Even in your body. I've been laid off after 20 years with one firm. I've been in a bad, bad car accident. I've experienced the death of a daughter to suicide related to drugs. And now my heart problem. The world is a dangerous place. Maybe even more dangerous than I'm willing to admit.
>
> — 52-year-old unemployed executive from New York City
> with serious coronary artery disease

My grandfather told it to my father during the Warlord Period. My father told it to me during the war with the Japa-

---

[33] Arthur Kleinman, *The Illness Narratives* (New York: Basic Books, 1988).

nese. And I told it to my son and daughter during the Cultural Revolution. He understood it, but what could he do? He was murdered. Even in these prosperous times I'm sure my daughter tells my granddaughter: be careful! Be very careful! Times change. History changes. The world is not the same. But social life is always very dangerous.

— 68-year-old Chinese intellectual from Beijing

These two excerpts from research interviews in two very different social spaces are chosen to illustrate the emphasis I have given to the sheer practical relevance of ordinary experience and its orientation around an acute appreciation of local dangers. There is not much question in either instance about what matters and why what matters absorbs the concern of members of a local world. Nor can there be much question about why these dangers are threatening, and why social suffering is perceived as dangerous. This is not because these experiences are natural or universal in some banal sense, but because, given the finite number of ways of being human owing to the constraints of social life (including social psychobiological processes creating certain practical limits in human conditions), we are well aware of the social consequences of these experiences, even while at the same time we cannot be certain what their distinguishing cultural meanings and subjective feelings are like.

The excerpts also illumine the intersubjectivity of experience. These dangers, along with the requirement for practical engagement with them, are faced by individuals in networks. They are both outside and inside the person, both social and subjective. Thus, they break down the sharp dichotomy between public and private spaces. Surely, there are public and private spaces at the level of the most macro- and most micro-processes. But much of lived experience in a local world occurs not in that realm of policy deliberation versus the deepest strata of innermost dreams and terrors, but rather in the mediating medium I described earlier as an intersubjective level of words, gestures, meanings, images, feelings, engagements with and amongst others, including others with whom we are in long-term, even intimate interactions as well as those who pass through our lives obliquely and infrequently, yet with real impact.

Our felt experience of the flow of lived time and space is both part of the intersubjective stream of cultural practices and social engagements and part of our inner being. Symbolic forms — language, music, cultural images — belong to both the social world of values and the interior world of feelings. They link norms with emotions, creating mediating processes that I call *sociosomatic*.[34] I have, at various times, used the image of a tidal stream to convey the interpenetration of the moral and the emotional, the social and the subjective. Experience, like a tidal stream, washes in among the feelings of inner life and rushes out among values, norms, and relationships. Moreover, as fresh water and salt water intermingle but also maintain their own forms in a tidal stream, so too do subjective and collective processes create a mediating world of intersubjectivity while still at times possessing their own characteristics. Social theorists have used different metaphors to capture this basic ethnographic and social historical understanding. Theorists have innovated new terms or revitalized old ones to express this mediating quality of human conditions. Traditional Chinese thought is not the only non-Western tradition also to describe lived experience as intersubjective interaction—notably, *renqing quanxi*, social connections and their affective dynamics — but because thinkers in that tradition (like those in many other non-Western traditions) were not steeped in mind-body dualism the dichotomy between body and society did not weigh as heavily on them as it has in the West. Therefore, thoroughgoing interpenetration between the world of values and the world of feelings was not a notion in a marginal intellectual stream but a canonical orientation in the Chinese tradition. That is to say, in traditional Chinese orientations society, body, and self are in constant relationship so that one

[34] Kleinman and Becker, "Introduction."

can speak of moral-somatic and moral-emotional processes: what I am calling today the moral modes of experience.[35]

That things actually at stake in the social world are interconnected with what is felt to be at stake in one's innermost being does not mean that what is involved is a process of social replication. The relationship between moral engagements and moral sentiments has been described as dialectical, open-ended, and indeterminante. As James Scott has shown, the inner transcript of a person may remain hidden because it resists the dominant public transcript in the infrapolitics of a village, where its open expression can injure that person, and we may extend his analysis to a social movement or a business organization.[36] Personal obsession with a perceived threat may seem to have little to do with collective concerns; nonetheless, even an idiosyncratic fear may begin from collective suspicions and surely also may feedback to reinforce or call into question the authenticity of those public worries.

What gives our local worlds their immense power to absorb our attention so as to direct our action, sometimes even away from personal interests, into collective projects and thereby force conformity or pressure one to contest and resist local conditions has to do with the character of danger at the core of interpersonal engagement that imparts a legitimate sense of threat to what is most at stake. We fear that what we hold dearest could be seriously menaced, even lost entirely. Loss of a world, through forced uprooting or massive historical transition, produces a collective feeling akin to grief, a cultural bereavement. Feelings of menace can be a powerfully motivating force for violent actions, as when they are whipped up for political purposes into a frenzy of ethnic nationalist conflict. Feelings of menace occur also in the most deeply personal ways, as when we feel alienated from what was formerly

[35] Kleinman and Kleinman, "Moral Transformations of Health and Suffering"; Kleinman and Kleinman, "Suffering."

[36] James C. Scott, *Domination and the Art of Resistance* (New Haven: Yale University Press, 1990).

at stake for us and fear that we will float, disoriented, without a clear stake in things. One may perceive such a fundamental divide between personal and social orientations that one develops basic distrust in one's local world. One fears being overcome by others, forced to betray inner secrets of such vital significance that one panics over being thoroughly lost or compromised without them. Over time passionate commitment to a social cause later shown to be unworthy or worse can yield a deep disquiet of misplaced loyalty. The absence of that sense of threat or betrayal can impart a feeling of comfort with one's living condition, a sense of success in having crossed over to safety. Joy may arise as much from that sense of liberty as from its opposite: the resonant feeling of belonging to a community of shared faith and practice. Either way, these are the moral-emotional dynamics of experience.

Ethnographers have also shown that trance and possession states, rather than alienating members from their social groups, as a form of personal pathology, frequently offer an authorized channel for conveying personal problems, criticism, and accusation into collective space so that they are made more acceptable and can be acted on.[37] Alternatively, this cultural psychology channel of what we now call dissociation can be seen to make available to individuals a language and a voice that appropriate collective fears as authenticated subjective realities. Hence we get two-way traffic: the social world haunts the person with personified dangers; the individual animates a legitimate social strategy to express individual doubt and desire collectively. Thus, authorized mythology about demons, witches, and other forms of malign influence (e.g., today perhaps early childhood traumas or the threat of environmental pollution) becomes verified states of personal being:

[37] Among others, this point is illustrated in the ethnographic descriptions of trance and possession states by Janice Boddy, *Wombs and Alien Spirits: Women, Men, and the Zar Cult in Northern Sudan* (Madison: University of Wisconsin Press, 1989); I. M. Lewis, *Ecstatic Religion: An Anthropological Study of Spirit Possession and Shamanism* (Hammondsworth: Penguin, 1971); Aihwa Ong, *Spirits of Resistance and Capitalist Discipline: Factory Women in Malaysia* (Albany: State University of New York Press, 1987).

cultural epistemology becomes local ontology.[38] Multiple personalities, chronic fatigue, multiple chemical sensitivities may be our contemporary examples.[39] The psychophysiological process of dissociation, then, like memory and emotion, connects a particular outward shape of the social world to particular inward forms of the body-self: in Bryan Turner's arresting terms, "ontological frailty" and "social precariousness" change in relation to each other and in relation to changing societal responses (see note 12).

I have said that to understand historical changes and cultural differences in this dynamic field of local experience we need to understand how cultural representations, collective processes, and subjectivity intersect and change under the impress of the large-scale transformations in politics and economics that define an era or a place. I will illustrate this process of change and difference in modes of moral experience with respect to suffering and lay and professional responses to it.

The early Christian era provides a serviceable example. Second-century Christian discourse fashioned a self that was centered around suffering. Suffering became a religious identification with divinity and a political alternative to the Stoic persona that was a key representation of the self for Romans (for whom suffering was not a virtue). As one historian of religion puts it: "Thus discourse created a new paradigm for understanding suffering and death, and, consequently, the experiential world. . . . Things that had universally been thought bad and contemptible were suddenly seen as valuable. . . . This empowerment, together with the emphasis on the resurrected body, display the subversive underpinnings of this discourse." [40]

---

[38] See Allan Young, *The Harmony of Illusions* (Princeton, N.J.: Princeton University Press, 1995); Ian Hacking, *Rewriting the Soul: Multiple Personality and the Sciences of Memory* (Princeton: Princeton University Press, 1995).

[39] Norma Ware and Arthur Kleinman, "Culture and Somatic Experience," *Psychosomatic Medicine* 54 (1992): 546–60.

[40] Judith Perkins, *The Suffering Self: Pain and Narrative Representation in the Early Christian Era* (London: Routledge, 1995), pp. 122–23.

This was no more and no less than a transformation in subjectivity. The new subjective self took institutional form around the organized collection of funds, administration of hospitals and poorhouses, and experiences of religious transformation. The entire cluster of representation, self, and institutions became a vehicle of political power.

Historical studies of witch burning in the medieval period tell a story of a transformation in subjectivity as well. The circle of religious obsession with sin and with the role of the devil, moral fears about the threat of sexuality, the social marginality of certain groups of women, church politics, and the development of new religious institutions reveal a reorganization of cultural representations, collective processes, and personal memory and affect that created a terrifying form of interpersonal experience in European towns and villages that had dire consequences for many.[41] By the turn of the Enlightenment not only was witch burning proscribed, but the experiential reality that featured and realized fear of witches, inquisitional practices, and the institutional support of civil authority had disappeared. Consider the possibility that the Nazi era in Germany, Stalin's era of terror in the Soviet Union, and Mao's Cultural Revolution in China as well, perhaps, as the Cambodian genocide and more recently Bosnia's ethnic cleansing might support similar analysis of the transformation of the political, moral, and subjective structure of experience.[42] Are the dif-

[41] Norman Davies, *Europe: A History* (Oxford and New York: Oxford University Press, 1996), pp. 566–67.

[42] This kind of argument is made, albeit in distinctive ways and with varying degrees of success, in such works as those of Browning, *Ordinary Men*; and Daniel Goldhagen, *Hitler's Willing Executioners: Ordinary Germans and the Holocaust* (New York: Knopf, 1996), on Nazi Germany and the Holocaust; and see David Apter and Tony Saich, *Revolutionary Discourse in Mao's Republic* (Cambridge, Mass.: Harvard University Press, 1994); and Wei-Ming Tu, "Destructive Will and Ideological Holocaust: Maoism as a Source of Social Suffering in China," in A. Kleinman et al., *Social Suffering*, on Maoist political violence; and Mark Danner, "Bosnia: 'The Great Betrayal,'" *New York Review of Books*, March 26, 1998, pp. 40–52, and his other pieces on Bosnia in the *NYRB*, November 20, 1997, December 4, 1997, February 5, 1998, February 19, 1998, reviewing the major themes

ferences in sense and sensibility in different eras simply an example of identifying key features in these changing structures? Humiliation in the Middle Ages of Christian theological hegemony: was it a means of creating loving obedience as a virtue so as in turn to create subjects appropriate to that time and place, as the social anthropologist Talal Asad argues?[43] In the same historical period, we can also easily see that suffering was organized into something profoundly different than it is in Western Europe or North America today: namely, disdain for bodily pain and valuing of suffering of the self (or soul) as a salvational practice.

In Colonial New England, Puritan modes of experiencing suffering emphasized discipline, prayer, and the positive virtues of self-negation, reflection, moral regeneration, and spiritual redemption. Suffering was a test of faith; a sign of impaired virtue; an occasion for salvation. Theology and moral practices and bodily sensibility were supported by the community's key institutions: church, school, workplace, family. In New England in the 1990s, where I live and work, the popular culture and leading social institutions support a fundamentally different mode of experience. Pain and suffering, especially chronic forms, are dealt with as if they were without positive value, a thoroughly bad thing. (Sotto voce, I explicitly exclude here the "no pain, no gain" mentality of our sports culture because it appropriates such a thin and limited and nontranscendent notion of suffering.) No one is expected anymore to merely *endure* pain and suffering. The methods for socializing children and the societal institutions that support moral meanings and practices do not reward endurance of misery or acceptance of the limits of repair and rescue. The salvific potential of suffering is at an all-time low. Even the experiential realities of old age and dying have been reorganized to emphasize that

---

of the leading works on Serbian atrocity in Bosnia. See also the chapters in Veena Das et al., eds., *Violence and Subjectivity* (Berkeley: University of California Press, in press); and Daniel, *Charred Lullabies.*

43 Asad, *Genealogies of Religion.*

pain, disability, and the end of living can be so managed as to
avoid or minimize suffering, which is seen as extraneous, no longer
a necessary part of these terminal realities. When the pope, visiting Cuba for the first time in January 1998, uses the words of suffering of self, soul, and society, they seem almost anachronistic,
quaintly out of keeping with the words used by the globalized
media, especially those used to describe human adversities. The
same commercial processes that sell suffering at a distance, a safe
distance, deny that anyone need experience suffering up close —
all one need do is buy something to relieve the pain.[44] The mix
of technology, legal procedure, and policy analysis that is the dominating global technical rationality of our times projects the idea
that all forms of suffering are manageable, if in no other way then
by insurance and forecasting.[45] Perhaps this disguise is what Mon-
tesquieu had in mind when he observed "the truth would be a terrible one, and we should have to conceal it from ourselves." [46] Or
perhaps what is truly ominous is that our political economy, via
advertising, even commodifies this sobering self-reflection.

This characterization of distinctive eras is necessarily crude;
community-based studies give a more nuanced understanding.
Here the cross-cultural record of ethnography can be cited. In a
study of AIDS and poverty in rural Haiti at the outset of the HIV
pandemic, for example, Paul Farmer shows how both the local culture of blame and the global discourse of accusation that pointed a
finger at Haitians as the supposed source of AIDS at the time led

[44] Arthur Kleinman and Joan Kleinman, "The Appeal of Experience; the Dismay of Images: Cultural Appropriations of Suffering in Our Times," *Daedalus* 125,
no. 1 (1996): 1–23; compare with Luc Boltanski, *La souffrance à distance* (Paris:
Métailie, 1993); and with Pierre Bourdieu, *La misère du monde* (Paris: Editions
du Seuil, 1993).

[45] Asad, "On Torture"; see also Nicholas Christakis, "The Self-fulfilling Proph-
ecy in Medicine," paper presented W. H. R. Rivers Lecture, 1998, Harvard Medical
School, forthcoming, for an account of risk, prognosis, and forecasting in medicine
as well as risk and forecasting in society generally; for more on the latter, see Ulrick
Beck, *Risk Society: Towards a New Modernity* (London: Sage Publications, 1992).

[46] Cited in Todorov, *On Human Diversity*, p. 365.

to a figuring of the problem in which victims — usually poor rural women — were routinely accused and societal responses to their suffering both minimized their need and blunted their agency because of huge differences in political-economic power.[47] Lawrence Cohen's field research in Benares, India, shows that dementia of the aged was earlier neither culturally marked as an experience of suffering nor understood by family members or professionals as a reason for medical (or religious) intervention.[48] All that is changing, the teeming humanity of this rich ethnography reveals, as geriatrics emerges as a professional field in India and as the global media present lifestyle alternatives that lead to marketing innovations that change local attitudes to the elderly. The upshot is a socially constructed yet locally experienced epidemic of "dementia." Anne Becker's research in rural Fiji suggests that a consistent pattern of social support for women during and after pregnancy, quite different than in North America, makes the experience of postpartum depression virtually absent in Fiji.[49] Here cultural representations and collective processes remake the psychobiology of subjective experience to prevent this form of suffering. Linda Green, exploring fear as a way of life among Mayan villagers during Guatemala's era of terror in the 1980s, observes that "memories of horror are experienced as bodily complaints by widows and others as a moral response, an emotional survival strategy, to the political repression they have experienced. . . ."[50] The research that Joan Kleinman and I conducted in Hunan among survivors of China's vastly destructive Cultural Revolution showed how three common symptoms — dizziness, fatigue, pain — acted as

[47] Paul Farmer, *AIDS and Accusation: The Geography of Blame in Haiti* (Berkeley: University of California Press, 1992).

[48] Lawrence Cohen, *No Aging in India* (Berkeley: University of California Press, 1998).

[49] Anne Becker, *Body, Self and Society* (Philadelphia: University of Pennsylvania Press, 1995).

[50] Linda Green, "Fear as a Way of Life," *Current Anthropology* 9, no. 2 (1994): 227–56.

bodily metaphors of collective and subjective disorientation, exhaustion, and hurt in that exceptionally dangerous time.[51] These symptom symbols authorized alternative history and disguised intersubjective remembering of political criticism and social resentment and moral recrimination. Many other ethnographic studies add support to the notion that distinctive cultural representations of suffering and processes of socializing people as sufferers (and as healers) constitute and express different collective and subjective experiences of suffering (or its opposite).[52]

Shigehisa Kuriyama notes, for example, that "tension" in earlier times in Western history was a "prized virtue, a quality to be sought and cultivated."[53] He goes on to comment on its altered meaning today, where "it almost invariably signals anxiety and alarm. Once upon a time, tenseness announced vigor and health, it declared the power of life; now it speaks of distress, and names a source of sickness." Kuriyama relates the change to both a professional and popular change in understanding what atmosphere is and how it relates to health and sickness. In earlier eras barometric pressure in the air was seen to correlate with vitality or its diminution in the body. Kuriyama associates the banishment of vitalism from science and medicine in the West and the use of tension and pressure as social metaphors to talk about "the demands of a competitive marketplace, the pace of modern life," and their health effects on the person with a change not only in dis-

[51] Arthur Kleinman and Joan Kleinman, "How Bodies Remember," *New Literary History* 25 (1994), 707–23.

[52] As Marshall Sahlins (*Islands of History* [Chicago: University of Chicago Press, 1985], p. xiv) configures social experience generally this "structure of conjuncture" involves "the practical realization of cultural categories in a specific historical context, as expressed in the interested action of the historic agents, including the microsociology of their interaction," creating a "relation between a happening and a structure (or structures)."

[53] Shigehisa Kuriyama, *The Expression of the Body: The Divergence of Greek and Chinese Medicine* (New York: Zone Books, in press). But clearly the cross-cultural picture is a lot more complex. In Greece today, for example, Michael Herzfeld (*The Poetics of Manhood: Contest and Identity in a Cretan Mountain Village* [Princeton: Princeton University Press, 1985]) shows that tension is highly valued and cultivated.

course but in the experience of health and suffering. Like tension and pressure in the West in earlier centuries, *qi* (vital energy) in the Chinese cultural tradition, Kuriyama suggests, is a different sensibility that results from a particular cultural constitution of experience. Pressure, tension, and *qi* may be taken as examples of "local biology." The interaction of psychobiology, cultural discourse, and social institutions such as medicine and business elaborates a distinctive experiential world that includes different sensations, different sensibility, and differences in the common sense understanding of what they signify with respect to health and disease. Indeed, the result of such historical change is a particular cultural organization of body-self-society processes or in other words: a distinctive local biology. In keeping with the analysis advanced in this lecture, such a local biology could also be referred to as a moral biology, one in which the moral, the political, and the medical are inseparable. Anthropological studies in support of this point include notably Margaret Lock's demonstration of distinctive symptoms, meanings, and responses to menopause among Japanese and North American women.[54] Other research demonstrates the local patterning of hormonal, cardiovascular, and immunological responses to distinctive social conditions.[55]

There is also intriguing evidence that in our own times in the West self-expression of the deepest kind has increasingly become a public performance that would have astonished our forebears. Many have been utterly amazed by ordinary people's overt reaction

[54] Margaret Lock, *Encounters with Aging: Mythologies of Menopause in Japan and North America* (Berkeley: University of California Press, 1993).

[55] Ellison, "Reproductive Ecology"; Kleinman and Becker, "Introduction"; see also list of references in Richard Wilkinson, *Unhealthy Societies: The Afflictions of Inequality* (New York and London: Routledge, 1996); as well as Anne Harrington, ed., *The Placebo Effect* (Cambridge, Mass.: Harvard University Press, 1997); and John Cacioppa and R. Peltz, eds., *Social Psychophysiology* (New York: Guilford, 1983), among many other relevant works that illustrate, for instance, the effect of bereavement on mortality; variation in mortality and morbidity with religious affiliation and religiosity; and variation in physiological parameters such as heart rates, blood pressure, or T-cell levels across sociodemographic groups.

of deep emotionality in the public display of private grief that followed the death of Princess Diana. But should we be so surprised? Clearly we have passed over into a new era: one in which the highly proclaimed emotional continence of British society of the past (itself something of a cultural stereotype) has given way to its opposite. Not only does the inhibited and deeply private sensibility that characterizes Henry James's paradigmatic depiction of upper-middle-class Victorian Britons and Americans describe a different world, but that portrayal of the world in recent movies like *The Wings of the Dove* makes it over into something much more akin to the way we are now.[56] Our globalized age of talk shows, sit coms, and glamour world photojournalism sponsors a different subjectivity of self-disclosure, outed performances of arousal, vicarious suffering, and perhaps also a thinning out and simplifying of grief, shame, and other complex emotions, which, as one commentator wondered, may be "now real only if we are seen having them?":[57] if "human nature" can be so malleable owing to changing times and circumstances you can appreciate why I question this overused concept (and the ways it is employed) ; why I insist that our subjectivities are not fixed any more than is our social circumstance or, as we will now see, our alleged moral compass.[58]

[56] Henry James, in his "Preface" to the novel *The Wings of the Dove* (New York: Scribner and Sons, 1902), describes the sensibility of the character of his age in an extraordinary depiction of the subtlest, most indirect, and complex emotions that emphasizes privacy and continence and elaborate sensitivities that have little to do with the way they are portrayed in the recent film version as overt, single-dimensional, and rather coarsely functional sentiments.

[57] Adam Phillips, "Grief on Demand," *New York Times*, Sunday, September 7, 1997, p. E17.

[58] Julia Raiskin, conducting an ethnography of a psychiatric telephone consultation service in Moscow in 1997, provides telling evidence of the way historical changes in subjectivity allow for people's selective memory and forgetting and therefore for renarratizing in 1997's Russia how experience was lived in the 1950s and 1960s in the Soviet Union. Here is an exchange between her and two Russian psychotherapists talking about the late Professor Andrei Snezhnevsky, who played a key role in the political abuse of Soviet psychiatry:

> Psychotherapist A: "I knew him, I was his graduate student. Yes, he loved his students, that is true. But he was one hell of a bastard. He had these awful squinty eyes and if you disagreed with anything he said he would

THE MORAL EPIDEMIOLOGY OF SOCIAL SUFFERING
IN A DISORDERING AGE

Suffering can be called "social" in several senses.[59] Their combined significance is to give emphasis to the idea that social suffering can be an index of moral disorder; or put differently, in a disordering time we can speak of the moral epidemiology to which findings on social suffering contribute. First, in what ways can suffering — the experience of going through, enduring, or transcending pain and tribulation — be considered social? To begin with, experiences of diseases, dying, bereavement, trauma from

> just throw this awful look in your direction. He was not half bad a scientist either, he did a lot for the diagnosis of schizophrenia, but he went too far, with the *sluggish* [schizophrenia, a diagnosis used to label dissidents.]"
>
> Julia Raiskin: "What do you think about that as a diagnosis?"
>
> Psychotherapist A (pointing at Psychotherapist B): "She would know a lot about that. She was the head of a whole department at the KGB Hospital."
>
> Psychotherapist B: "It was not the KGB! It was many years ago. Ay, just forget it. Leave me alone."
>
> Psychotherapist A: "She was, she was. She will tell you all about *sluggish*."
>
> Psychotherapist B: "It was a diagnosis like any other. Some are really *sluggish schizophrenics*, their symptoms and all. Of course, it is a category like any other. Somewhere there must have been misdiagnosis."
>
> Psychotherapist A: "Somewhere, right there under your nose. I am sure you sent away a few yourself."
>
> Psychotheraist B: "For God's sake, just leave me alone. You have to agree that no reasonable person would have opened his mouth in those years. Anyway, do you really think it is better for someone to be sent to Siberia for life, or just to spend a few months in a hospital and then come out and live a normal life?"
>
> Psychotherapist A: "You call that a normal life? Your whole life you are on the same insane registry, and that means no work, no traveling abroad. You call scientists' street sweeping a life? I would rather go to Siberia."
>
> Psychotherapist B: "It's better than Siberia. I am going to do some work."
> (She walks out and heads for her cubicle.)
>
> (Julia Raiskin, chapter 3, Senior Honors Thesis,
> Department of Anthropology, Harvard University, 1998)

One can see here the way memory and forgetting first suppress and then revivify former kinds of subjectivity and being-in-the-world (as professional collaborators in the police state) that now are neither acceptable nor experienced as real anymore.

[59] Arthur Kleinman, Veena Das, and Margaret Lock: "Introduction," in Kleinman, Das, and Lock, *Social Suffering*.

natural catastrophes, and violence are most often intersubjective. Think of Alzheimer's disease in an elderly woman, the mother of three adult children with families of their own. Their mother may have such devastating cognitive impairment that she can neither recognize them nor realize the degree of her own disability. Yet they are overcome by their hurt, loss, and frustration. Where is the experience of suffering? Contrary to our pronounced Western ideological tendency to emphasize the tragedy of a single person, the locus of suffering in this instance and in many, many others is in the intersubjective space between the demented patient and her closest family members.[60] In bereavement, in domestic violence with family breakdown, in business failure accompanied by unemployment, and in end-of-life care, it is clear that suffering itself is intersubjective. In that intersubjective space, suffering is taken up in engagement with what matters most. Indeed, what is most at stake may be suffering itself and responses to it. After thirty years of working with patients with chronic illness, their family caregivers, and the professionals who help them, I have come to the strong impression that most of the time cancer, heart disease, diabetes, asthma, depression, and most other chronic conditions evoke an interpersonal experience, a relational style of suffering.[61]

[60] The powerful entailment of the Western tradition's emphasis on the individuality of suffering can lead even such a dialectical theorist as William James to focus solely on the sick person, made more compelling in his case by his recognition that illness, at least as constructed in the West (in this instance his disease), frequently isolates and self-absorbs the sick person to an inordinate degree. "I find myself in a cold, pinched, quaking state when I think of the probability of dying soon with all my music in me. My eyes are dry and hollow, my facial muscles won't contract, my throat quivers, my heart flutters, my breast and body feel as if stale and caked. . . . I have forgotten, really *forgotten* that mass of this world's joyous facts which in my healthful days filled me with exultation about life. . . . The increasing pain and misery of more fully developed disease — the disquiet, the final strangulation, etc., begin to haunt me, I fear them; and the more I fear them, the more I think about them. I am turned into a pent-in egoist, beyond a doubt, having in my spiritual make-up no rescuing resources adapted to such a situation" (cited in Simon, *Genuine Reality*, p. 296). But as James's own illness experience actually shows, his was as intersubjective an engagement with body and death as it is possible to imagine, with family and friends deeply involved.

[61] Kleinman, *The Illness Narratives.*

But suffering is "social" in a second, and rather different, sense as well. That is to say, certain mental and social health problems have social roots. Illicit drug and alcohol abuse, related violence, sexually transmitted diseases, many neuropsychiatric disorders, and suicide are on the increase in many areas of the world, rich and poor alike.[62] A leading hypothesis is that these conditions are more adequately configured as forms of social suffering that result from massive political, economic, and cultural changes of our era of triumphal global capitalism. This is surely the case with the spread of tobacco and alcohol use, and the health problems associated with such use, in low-income societies. It can also be seen in the statistical correlation of greater infant and maternal morality and child and adult morbidity with the widening gap between the richest 20 percent and poorest 20 percent of the population globally.[63] All societies have a health gradient in which by far the greatest burden of disease and premature death is carried by their poorest members. The World Health Organization (WHO) calls poverty the greatest killer and maimer of people.[64] But while poverty may be the most deadly social cause, it is not the only one. Race in America also correlates (even when poverty is statistically controlled) with worse health and health care outcomes. Hence social suffering is a marker of disadvantage, relative powerlessness, and devastating effects of social change, and in this sense is a moral indicator of cultural or societal disorder. Inasmuch as we are living through a pandemic of mental health and social health problems that is occurring at the very time, we are informed, that economies are growing faster than ever before and societies are becoming materially richer than before, and because that pandemic does not relent but perhaps even intensifies in "richer societies," it is not unreasonable to consider current global political economic and cultural transformations as disordering, a major cause of social

[62] Desjarlais et al., *World Mental Health*.

[63] Richard Wilkinson, *Unhealthy Societies*.

[64] *World Health Report, 1996* (Geneva, Switzerland: WHO, 1997).

suffering, here understood as disordered moral experience in a disordering epoch.[65] For example, as China, under economic reform and so-called market socialism, has moved from a terribly poor society to the world's most rapidly growing and, as measured by Purchasing Power Parity, the world's third largest economy, rates of alcoholism, illicit drug abuse, violence, suicide (330,000 deaths per year; 40 percent of suicides globally), depression, STDs (sexually transmitted diseases), AIDs, and family and community breakdown are all increasing (see fig. 2).[66]

Suffering carries yet another, equally troubling social meaning: namely, the way that health and problems such as drug abuse, violence, and the sedimentation of HIV/AIDS, STDs, tuberculosis, and related conditions among the members of the poorest strata of society are divided up and managed differently by the medical, welfare, legal, religious, and other institutions of contemporary society. The result of this division of labor is that institutional responses tend to fragment these problems into differentiated, smaller pieces that then become the subject of highly particularized technical policies and programs, increasingly ones that last for short periods and then are replaced by yet others that further rearrange and fracture these problems. The upshot sometimes can be effective policies and programs. But all too often there is another result altogether. Institutional practices make health and social problems more intractable and deepen both the sense and substance of misery. At the same time, narrow technical categories strip away the moral significance of these problems, and practitioners appropriate the authentic voices of sufferers for their own institutional ends.

Let me use one of my own professions — psychiatry — as a sad but telling example. First, I want to make clear that I am not anti-

[65] Desjarlais et al., *World Mental Health.*

[66] Arthur Kleinman and Joan Kleinman, "Transformation of Everyday Social Experience in Chinese Communities," in *Culture, Medicine and Psychiatry* (in press); Sing Lee and Arthur Kleinman, "Epidemiology of Mental Illness in China," *Harvard Review of Psychiatry* 5 (1997): 43–46.

FIGURE 2. CHINA'S MENTAL/SOCIAL HEALTH INDICES
(1978–98)

Rates over 20 years

- Alcohol Abuse   ↑
- Illicit Substances   ↑
- Depression   ↑
- STDs   ↑
- HIV/AIDS   ↑
- Violence   ↑
- Crime   ↑
- Gambling   ↑
- Displacement   ↑

psychiatry. There are many important contributions that psychiatrists and psychiatric institutions make, including providing more effective recognition, diagnosis, and treatment of mental illnesses than in the past.[67] The knowledge base of psychiatry has grown substantially, and with it has come more effective and efficient mental health care for thousands. But psychiatry is in a unique position vis-à-vis other medical specialties; it is the only one for which its core disorders do not have biological markers.[68] There is no x-ray or blood test to diagnose a case. Hence the diagnosis of depression, even schizophrenia, and postraumatic stress disorder is decided entirely on interview criteria, making it difficult or even impossible to delimit the borders of these disorders. Thus, when the WHO claims that there are more than 300 million people worldwide at this moment who suffer from depressive disorder, although we know the actual number is high, we do not know how valid this number is.

Take the difference between normal bereavement and clinical depression (a pathological state). When I was trained to be a clinical psychiatrist, in the early 1970s, the official psychiatric diag-

[67] See Arthur Kleinman, *Rethinking Psychiatry* (New York: Free Press, 1988).

[68] Arthur Kleinman and Alex Cohen, "Mental Illness," in *ENCARTA Encyclopedia* (Redmond, Wash.: Microsoft, 1998).

nostic criteria in our country taught that normal bereavement lasted for one year. After thirteen months (to avoid misdiagnosis because of anniversary reactions), a bereaved person could be diagnosed as depressed. Inasmuch as the symptoms of bereavement and depression are the same, only the time criterion can determine when the diagnosis is appropriate. Today DSM-IV, the official diagnostic system of the American Psychiatric Association, lists two months as the normal course of bereavement. Slightly more than eight weeks following the death of a spouse, a parent, or a child, a grieving family member is diagnosable as a case of depressive disorder. In fact, the cross-cultural data on bereavement are so thin that it is really not known in a scholarly sense what the course of bereavement is, and how it may vary by age, gender, or culture. Because around 2 million people die each year in our own country, the number of bereaved is quite high. That means that so is the number of potential patients. Does political economy play a role in the institutional conversion of the bereaved into patients? Almost certainly it does. But this is not the only problematic side to this story. What effect does an antidepressant have on the experience of bereavement? What does it mean to the sufferers, to their family members, and to society to convert a moral problem (grief) into a medical one (depression)? Does changing how we categorize normal bereavement influence the subjective and interpersonal experience of grieving? Anthropologists and historians of science have described how the idea of "normality" has been expanded from medicine to infiltrate almost every area of society.[69] The infiltration has been attributed to the modern nation state and its institutional forms of social control. Now, for example, there is as I mentioned "normal" bereavement and pathological bereavement. This is a process of remaking social

[69] Margaret Lock, "Displacing Suffering: The Reconstruction of Death in North America and Japan," *Daedalus* 125, no. 1 (1996): 207–44; see also George Canquilham, *The Normal and the Pathological*, trans. Carolyn Faucett and Robert Cohen (New York: Zone, 1989); and Ian Hacking, *The Taming of Chance* (Cambridge: Cambridge University Press, 1990), p. 160.

experience that is called "medicalization." What are the negative effects of medicalization? Victims may be turned into patients, as when victims of political violence are labeled as cases of post-traumatic stress disorder. While this may lead to financial benefits and services, what is the moral, political, and health significance of this transformation in social experience? I don't think we know.

When we call a dying patient who is receiving end-of-life-care for metastic breast or prostate cancer "depressed," we end up in the same situation. Most patients with end-stage cancers and also terminal heart disease, liver failure, renal failure, and stroke can make the technical interview-based criteria for clinical depression, because their often serious appetite, sleep, and energy disturbances as well as their pain, agitation, and sadness are produced by their end-of-life medical conditions and also by the treatments they receive and by the tribulations of coming to terms with death and crafting a way to die. But these are the same symptoms as those of depressive disease. There is no scientific means to separate the two. It would be grotesque to label all these patients as mentally ill with depressive disorder: an extreme example of the institutional transformation of suffering into disease. And yet this is increasingly happening. The momentum seems to be inexorable. Here then is another illustration of social suffering, one in which professionals and institutions transform the recalcitrance of a moral problem into the corrigibility of a medical one. Programs that manage welfare, legal, and religious responses to social suffering tell much the same story. Not only does social power break persons and bodies in the causation of disease, but it remakes people into the objects of institutional control.[70] Structural violence and welfare policy, and the cycle of political violence, forced uprooting, search for refuge, and management of trauma, are telling instances. Sometimes this transformation is helpful, at other times it is not. But either way it reveals the inseparability of the moral, the medical, and the political.

[70] Kleinman, Das, and Lock, "Introduction."

Ethical discourse can play a potentially useful role of reflexive awareness of how an institution and its members come to understand the way societal values and professional commitments influence their functioning. But it is equally crucial to focus on moral processes so that we can come to see how the subjects of institutional practices (as well as the practitioners) are caught up in the very transpersonal processes of social experience that create, sustain, and appropriate suffering. A small but telling example from California is Anne Fadiman's arresting account of how a Hmong family with an epileptic child in Merced, whose loving attention to a seriously ill daughter is quite extraordinary, is made over into child abusers whose child is forcibly removed by this state's governmental agencies not because her physicians are incompetent or unfeeling, but precisely because their high standards of professionalism lead to dedication but also to inflexibility. These cultural standards of practice will not allow them to share control of the treatment, not to grant respect to another cultural reality.[71]

The prolific book reviewer and social critic Ian Buruma defines another sense in which social suffering holds salience for our times.[72] Analyzing the social uses of suffering in the cases of the commercialization of Anne Frank's diary, and in the preoccupation of American Jews with the Holocaust as a uniquely defining religious as well as cultural event, and in the constant rehearsals of victimization in Serbian national identity that so frequently justify horrific brutality to outsiders, and in the insistent claims by some in the Chinese American community that the Japanese Army's "rape" of Nanking in the 1930s is another "holocaust" to be treated on the same level as the Nazi extermination of European Jewry, Buruma concludes ruefully that ethnic, racial, and

---

[71] Anne Fadiman, *The Spirit Catches You and You Fall Down* (New York: Farrar, Straus and Giroux, 1997).

[72] Ian Buruma, "The Afterlife of Anne Frank," *New York Review of Books* 45, no. 3 (February 19, 1998): 4–8.

national overidentification with suffering (including competition over whose people's suffering is greater) is a powerful collective appropriation that can have dangerous consequences in creating cycles of vengeance, distorting sentimentality, a sense of moral superiority, and failure to come to terms with changed times with new problems and opportunities.[73] Buruma's criticisms can be all too readily waved away as a kind of backlash from the unaffected, but he identifies a disturbing tendency.

Social suffering, then, points to the intersection of the great cultural and political economic forces of our epoch with human conditions, such that normality and disorder are being recast into new forms of social experience — forms that have as much to tell us about the moral transformation in local worlds and globally in our time as they do about our engagement with and responses to those transformations. Perhaps no other aspect of that transformation is deeper and more dangerous than the changes in subjectivity that affect suffering and our responses to it. I turn now to that difficult and potentially ominous question.

A Deep and Most Dangerous Transformation

I earlier adverted to the changes in subjectivity that in combination with changing cultural representations and collective processes characterize the modes of moral experience of a particular time and place. But what sort of transformation in subjectivity animates and constrains moral experience in our own era in this society?

---

[73] W. S. DiPiero writes in the *New York Times Book Review* (March 8, 1998, p. 4) "a sour whiff of suffering as privilege rises from their [memoirs of suffering] pages, and I feel as though I'm expected to envy or even covet such privilege." Seamus Heaney in his play *The Cure at Troy*, based on Sophocles' *Philoctetes*, writes of "the swank of victimhood . . . the wounded one whose identity has become dependent on the wound. . . ." However, the identification by African Americans of slavery and its long-term effects with "time on the cross," suffering as an explicitly Christian religious experience, seems to suggest how powerful suffering can be as a source of social movements and change. It is also a reminder of the locality for the coming together of religious, political, ethnic, and individual identity in particular worlds of pain that to outsiders may carry a very different signification.

Adam Smith in his *Theory of Moral Sentiments* reckoned that pity and compassion were part of human nature.[74] They were the primary source of our fellow feeling for the misery of others. As Smith put it with a characteristic balance of jaundiced eye and one big economic reason for expectant faith, "How selfish soever man may be supposed, there are evidently some principles in his nature, which interest him in the fortune of others. . . ."

Smith went on to argue that human nature assured that people were the bearers of a much stronger feeling of tenderness toward children than filial piety toward parents — a point whose reversal in the Confucian tradition doesn't lend confidence to our reception of his claim to natural and universal standards. In our own era, the distinguished Canadian moral theorist Charles Taylor writes that "we should treat our deepest moral instincts, our ineradicable sense that human life is to be respected, as our mode of access to the world in which ontological claims are discernible and can be rationally argued about and sifted." [75] Taylor goes on to observe that the modern situation in the West is such that while many contemporaries concur that "some ground in human nature . . . makes human beings fit objects of respect" (pp. 10–11), that respect has come to be formulated in terms of human rights. As a result, the autonomy of the individual is fundamental to the Western moral outlook, and great importance is given to avoiding and relieving suffering and affirming ordinary life. In this way, questions of personal identity (read subjectivity) and questions of moral action interfuse. "We are," writes Taylor with characteristic concision, "selves only in that certain issues matter for us" (p. 34). And he points to the social space of ordinary life and moral questions that hold considerable resonance with the definition I offered at the outset of experience (p. 35, for example). And yet, for Taylor the

[74] Adam Smith, *Theory of Moral Sentiments* (Indianapolis: Liberty Classics, 1983 [1759], p. 9.

[75] Charles Taylor, *The Sources of the Self* (Cambridge, Mass.: Harvard University Press, 1989), p. 8.

idea of human nature, despite the social space of moral action and the fact that we come to our identity through historically situated narrative forms, remains crucial. We have, he avers, an inner "craving which is ineradicable from human life. *We have to be rightly placed in relation to the good*" (p. 44; emphasis mine).

But we have already seen that the case for a single, universal human nature is unconvincing at best. At worst it is a means of begging a greatly troubling question: namely, if there is no fixed and final human nature, then what guarantees, in different times and places, moral responses and responsivity to those in misery and to social suffering more generally?

Here I wish to argue that anthropologically speaking there is no guarantee. Indeed, I believe we are now undergoing, thanks to an unprecedented infiltration of globalization into every nook and cranny of local worlds, a deep and a most dangerous transformation in subjectivity; and such a transformation in personhood, affect, and sensibility, as Taylor suggests, must mean a transformation as well in moral processes — perhaps not on the order of some of the earlier horrors I recounted, yet ominous nonetheless. What evidence is there to support so dismaying an assertion?

Elsewhere Joan Kleinman and I have written of the commercial appropriation of images and voices of suffering as infotainment on the nightly news to gain audience share.[76] The arresting artistry of photojournalism and the ubiquitous real-time video recorder are making over witnessing into voyeurism. We are no longer merely titillated by appalling images of brutality, trauma, and carnage. Now we need to see them in order to feel that stories have been authenticated. But these images, to be effective, must be

---

[76] Arthur Kleinman and Joan Kleinman, "The Appeal of Experience, the Dismay of Images: Cultural Appropriations of Suffering in Our Times," *Daedalus* 125, no. 1 (1996): 1–24; on the subject of the uses of images, see also Martin Jay, *Downcast Eyes: The Denigration of Vision in Twentieth-Century Thought* (Berkeley: University of California Press, 1993); and David Michael Levin, *Modernity and the Hegemony of Vision* (Berkeley: University of California Press, 1993).

of suffering at a distance, usually a great distance.[77] There is nothing we need do (or in fact can do) in these circumstances. So that both the suffering and our responses to it become gratuitous. Sometimes, as when images involve sexual imagery, there seems to come to pass a stunning conversion of empathy into desire, a transformation that the extraordinary photographic artistry of our age clearly aims to achieve. And so powerful are TV images that they may seem more real than lived experience, so that images provide the occasion for exhibition of moral-emotional responses of a kind previously kept private, as in the outpouring of grief for Princess Diana. Does such a transformation in cultural representation and collective response, under the immense pressure of commercial power, also bespeak a transformation in moral-emotional processes themselves? Are empathy and compassion being thinned out by the sheer enormity of exposure to wounds and horrors? Does the absence of a close connection that demands action mean that we are seeing a dissociation of sensibility and responsivity, of feeling and obligation to be there, to do something, to be engaged? Or put in terms of the argument of this lecture, are those very expectations to be understood as specific to a particular societal configuration of the political, the economic, the psychological, and the moral?

Let me illustrate what I have in mind with a brief tale of something that happened to me last summer.

Midnight in an old apartment block. I am drawn by sounds to an open window. It faces onto an interior courtyard. Dried leaves stick to its panes. The heavy midsummer's air fills with sobs, with crying, with the long loud wails of a single female voice. "Dead! Do you want me dead? Is that it? Do you want to take everything away from me? Everything in me? Do you? Do you? You go on upward. And what about me? About me? I'm left

---

[77] Boltanski, *La souffrance.* Consider also the idea of a proper distance for emotional response in Thomas Scheff, *Catharsis in Healing, Ritual and Drama* (Berkeley and Los Angeles: University of California Press, 1979).

behind, damn you, like an old coat . . . Left behind? Left alone!
Left to die! Left to die! Ayeh . . . Ayeh . . . Ayeh!"

Deep, distressing moans follow. The distraught voice stops me
completely with its pain. The wrench of loss sounds absolute. I
can feel the ache of breathing broken by sobs reverberate in my
own chest! The clutching sensation makes me, an asthmatic, gasp
for air. Framed by so muted and minimal a response from a thin
male voice, it keeps me still, listening in the darkness, long after
an upstairs window snaps shut and all sounds cease.

The end of a marriage? The close of a long affair? The tone
color of the domestic threnody — dark, ominous, filled with bitter
hurt — makes me think it will end as a court case. So much passionate energy overflows that for a few menacing moments I even
worry about the risk for suicide; but there is neither direct threat
nor action. Nonetheless the thought stays in mind, as it would for
a psychiatrist, faint but still present, an indistinct remainder of the
danger of words.

I am a sojourner in a foreign city, staying in the apartment of
others, who are on vacation far away. I know no one here. There
is no sensible reason for me to be so engaged with the aftereffects
of the commotion. There are no faces, no stories I can affix to the
disembodied voices to give them personal shape; no history known
to me can bring the event into a context of significance. Yet, inside, hours afterward, I can still feel the anguished pain. Here
before me was a riveting instance of break-up and loss; an experience about which I knew nothing and could do nothing, but still I
was held by its sheer intensity, its insistent force, which caused the
sounds to echo down the corridors of memory, drawing taut the
filaments of sympathy.

But still, the anonymity of the occasion leaves an aftertaste of
lingering disquiet. I am but the spectator of a transitory event.
One that has for me neither a beginning nor an ending. Nothing
is required of me. There is freedom to listen in or not, but no responsibility, no obligation to be engaged. Now this can happen to

anyone at anytime. But suppose we are repeatedly experiencing such anonymous suffering. Owing to the global changes in communication, travel, entertainment, and the like, suppose we are recreating the world so that we are awash in exposures to suffering that are primarily gratuitous. What then does it do to us? Does it eventually lead us to tune out, close off, and disregard? Does it alter the moral response to suffering?

Musing in the early morning quiet, I think back to a TV news program I saw some months before. Film flickers across my memory of wounded refugees dying in the bush in a Zaire that no longer exists. One of the wounded, a teenage boy, speaking very quietly, almost inaudibly, his ebony face an immobile mask of resignation, recounts the horrors his family has experienced on the long, long journey. The commentator mentions the uncertainty of whether this victim was also, earlier, a victimizer. The film clip ends on this point of uncertainty, a fragment of pain followed immediately by an advertisement for beer. Healthy, playfully happy, eroticized white bodies frolic at the beach. The juxtaposition of real agony and commercialized joy, black and white, is shocking. Is there a message here? Is it that experiences come and go, some die, some have fun, it's all a matter of switching channels? Is it a commentary on the lack of moral engagement? Nothing need matter to the viewer, save self-interest. Am I worrying over a sign of some fundamental rupture in what I had been educated to believe to be the existential order of things? Has there been, imperceptibly, a seismic shift in the self and in moral sensibility? So that the rock-certain claim about the Judeo-Christian tradition of the late European ethicist Emmanuel Levinas, that moral practice begins with the empathic suffering of the witness in engagement, in solidarity with the sufferer, no longer holds, because we have changed in some basic way?[78] If this is our new condition, what would be the implications of such a change in

---

[78] Emmanuel Levinas, "Useless Suffering, In *The Provocatoin of Levinas*, ed. R. Beraconi and D. Wood (London and New York: Routledge, 1988).

subjectivity, in who we are, when writ large as a transition in society's collective sensibility and behavior? Can a disordering time such as ours break Western societal traditions of human engagement and substitute in their place something more sinister, more destabilizing for our future, as has happened in the past and is still happening around the world?

Here you have the question at the heart of this exploration. We live in a time of immense transformations in financial systems, in trade, in communication, in technology, in transportation, in global culture—transformations that in turn are reshaping societal structures such as the city and the workplace and the home as well as creating new lifestyles and perhaps even new forms of behavior. The unsettling compression in time and space and the fragmentation of cultural practices and confusion of virtual and lived realities that characterize this age — are they also altering the collective and personal poles of everyday experience? If there is reason, as I believe there is, to justify such a query, what significance does a potential change in the ordinary existential roots of experience — the way we feel and act — hold for our understanding of moral questions and practices? Either human nature is malleable to a degree we have never imagined and we are participating right now in a sea change in its elements, or our era, like other momentous times of epochal change before it, is ushering in another form of subjectivity altogether, a new type of personhood. Suppose this were the case.

Several objections to this train of thought can be lodged, of course. Globalization also carries with it greater attention to international relations, greater familiarity with other cultures, and arguably more respect for differences (e.g., in ethnicity and gender). And one can point almost endlessly as well to evidence that all of human history has its share of misery, in response to which not only has empathy been tested but, at crucial points, it has failed. Forgetting and denial have made the moral effects of such failure tolerable, allowing ordinary men and women to live through bad times while not feeling such despair that they have given up or experiencing such hypocrisy that they have annulled projects of tradition and modernity of those who follow them.

Global social change is indeed complex, multisided, and likely to have several (perhaps contradictory) effects. The alteration in collective and individual experience that I have identified may be offset by other changes. Nonetheless, for all that, the transformation of moral and emotional processes seems real enough and consequential. That it is flanked by other changes with potentially different effects makes the story told in these pages both more complexly human and more interesting.

It is reflections like this one that in past eras and in other societies have led concerned people to wonder aloud whether such changes can be fundamental enough to cause the loss of the human.[79] There is a sense today that this fear of the loss of the human is not entirely romantic or unwarranted. Like some universal solvent the disordering effects of advanced capitalism appear to be dissolving much that really matters to ordinary men and women globally. Is this merely an essentializing millenarian dismay? Is it the kind of apperception of danger to what is at stake that I characterized earlier as itself a spur of desperate and inhuman acts? Or is it our enormous preoccupation with, say, the threat of alien invasions that is itself a sign of our recognition of the alien lineaments of our time and even a self-reflexive sensibility that we are ourselves becoming alien?

So much depends on maintaining the fiction that nothing has changed all that much. That at base we can change political economy, political practices, technology, social institutions, and cultural forms, and yet ourselves remain the same. Because that is the way

---

[79] I am indebted to Gerald Bruns for this idea; but I accept responsibility for the way I use it here, which differs in a fundamental way from Bruns's sense that there may be a useful effect of widening and remaking what is meant by the "human" within a moral community. See his Roger Allan Moore Lecture, "On Ceasing to Be Human," Department of Social Medicine, Harvard Medical School, April 23, 1998.

things seem to have been and will be. But things clearly are not the same. What if it isn't just material things like information and entertainment technologies that are different, but relationships and sensibilities and all the other dense package of moral-emotional things that constitute and express subjectivity, intersubjectivity, experience?

I realize I may not have convinced you that there is a widening gap between the witnessing of disaster and the feeling of an obligation to respond. I simply don't have the space needed to review the various sorts of data that would be necessary to better substantiate my case. In any event, nothing but the years to come will show if this be prescience or alarmism.

Rather, I want to spend the second of my lectures to address the chief implication of this analysis for scholarship, for practice, and for policy. My purpose here is not to level a moral indictment of our times, not to conjure up prudishly the tawdriness, the squalor, or the horrors that would make for a *fin-de-siècle* call for moral rejuvenation. Actually, there are many positive sides to our epoch — in technology, in social policy, in legal procedure, in respect for cultural, gender, and other difference, and even in other domains where self-reflective awareness is ramifying — that do at times make me feel cautiously optimistic about other aspects of our future.[80] No, rather I seek to press home the point about a transformation in experience and its moral modes in order to figure out what that transformation specifically may mean for practices, policies, and programs concerned with social suffering.

---

[80] See, for example, Alan Wolfe, *One Nation after All* (New York: Viking, 1998).

LECTURE II. THE MORAL, THE POLITICAL, AND THE
MEDICAL: ETHNOGRAPHIC AND CLINICAL
APPROACHES TO HUMAN ENGAGEMENT

Images in the popular media are not the only materials I can
present to make a case for a moral mutation in experience. Take
my own field of medicine, and the patient-practitioner-family relationship that is so central to health care. The managed care revolution that we are living through today — a transformative part of
transnational political economic developments — in its unprecedented search for efficiency (and profits) has altered this core
clinical relationship almost beyond recognition and raised a serious
question as to whether the core skills of doctoring can be preserved. (Of course, managed care has also done certain useful
things like reduce unnecessary medical costs and improve regulation of practice standards.) A typical scenario in managed primary
care is that a physician has between twelve and fifteen minutes
to see a seriously ill patient on a follow-up visit for a complicated
chronic condition such as diabetes, cancer, heart disease, or clinical
depression. During that time the clinician needs to check the results of blood tests and other lab values, read the x-rays (or the
radiologist's report), take a history of symptoms, current functioning, and response to new treatments, perform a physical examination and write prescriptions, and plan the further course of care
(including rearranging a regimen of diet, exercise, and lifestyle,
making referrals, discussing disability assessment, and the like).
There is such a compression of time that there is hardly time to
accomplish these tasks. There is literally no time to do what that
clinician has been trained to do to provide quality care: namely,
solicit the patient's illness narrative, engage the emotional, family,
and work issues that together constitute the social course of the
disorder and the response to treatment, and communicate sensi-
tively about the prognosis and next phase of care. Engagement
with issues of cultural, religious, gender, and other sources of dif-

ference in clinical case management that requires additional time and effort is almost certain to be short-changed. The practitioner, that is to say, cannot adequately deal with the patient's suffering.

The upshot, as we are now becoming aware, is frustration, anger, and a deep sense of disaffection on behalf of patients, family members, and practitioners. That is what these voices mean to convey:

> They rush me in for a visit. There is hardly time to talk about what is happening. No one asks anymore how I am feeling. And then I am rushed out. I don't get a chance to tell all that has happened. Or even to ask about what is coming next. I am very angry and very disappointed. What good does it do?
>
> — 65-year-old man with worsening diabetes and associated kidney, visual, and metabolic problems

> You would think I was irrelevant to my disease from the way I get treated. Nobody asks me about my ideas. When I make a suggestion, it's taken as if it came from left field. It makes me angry, and it makes me want to do something, anything really to show them that I am part of this. Sometimes I purposefully miss an appointment or don't comply with the treatment — as silly and futile as it is. I'm sore because I want to have my opinion respected, taken into account.
>
> — 39-year-old college teacher with a chronic intestinal condition

> I'm just so angry at them. They don't listen. I want to shake them by the scruff of the neck and tell 'em: Here, don't you disregard me. What can you do? They make me so angry sometimes that I want to stop coming . Sometimes I don't show up. But it only makes things worse for me.
>
> — 64-year-old mechanic with chronic liver disease

> My mother is 93. She doesn't hear well. She needs someone to speak with her who can slowly explain what her dizziness is about and why it is so difficult to control. But the doctors and nurses don't even seem to have the time to speak to me so that I can explain to her what's happening. It's very frustrating. How can they use the word "quality" to describe the care she gets? But there is no alternative.
>
> — 55-year-old woman who is a real estate agent

I was so scared that they would not give my dad all he requires. They might write him off. Another 80-year-old. Time to pull the plug. I read the papers. I know what doctors are doing to keep costs down, and to ration care. If you don't push 'em, you don't get what you should. Well, I pushed 'em for Dad. I simply don't trust people in the hospital. I watch what they are doing and I speak up.

> — 40-year-old African-American lawyer whose 81-year-old father was in a teaching hospital with stroke and heart disease

Something very deep and very bad has happened, is happening to medicine. There is so little time, and so little emphasis on spending time with patients, talking to them, asking about their problems, explaining what needs to be done, responding to their fears and wants. It's all a new language: cost, efficiency, management talk. This isn't the language of clinical practice I was trained in. I feel frustrated and very, very alienated. I'm beginning to think it is not for me. I need to get out of it.

> — 60-year-old primary care physician in a managed care practice in a Health Maintenance Organization (HMO)

We all know medicine is going through a revolution. But you like to believe — have to believe — that the change offsets only the nonclinical aspect of care. But that's preposterous. So we can't even tell ourselves lies we can believe in. My institution doesn't seem to value any longer those things I was trained to believe are central to good care: a close trusting relationship with your patients, good communicative skills, enough time to talk things over with patients who are going through bad times with their diseases, attention to what bothers them. That is not only the "soft" side of care. You need to do these things because they really are essential. And if you don't, don't do them I mean, then what kind of doctor are you? What kind of care are you giving? It's really a moral issue. The managed care institution with all its paraphernalia has become more important than the patient. The relationship should be called "patient-doctor-managed care provider," because we spent most of our time on the management issues. I think that is a dangerous slide in the moral content of doctoring.

> — 48-year-old primary care physician in a large HMO

Sometimes I feel like a hypocrite. I am standing up before a room of medical students and teaching them things about communication and psychosocial skills in doctoring, and acting as if they have the time to do these things once they get into practice. They don't; they won't! They can't take the time, and they will not get the support they need from practice managers to do the things they know how to do and know they should do. So there we are. That is medical education today. Wouldn't you call that a pedagogic crisis? But for a medical educator it is also a moral crisis. What to do?

> 57-year-old medical educator at a leading
> American medical school

Of course, I have selected these excerpts from interviews to make my point. They are a biased sample. Some of the same complaints have been leveled against medical practice for a long time, well before the current era of managed care and the corporatization of medicine. The problems may be intensifying, yet they have been around for decades. But I could provide many, many more complaints in support of the overall theme. The engagement with patient and families' experiences of suffering appears to many to be thinning out and even disappearing under the managerial pressure of health care financing and delivery "reform." The change is a change in the clinical relationship (and in self-identity of the health professional from healer to businessperson, technician, or bureaucrat), but over time it also shapes expectations and practices so that the intersubjective experience of clinical care is changing. (Is self-identity of the patient also transmuting from sufferer to consumer and co-payer and commodified object of technological and managerial manipulation?) That change is a transformation in the moral processes of illness experience and doctoring.

In the social transformation of American medicine today, several things are happening in concert. The human engagement with pain and suffering is being reformulated, as part of a century-long institutional transition, into purely technical issues that are managed by technology and technical rationality. Thus, the ethos of end-of-life care is being converted from a religious and moral one into a psychiatric question of using psychotropic medication to treat clinical depression. At the same time, the political-economic transformations of health care financing and delivery are compressing time to a minimum that is consistent with the greatest efficiency and profits. In that squeeze moral processes in the patient-family-doctor relationship either are left unaddressed or are converted into their technological equivalent, professional ethical discourse, which itself has become a subspecialty of biomedicine (to wit: bioethics), and subject to some of the same pressures of time and efficiency. Hence the curiously disquieting image of the clinical bioethicist, beeper in hand, responding to emergency pages to render definitive ethical judgments immediately so that business can get under way expeditiously. In either case, there is in practice a revaluation of values. But the revaluation is not out of keeping with cultural and political processes in the Western tradition — not at all. Thus, mind-body dualism, with its supporting ideas of the body as a machine and rejection of matter (physical stuff) encompassing spirit, points the way toward the transformation of medical care into industrial models such as the servicing of automobiles or the training of airline pilots in safe practices. And this moral transformation of meanings and experience works hand in glove with the political-economic transformation of medicine into more highly institutionalized systems in which the proletarianization of professionals and the commoditization of health and health care are tied up with greater bureaucratic efficiency and control.[81]

The deep connections between the moral, the political, and the medical are particularly visible in the management of pain, par-

[81] In this sense of the triumph of managerial and institutional rationality as a source of "efficiency," we are watching the working out of the Weberian forecast for society as a whole within medicine, perhaps the last major holdout from the dominance of technical rationality and institutional control (see John Patrick Diggins, *Max Weber — Politics and the Spirit of Tragedy* [New York: Basic Books, 1996], pp. 12–16, 99–101, 106–9).

ticularly chronic pain. Elaine Scarry has tellingly put it for our Western tradition: "So, for the person in pain, so incontestably and unnegotiably present is it that 'having pain' may come to be thought of as the most vibrant example of what it is to 'have certainty,' while for the other person it is so elusive that 'hearing about pain' may exist as the primary model of what it is 'to have doubt.' Thus pain comes unsharably into our midst as at once that which cannot be denied and that which cannot be confirmed." [82]

The problem of pain is posed as a cognitive one: a truth that cannot be denied and cannot be confirmed. It is established as the kind of issue that requires legal procedure. No wonder so many chronic pain patients complain that medical care has failed them because they feel they are treated without respect for their suffering and without trust, as if they were deliberately deceiving their caregivers. Ask physician pain experts and you all-too-often see the mirror-image: complete distrust of patients' complaints. [83]

Surely, there is another way to proceed here. The value commitment of engagement with the person in pain that holds for practitioner or family caregiver in various formulations of ethics and the moral requirement of such engagement in many local worlds of medicine are not the same as the rational technical detection of truth or deception. Acknowledgment of the words and feelings of the other in pain is what is called for. [84] Failure to acknowledge the other's condition is a moral (and cultural) failure, no matter what is the cognitive issue at hand. Ethical discourse about the principle of beneficence is not what I have in mind; but rather a reform in local moral processes and in the application of ethical formulations for those circumstances.

[82] Elaine Scarry, *The Body in Pain* (New York: Oxford University Press, 1985), p. 4.

[83] See, for example, Marian Osterweis, Arthur Kleinman, and David Mechanic, eds., *Pain and Disability* (Washington, D.C.: American Academy Press, 1987).

[84] See the way this point is made by Stanley Cavell, "Comments on Veena Das," *Daedalus* 125, no. 1 (1996): 93–98.

Take the Confucian approach to suffering, as a telling alternative. Mencius remarked, "For every man there are things he cannot bear. To extend this to what he can bear is benevolence (or humaneness)" (VIIB:31). Wei-Ming Tu has shown that this implies, on the moral level, engagement with others' pain and suffering.[85] It is the extension of the moral-emotional capacity of the person to engage the other that is the issue. That exercise of human capability begins with acknowledgment and includes embodying the experience of the other's pain as compassion and responsiveness. The Jewish and Christian religious traditions in the West also contain a central commitment to the idea that the suffering other is to be engaged with compassion, so that, as Levinas puts it, the suffering of the witness on behalf of the sufferer provides the moral usefulness of the latter's plight.[86] "For Levinas," as Gerald Bruns so tellingly puts it, "the face-to-face [relation] is an ethical [in our terms 'moral'], not a cognitive relation; it is ethical precisely because non-cognitive. . . . 'The face [of the other] speaks to me and thereby invites me to a relation incommensurate with a power exercised.' . . . This incommeasurable relation is that of the ethical claim."[87] Levinas insists that there is no human nature; every human being (and every human relation) is unique and refractory to categorization.[88]

Talal Asad, an influential anthropologist of religion, argues that the hegemonic global ideology of the present time — namely, an amalgam of technology, the technical rationality of policy decision making, and legal procedure — drives such religious and ethi-

---

[85] See Wei-Ming Tu, "A Religiophilosophical Perspective on Pain," in *Pain and Society*, ed H. W. Kosterlitz and L. Y. Terenius, Dahlen Conference, 1980 (Weinheim: Verlag Chemie Gmbh, 1982), pp. 63–78.

[86] Levinas, "Useless Suffering."

[87] Bruns, "On Ceasing to Be Human."

[88] Bruns (ibid.) cites Stanley Cavell's *The Claim of Reason* (New York and London: Oxford University Press, 1979), p. 397, as a further development of this position on the primacy of moral engagement with others: "Being human is the power to grant being human. Something about flesh and blood elicits this grant from us, and something about flesh and blood can also repel it."

cal framings of suffering as well as their consequences in moral processes out of the mainstream and onto the sidelines.[89] This analysis is in keeping with Max Weber's argument that institutional forms in society would come to occupy a central place because they would be the strongest source of rational technical control and its efficiencies. The result would mean that religion, tradition, sentiment, and the ad hoc would be deprived of a central place in public discourse and in social process, in favor of the hegemonic rational technical discourse.[90] In both visions, intersubjective moral processes in human relationships would lose their centrality, or rather would be reframed as cognitive questions for bureaucratic adjudication. This would seem to be an accurate portrayal of what is happening in the health care domain, and perhaps this reframing is happening even more generally in everyday social life. But if this is the reason why the current coming together of the medical, the moral, and the political is creating a problem for moral experience, then what alternatives are there that would sponsor a different and more humane approach to clinical practice, and more generally in human interactions? In this lecture, I seek to address the questions by employing an anthropological understanding of ethnography (and of clinical work as a kind of ethnographic application) as a model for moral engagement.[91]

Conclusion: Moral Engagement — Ethnography as a Human Practice

Ethnography is an engagement with others that brings the ethnographer into the ordinary, everyday space of moral processes in a local world. As part of the anthropological program, ethnographic description and interpretation is called "experience near"; it precedes from the general to the particular, and only after privi-

---

[89] Asad, *Genealogies of Religion*.

[90] Denis Wrong, "Oversocialized Conceptions of Man in Modern Sociology," in his *Skeptical Sociology* (New York: Columbia University Press, 1976), p. 247.

[91] Arthur Kleinman, chapter 15 in *The Illness Narratives*.

leging the local does it extend back to a general framework that enables comparisons. The ethnographer, no matter how successful she is in participant observation, is always an outsider. She will come to understand local categories and even perhaps to feel the weight of local obligations, and she will almost certainly at some point get caught up in the give and take of daily life, but, for all that, she is not so fully absorbed by what is most at stake for local stake-holders that their world of experience becomes hers as well. She is aware (often acutely so) of that difference, that separation. (This even becomes true for the indigenous ethnographer.) Indeed, the ethnographer feels the pull of ties that bind her elsewhere, to her own network and to the world of scholarly discourse. That creates a defining marginality, and perhaps is one reason why many anthropologists end up studying marginal persons and groups. Even her involvement with global processes differs from that of those around her. And it is this positioning that makes ethnography, despite certain limitations in reliability of its findings, an interesting approach for moral theory — one that also holds potential significance for practice and policy.

What is special about ethnography, then, is the practice it realizes, not the qualities of the ethnographer. With respect to the subject at hand, the ethnographer can claim no special human virtues, and history shows that all sorts of people have taken up the practice with varying results. What they do share usually is the burden of the almost impossible requirement of participating in local moral processes yet also being outside them. This form of insider-outsider engagement with a world of social experience has led to ethnographers being described, especially in earlier eras, at worse, as double agents or, in a somewhat nicer expression, professional strangers. It is not easy on the ethnographer, or on her informants and friends. But it confers, in this instance, one large advantage. The ethnographer's angle of exposure places her so uncomfortably between distinctive moral worlds and local and global ethical discourses and, what is more, creates such a destabilizing tension between them that she is forced to become, even at times it seems from published accounts against her will, self-reflexively critical of her own positioning and the commitments and problems it leads to as well as attentive to the new and unexpected possibilities that can (and so often do in real life) emerge.

The situation is clearest with respect to moral processes, which, as I have described them here, could be said to be the actual stuff (the subject matter) of ethnographic enquiry, even if many ethnographers have used other names or categories to deal with them. The ethnographer's very marginality, as professionally discomfiting and personally burdensome as it often becomes, enables a comparison of the moral processes she comes to understand (withstand?) in her fieldwork with the moral processes that she is usually so taken up with in her own world that she (like most of the rest of us) takes them for granted to such an extent that they operate behind her back. There are probably other forms of engagement that give somewhat similar access to the moral modes of different worlds of experience — psychotherapy, social history, comparative religion, cross-cultural medicine, certain forms of literary criticism come to mind (not to mention the experience of immigrants) — all of which either share the comparative method or create the opportunity for destabilizing comparative engagement with experience of equal depth. But for the purpose of this analysis I will focus on ethnography.

Besides the critical self-reflection on different cultural processes that it realizes in actual interpersonal engagements, ethnography more or less demands that the ethnographer take both indigenous ethical discourse and global ethical discourse into account simultaneously, and also that she examine how both are rooted in particular forms of moral experience. That ethnographers often find ways to avoid the responsibility must be one of the arresting ironies of scholarship. The disciplined professional skill with which the ethnographer tries to get things right from the native point of view means that ethnographic description can at best establish ethnoethical categories and describe how they are deployed in indigenous ethical discourse and relate to global framings. Were most ethnographers better prepared in ethical discourse, they would be in an almost ideal place to project the local into the global (and vice versa). This is the scholarly contribution that ethnographers could make to moral theory. Because ethnography, at least as I describe it here, is not merely a social science methodology, and a demanding one, but also an intrinsic part of social and cultural anthropology, if moral theorists decide they wish to participate in this approach they need training in anthropology.

Ten years ago, in *The Illness Narratives*, I suggested that clinical work can be modeled on ethnography.[92] I went on to describe how clinicians can undertake a mini-ethnography of the illness experience and interpretation of illness narratives as both collective and individual to the benefit of care. In particular, I sought to emphasize the ethnographer's willingness to listen to others, to solicit and attend to their stories, and her skill in getting at what matters to people going about all the things that make up everyday life. I thought that this disciplined yet open-ended engagement could be a model for caregiving. But because of what I have already said about the dire effects of the managerial transformation of health care services on clinical practice I have no illusion that this is feasible under the current regime of the corporatization

[92] Ibid. In recent years the call for ethnography in bioethics has become louder and voiced by many. See, for example, Barry Hoffmaster, "Can Ethnography Save the Life of Medical Ethics?" *Social Science and Medicine* 35, no. 12 (1992): 1421–32; and multiple authors writing in Raymond DeVries and Janardan Sabede, eds. *Bioethical Society: Constructing the Ethical Enterprise* (Upper Saddle River, N.J.: Prentice Hall, 1998). But as Renee Fox and Raymond DeVries, writing in the same volume, point out, this new fashion has raised so much enthusiasm that the point is often missed that ethnographic study is a scholarly discipline requiring rigorous training and disciplined application (p. 275). In a recent workshop on "Ethics, Medicine, and Social Science," Harvard Medical School, March 12, 1998, the same resonant interest in ethnography within bioethics and same caution were raised. Here I am less interested in the example of ethnography as a research method based in social theory and anthropological training than I am in the sensibility that ethnography requires of (and creates for) the ethnographer in the actual practice of doing fieldwork. (But see note 95 for a brief reflection on ethnography's contributions to scholarship.)

of medicine. Nonetheless, ethnography still seems to me appropriate for educating medical students about illness as experience and for the practice of medical ethicists. And there are now available several impressive models of what this practice entails.[93] Ethnography as ethical practice in health and medicine, then, is a going concern that deserves another lecture all to itself. Not the least of its potential contributions is that it makes unavoidable the moral requirements of doctoring, which are so readily distorted by analytic preoccupation with business practices and technical efficiencies.

In the complex, changing, diverse, and divisive local worlds of our era, the uneasy, divided sensibility that ethnography brings of being both within and without the flow of experience is not inappropriate *modus vivendi*. The ethnographer's self-reflective criticism of her own positioning and its limitations, her hesitancy to prescribe interventions, at least until their human consequences can be better understood, her newly emergent readiness to make a commitment not just to study others, but to engage them and to witness their problems so as to be of use (based as it would be in her acutely dismaying understanding of the failure of earlier generations of fieldworkers to do so), and her willingness to compare local processes and nonlocal discourse so that they can come into relation with each other are not irrelevant to the thrust of argument in this lecture. Nothing about ethnography is anything like a panacea or proven preventative. Yet, in the absence of any ultimate guarantee of compassion and willingness to acknowledge and respond to the suffering of others, the epistemological scruples, the ontological uncertainties, and the moral sensibilities (and predicaments) of the ethnographer offer themselves up as one means (limited and unpredictable though it be) of sustaining empathy and engagement that deserves serious consideration. That is to say, the ethnographer is "called" into the stories and lives of others by

[93] The "Ethics, Medicine and Social Science" workshop featured the ethnographic contributions of Veena Das, Barbara Koenig, Charles Bosk, Renee Fox, Nicholas Christakis, Mary-Jo Delvecchio Good, and Alexander Capron, among others.

the moral process of engaged listening, the commitment to witnessing, and that call to take account of what is at stake for people becomes an instructive aspect of the ethnographer's sensibility.

Were this sensibility to be encouraged among ordinary men and women as a mode of moral experience (and ethical reflection), would there be the possibility of a countervailing social process in our globalized times? Could it broaden the horizon of moral imagination so as to encourage engagement with the marginal and solidarity with the afflicted? The expectation of what could be achieved would, of course, need to be quite limited, in keeping with the modesty of an anthropological intervention that amounts to rather little when put up against the driving force of political-economic, technological, and social-institutional change in our disordering epoch, or the equally dangerous political and religious and ethnic-nationalist fundamentalisms that have intensified in order to resist such transformation. The only thing perhaps to recommend it is that it is the only thing I can think of that emerges from (and seems valid within) my own circumstances.

Some of us have argued for such an ethnographic moment in policy and programs directed at social suffering.[94] The obstacles to the realization of that moment are formidable, because the language of policy is so powerfully controlled by economics and decision analysis and legal procedure that it is difficult to pry open even a small space for ethnography. Nonetheless, efforts are underway to try to produce a change. What I am now suggesting is that the ethnographic approach be developed more generally as a means of teaching about moral processes and examining their practical implications.[95] How this might be accomplished in a society

---

[94] See Kleinman, Das, and Lock, "Introduction"; and Desjarlais et al., *World Mental Health*.

[95] That brings us, at the close, to scholarship. Ethnography is, in a certain way, a backward-looking methodology, more nineteenth than twenty-first century. It emphasizes face-to-face engagements, including both indirect participant observation and direct interviews, with a relatively small number of informants. It takes times, a good deal of time: months and years, not days or weeks. It tacks back and forth

such as ours goes far enough beyond the limits of this lecture to suggest that it would be most prudent to break off here with merely the barest outline of this modest proposal. Yet I do think that it may well be in the sphere of applied moral theory that ethnography, *pace* the usual fear among ethicists about its encouragement of cultural relativism, could well hold most promise. Such a seeming irony would be quite in keeping with the deeply human roots and consequences of ethnographic engagement. Without relinquishing my own tendency to see the future in Weberian terms as the propensity of unfolding into newer and deeper historical tragedies, I am willing to propose ethnographic sensibility as a way of living with the challenges that the next millennium has already

---

between description and interpretation based on social theory. Thus, it proceeds from the general to the minutely particular, and then it struggles to go back toward the general, which it tends to recast in light of the findings. It requires the capaciousness of the book--length monograph to work out its findings and establish their significance. Thus, it seriously goes against the grain of space-time compression. It is inefficient. It is not oriented toward reliability — the verification of observations — nearly as much as it is toward validity — the verification of the concepts that stand behind and shape those observations. It is curious in that it is an approach that combines humanistic and social science methodologies, not at all inappropriate for an academic discipline, anthropology, that crosses the three great intellectual divides of the academy: natural science, social science, humanities.

It is not a compelling way of providing causality, but it does lend itself to laying out the social dynamics of ordinary experience and offering a comparative analysis as well. Indeed, it seems ready made to describe and interpret and compare moral processes. Because it can be combined with quantitative social science techniques and with physiological measurement, it has the potential (all too infrequently realized in practice, to be sure) to relate the moral to the medical, the political, and the economic. A methodology that can encompass narratives as well as numbers has a certain advantage in interdisciplinary enterprises. In an era that is witnessing the hegemony of analyses based in economic, molecular biological, and engineering framings of research questions, ethnography has a certain utility to get at the human aspects of a wide range of subjects.

Although it includes formal methods for getting at things like kinship relations, indigenous categories, linguistic data, and the like, ethnography relies as much on the ethnographer as a calibrated instrument of evaluation as on questionnaires, structured and semistructured interview guides, content analysis of narratives, historical archives, economic data, and psychological tests. Perhaps there is no better use of ethnography than when the researcher is a disciplined observed and interpreter in the engagement with moral issues. For this reason ethnography is a highly appropriate methodology for scholarship in the relation of moral theory to everyday experience of moral processes, for bringing together in the same context moral and ethical materials. This is also why it is appropriate as a method for evaluating the moral processes and social consequences of policies and programs.

brought us that at least clarifies the magnitude and form of that threatening future. Of course, such a change in sensibility will amount to too little too late unless it helps to usher in new political and economic policies to address the social roots of social suffering.[96]

    [96] For a cautionary discussion of why any engagement with ethical issues concerning social suffering must contain explicit engagement with political-economic issues, especially as regards the developing world and the poor in the technologically advanced world, see Solomon Benatar, "Just Health Care beyond Individualism: Challenges for North American Bioethics," *Cambridge Quarterly of Healthcare Ethics* 6 (1992): 317–415; Solomon Benatar, "World Health Report 1996: Some Millennial Challenges." *Journal of the Royal College of Physicians of London* 31, no. 4 (1997): 456–57 and Paul Farmer et al., eds., *Women, Poverty and AIDS* (Boston: Common Courage Press, 1996).
    Readers will doubless note that I cut the conclusion short wtihout providing a fully developed theoretical summary. I do this intentionally. I plan to provide that summary in the book that I am now preparing. That book extends these two lectures into a more fully developed theory of how moral processes and ethical discourse can be related. It does so by setting out an anthropological method for medical ethics and an ethnographic grounds for advancing human rights that also privileges the way both are realized in local worlds.

THE TANNER LECTURERS

1976–77

OXFORD — Bernard Williams, Cambridge University

MICHIGAN — Joel Feinberg, University of Arizona
"Voluntary Euthanasia and the Inalienable Right to Life"

STANFORD — Joel Feinberg, University of Arizona
"Voluntary Euthanasia and the Inalienable Right to Life"

1977–78

OXFORD — John Rawls, Harvard University

MICHIGAN — Sir Karl Popper, University of London
"Three Worlds"

STANFORD — Thomas Nagel, Princeton University

1978–79

OXFORD — Thomas Nagel, Princeton University
"The Limits of Objectivity"

CAMBRIDGE — C. C. O'Brien, London

MICHIGAN — Edward O. Wilson, Harvard University
"Comparative Social Theory"

STANFORD — Amartya Sen, Oxford University
"Equality of What?"

UTAH — Lord Ashby, Cambridge University
"The Search for an Environmental Ethic"

UTAH STATE — R. M. Hare, Oxford University
"Moral Conflicts"

1979–80

OXFORD — Jonathan Bennett, University of British Columbia
"Morality and Consequences"

CAMBRIDGE — Raymond Aron, Collège de France
"Arms Control and Peace Research"

HARVARD — George Stigler, University of Chicago
"Economics or Ethics?"

[421]

MICHIGAN Robert Coles, Harvard University
"Children as Moral Observers"

STANFORD Michel Foucault, Collège de France
*"Omnes et Singulatim: Towards a Criticism
of 'Political Reason' "*

UTAH Wallace Stegner, Los Altos Hills, California
*"The Twilight of Self-Reliance: Frontier Values
and Contemporary America"*

1980–81

OXFORD Saul Bellow, University of Chicago
"A Writer from Chicago"

CAMBRIDGE John Passmore, Australian National University
"The Representative Arts as a Source of Truth"

HARVARD Brian M. Barry, University of Chicago
*"Do Countries Have Moral Obligations? The Case
of World Poverty"*

MICHIGAN John Rawls, Harvard University
"The Basic Liberties and Their Priority"

STANFORD Charles Fried, Harvard University
"Is Liberty Possible?"

UTAH Joan Robinson, Cambridge University
"The Arms Race"

HEBREW UNIV. Solomon H. Snyder, Johns Hopkins University
"Drugs and the Brain and Society"

1981–82

OXFORD Freeman Dyson, Princeton University
"Bombs and Poetry"

CAMBRIDGE Kingman Brewster, President Emeritus, Yale University
"The Voluntary Society"

HARVARD Murray Gell-Mann, California Institute of Technology
"The Head and the Heart in Policy Studies"

MICHIGAN Thomas C. Schelling, Harvard University
"Ethics, Law, and the Exercise of Self-Command"

STANFORD Alan A. Stone, Harvard University
"Psychiatry and Morality"

UTAH   R. C. Lewontin, Harvard University
"Biological Determinism"

AUSTRALIAN
NATL. UNIV.   Leszek Kolakowski, Oxford University
"The Death of Utopia Reconsidered"

1982–83

OXFORD   Kenneth J. Arrow, Stanford University
"The Welfare-Relevant Boundaries of the Individual"

CAMBRIDGE   H. C. Robbins Landon, University College, Cardiff
*"Haydn and Eighteenth-Century Patronage
in Austria and Hungary"*

HARVARD   Bernard Williams, Cambridge University
"Morality and Social Justice"

STANFORD   David Gauthier, University of Pittsburgh
"The Incompleat Egoist"

UTAH   Carlos Fuentes, Princeton University
"A Writer from Mexico"

JAWAHARLAL
NEHRU UNIV.   Ilya Prigogine, Université Libre de Bruxelles
"Only an Illusion"

1983–84

OXFORD   Donald D. Brown, Johns Hopkins University
"The Impact of Modern Genetics"

CAMBRIDGE   Stephen J. Gould, Harvard University
"Evolutionary Hopes and Realities"

MICHIGAN   Herbert A. Simon, Carnegie-Mellon University
*"Scientific Literacy as a Goal in a High-Technology
Society"*

STANFORD   Leonard B. Meyer, University of Pennsylvania
"Music and Ideology in the Nineteenth Century"

UTAH   Helmut Schmidt, former Chancellor, West Germany
"The Future of the Atlantic Alliance"

HELSINKI   Georg Henrik von Wright, Helsinki
"Of Human Freedom"

1984–85

OXFORD   Barrington Moore, Jr., Harvard University
"Authority and Inequality under Capitalism and Socialism"

CAMBRIDGE   Amartya Sen, Oxford University
"The Standard of Living"

HARVARD   Quentin Skinner, Cambridge University
"The Paradoxes of Political Liberty"

Kenneth J. Arrow, Stanford University
"The Unknown Other"

MICHIGAN   Nadine Gordimer, South Africa
"The Essential Gesture: Writers and Responsibility"

STANFORD   Michael Slote, University of Maryland
"Moderation, Rationality, and Virtue"

1985–86

OXFORD   Thomas M. Scanlon, Jr., Harvard University
"The Significance of Choice"

CAMBRIDGE   Aldo Van Eyck, The Netherlands
"Architecture and Human Values"

HARVARD   Michael Walzer, Institute for Advanced Study
"Interpretation and Social Criticism"

MICHIGAN   Clifford Geertz, Institute for Advanced Study
"The Uses of Diversity"

STANFORD   Stanley Cavell, Harvard University
"The Uncanniness of the Ordinary"

UTAH   Arnold S. Relman, Editor, *New England Journal of Medicine*
"Medicine as a Profession and a Business"

1986–87

OXFORD   Jon Elster, Oslo University and the University of Chicago
"Taming Chance: Randomization in Individual and Social Decisions"

CAMBRIDGE   Roger Bulger, University of Texas Health Sciences Center, Houston
            "On Hippocrates, Thomas Jefferson, and Max Weber: The Bureaucratic, Technologic Imperatives and the Future of the Healing Tradition in a Voluntary Society"

HARVARD   Jürgen Habermas, University of Frankfurt
            "Law and Morality"

MICHIGAN   Daniel C. Dennett, Tufts University
            "The Moral First Aid Manual"

STANFORD   Gisela Striker, Columbia University
            "Greek Ethics and Moral Theory"

UTAH   Laurence H. Tribe, Harvard University
            "On Reading the Constitution"

1987–88

OXFORD   F. Van Zyl Slabbert, University of the Witwatersrand, South Africa
            "The Dynamics of Reform and Revolt in Current South Africa"

CAMBRIDGE   Louis Blom-Cooper, Q.C., London
            "The Penalty of Imprisonment"

HARVARD   Robert A. Dahl, Yale University
            "The Pseudodemocratization of the American Presidency"

MICHIGAN   Albert O. Hirschman, Institute for Advanced Study
            "Two Hundred Years of Reactionary Rhetoric: The Case of the Perverse Effect"

STANFORD   Ronald Dworkin, New York University and University College, Oxford
            "Foundations of Liberal Equality"

UTAH   Joseph Brodsky, Russian poet, Mount Holyoke College
            "A Place as Good as Any"

CALIFORNIA Wm. Theodore de Bary, Columbia University
            "The Trouble with Confucianism"

BUENOS AIRES Barry Stroud, University of California, Berkeley
            "The Study of Human Nature and the Subjectivity of Value"

MADRID   Javier Muguerza, Universidad Nacional de Educación a
             Distancia, Madrid
             "The Alternative of Dissent"

WARSAW   Anthony Quinton, British Library, London
             "The Varieties of Value"

1988–89

OXFORD   Michael Walzer, Institute for Advanced Study
             "Nation and Universe"

CAMBRIDGE   Albert Hourani, Emeritus Fellow, St. Antony's College,
             and Magdalen College, Oxford
             "Islam in European Thought"

MICHIGAN   Toni Morrison, State University of New York at Albany
             *"Unspeakable Things Unspoken: The Afro-American
             Presence in American Literature"*

STANFORD   Stephen Jay Gould, Harvard University
             "Unpredictability in the History of Life"
             *"The Quest for Human Nature: Fortuitous Side,
             Consequences, and Contingent History"*

UTAH   Judith Shklar, Harvard University
             "American Citizenship: The Quest for Inclusion"

CALIFORNIA   S. N. Eisenstadt, The Hebrew University of Jerusalem
             *"Cultural Tradition, Historical Experience, and Social
             Change: The Limits of Convergence"*

YALE   J. G. A. Pocock, Johns Hopkins University
             *"Edward Gibbon in History: Aspects of the Text in
             The History of the Decline and Fall of the
             Roman Empire"*

CHINESE
UNIVERSITY OF
HONG KONG   Fei Xiaotong, Peking University
             *"Plurality and Unity in the Configuration
             of the Chinese People"*

1989–90

OXFORD   Bernard Lewis, Princeton University
             "Europe and Islam"

CAMBRIDGE	Umberto Eco, University of Bologna *"Interpretation and Overinterpretation: World, History, Texts"*
HARVARD	Ernest Gellner, Kings College, Cambridge *"The Civil and the Sacred"*
MICHIGAN	Carol Gilligan, Harvard University *"Joining the Resistance: Psychology, Politics, Girls, and Women"*
UTAH	Octavio Paz, Mexico City *"Poetry and Modernity"*
YALE	Edward N. Luttwak, Center for Strategic and International Studies *"Strategy: A New Era?"*
PRINCETON	Irving Howe, writer and critic *"The Self and the State"*

1990–91

OXFORD	David Montgomery, Yale University *"Citizenship and Justice in the Lives and Thoughts of Nineteenth-Century American Workers"*
CAMBRIDGE	Gro Harlem Brundtland, Prime Minister of Norway *"Environmental Challenges of the 1990s: Our Responsibility toward Future Generations"*
HARVARD	William Gass, Washington University *"Eye and Idea"*
MICHIGAN	Richard Rorty, University of Virginia *"Feminism and Pragmatism"*
STANFORD	G. A. Cohen, All Souls College, Oxford *"Incentives, Inequality, and Community"* János Kornai, University of Budapest and Harvard University *"Market Socialism Revisited"*
UTAH	Marcel Ophuls, international film maker *"Resistance and Collaboration in Peacetime"*

YALE   Robertson Davies, novelist
                  "Reading and Writing"

PRINCETON   Annette C. Baier, Pittsburgh University
                  "Trust"

LENINGRAD   János Kornai, University of Budapest and Harvard
                     University
                  "Transition from Marxism to a Free Economy"

1991–92

OXFORD   R. Z. Sagdeev, University of Maryland
                  "Science and Revolutions"

CALIFORNIA

LOS ANGELES   Václav Havel, former President, Republic of Czechoslovakia
                  (Untitled lecture)

BERKELEY   Helmut Kohl, Chancellor of Germany
                  (Untitled lecture)

CAMBRIDGE   David Baltimore, former President of Rockefeller
                     University
                  "On Doing Science in the Modern World"

MICHIGAN   Christopher Hill, seventeenth-century historian, Oxford
                  "The Bible in Seventeenth-Century English Politics"

STANFORD   Charles Taylor, Professor of Philosophy and Political
                     Science, McGill University
                  "Modernity and the Rise of the Public Sphere"

UTAH   Jared Diamond, University of California, Los Angeles
                  "The Broadest Pattern of Human History"

PRINCETON   Robert Nozick, Professor of Philosophy, Harvard University
                  "Decisions of Principle, Principles of Decision"

1992–93

MICHIGAN   Amos Oz, Israel
                  *"The Israeli-Palestinian Conflict: Tragedy, Comedy,
                     and Cognitive Block—A Storyteller's Point of View"*

CAMBRIDGE   Christine M. Korsgaard, Harvard University
                  "The Sources of Normativity"

UTAH   Evelyn Fox Keller, Massachusetts Institute of Technology
"Rethinking the Meaning of Genetic Determinism"

YALE   Fritz Stern, Columbia University
"Mendacity Enforced: Europe, 1914–1989"
"Freedom and Its Discontents: Postunification Germany"

PRINCETON   Stanley Hoffmann, Harvard University
"The Nation, Nationalism, and After: The Case of France"

STANFORD   Colin Renfrew, Cambridge University
"The Archaeology of Identity"

1993–94

MICHIGAN   William Julius Wilson, University of Chicago
"The New Urban Poverty and the Problem of Race"

OXFORD   Lord Slynn of Hadley, London
"Law and Culture — A European Setting"

HARVARD   Lawrence Stone, Princeton University
"Family Values in a Historical Perspective"

CAMBRIDGE   Peter Brown, Princeton University
"Aspects of the Christianisation of the Roman World"

UTAH   A. E. Dick Howard, University of Virginia
"Toward the Open Society in Central and Eastern Europe"
Jeffrey Sachs, Harvard University
"Shock Therapy in Poland: Perspectives of Five Years"
Adam Zagajewski, Paris
*"A Bus Full of Prophets: Adventures of the
Eastern-European Intelligentsia"*

PRINCETON   Alasdair MacIntyre, Duke University
*"Truthfulness, Lies, and Moral Philosophers:
What Can We Learn from Mill and Kant?"*

CALIFORNIA   Oscar Arias, Costa Rica
"Poverty: The New International Enemy"

STANFORD   Thomas Hill, University of North Carolina at Chapel Hill
"Basic Respect and Cultural Diversity"
"Must Respect Be Earned?"

US SAN DIEGO   K. Anthony Appiah, Harvard University
"Race, Culture, Identity: Misunderstood Connections"

1994–95

YALE   Richard Posner, United States Court of Appeals
                    "Euthanasia and Health Care: Two Essays on the
                    *   Policy Dilemmas of Aging and Old Age"*

MICHIGAN   Daniel Kahneman, University of California, Berkeley
                    "Cognitive Psychology of Consequences and
                    *   Moral Intuition"*

HARVARD   Cass R. Sunstein, University of Chicago
                    "Political Conflict and Legal Agreement"

CAMBRIDGE   Roger Penrose, Oxford Mathematics Institute
                    "Space-time and Cosmology"

PRINCETON   Antonin Scalia, United States Supreme Court
                    "Common-Law Courts in a Civil-Law System:
                    *   The Role of the United States Federal Courts*
                    *   in Interpreting the Constitution and Laws"*

UC SANTA CRUZ Nancy Wexler, Columbia University
                    "Genetic Prediction and Precaution Confront
                    *   Human Social Values"*

OXFORD   Janet Suzman, South Africa
                    "Who Needs Parables?"

STANFORD   Amy Gutmann, Princeton University
                    "Responding to Racial Injustice"

UTAH   Edward Said, Columbia University
                    "On Lost Causes"

1995–96

PRINCETON   Harold Bloom, Yale University
                    I. *"Shakespeare and the Value of Personality,"* and
                    II. *"Shakespeare and the Value of Love"*

OXFORD   Simon Schama, Columbia University
                    "Rembrandt and Rubens: Humanism, History, and the
                    *   Peculiarity of Painting"*

CAMBRIDGE   Gunther Schuller, Newton Center, Massachusetts
                    I. *"Jazz: A Historical Perspective,"* II. *"Duke Ellington,"*
                    and III. *"Charles Mingus"*

RIVERSIDE   Mairead Corrigan Maguire, Belfast, Northern Ireland
"Peacemaking from the Grassroots in a World of Ethnic Conflict"

HARVARD   Onora O'Neill, Newham College, Cambridge
"Kant on Reason and Religion"

STANFORD   Nancy Fraser, New School for Social Research
"Social Justice in the Age of Identity Politics: Redistribution, Recognition, and Participation"

UTAH   Cornell West, Harvard University
"A Genealogy of the Public Intellectual"

YALE   Peter Brown, Princeton University
"The End of the Ancient Other World: Death and Afterlife between Late Antiquity and the Early Middle Ages"

1996–97

TORONTO   Peter Gay, Emeritus, Yale University
"The Living Enlightenment"

MICHIGAN   Thomas M. Scanlon, Harvard University
"The Status of Well-Being"

HARVARD   Stuart Hampshire, Emeritus, Stanford University
"Justice Is Conflict: The Soul and the City"

CAMBRIDGE   Dorothy L. Cheney, University of Pennsylvania
"Why Animals Don't Have Language"

PRINCETON   Robert M. Solow, Massachusetts Institute of Technology
"Welfare and Work"

CALIFORNIA   Marian Wright Edelman, Children's Defense Fund
"Standing for Children"

YALE   Liam Hudson, Balas Copartnership
"The Life of the Mind"

STANFORD   Barbara Herman, University of California, Los Angeles
"Moral Literacy"

OXFORD   Francis Fukuyama, George Mason University
"Social Capital"

UTAH   Elaine Pagels, Princeton University
"The Origin of Satan in Christian Traditions"

1997–98

UTAH	Jonathan D. Spence, Yale University *"Ideas of Power: China's Empire in the Eighteenth Century and Today"*
PRINCETON	J. M. Coetzee, University of Cape Town *"The Lives of Animals"*
MICHIGAN	Antonio R. Damasio, University of Iowa *"Exploring the Minded Brain"*
CHARLES UNIVERSITY	Timothy Garton Ash, Oxford University *"The Direction of European History"*
HARVARD	M. F. Burnyeat, Oxford University *"Culture and Society in Plato's* Republic*"*
CAMBRIDGE	Stephen Toulmin, University of Southern California *"The Idol of Stability"*
UC IRVINE	David Kessler, Yale University *"Tobacco Wars: Risks and Rewards of a Major Challenge"*
YALE	Elaine Scarry, Harvard University *"On Beauty and Being Fair," and "On Beauty and Being Wrong"*
STANFORD	Arthur Kleinman, Harvard University *"Experience and Its Moral Modes: Culture, Human Conditions, and Disorder"*

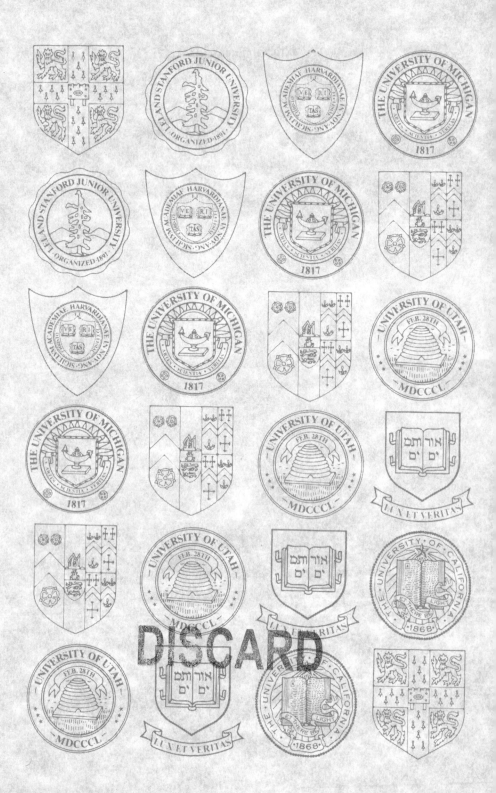